61401623   D1759837

Songwriters of the American Musical Theatre

From the favorites of Tin Pan Alley to today's international block-busters, the stylistic range required of a musical theatre performer is expansive.

Musical theatre roles require the ability to adapt to a panoply of characters and vocal styles. By breaking down these styles and exploring the output of the great composers, *Songwriters of the American Musical Theatre* offers singers and performers an essential guide to the modern musical. Composers from Gilbert and Sullivan and Irving Berlin to Alain Boublil and Andrew Lloyd Webber are examined through a brief biography, a stylistic overview, and a comprehensive song list with notes on suitable voice types and further reading.

This volume runs the gamut of modern musical theatre, from English light opera through the American Golden Age, up to the "mega musicals" of the late Twentieth Century, giving today's students and performers an indispensable survey of their craft.

Nathan Hurwitz is a tenured associate professor of music theatre at Rider University, USA. He is the author of *A History of American Musical Theatre: No Business Like It* (2014).

Library
University of Cumbria

POL—18943
03/19
£36.99
782.140973Hur
B-pert

Songwriters of the American Musical Theatre

A Style Guide for Singers

Nathan Hurwitz

 Routledge
Taylor & Francis Group

LONDON AND NEW YORK

First published 2017
by Routledge
2 Park Square, Milton Park, Abingdon, Oxon OX14 4RN

and by Routledge
711 Third Avenue, New York, NY 10017

Routledge is an imprint of the Taylor & Francis Group, an informa business

© 2017 Nathan Hurwitz

The right of Nathan Hurwitz to be identified as author of this work has
been asserted by him in accordance with sections 77 and 78 of the Copyright,
Designs and Patents Act 1988.

All rights reserved. No part of this book may be reprinted or reproduced or
utilised in any form or by any electronic, mechanical, or other means,
now known or hereafter invented, including photocopying and recording,
or in any information storage or retrieval system, without permission in
writing from the publishers.

Trademark notice: Product or corporate names may be trademarks
or registered trademarks, and are used only for identification and explanation
without intent to infringe.

British Library Cataloguing in Publication Data
A catalogue record for this book is available from the British Library

Library of Congress Cataloguing in Publication Data
A catalog record for this book has been requested

ISBN: 978-1-138-91441-4 (hbk)
ISBN: 978-1-138-91442-1 (pbk)
ISBN: 978-1-315-69084-1 (ebk)

Typeset in Sabon
by Out of House Publishing

Contents

Introduction

As a singer of the songs of the musical theatre, the more informed you can be about the material you are singing – why it was written the way that it was, what kinds of interpretations have been more successful or less successful – the better equipped you are to make smart, interesting choices. Of course you are absolutely not required to perform any song in the style in which it was originally written or the way it has traditionally been performed; new and interesting interpretations can be very exciting. But the more you know about the song, its history, the composer and lyricist and their body of work, the better able you are to make informed choices about the material.

That is the impetus behind the creation of this book. You should use this book not just to find material but as the first stop on an exploration of the great writers of the American musical theatre and the popular songs of the American Songbook. While this book does not prescribe a set of rules for each period or writer, it is an introduction to a set of performance traditions. There are wonderful sources that offer complete, encyclopedic lists of song titles, performances, audio recordings and so on; this book is not intended to be that kind of reference. With only so much space in one book, there are wonderful composers and lyricists who have not found space here, writers whose work you should seek out.

The first goal of this book is to touch on the major artists – the ones whose work marked a step forward in the craft of songwriting or who epitomize a particular style or period. After identifying these writers, this book looks at the vocal styles for which they wrote, as well as at the vocal styles that have been applied to their body of work since. This book is a starting point, a jumping off place for further, more specific research to begin. To that end, listening and viewing recommendations are made throughout the book to help the reader find further information.

The stylistic range a musical theatre performer is expected to have at his or her fingertips is huge. Musical theatre composers employ vocal styles from *bel canto* and the chanting of a Greek chorus, to madrigal singing, to imitating Elvis, Frankie Valli, Judy Garland or Billie Holiday, to the latest in house, hip-hop and alternative rock and everything in between. The most stylistically versatile musical theatre performers are, naturally, the most employable. Besides the classical repertoire of the musical theatre, today's musical theatre borrows more and more from other forms of popular music. Beyond the obvious example of the Broadway smash *Hamilton*, recent Broadway seasons alone have offered musicals featuring tangos, the music of the Beatles, Carole King, Burt Bacharach and Janis Joplin, a folk musical by a hippie rabbi and a transsexual punk musical. Jukebox musicals like *Mamma Mia, Moving Out* and *Jersey Boys* take pre-existing songs from the catalogs of great rock and popular composers and successfully integrate them into musicals. The young musical theatre singer's potential for work increases in direct correlation to the degree of familiarity and comfort he or she has with as wide a range of popular music styles as possible.

Musical theatre training programs are cropping up and thriving at colleges, universities and conservatories across the US and around the world. Most of these programs require a course introducing the students to the literature of the musical theatre and popular song. But with so much material to cover, most of these courses have to be structured as surveys, where young singers encounter a different composer or period in each class session. These survey courses expose the singer to a large wealth of material, but frequently lack the class time to engage the material in depth. Many of these classes leave the students with a general "feel" of the composers' styles but fall short of actually coming to terms with the specifics that define these styles and genres. Frequently these courses introduce the students to songs from the repertoire with a brief overview or recap of the composer, style or period. But there is usually not the time for an in-depth examination; nor is there a comprehensive guide in print to supplement these classes. Within most musical theatre training programs, students are introduced to a wealth of material. While great emphasis rests on exposure to as much material as possible, little is placed on the articulation of the different genres and styles of the material of the musical theatre and the canon of popular songs. This book offers a style guide for songs of the musical theatre, a composer-by-composer analysis. To that end, this book is intended to augment and deepen the material covered in musical theatre repertoire classes, a guide to understanding many of the most prevalent vocal styles encountered in the musical theatre. This book should be an invaluable addition to the library of any musical theatre performer, any singer of popular music, any voice teacher, vocal coach or teacher of the musical theatre repertoire.

There are many sources that offer song titles or lists of songs from the various composers, periods or styles. Several of the best sources are the listening and viewing sites including Spotify, iTunes and youtube. Other online sources include the Songwriters Hall of Fame, (www.songwritershalloffame.org/) and the Internet Broadway Database (www.ibdb.com), while in print David P. DeVenney's *The New Broadway Song Companion: An Annotated Guide to Musical Theatre Literature by Voice Type and Song Style*[1] is an excellent and useful resource. But there is no comprehensive source to help the young singer begin to grapple with defining and articulating the musical styles used in the literature of the musical theatre. This book is unique in that it aims to help the young singer understand this repertoire better from a stylistic perspective.

That is not to say that because a song was written in a particular style, or even in a particular vocal range, that it must always be performed that way. Indeed, taking a song that has traditionally been performed in a certain way and reconsidering it in the context of another style can prove tremendously fruitful. Jazz singers, rock singers, rhythm and blues singers, gospel singers, even grunge bands have all tried their hand at interpreting the great songs of the American musical theatre – some more successfully, some less. In 1994 George Martin, producer of The Beatles' albums, produced a CD of Gershwin songs featuring rock artists like Peter Gabriel, Sting, Elton John, Elvis Costello, Cher and Sinéad O'Connor; it was a great re-examination of songs that had originally been sung in a relatively legitimate style and had become the domain of crooners or jazz singers through the prism of the rock singer.

Each chapter of this book examines a period or stylistic movement beginning by tracing how and why these styles came to be. The structure of each chapter includes:

- An *overview* of the period or movement from the perspective of a performer preparing to sing the songs as the composer and lyricist intended them. These historical overviews contextualize the styles to help the singer understand and integrate the composers' and lyricists' intent, their style.

- A discussion of each composer or lyricist in some detail then follows. An examination of the composer or lyricist's *stylistic approach* begins each composer/lyricist section. This includes information such as a discussion of their background, the range of styles in which they most often (and most successfully) wrote, and major artists who have had success singing or recording their songs.

- This is followed by a relatively comprehensive catalog of their *body of work*, which includes lists of the stage and film musicals they wrote and a list of their most important, popular or best-remembered songs. Where it is significant, the original vocal register of the song is indicated in the catalog. This is not meant to suggest that a song originally written for a baritone can never be sung by a mezzo-soprano, for instance; in fact, many of these songs have been published in keys for other vocal ranges, and the advent of computer programs like *Finale*, and websites like www.musicnotes.com, make it very easy to get sheet music of practically any song in just about any key. Taking one of these songs and reconceiving them for a different gender or voice type can shed new light on it, yielding a fresh interpretation of the text.

- The body of work is followed by a brief *biography*, focusing on those biographical facts that might be most germane to the singer preparing to sing their work. These facts might include date and place of birth and death, where they grew up, went to school, early work, important collaborators and an overview of their career.

- The final section for each composer or lyricist is a brief mention of additional primary *resources*. The reader of this book is encouraged to take an active interest in further exploring the works and lives of the writers included in this book.

The twelve chapters of this book are broken down as follows:

Chapter 1, Light opera, looks at the most successful musicals of the late nineteenth and early twentieth century: the operettas. This chapter includes the operettas of Viennese waltz king, Johann Strauss II (1825–1899); the French operettas of Jacques Offenbach (1819–1880); operettas by Franz Lehár (1870–1948), the composer of *The Merry Widow,* the biggest hit at the beginning of the twentieth century; the first great English-language music theatre writing team, W.S. Gilbert (1836–1911) and Sir Arthur Sullivan (1842–1900); and the three great American operetta writers, Victor Herbert (1859–1924), Rudolf Friml (1879–1972) and Sigmund Romberg (1887–1951).

Chapter 2, Popular musical theatre songs of the early 1900s, explores the styles of the three greatest early twentieth-century American songwriters of musical theatre scores, who also happen to be three of the greatest American composers of popular music of their time. These include George M. Cohan (1878–1942), Irving Berlin (1888–1989) and Jerome Kern (1885–1945).

Chapter 3, The great songwriters of Tin Pan Alley, offers a brief history of Tin Pan Alley, the center of popular American music in the early twentieth century. It examines the works of the most important songwriters of this period: Harry Warren (1893–1981), Jimmy McHugh (1894–1969), B.G. "Buddy" DeSylva (1895–1950), Lew Brown (1893–1958), Ray Henderson (1896–1970), George Gershwin (1898–1937), Ira Gershwin (1896–1983), Arthur Schwartz (1900–1984), and Howard Dietz (1896–1983), and Harold Arlen (1905–1986). The works of these composers took the European model of a song but infused it with a distinctly American sound that borrowed heavily from African American blues traditions and Jewish folk and liturgical music. These writers provided the foundation of what has become known as the American Songbook. Many of their songs have been re-examined and re-interpreted through each ensuing generation and popular musical style.

The subject of Chapter 4, The great wits and sophisticates, is the witty, urbane and sophisticated set of songwriters in the 1920s and 1930s, most of whom continued to make substantial contributions into the 1940s and 1950s; but their spectacular entrance onto the scene took place in the 1920s and 1930s. These writers include Cole Porter (1891–1964), Richard Rodgers (1902–1979) and Lorenz Hart (1895–1943), E.Y. "Yip" Harburg (1896–1981), Johnny Mercer (1909–1976), Dorothy Fields (1905–1974) and Vernon Duke (1903–1969). These were the writers whose music and lyrics call attention to themselves; the "star attraction" of these songs is the verbal and musical dexterity that these writers display.

Unlike the other chapters, Chapter 5, The great jazz composers, looks at American jazz composers who have never written a musical per se, although their songs have certainly appeared on the Broadway stage. These composers include Eubie Blake (1887–1983), Jelly Roll Morton (1890–1941), Duke Ellington (1899–1974), Hoagy Carmichael (1899–1981) and Thomas "Fats" Waller (1904–1943). By its nature, jazz is a highly interpretive art. To understand jazz styling, one needs as great an appreciation for and understanding of the different jazz singers as of the literature of jazz standards; and so this chapter takes a brief look at some of the great jazz singers whose style has helped to define vocal jazz music. These singer include Ma Rainey (1886–1939), Bessie Smith (1894–1937), Adelaide Hall (1901–1993), Louis Armstrong (1901–1971), Cab Calloway (1907–1994), Billy Eckstein (1914–1993), Billie Holiday (1915–1959), Frank Sinatra (1915–1998), Ella Fitzgerald (1917–1996), Nat "King" Cole (1919–1965), Jon Hendricks (b. 1921), Carmen McRae (1922–1994), Sarah Vaughan (1924–1990), Dinah Washington (1924–1963), Mel Tormé (1925–1999), Tony Bennett (b. 1926), Ray Charles (1930–2004), Nina Simone (1933–2003), Al Jarreau (b. 1940), George Benson (b. 1943), Bobby McFerrin (b. 1950). This list is in no way comprehensive, and is meant merely as an introduction to the various sub-genres of jazz and to give the beginning singer a good list from which to begin listening to various jazz singers' styles.

In 1943, Rodgers and Hammerstein's *Oklahoma!* opened and almost immediately changed the model of the musical theatre. From that point forward, composers and lyricists were obligated to be musical dramatists first and foremost, to use songs to either advance plot or reveal character. The specificity of the model that *Oklahoma!* established constrained these writers, but also freed them to create in what became a golden age. As the social, cultural and political facts of Ancient Greece in the 400s BC created the conditions enabling a golden age of playwriting, so the 1940s–1960s allowed for a golden age of writing in the American musical theatre.

Chapter 6, The Golden Age – The integrated musical, looks at the works of Richard Rodgers (1902–1979) and Oscar Hammerstein II (1895–1960), Alan Jay Lerner (1918–1986) and Frederick Loewe (1901–1988), Frank Loesser (1910–1969), Kurt Weill (1900–1950), Burton Lane (1912–1992), Leonard Bernstein (1918–1990), Betty Comden (1917–2006) and Adolph Green (1914–2002), and Jule Styne (1905–1994). As the music and lyrics had been the drawing attraction in the period preceding this, in this period the character and story are the "stars." As microphones were the exception rather than the rule in the theatre at this time, vocally this is the age of the big bright sound with the frontal placement, either in chest voice or head voice. All of these writers assume a strong, legitimate vocal technique from singers of their songs.

Chapter 7, The culmination of the Golden Age of the American musical, examines the writers who had their earlier successes at the end of the Golden Age and early into the transition to the concept musicals of the 1970s. The writers whose works are examined in this chapter include: Jerry Herman (b. 1931), Charles Strouse (b. 1928), Tom Jones (b. 1928) and Harvey Schmidt (b. 1929), Jerry Bock (1928–2010) and Sheldon Harnick (b. 1924), Cy Coleman (1929–2004), and John Kander (b. 1927) and Fred Ebb (1928–2004). These were the last musical theatre writers to come of age in a time of unamplified voice; they knew how to write in such a way as to help the singer get the melody and lyrics out over a full orchestra pit. Writers in later periods never had to take this into consideration. Vocal registers are given for these songs as they were originally performed in the shows for which they were written. Many of these songs have been sung and recorded in different voices in different keys, sheet music for many of which is commercially available; when it is not commercially available services such as musicnotes.com and independent arrangers can transpose appropriately.

Chapter 8, *Sui generis* – Stephen Sondheim, looks at the work of Stephen Sondheim. While a tremendous amount of excellent critical work has been published on Sondheim and his writing, this chapter looks at how each of Sondheim's scores is unique in and of itself. Since the styles are so wide-ranging, a unique and specific vocal approach would appear to be called for by each of Sondheim's scores.

Chapter 9, New sounds – The 1970s, describes how writers who were born mostly in the late 1930s into the early 1950s experienced their formative years as listeners of music when rock and roll was in the ascendant. The musical vocabulary from which they drew their inspiration had a more diverse range of sounds than their predecessors, and the sounds of their childhoods and adolescences readily found its way into what they wrote. Not only were many of their songs written with pop, rock and folk inflections, but also they call out for singers to supply style and embellishments from those genres that previous writers did not. These writers include: Galt MacDermot (b. 1928), Stephen Schwartz (b. 1948), Marvin Hamlisch (1944–2012), Maury Yeston (b. 1945), Howard Ashman

(1950–1991) and Alan Menken (b. 1949), Richard Maltby Jr (b. 1937), and David Shire (b. 1937), and William Finn (b. 1952)

Chapter 10, The mega-musical, explores the vocal requirements and possibilities for the songs from the mega-musicals of the 1980s and 1990s. The greatest songwriters of mega-musicals, the ones examined in this chapter, are Andrew Lloyd Webber (b. 1948), and Claude-Michel Schönberg (b. 1944) and Alain Boublil (b. 1941). Both Lloyd Webber and the team of Schönberg and Boublil frequently call for vocalists who have a decidedly classical vocal technique informed by contemporary stylings. Some of their shows, like *Jesus Christ, Superstar*, are more rock-based, while others, like *Aspects of Love*, call for a more classical vocal sound. Their works are examined in this chapter, as is the effect on vocal production of a business model that requires duplicate productions to be mounted simultaneously around the world.

Chapter 11, Musicals of the 1990s and 2000s, discusses the styles of the composers and lyricists of the last 25 years. Throughout popular culture, the 1990s and 2000s were a time of "repurposed" or "recycled" culture, when artists referenced, pulled from and cited earlier works. This is true across a wide spectrum of popular and high art forms, and the musical theatre was no exception. Repurposed styles "mashed up" and co-joined has defined the musical theatre of this period. The most successful composers and lyricists in this chapter have all cited a wide range of influences, which are explored in this chapter. Facility with a wide range of styles is important for the vocalist in approaching the material of these writers. Writers explored in this chapter include: Elton John (b. 1947), Jonathan Larson (1960–1996), Frank Wildhorn (b. 1958), Lynn Ahrens (b. 1948) and Stephen Flaherty (b. 1960), Michael John LaChiusa (b. 1962), Jason Robert Brown (b. 1970), Andrew Lippa (b. 1964), Adam Guettel (b. 1964), Tom Kitt, Ricky Ian Gordon (b. 1956), and Jeanine Tesori (b. 1961).

Chapter 12, Other popular styles: The jukebox musicals, looks at the exponential growth in the number of "jukebox" musicals: stage productions using pre-existing songs rather than original scores. Many of these shows have plots (usually fairly thin) written to weave the songs together. Shows like *Jersey Boys*, *Mamma Mia*, *Ring of Fire* and *A Night With Janis Joplin* have proliferated. They have made the understanding of a vast range of styles of composition and performance vital for the aspiring musical theatre performer. This chapter clarifies the styles of popular music, explores their offshoots and offers sources for gaining a deeper knowledge of them. Styles explored in this chapter include: country music (both old country and new country), pop music of various traditions, rock music including classic rock, alternative, R&B, rap, house, blues, gospel, American folk music, yodeling and folk music of various other nations. This chapter take a brief look at what has appeared on the musical theatre stage – what has yet to appear could, in truth, be anything. Being able to listen, discern, study and learn styles is vitally important to the musical theatre performer of the twenty-first century.

This book should be used as a springboard for further investigation. It is not a comprehensive catalog of song titles, rather a selective catalog that should lead readers further into their study of these composers and the styles in which their songs can most effectively be sung. In addition to further reading and finding copies of the songs yourself, the best thing you could do to build on this book is to listen to absolutely as many different recordings, versions and interpretations as possible.

Using this book

In connection with most of the writers discussed throughout this book, examples of recordings are offered for various songs. Most of these recordings are available to either listen to online or download for a nominal price. Describing singing styles in words is limited and approximate at best. If the reader of this book is able to take the time to listen to the examples of these styles recommended, the styles should become much more concrete than they would by simply reading. Listening to more than simply the recommended examples can only further enhance the listener's grasp of and ability to perform these styles. Always try to listen to the original cast recordings of the musical theatre writers, the movie soundtracks or video clips for movie musical writers. Follow this up with popular recordings by artists in a variety of genres (jazz, rock, pop, country, and so on), and your understanding of the writer is only enhanced and expanded.

Vocal ranges are given for songs in many cases in this book. A soprano could certainly sing a song originally sung by a baritone, tenor or mezzo, although she would likely need to have the song transposed, as mentioned above. Throughout the book vocal ranges are indicated as follows:

* Soprano
** Mezzo-soprano
† Tenor
†† Bass/Baritone

Vocal styles encountered in this book include *bel canto*, swing singing, crooning, various styles of jazz singing, belting, talk-singing (*Sprechstimme*), gospel, rock, pop and folk. Vocal styles are not one easily definable thing; they are fluid; in fact many contemporary composers borrow from a great range of styles in a single song. However, the following chapters give brief descriptions of these vocal styles.

Note

1 David P. DeVenney, *The New Broadway Song Companion: An Annotated Guide to Musical Theatre Literature by Voice Type and Song Style*, New York, NY: Scarecrow Press, 2009.

Chapter 1

Light opera

Jacques Offenbach, Johann Strauss II,
W.S. Gilbert, Sir Arthur Sullivan,
Franz Lehár, Victor Herbert,
Rudolf Friml, and Sigmund Romberg

While opera dates back to the late sixteenth century, light opera began in the late seventeenth century. By the mid-eighteenth century, light opera had become *opera buffo*, and by the mid-nineteenth century had evolved further into operetta. Operetta thrived throughout Europe, particularly in France, whose star composer was Jacques Offenbach and in Germany/Austria, whose star composer was the Austrian Johann Strauss II. Perhaps the biggest hit operetta was *The Merry Widow*, by Austro-Hungarian composer Franz Lehár. Gilbert and Sullivan created English-language operetta, which became immensely popular around the world. The works of these men were embraced, emulated, imitated and advanced by the three great American writers of operetta, Victor Herbert, Rudolf Friml and Sigmund Romberg.

In the eighteenth and early nineteenth centuries, several important vocal styles existed, such as *canto spianato*, *cantabile*, *canto fiorito* and *canto declamato*. But by far the most important and widely respected vocal style of this time was *bel canto*, which translates as "beautiful singing." *Bel canto*, which can be traced back to the sixteenth century, had become firmly entrenched as the most common operatic vocal technique by the nineteenth century. Aspects of *bel canto* technique include

- an impeccable legato production throughout the singer's registers (a seamless range)
- the use of a light tone in the higher registers
- an agile, flexible technique capable of dispatching ornate elements, embellishments such as singer-supplied cadenzas
- the ability to execute fast, accurate divisions (articulating rapid notes with pitch-perfect precision)

- the avoidance of aspirates and the eschewing of loose vibrato
- a pleasing, well-focused timbre
- a clean attack
- limpid diction
- graceful phrasing rooted in a complete mastery of breath control.[1]

Bel canto singers used the following tools to bring color and inflect their text, to be convincing in their acting:

> accent, emphasis, tone of voice, register, phrasing, legato, staccato, portamento, messa di voce, tempo, vibrato, ornamentation and gesture. *Bel Canto* performers sang in an emphatic way, accenting individual syllables appropriately, matched register and tonal quality […] to the emotional content of the words; employed a highly articulate manner of phrasing; varied their delivery with several types of legato and staccato; liberally applied more than one type of portamento; considered *messa di voce* to be one of the principal sources of expression; altered tempo frequently through rhythmic rubato and the quickening and slowing of the overall time; introduced a wide variety of graces and divisions into the music they sang; and regarded gesture as a powerful tool for enhancing the effect of their delivery. They reserved vibrato, however, for heightening the expression of certain words and for gracing longer notes.[2]

Coming from Italian opera, *bel canto* is a vocal technique in which the quality of the voice is judged on the smoothness of the vocal line, both in terms of its legato quality and the lack of any perceptible register shift. The technique results in "resonance and purity of tone, consistency of tone across the registers of the voice."[3] According to *bel canto* acolyte Chris Tondreau, the fours stages of the *bel canto* technique are 1) the lift of the throat, using the hard resonant surfaces of the vocal mechanism such as teeth and the hard palate to create vocal size, 2) placing the voice high in the face and using the mask of the face to create resonance, 3) using the visualization of the inhalation of sound and 4) holding the breath rather than using the diaphragm to force air out. In the eighteenth and early nineteenth century Italian opera singers were judged on their ornate embellishments such as trills and runs. In order to accomplish these with a sense of effortlessness, this *bel canto* style offered an agility through the lightness of the technique and the lack of any discernible break between registers.

As operettas were reaching the peak of their popularity in Europe, the traditional *bel canto* style of singing had given way to the newer *verismo* style, which replaced pure beauty of tone with intensity of dramatic situation, heightened emotions and the need to get the voice out over a thicker orchestral accompaniment.

By the later nineteenth century the *verismo* style had replaced the earlier Italian style, and opera composers were writing heavier vocal lines, pushing singers higher in their ranges, and requiring singers to extend vocal registers. Tenors, for instance needed to produce high Cs and even Ds in their full voice rather than falsetto to create the desired emotional truth and to overcome the thicker instrumental accompaniment. While *bel canto* singers had been judged by the beauty of line (the legato quality) and the singer's agility, *verismo* vocal technique was judged on the power of the voice and the emotional "truth." *Verismo* required substantially more muscling of sound than *bel canto*, and frequently singers would combine techniques; the demands of such muscular singing as a sole means of sound production would endanger the longevity of a singer's career.

Operettas were through-composed, with substantial recitative and minimal dialogue. The melodies of the arias were not particularly repetitive, and they took advantage of the singers' full ranges. Performing these pieces required an embrace of a bombastic acting style, commitment to a larger-than-life world as well a high degree of vocal technique and a high level of musicianship.

For the most part, operetta performers tended to be opera singers who were exploring a lighter, frothier art form, rather than singing actors. Although critics and music fans sometimes wondered at opera stars straying from the genre at which they excelled, the stars themselves enjoyed performing operetta and frequently became attached to one or more composers of operetta. When Austrian operatic star tenor Richard Tauber announced that he would be giving up opera to dedicate himself to operetta, he was reproached in the press, but proudly responded, "I'm not singing operetta, ... I'm singing Lehár."[4]

At roughly the same time at the Bayreuth Festival, the opera house that Richard Wagner had built to mount his own operas, a new style of vocal attack was being developed by Richard and Cosima Wagner. This Wagnerian style included a strong element of declamatory singing in which clear enunciation of the text can be as important as the purity of tone or vocal quality. This talk-singing has become what we now refer to as *Sprechgesang* or *Sprechstimme*.

Many nineteenth-century critics and opera fans alike bemoaned the loss of their beloved *bel canto* to the less subtle *verismo* and referred to the Wagnerian variation as the "Bayreuth bark." Nonetheless, it was the heavier vocal style and the clarity of diction that came to define the vocal styles of the European operetta (French and German) as well as the English-language operettas.

Jacques Offenbach (1819–1880)

Stylistic approach

French composer Jacques Offenbach wrote very much in the style of the popular music of his time; there is nothing formal or stuffy about his compositions. Offenbach's music is light, fun, popular, playful and sexy – and it required that the singer embrace all of those elements in the vocal production and dramatic interpretation. Offenbach did not always write for the most highly trained voices, as many of his pieces were written for performance at private gentlemen's clubs, sometimes by professional singers and sometimes by amateurs or even courtesans. Over the years, as his work has entered the popular canon it has been given an ever-increasing respectability, sometimes at a loss of the fun of the pieces. But they hold up well to either a classical or a rougher, less trained vocal quality. One needs only imagine the absinthe-filled nights in smaller Paris theatres shared by Offenbach, Toulouse-Lautrec and other denizens of the Paris nightlife to realize that Offenbach accurately captured the "vigorous, earthy and gloriously vulgar" hedonism of the world he inhabited. It is incumbent upon the singer to evoke that world in their singing, even if this means choosing some moments that are more earthy than ethereal. Applying some folk inflections of the French chanteur will help the singer's approach to Offenbach.

With the continuing popularity of light opera, and light opera companies around the world producing these works regularly, the Internet abounds with recordings of most Offenbach works. Recordings of most of Offenbach's songs and complete operas are as close as youtube.com. Listening to several different recordings of a piece of Offenbach's is a terrific way to begin preparing your own interpretation – not to imitate, but to better understand the style and to build on the stylistic choices of other singers.

Body of work

Jacques Offenbach was one of the most popular and prolific composers of operetta of his time. All told, he wrote over 100 stage works between 1847 and 1880. Although all but two of these are now considered operettas, Offenbach himself designated them differently. He called 30 of them *opéra bouffes*, 24 of them *opérette bouffes*, 24 *opéra comiques*, and the others he put into several other categories, some of which he created himself, such as *opéra bouffon*, *bouffonnerie musicale*, *saynéte*, *pièce d'occasion* and revue. Offenbach's works are known for focusing on their ribald subject matter; grotesque, shocking and practically pornographic for their day, they have come down to us in fairly distilled and "sanitized" versions. Despite this cleansing, many of Offenbach's works remain in the repertoire into the twenty-first century.

Offenbach's stage compositions include:

L'alcôve (The Alcove, opéra comique, 1847)

Blanche (White, opéra comique, unperformed, 1847)

La Duchesse d'Albe (The Duchess of Alba, unperformed, 1848)

Le trésor à Mathurin (The Treasure of Mathurin, tableau villageois, 1853; also revised as *Le mariage aux lanternes*, an opérette in 1857)

Pépito (opéra comique, 1853)

Luc et Lucette (opéra comique, 1854)

Le décaméron, ou La grotte d'azur (légende napolitaine, 1855)

Entrez, messieurs, mas-dames (Come in Ladies and Gentlemen, pièce d'occasion, 1855)

Une nuit blanche (One White Night, opéra comique, 1855)

Les deux aveugles (The Two Blind Men, bouffonnerie musicale, 1855)

Le réve d'une nuit d'été (The Dream of a Summer Night, saynète, 1855)

Oyayaye, ou La reine des îles (Oyayaye, or the Queen of the Islands, anthropophagie musicale, 1855)

Le violoneux (The Fiddler, lègende bretonne, 1855)

Madame Papillon (Mrs. Butterfly, opérette, 1855)

Paimpol et Périnette (saynète, 1855)

Ba-ta-clan (chinoiserie musicale, 1855)

Trafalgar – Sur un volcan (Trafalgar – or, On a Volcano, comédie à ariettes, 1855)

Un postillon en gage (opérette, 1856)

Tromb-al-ca-zar, ou Les criminels dramatiques (Tromb-al-ca-zar, or The Dramatic Criminals, bouffonnerie musicale, 1856)

La rose de Saint-Flour (opérette, 1856)

Les dragées du baptême (The Candied Almonds of Baptism, pièce d'occasion, 1856)

Le 66 (opérette, 1856)

Le financier et le savetier (The Financier and the Cobbler, opérette bouffe, 1856)

Le bonne d'enfant (The Nanny, opérette bouffe, 1857)

Les trois baisers du diable (The Three Kisses of the Devil, opérette fantastique, 1857)

Croquefer, ou Le dernier des paladins (Croquefer or Last Paladin, opéra bouffe, 1857)

Dragonette (opéra bouffe, 1857)

Vent du soir, ou L'horrible festin (Evening Breeze, or The Horrible Feast, opérette bouffe, 1857)

Une demoiselle in loterie (A Damsel in Lottery, opérette, 1857)

Les deux pêcheurs, ou Le lever du soleil (The Two Fishermen, or The Sunrise, opérette bouffe, 1857)

Mesdames de la Halle (Ladies of the Hall, opérette bouffe, 1858)

La chatte métamorphosée en femme (The Cat Transformed Into a Woman, opérette, 1858)

Orphée aux enfers (Orpheus in the Underworld, opéra bouffon, 1858)

Un mari à la porte (A Husband at the Door, opérette, 1859)

Les vivandières de la grande-armée (The Vivandiers [canteen-keepers] of the Grand Army, opérette bouffe, 1859)

Geneviève de Brabant (opéra bouffon, 1859)

Le carnival des revues (The Carnival Magazine, revue, 1860)

Daphnis et Chloé (Daphnes and Chloe, opérette, 1860)

Barkouf (opéra bouffe, 1860)

Le Papillon (The Butterfly, ballet fantastique, 1860)

La chanson de Fortunio (The Song of Fortunio, opéra comique, 1861)

Le pont des soupirs (The Bridge of Sighs, opéra bouffon, 1861)

M. Choufleuri restera chez lui le … (Mr. Cauliflower Will Be at Home, opéra bouffe, 1861)

Apothicaire et perruquier (Apothecary and Barber, opéra bouffe, 1861)

Le roman comique (opéra bouffon, 1861)

Monsieur et Madame Denis (Mr. and Mrs. Denis, opéra comique, 1862)

Bavard at bavarde (The Chatterboxes, opéra bouffe, 1862)

Le voyage de MM. Dunanan pére et fils (The Journey of Misters Dunanan, Father and Son, opéra bouffe, 1862)

Jacqueline (opérette, 1862)

La baguette (opéra comique, unperformed, 1862)

Il signor Fagotto (opérette, 1863)

Lischen et Fritzchen (conversation alsacienne, 1863)

L'amour chanteur (The Love Singer, opérette, 1864)

Les géorgiennes (opéra bouffe, 1864)

Le fifre enchanté, ou Le soldat magician (The Enchanted Fife Player, or The Soldier Magician, opéra comique, 1864)

Jeanne qui pleure et Jean qui rit (Jeanne Crying and Jean Laughing, opérette, 1864)

Die Rheinnixen (The Rhine Nixes, opéra, 1864)

La belle Hélène (opéra bouffe, 1864)

Coscoletto, ou Le lazzarone (opéra comique, 1865)

Les refrains des bouffes (The Choruses of The Comics, fantaisie musicale, 1865)

Les bergers (The Shepherds, opéra comique, 1865)

Barbe-bleue (Bluebeard, opéra bouffe, 1866)

La vie parisienne (Parisienne Life, opéra bouffe, 1866)

La Grande-Duchesse de Gérolstein (The Grand Duchess of Gerolstein, opéra bouffe, 1867)

La permission de dix heures (Permission of Ten Hours, opéra comique, 1867)

La leçon de chant électromagnétique (The Electromagnetic Singing Lesson, bouffonnerie musicale, 1867)

Robinson Crusoé (opéra comique, 1867)

Le château à Toto (The Castle at Toto, opéra bouffe, 1868)

L'île de Tulipatan (The Island of Tulipatan, opéra bouffe, 1868)

La Périchole (opéra bouffe, 1868)

Vert-Vert (opéra comique, 1869)

La Diva (opéra bouffe, 1869)

La princesse de Trébizonde (opéra bouffe, 1869)

Les brigands (opéra bouffe, 1869)

Le romance de la rose (The Romance of the Rose, opérette, 1869)

Le roi Carotte (The Carrot King, opéra bouffe féerie, 1872)

Fantasio (opéra comique, 1872)

Der schwarze Corsar (The Black Pirate, opéra comique, 1872)

Les braconniers (The Poachers, opéra bouffe, 1873)

Pomme d'api (opérette, 1873)

La jolie perfumeuse (The Beautiful Perfumer, opéra comique, 1873)

Bagatelle (Trifle, opéra comique, 1874)

Madame l'archiduc (opéra bouffe, 1874)

Whittington (opéra bouffe féerie, 1874)

Les hannetons (June Bugs, revue, 1875)

La boulangère a des écus (opéra bouffe, 1875)

Le voyage dans la lune (The Trip to the Moon, opéra féerie, 1875)

La créole (opéra comique, 1875)

Tarte á la crème (The Cream Pie, valse, 1875)

Pierrette et Jacquot (opérette, 1876)

La boîte au lait (The Milk Box, opéra bouffe, 1876)

Le docteur Ox (Dr. Ox, opéra bouffe, 1877)

La foire Saint-Laurent (The Saint Lawrence Fair, opéra bouffe, 1877)

Maître Péronilla (The Woman with Two Husbands, opéra bouffe, 1878)

Madame Favart (opéra comique, 1878)

La marocaine (The Moroccan, opéra bouffe, 1879)

La fille du tambour-major (The Drum Major's Daughter, opéra comique, 1879)

Belle Lurette (opéra comique, 1880)

Mam'zelle Moucheron (Miss Moucheron, opérette bouffe, 1881

Les contes d'Hoffmann (The Tales of Hoffmann, opéra, 1881)

With such a prodigious output, a complete list of Offenbach's arias would be overwhelming. Here is a highly abbreviated list of some of his most popular arias from his operettas and from his final opera, *Les Contes d'Hoffmann*, separated by voice type.

Soprano

Il était une fois á la cour d'Eisenach (Once Upon a Time in the Court of Eisenach, *Les Contes d'Hoffmann*)

Allons! Courage et confiance … Ah! Vivre deux! (Come! Courage and Confidence … Ah! Two Live!, *Les Contes d'Hoffmann*)

Amis, l'amour tendre et
rêveur (Friends,
Dreaming and Tender
Love, *Les Contes
d'Hoffmann*)
O Dieu! De quelle ivresse
(Heavens, with what
rapture, *Les Contes
d'Hoffmann*)
Jour et nuit je me mets en
quatre (Day and Night
I Bend Over Backwards
For Him, *Les Contes
d'Hoffmann*)
Ce qu'j'ai, tu demandes (That
Which I Have, You Ask, *La
Boulangère a des Écus*)
Je voyais bien votre tendresse
(I Could See Your
Tenderness, *La créole*)
Prenez les grappes empour-
prées (Take the Crimson
Clusters, *La fille du
Tambour-Major*)
Eh bien! En voilà des
maniéres (Ah Well! Here
are Ways, *La fille du
Tambour-Major*)
Doux jus de la pomme (Sweet
Apple Juice, *Jeanne qui
pleure et Jean qui rit*)
Ce qu'il me faut servie (What I
Need, *La Jolie parfumeuse*)
Où je vais? J'n'en savons rien
(Where Do I Go? I Do Not
Know, *Madame l'archiduc*)
Le femme dont le coeur rêve
(The Woman With the
Dream Heart, *Orphéeaux
enfers*)

On va courir, on va sortir (It
Will Run, It Will Come
Out, *La vie parisienne*)
Je suis nerveuse, je suis
fiévreuse (I'm Nervous, I'm
Feverish, *Le voyage dans la
lune*)
Au chapeau je porte une
aigrette (In My Hat I Wear
a Plume, *Les Brigands*)
Ma chère eau pure (My Dear
Pure Water, *La chanson de
fortunio*)
Grâce à vous (Thanks to You,
Geneviéve de Brabant)
Ah! Vraiment, c'est charmant
(Ah! Really It Is Charming,
Les Géorgiennes)
J'ai perdu mon ami (I Lost My
Friend, *L'île de Tulipatan*)
Je suis la petite fruitière (I
Am the Little Fruit-seller,
Mesdames de la halle)
La mort m'apparaît souri-
ante (Death Appears to
Me Smiling, *Orphée aux
enfers*)
Conduisez-moi vers celui que
j'adore (Take Me To the
One I Love, *Robinson
Crusoé*)
Mon gros chéri, mon petit roi
(My Big Baby, My Little
King, *Le roi Carotte*)
Petit bébé, sous le rameau
(Little Baby Under the
Branch, *Vent du soir*)
Je suis veuve d'un colonel
(I Am a Widow of a
Colonel, *La vie parisienne*)

Mezzo-soprano

J'ai des yeux (I Have Eyes, *The Tales of Hoffmann*)

Scintille, diamant (Sparkle, Diamond, *The Tales of Hoffmann*)

Dans les rôles d'amoureux langoureux (In the Roles of Languid Love, *The Tales of Hoffmann*)

Amours divins! Ardentes flames! (Divine Love! Burning Flames!, *La Belle Hélène*)

On me nomme Hélène la blonde (They Call Me Blond Helene, *La Belle Hélène*)

Lá! Vrai, je ne suis pas coupable (There! Indeed I Am Not Guilty, *La Belle Hélène*)

Examinez ma figure (Look at My Figure, *La fille du tambour-major*)

Ah! Que j'aime les militaires (Ah! I Love the Military, *La Grande-Duchesse de Gérolstein*)

Je passé sur mon enfance (I Passed My Childhood, *Madame Favart*)

Ah! Quel dîner je viens de faire (Ah! What a Dinner I Have, *La Périchole*)

Tu n'es pas beau, tu n'es pas riche (You're Not Beautiful, You're Not Rich, *La Périchole*)

Vous souvient-il, ma belle (You Remember It, My Beauty, *La vie parisienne*)

C'est ici l'endroit redouté des meres (This Is the Place That Mothers Dreaded, *La vie parisienne*)

Y'a des berger dans le village (There Are Shepherds In the Village, *Barbe-bleue*)

Quand tu me fis l'insigne honneur (When You Did Me the Honor, *Les brigands*)

J'suis ainsi, v'là mon caractère (I'm Well, That's My Character, *Le château á Toto*)

Dites-lui qu'on l'a remarqué (Tell Him That It Has Been Noticed, *La Grande Duchesse de Gérolstein*)

Allons, voyons je sais comprendre (Come, Now I Understand, *Madame l'Archiduc*)

Catarina, je chante (Catarina, I Sing, *Le pont des soupirs*)

Une jeune fille passait (A Girl Going, *La princesse de Trébixonde*)

Fleur qui se fane avant d'éclore (Flower That Fades Before Blooming, *La princesse de Trébizonde*)

Tamayo mon frère (*Robinson Crusoé*)

Étudiant de cette ville (Student of the City, *Le roi Carotte*)

Je regarde vos jolis yeux (I Look at Your Pretty Eyes, *Le voyage dans la lune*)

Tenor

Les oiseaux dans la charmille
(The Birds in the Bower,
The Tales of Hoffmann)
Elle a fui, la tourterelle (She
Fled, the Dove, *The Tales
of Hoffmann*)
Au mont Ida (At Mount Ida, *La
Belle Hélène*)
On connaît nom partout
(Name Is Known Over All,
La Créole)
Tout en tirant mon aiguille
(While Pulling My
Needle, *La fille du
tambour-major*)
Pour épouser une princesse
(To Marry a Princess,
*La Grande-Duchesse de
Gérolstein*)
La ruisseau qui prend sa source
(The Creek That Rises,
*Jeanne qui pleure et Jean
qui rit*)
Suzanne est aujourd'hui ma
femme (Suzanne Is Now
My Wife, *Madame Favart*)
Moi, je suis Aristée (Me, I Am
Aristée, *Orphée aux enfers*)
Heureuses divinités (Happy
Gods, *Orphée aux enfers*)
On me proposait d'être infâme
(I Was Offered Infamy, *La
Périchole*)

Ô mes amours, ô mes
maîtresses (Oh My Love,
Oh My Mistress, *Les
Brigandes*)
C'est moi qui suis le petit clerc!
(It Is I Who Am The Little
Clerk, *La Chanson de
Fortunio*)
Une poule sur un nur (A Hen
On a Wall, *Geneviéve de
Brabant*)
Quand j'étais Roi de Béotie
(When I Was King of
Boetia, *Orphée aux enfers*)
Mon oncle, ne vous fâchez pas
(My Uncle, Do Not Get
Angry, *Pomme d'Api*)
Ah! Qu'il était doux mon beau
rêve (Ah! It Was My Sweet
Beautiful Dream, *Le pont
des soupirs*)
Me maquillé-je comme on dit?
(I Disguised Myself, As
They Say, *La Princess de
Trébizonde*)
Salut, chaumiére (Hello
Cottage, *Robinson Crusoé*)
L'amour, c'est ton jeune cour-
age (Love is Your Young
Spirit, *Le Roi Carotte*)
Pour découper adroitement
(To Cut Deftly, *La vie
parisienne*)

Baritone/Bass

Une poupée aux yeux d'émail
(A Doll With Dynamic
Eyes, *The Tales of
Hoffmann*)

Voyez-la sous son éventail (See
It under Her Fan, *The Tales
of Hoffmann*)

C'est l'amour vainqueur (It is
   Love The Conqueror, *The*
   Tales of Hoffmann)
À cheval sur la discipline
   (Straddling Discipline,
   La Grande-Duchesse de
   Gérolstein)
Dans une cave obscure (In
   a Dark Cave, *Madame*
   Favart)
Quand du four on le retire
   (When the Oven is
   Removed, *Madame Favart*)
Quand il cherche dans sa
   cervelle (When he Looks In
   His Mind, *Madame Favart*)

L'employé m'a dit: De quel âge
   (The Clerk said, What Age
   (do You Want), *Pomme*
   D'api)
Elles sont tristes les marquises
   (The Nobelwomen are Sad,
   La vie parisienne)
Je suis brésilien, j'ai de l'or (I
   am Brazilian, I Have Gold,
   La vie parisienne)
Dans cette ville toute pleine (In
   This City So Full, *La vie*
   parisienne)
V'lan, V'lan, je suis V'lan
   (V'lan, V'lan, I Am V'lan,
   Le voyage dans la lune)

Biography

Jacques Offenbach was born in Cologne, Germany, the son of a Jewish cantor. As a young cellist he formed a trio with his brother, a violinist and his sister, a pianist. With greater opportunities open to Jews in France, he moved to Paris and began studying cello at the Paris Conservatoire, and changed his name from Jacob to Jacques. He was quickly offered a prestigious job, playing the cello in the orchestra of the *Opéra-Comique*. He had become one of the leading cellists in Europe by the age of 19 in 1838. By the age of 31 he became the conductor at the *Théâtre Française* and at the age of 36 opened his own theatre, the *Bouffes-Parisiens,* to produce the kind of light operetta he wanted to write.

Offenbach continued to write, conduct and produce, writing what is considered his finest composition, *The Tales of Hoffmann,* at the end of his life. His work set the standard for light French opera. Composer Rossini referred to him as "our little Mozart of the Champs-Elysées." He was the most prolific of his time, and the best remembered and most often produced today from his time.

References

While there are only a few biographies of Offenbach, there are a great many books and websites outlining the lives of famous composers.

Productions of Offenbach works are plentiful. Offenbach is so popular with performers that a great many arias and some entire operettas are available for viewing on youtube.com and other websites.

Johann Strauss II (1825–1899): The Waltz King

Stylistic approach

Johann Strauss II has been called "the most famous and enduringly popular composer of 19th century light music."[5] Today Johann Strauss' music sounds classical and austere to us, but Strauss wrote the popular music of his day. His dance music and operettas were as exciting and "of the moment" as The Beatles were in the 1960s, or the musical *Rent* was in the 1990s. Strauss' melodies soar, and yet they leave room for the singer to be the star, rather than the song or the composer. They ask for a traditional *verismo* style of vocal production, but there is a lightness required of Strauss' arias and solos. The serious operas of Verdi, Wagner, Rossini and Puccini require more "weight" in the voice; Strauss, existing in the world of the light opera, the world of the popular music of his day, calls for a vocal quality that floats more. Strauss' music exudes a sense of effervescence and exuberance, and the singer of Strauss needs to be aware of keeping the tone spinning. One must give the appearance of effortlessness, despite the fact that this in and of itself takes a great deal of both effort and technique.

As with Offenbach, recordings of most of Strauss' work are readily available. Listening to several different recordings will help you prepare your own interpretation – not to imitate, but to better understand the style and to build on the stylistic choices of other singers.

Body of work

The more than 500 pieces of dance music Strauss composed include waltzes, polkas, quadrilles and marches; the most famous of these include "The Blue Danube Waltz," "Tales from the Vienna Woods," "Tritsch Tratsch Polka," "The Artist's Life" and "Wine, Women and Song." He composed the score for the ballet *Cinderella*. For the theatre he saw 16 of his light and comic operettas successfully produced between 1871 and 1897; two earlier works, operetta burlesques, were never completed or produced. The most enduring of his operettas are "A Night in Venice," "The Gypsy Baron" and "Die

Fledermaus" ("The Bat"), which has become a New Year's Eve tradition with opera companies around the world.

Strauss wrote his first composition, a waltz, when he was only 6 years old. By the age of 19 he had become an important orchestra leader in Vienna, competing with his own father's orchestra. After being encouraged to try writing light opera by French composer Jacques Offenbach, and at the urging of his wife, Jetta, Strauss made his first attempt at writing an operetta burlesque, "The Merry Wives of Vienna" at age 43. This piece and his next endeavor, *Romulus*, were never completed and never saw production. However, his next operetta, *Indigo and the Forty Thieves*, opened successfully in 1871, seeing productions in Paris and London under the title *Queen Indigo* and later *A Night on the Bosphorus*. It has been retitled *The Thousand and One Nights* and remains popular to this day.

Many of Strauss' waltzes were composed for solo voice, and have been performed and recorded by singers in addition to their orchestral versions. Some of Strauss' solo vocal pieces outside of his stage works include:

Weiner Bonbons Waltz †

Am Donaustrande (On the
   Banks of the Danube),
   Improvisation for Voice and
   Piano *

Bauersleut' in Künstlerhaus
   (Country Bumpkins in the
   Art Gallery) tone poem for
   voice and piano ††

D'Hauptsach (The Main
   Thing), song for voice and
   orchestra ††

Dolci Pianti, song for voice
   and orchestra *

Draussen in Sievering
   (Out There in Sievering),
   aria for voice and
   orchestra */†

Ein Gstanzl vom Tanzl
   (A Verse for Dancing)

I'm in Love with Vienna, song
   based on Geschichten aud
   dem Weinerwald for voice
   and piano *

* soprano
† tenor
†† baritone

A full list of Strauss' operettas includes:

The Merry Wives of Vienna
   (never completed, 1868)

Romulus (never
   completed, 1871)

Indigo and the Forty Thieves
  (later retitled *Queen
  Indigo, A Night on the
  Bosphorus* and *The
  Thousand and One
  Nights*,1871)
The Carnival in Rome (1873)
Die Fledermaus (The Bat)
  (1874)
Cagliostro in Vienna (1875)
Prince Methusela (1877)
Blind Man's Bluff (1878)
*The Queen's Lace
  Handkerchief* (1880)

The Merry Way (1881)
A Night in Venice (1883)
The Gypsy Baron (1885)
The Rogue from Bergen (never
  completed or produced,
  1886)
Adventurous Simplicius
  (1887)
Knight Pázáman (1892)
Princess Ninetta (1893)
The Apple Festival (1894)
Woodruff (1895)
The Goddess of Reason
  (1897)

Among Strauss' most popular and enduring arias (listed by operetta) are:

Soprano

Adele's Laughing
  Song (*Die
  Fledermaus*)
The Audition Song
  Die Fledermaus)

Oh, How I Burn Inside (*A
  Night in Venice*)
Frutti Di Mare (*A Night in
  Venice*)
Saffi's Aria (*The Gypsy Baron*)

Mezzo

Chacun à son goût (Orlovky's
  Song, *Die Fledermaus*)
I Love to Invite my Friends
  (*Die Fledermaus*)

The Audition Song
  (*Die Fledermaus*)

Tenor

Take a Little Noodle (*A Night
  in Venice*)
Gondolier's Song (*A Night in
  Venice*)
Lagoon Waltz (*A Night in
  Venice*)

Als Flotter Geist (*The
  Gypsy Baron*)
Homonay's Song (*The
  Gypsy Baron*)

Baritone

I Love to Invite my Friends   Zsupan's Battle Song (*The*
   (*Die Fledermaus*)   *Gypsy Baron*)

Biography

Born in Vienna, the son of Johann Strauss, the "Father of the Waltz," Johann Strauss II (1825–1899) was the leading composer of light Viennese music in the latter half of the nineteenth century. Strauss the son built on his father's work and himself became known as the "Waltz King." Dancing and dance bands were all the rage in Vienna at the time.

Respecting his father's wishes that he not become a musician, the younger Strauss took a job as a bank clerk. However he began studying the violin in secret and began conducting a dance orchestra that was a rival of his father's at the age of 17. One year later he formed his own orchestra and began composing his own dances. After his father's death he combined his father's orchestra with his own. For this larger orchestra he composed, conducted and managed. This orchestra became so successful that he brought in his two younger brothers to take over management as the orchestra continued to perform in Vienna and on tour across Europe.

By age 46 Strauss began seeing his operas produced and, although initially critics claimed that he was simply writing dances with lyrics attached to them, he found himself pleasing audiences and ultimately winning critics over. Strauss died of pneumonia at the age of 73 in his beloved Vienna.

Resources

There are many fine biographies of Strauss, including David Ewen's *Wine, Women and Waltz: A Romantic Biography of Johann Strauss, Son and Father*[6] and H.E. Jacob's *Johann Strauss – Father and Son – A Century of Light Music.*[7]

W.S. Gilbert (1836–1911) and Sir Arthur Sullivan (1842–1900)

Stylistic approach

Quite possibly no songwriters' works are as surrounded by performance traditions than the works of Gilbert and Sullivan.

The D'Oyly Carte Opera Company was the original producer of Gilbert and Sullivan's operettas. The company, founded by Richard D'Oyly Carte, was solely dedicated to the production of the Gilbert and Sullivan operettas from 1881 to 1982, when the company fell upon hard times. The company received national money and reopened, producing the Gilbert and Sullivan operettas again from 1988 to 2003, when the company finally permanently folded.

Throughout all of those years, sets, costumes, props, staging, acting and tempi – all aspects of production – were kept relatively intact since their original mountings, with only the most occasional and thoughtful revisions finding their way into production. Many company members stayed with the company for great portions of their careers, sometimes more than 30 years. So the roles that the actors played year after year came to be firmly entrenched in performance traditions. When actors did ultimately retire and new actors took their roles over, they took on the traditions of the actor whom they were replacing, much like the traditions of the *commedia dell'arte* companies.

Prior to the 1870s, the artistic traditions of England tended to be weighted heavily towards the literary, and not towards the musical. Gilbert and Sullivan's operettas clearly did develop as an outgrowth of European operatic traditions and traditions of operetta. But in the context of nineteenth century British writers and production, emphasis was placed more squarely on the lyrics, a fact that rankled Sullivan and ultimately contributed to the dissolution of their collaboration. The melodies are delightful and tuneful, but they take second place to the lyrics. In terms of performance style, clarity of diction above all in this series of operettas filled with verbal wit, obscure jokes and imagery and frequent patter songs only makes sense.

Performances of Gilbert and Sullivan tend to be traditional. Many individual recordings and two complete sets of recordings of the complete canon of the Gilbert and Sullivan operas exist and are still available. These two sets of complete recordings were made in the 1960s and 1970s by the D'Oyly Carte Opera Company. Because the Company kept the performance tradition so carefully throughout most of the twentieth century, the performances on these recordings are stylistically authentic in every aspect. Listening to these recordings is a great way to enhance your sense of this style.

Body of work

Gilbert and Sullivan created a very successful model on which they based their operettas. These operettas have been produced and enjoyed around the world and translated into Portuguese, Yiddish, Hebrew, Swedish, Dutch, Danish, Estonian, Hungarian, Russian, Japanese, French, Italian, Spanish and more. They continue to be produced and enjoyed around the world, but hold a particular place in the hearts of audiences of the English-speaking musical theatre.

Each of their operettas takes place in fanciful worlds of "topsy-turvy," in which the absurdities of the world are taken to their extremes. In this way Gilbert and Sullivan were able to gently mock the rigid rules of English Victorian society, both written and unwritten. The model that Gilbert and Sullivan followed for almost all of their operettas features a heroic tenor protagonist, his soprano love interest, a sharp-tongued older alto or mezzo, the girl's befuddled baritone father, a bass-baritone villain and the comic patter-singing baritone.

Gilbert and Sullivan collaborated on 14 operettas between 1871 and 1896. They firmly established the tradition of English-language operetta and paved the way for all of the English-language music theatre to come. These 14 operettas continue to be the most frequently performed series of operettas in history; they include:

Thespis (1871)	*Princess Ida* (1884)
Trial By Jury (1875)	*The Mikado* (1885)
The Sorcerer (1877)	*Ruddigore* (1887)
H.M.S. Pinafore (1878)	*The Yeomen of the Guard* (1888)
The Pirates of Penzance (1880)	*The Gondoliers* (1889)
Patience (1881)	*Utopia Limited* (1893)
Iolanthe (1882)	*The Grand Duke* (1896)

Some of Gilbert and Sullivan's best-loved songs are their comic patter songs, originally written for the comic patter-singing baritone character in each of their shows. As with most of the catalog of Gilbert and Sullivan songs, these were written to suit the talents of a specific actor, originally Sullivan's older brother, Fred in *Thespis* and *Trail By Jury* and after Fred Sullivan's death, George Grossmith in *The Sorcerer* through *Yeomen of the Guard*.

Taken from their operettas, here is a list of the more popular
Gilbert and Sullivan arias, separated by voice type:

Soprano

How Would I Play This Part
(*The Grand Duke*)
So Ends My Dream (*The
Grand Duke*)
Simple Sailor Lowly Born
(*H.M.S. Pinafore*)
Sorry Her Lot Who Loves
Too Well (*H.M.S. Pinafore*)
The Sun Whose Rays
Are All Ablaze (*The
Mikado*)
I Cannot Tell What This Love
May Be (*Patience*)
Love Is a Plaintive Song
(*Patience*)

Poor Wand'ring One (*The
Pirates of Penzance*)
Oh, Goddess Wise
(*Princess Ida*)
I Built Upon a Rock
(*Princess Ida*)
A Lady Faire of Lineage High
(*Princess Ida*)
If Somebody There Chanced to
Be (*Ruddigore*)
When He Is Here (*The Sorcerer*)
Happy Young Heart (*The
Sorcerer*)
'Tis Done! I Am a Bride (*The
Yeomen of the Guard*)

Mezzo-soprano

When Fredric Was A Lad
(*The Pirates of Penzance*)
To A Garden Full of Posies
(*Ruddigore*)
Alone, and Yet Alive (*The
Mikado*)
A Lady Fair (*Princess Ida*)
Cheerily Carols the Lark
(*Ruddigore*)
Come Mighty Must!
(*Princess Ida*)
My Lord, A Suppliant At
Your Feet (*Iolanthe*)
On the Day When I Was
Wedded (*The Gondoliers*)
Sir Rupert Murgatroyd
(*Ruddigore*)

When But a Maid of Fifteen
Years (*Utopia Limited*)
When Our Gallant Norman
Foes (*The Yeomen of the
Guard*)
(I'm Called) Little Buttercup
(*H.M.S. Pinafore*)
Were I Thy Bride (*The Yeomen
of the Guard*)
When Maiden Loves, She Sits
and Sighs (*The Yeomen of
the Guard*)
When a Merry Maiden
Marries (*The Gondoliers*)
Silver'd is the Raven Hair
(*Patience*)
Oh, Foolish Fay (*Iolanthe*)

Tenor

Rising Early in the Morning
(*The Gondoliers*)
Take a Pair of Sparkling Eyes
(*The Gondoliers*)
A Maiden Fair to See (*H.M.S. Pinafore*)
Spurn Not the Nobly Born
(*Iolanthe*)
A Wand'ring Minstrel (*The Mikado*)
Oh, Is There Not One Maiden
Breast (*The Pirates of Penzance*)
Twenty Years Ago
(*Princess Ida*)

Would You Know the Kind of
Maid (*Princess Ida*)
I Shipped, D'Ye See (*Ruddigore*)
For Love Alone (*The Sorcerer*)
It Is Not Love (*The Sorcerer*)
Oh, Gentlemen, Listen, I Pray
(*Trial By Jury*)
When First My Old, Old Love
I Knew (*Trial By Jury*)
A Tenor, All Singers Above
(*Utopia Limited*)
Free from His Fetters Grim
(*The Yeomen of the Guard*)
Is Life a Boon? (*The Yeomen of the Guard*)

Baritone/Bass

No Possible Doubt Whatever
(*The Gondoliers*)
When All Night Long a Chap
Remains (*Iolanthe*)
When You're Lying Awake
with a Dismal Headache
(*Iolanthe*)
Fair Moon to Thee I Sing
(*H.M.S. Pinafore*)
When I Was a Lad I Served a
Term (*H.M.S. Pinafore*)
As Some Day Soon May
Happen (*The Mikado*)
Willow, Tit-Willow (*The Mikado*)
I Am a Pirate King
(*The Pirates of Penzance*)

I Am the Very Model of a
Modern Major-General
(*The Pirates of Penzance*)
The Policeman's Song (*The Pirates of Penzance*)
If You Give Me Your Attention
(*Princess Ida*)
Whene'er I Spoke (*Princess Ida*)
My Boy, You May Take It From
Me (*Ruddigore*)
My Name Is John Wellington
Wells (*The Sorcerer*)
Time Was When Love and I
(*The Sorcerer*)
Engaged to So-and-So (*The Sorcerer*)
I've Jibe and Joke (*The Yeomen of the Guard*)

Biography

Gilbert was born in London in 1836. His father was a naval sur-
geon and occasional writer of novels and short stories. In 1861

Gilbert began publishing a series of illustrated poems under the title "Bab Ballads," "Bab" having been a childhood nickname. It was in these pieces that Gilbert began working out his "topsy-turvy" style in which the humor derives from extending the absurd premises of the world to their ultimate logical consequences.

Sullivan was born in London in 1842, the son of a military bandleader. Musically precocious, he received the first Mendelssohn Scholarship awarded in the United Kingdom at age 16 and began his musical studies at the Royal Academy of Music. His graduation composition was performed at London's Crystal Palace in 1862 and almost immediately Sullivan was recognized and acknowledged as one of England's most promising rising composers at age 20. In 1866 he tried his hand at comic opera with *Cox and Box*.

Producer John Hollingshead brought Gilbert and Sullivan together in 1871 to create a musical Christmas entertainment for him, *Thespis*, which proved highly successful. Between 1871 and 1875 Gilbert and Sullivan both continued to work with other partners and to grow in their reputations, public esteem and their respective crafts, until producer Richard D'Oyly Carte brought them together again to write *Trial By Jury*. Success followed success with D'Oyly Carte producing their works and ultimately building the Savoy Theatre as a home for his D'Oyly Carte Opera Company, established to produce the works of Gilbert and Sullivan.

By 1890 Gilbert and Sullivan had each grown to resent having to subjugate their talents to the needs and ego of the other. An argument over whether the replacement of a carpet in the theatre should be charged to the company's accounts or whether D'Oyly Carte should pay for it himself was the spark that immolated the relationship.

Resources

There is a wealth of excellent material available about Gilbert and Sullivan. Among them are: François Cellier's *Gilbert and Sullivan and Their Operas; With Recollections and Anecdotes of D'Oyly Carte & Other Famous Savoyards*,[8] Michael Ainger's *Gilbert and Sullivan: A Dual Biography*[9] and Harold Orel's *Gilbert and Sullivan: Interviews and Recollections*.[10] In addition to these resources, audio and video recordings of the operettas are plentiful, including full performances of all of their works as well as many concert performances of the songs on youtube.com and other websites.

Franz Lehár (1870–1948)

Stylistic approach

Lehár brought the can-can and other French elements to Viennese operetta, joining the best of Offenbach and his traditions and the best of Strauss and his. The music of Lehár is a little more technically demanding, requiring a slightly heavier sound and a little more vocally muscle-bound technical approach than the work of his predecessors.

Body of work

Lehár's greatest success was *Die lustige Witwe* (The Merry Widow), which was a worldwide phenomenon. It was successfully produced around the world, and played for 778 performances in London and for 416 performances in New York – both considered extraordinary runs in 1907. It has been made into five different film versions. In addition to *Die lustige Witwe*, Lehár wrote a great number of operas and operettas, which have proven very successful in many languages, including their English translations.

As with Offenbach and Strauss, recordings of most of Lehár's work is available online. Listening to several different recordings will help in preparing your own interpretation – not to imitate, but to better understand the style and to build on the stylistic choices of other singers.

Lehár's operas and operettas include:

Der Kürassier (The Cavalry, Oper, unperformed, 1891)

Rodrigo (Oper, unperformed, 1893)

Kukuška (Oper, 1896)

Arabella, der Kubanerin (Operette, never completed, 1901)

Das Klub-Baby (The Club Baby, Operette, never completed, 1901)

Der Klavierstimmer (The Piano Tuner, Operette, 1902)

Der Rastelbinder (The Tinker, Operette, 1902)

Weiner Frauen (Viennese Ladies, 1902)

Der Göttergatte (The Divine Husband, Operette, 1904)

Die Juxheirat (The Marriage Lark, Operette, 1904)

Die lustige Witwe (The Merry Widow, Operette, 1905)

Der Schüssel zum Paradies (The Key to Paradise, Operette, 1906)

Peter und Paul schlafen ins Schlaraffenland (Peter and Paul Sleep to Paradise, Zaubermärchen, 1906)

Mitislaw der Moderne (Mitislaw, the Modern, Operette, 1907)

Der Mann mit den drei Frauen (The Man With Three Wives, Operette, 1908)

Das Fürstenkind (The Prince's Child, Operette, 1909)

Der Graf von Luxemburg (The Count of Luxembourg, Operette, 1909)

Zigeunerliebe (Gypsy Love, romantische Operette, 1910)

Eva (*Das Fabriksmädel*) (Eva, The Factory Girl, Operette, 1911)

Rosenstock und Edelweiss (Rosebush and Edelweiss, Singspiel, 1912)

Die ideale Gattin (The Ideal Wife, Operette, 1913)

Endlich allein (Alone at Last, Operette, 1914)

Der Sterngucker (The Stargazer, Operette, 1916)

Wo die Lerche singt (Where the Lark Sings, Operette, 1918)

Die blaue Mazur (The Blue Mazurka, Operette, 1920)

Die Tangokönigin (The Tango Queen, Operette, 1921)

Frühling (Spring, Singspiel, 1922)

La danza delle libellule (The Dance of the Dragonflies, Operette, 1922)

Frasquita (Operette, 1922)

Die gelbe Jacke (The Yellow Jacket, Operette, 1923)

Libellentanz (The Dance of the Dragonflies, Operette, 1923)

Cloclo (Operette, 1924)

Paganini (Operette, 1925)

Gigolette (Operette, 1926)

Der Zarewitsch (The Tsarevich, Operette, 1926)

Frühlingsmädel (The Girl of Spring, Singspiel, 1928)

Friederike (Singspiel, 1928)

Das Land des Lächelns (The Land of Smiles, romantische Operette, 1929)

Schön ist die Welt (Beautiful World, Operette, 1930)

Der Fürst der Berge (The Prince of the Mountains, Operette, 1932)

Giuditta (musikalische Komödie, 1934)

Garabonciás diák (The Wandering Scholar, romantische Singspiel, 1943)

Here is a list of the more popular of Lehár's arias, listed by voice type:

Soprano

Mazurka (*Die lustige Witwe*)
Es lebt eine Vilja (There
    Lived a Vilja, *Die
    lustige Witwe*)
Meine Lippen, sie küsser so
    heiss (My Lips, they Kiss so
    Hot, *Giuditta*)
Einer wird kommen (Someone
    Will Come, *Der
    Zarewitsch*)

Liebe, du Himmel auf Erden
    (Love, Thou Heaven on
    Earth, *Paganini*)
Heut' noch werd' ich Ehefrau
    (*Der Graf von Luxemburg*)
Lied und Csárdás (Song and
    Dance, *Zigeunerliebe*)
Ich möcht' wieder einmal die
    Heimat she'n (*Das Land
    des Lächelns*)

Tenor

Da geh 'ich zu Maxim (You'll
    Find Me at Maxim's, *Die
    lustige Witwe*)
Wie eine Rosenknospe (At the
    First Kiss of April, *Die
    lustige Witwe*)
Dein ist mein ganzes Herz (You
    Are My Heart's Delight,
    Das Land des Lächelns)
Freunde, das Leben ist lebens-
    wert (Friends, Life is Well
    Worth Living, *Giuditta*)

Walgalied (*Der Zarewitsch*)
O Mädchen, mein Mädchen
    (Oh Maiden, My Maiden,
    Frederike)
Gern hab' ich die Frau'n
    geküsst (I Enjoyed
    Kissing the Women,
    Paganini)
Hab'ein blaues Himmelbett
    (My Little Nest
    of Heavenly Blue,
    Frasquita)

Baritone/Bass

Danillo's Song (*Die
    lustige Witwe*)
Adolar's Song (*Die blaue Mazur*)

Prince's Aria (*Das Land des
    Lächelns*)

Biography

Franz Lehár was born in Komáron in the Austro-Hungarian Empire. His father was a horn player and military bandleader. After being sent to Sternbeck in the Kingdom of Bohemia to live with and play violin under his uncle, the town musical director, Lehár began studies in violin and music theory at the Prague Conservatory at age 15. In 1888 he accepted his first professional position as theatre violinist in Barmen-Elberfeld, Germany, followed by a position as a military bandleader for the 50th Austrian regiment band.

His first opera, *Kukuška*, in 1896 was only a modest success, but a transfer to Vienna put him at the center of German-language opera, where his waltz "Gold and Silver" became immensely popular. Following several early pieces, which were marginal successes, his greatest success, *Die lustige Witwe (The Merry Widow)*, opened and became an international hit; in fact five different productions played simultaneously in Buenos Aires alone. Operetta had started its decline as a popular art form, and *Die lustige Witwe* is credited with single-handedly rekindling the public's infatuation with the genre.

Following World War I, Lehár's popularity flagged, but he revived it with a longstanding relationship with tenor Richard Tauber. During World War II, Lehár was forced to cultivate a relationship with the Nazis in order to protect his wife, who had been born Jewish. After the war his reputation suffered due to his wartime relationship with the Nazis.

Resources

Lehár biographies are relatively few. One is Bernard Grun's *Gold and Silver: The Life and Times of Franz Lehár.*[11] There are several sources available discussing Hitler's relationship with artists and with the arts, which may be useful. Those looking for further information on Lehár should begin by looking into general texts on operetta. Many performances of Lehár arias are available in audio and video recordings.

Victor Herbert (1859–1924)

Stylistic approach

While operetta was popular worldwide, three American writers were responsible for establishing the American tradition of operetta; the first and arguably the most successful of these was Victor Herbert. Born in Dublin, Ireland, and raised and trained in Stuttgart,

Germany, Herbert brought a traditional European sensibility in operetta traditions with him to America when he immigrated with his wife in 1886. Herbert used a huge range of styles, sounds and influences. He often developed a musical theme through a series of styles, pulling from the sounds of Spanish, Austrian, Italian and Hungarian music. Marches, waltzes, cakewalks and more were part of his musical vocabulary. As musical styles and tastes shifted, Herbert shifted with them; he comfortably kept up with ragtime, foxtrots, tangos and other popular forms.

European operettas had employed opera singers, and Herbert's operettas on Broadway did as well. Three of Herbert's favorite leading ladies were Americans Alice Nielsen and Fritzi Scheff and Italian-born Emma Trentini; all three were highly trained opera singers as well as accomplished actresses. By the time of Herbert's success, *bel canto* singing was no longer being practiced (although it would make a resurgence in the 1950s); voices were called on to have more size, often at the loss of purity. Recordings of Nielsen, Scheff and Trentini are all available online, singing Herbert's songs and others. These recordings are absolutely invaluable for getting a grasp of Herbert's songs as he originally intended them to be performed. To a contemporary ear these recordings may sound a little self-indulgent dynamically, with more vibrato than we are used to hearing, but this was the style that Herbert loved. These songs do not need to be sung in such a traditional style, but it is certainly a good place to begin when developing a performance of these works.

Body of work

Herbert's stage works were almost all operettas (except where noted below) and almost all were presented initially on Broadway.

Prince Ananias (1894)
The Wizard of the Nile (1895)
The Gold Bug (musical
     farce, 1896)
The Serenade (1897)
The Idol's Eye (1897)
The Fortune Teller (1897)
The Ameer (1899)
Cyrano de Bergerac (1899)
The Singing Girl (1899)

The Viceroy (1900)
Babes in Toyland (1903)
Babette (1903)
It Happened in Nordland
     (musical comedy, 1904)
Wonderland (fantastic musical
     play, 1905)
Miss Dolly Dollars (musical
     comedy, 1905)
Mlle. Modiste (1905)

The Red Mill (1906)
The Magic Knight (1906)
Dream City (1906)
The Tattooed Man (1907)
The Song Birds (1907)
Algeria (musical play, 1908)
Little Nemo (musical
    comedy, 1908)
The Prima Donna (comic
    opera, 1908)
The Rose of Algeria (musical
    play, 1909)
Old Dutch (musical
    farce, 1909)
Naughty Marietta (1910)
When Sweet Sixteen (musical
    comedy, 1911)
Natoma (opera, 1911)
The Duchess (1911)
The Enchantress (1911)
The Lady of the Slipper (musi-
    cal fantasy, 1912)
Sweethearts (musical
    play, 1913)
The Madcap Duchess (1913)
The Only Girl (musical
    comedy, 1914)

The Debutante (musical
    comedy, 1914)
The Princess Pat (1915)
The Century Girl (revue, 1916)
Eileen (1917)
Miss 1917 (revue, 1917)
Her Regiment (1917)
Madeleine (opera, 1918)
The Velvet Lady (musical
    comedy, 1919)
Angel Face (musical play, 1919)
My Golden Girl (musical
    comedy, 1919)
Ziegfeld Follies of 1920
    (revue, 1920)
Oui Madame (1920)
The Girl in the Spotlight (1920)
Ziegfeld Follies of 1921
    (revue, 1921)
Ziegfeld Follies of 1922
    (revue, 1922)
Orange Blossoms (musical
    comedy, 1922)
Ziegfeld Follies of 1923 (sum-
    mer edition) (revue, 1923)
The Dream Girl (musical
    comedy, 1924)

Herbert wrote what are still some of the most loved songs in American operetta; in addition, many of his individual songs outside operettas became very popular. Among Herbert's most popular songs by vocal range are:

Soprano

Toyland (Babes in Toyland)
A Kiss in the Dark (Orange
    Blossoms)
Art is Calling Me (The
    Prima Donna Song, The
    Enchantress)

Italian Street Song (Naughty
    Marietta)
Thine Alone (Eileen)
Kiss Me Again (Mlle. Modiste)
When You're Away (The
    Only Girl)

Romany Life (*The Fortune Teller*)
I'm Falling in Love With Someone (*Naughty Marietta*)

Ah! Sweet Mystery of Life (*Naughty Marietta*)
Sweethearts (*Sweethearts*)

Mezzo

My Heart is True (Op. 21, No. 2. Berlin: Luckhardte, 1891)
A Maiden Went Into the Field Alone (Op. 18, No. 2. Berlin: Luckhardte, 1891)
If You But Knew (date unknown)

Longing For Home (date unknown)
Love Song (New York: Schuberthe, 1896)
Peace (New York: Schuberthe, 1896)
Neath the Southern Moon (*Naughty Marietta*)

Tenor

In Dreamland (*The Wizard of the Nile*)
I Want What I Want When I Want It (*Mlle. Modiste*)
The Only Girl (*The Only Girl*)
I'm Falling In Love With Someone (*Naughty Marietta*)

Tramp, Tramp, Tramp (*Naughty Marietta*)
Every Day Is Lady's Day With Me (*The Red Mill*)
The Streets of New York (*The Red Mill*)
When You're Away (*The Only Girl*)
I Might Be Your "Once in a While" (*Angel Face*)

Baritone

Slumber On My Little Gypsy Sweetheart (*The Fortune Teller*)
Under an Oak (*Prince Ananias*)

Every Lover Must Meet His Fate (*Sweethearts*)
When You're Away (*The Only Girl*)

Many of Herbert's popular songs have been performed by singers with different vocal ranges and are available in a variety of keys. For that reason they are not listed by voice type. These songs include:

Fairy Tales
I Envy the Bird
Ah! Love Me
Love's Token
The Silent Rose
When I Was Born I Weighed
    Ten Stone
Jenny's Baby
Me and Nancy
What Is Love?
The Secret
The Tattooed Man
Gypsy Love Song
Mary's Lamb
The Serenades of All Nations
Hear Me
We'll Catch You at Last,
    Tivolini
Barney O'Flynn
I Can't Do the Sum
March of the Toys
If I Were on the Stage
When the Cat's Away the Mice
    Will Play
Moonbeams
The Streets of New York
Love Laid His Sleepless Head

The Friars' Song
Ask Her While the Band Is
    Playing
Love Is Like a Cigarette
Won't You Be My Valentine?
I Want to Be a Good Lamb
Naughty Marietta
To the Land of My Own
    Romance
Love's Hour
If Love Were What the Rose Is
The Love of the Lorelei
Remembrance
Sweet Harp of the Days
An Easter Dawn
Indian Summer
Molly
My Day Has Come
Equity Star
Dream On
Lora Lee Joseph
Mary Came Over to Me
When Knighthood Was
    in Flower
God Spare the Emerald Isle
Little Old New York
Heart o'Mine

Biography

Herbert was born in Dublin, Ireland, in 1859. Following his father's death, when he was two years old, he moved with his mother to the home of his grandfather, a painter, novelist and composer. By the time he was seven, his mother had remarried and moved the family to Stuttgart, Germany. Family financial conditions shifted Herbert's focus from medicine to music. By the age of 19 he had become famous throughout Germany as a cellist. In 1885 he met soprano Therese Forster, who had recently been discovered by Walter Damrosch of the Metropolitan Opera. Forster accepted a contract with the Metropolitan Opera in New York on the terms that employment was provided for Herbert.

Herbert quickly rose in the orchestral world in the United States as cellist, composer and conductor. Herbert's theatre scores helped stage entertainment transition from vaudeville and variety-based entertainments to story-based musical theatre. He was one of the first true giants of the American musical theatre.

As was the case with the writers in this chapter, most of Herbert's work is easily accessible online and on recordings. Listening to several different recordings, both from Herbert's day and later, will help in preparing your own interpretation. As with the others, this is not meant as in invitation to imitate, but to better understand the style and to build on the stylistic choices of other singers.

Resources

The most recent biographies of Herbert are Neil Gould's book, *Victor Herbert: A Theatrical Life*[12] and Joseph Kaye's *Victor Herbert: The Biography of America's Greatest Composer of Romantic Music*. Both of these provide an excellent source to start with. There are audio and video recordings of much of Herbert's repertoire available online.

Rudolf Friml (1879–1972)

Stylistic approach

Friml draws heavily on the work and style of Johann Strauss II and the Viennese school of operetta. Building on the American operetta tradition initiated by Herbert, Friml's musicals and operettas call for long legato vocal lines, a *verismo* style of singing and a highly dramatic and demonstrative style of acting. Many of Friml's stage works were successfully adapted into films. While his body of work has not yielded as many popular arias as Herbert's, those hits that he did have were just as substantial and lasting, and his popular operettas remain just as popular as Herbert's.

Body of work

Friml's stage productions include:

The Firefly (1912)   *The Peasant Girl* (1915)
High Jinks (1913)   *Katinka* (1915)

You're in Love (1917)
Kitty Darlin' (1917)
Sometime (1918)
Glorianna (1918)
Tumble In (1919)
The Little Whopper (1919)
June Love (1921)
Ziegfeld Follies of 1921 (1921)
The Blue Kitten (1922)
Cinders (1923)
Dew Drop Inn (1923)
Ziegfeld Follies of 1923 (1923)

Annie Dear (1924)
Rose Marie (1924)
The Vagabond King (1925)
No Foolin' (1926)
Ziegfeld's Palm Beach
    Girl (1926)
The Wild Rose (1926)
White Eagle (1927)
The Three Musketeers (1928)
Ruth Selwyn's 9:15 Revue (1930)
Luana (1930)
Music Hath Charms (1934)

In 1927 the film *The Jazz Singer* introduced talking and singing films to audiences. Just two years later the Great Depression began, and with it fewer live stage shows with shorter runs and less chance of making a living. With a surge in the production of singing movie musicals, a great majority of the Broadway community took refuge in Hollywood during the 1930s, and many never returned or they took up dual residence. Like so many other Broadway writers, performers, directors and so on, Friml reestablished his roots in Hollywood during the 1930s. Friml was less successful than many other displaced New Yorkers, but once he made it his home he never returned to New York full-time. Friml's full-length films include:

The Vagabond King (1930)
The Lottery Bride (1930)
Rose-Marie (1936)
The Firefly (1937)

Music for Madame (1937)
Northwest Outpost (1947)
Rose-Marie (1954)

Many of Friml's most famous songs have been sung by singers in different vocal ranges and are available in a variety of keys; for that reason, these songs are not listed by vocal type. Some of Friml's most famous songs include:

Giannina Mia (*The Firefly*)
Love Is Like a Firefly (*The Firefly*)
When a Maid Comes Knocking at Your Door (*The Firefly*)
Sympathy (*The Firefly*)

Something Seems a Tingle-ing-eling (*High Jinks*)
Love's Own Kiss (*High Jinks*)
Not Now but Later (*High Jinks*)

Katinka (*Katinka*)

'Tis the End, So Farewell (*Katinka*)

Allah's Holiday (*Katinka*)

Rackety Coo (*Katinka*)

You're in Love (*You're in Love*)

Cutie (*The Blue Kitten*)

The Door of My Dreams (*Rose-Marie*)

Rose-Marie (*Rose-Marie*)

The Song of the Mounties (*Rose-Marie*)

Indian Love Call (*Rose-Marie*)

Pretty Things (*Rose-Marie*)

Totem Tom-Tom (*Rose-Marie*)

Song of the Vagabonds (*The Vagabond King*)

Some Day (*The Vagabond King*)

Tomorrow (*The Vagabond King*)

Only a Rose (*The Vagabond King*)

Huguette Waltz (*The Vagabond King*)

Love Me Tonight (*The Vagabond King*)

Wild Rose (*The Wild Rose*)

One Golden Hour (*The Wild Rose*)

Give Me One Hour (*White Eagle*)

March of the Musketeers (*The Three Musketeers*)

My Sword and I (*The Three Musketeers*)

All For One and One For All (*The Three Musketeers*)

Ma Belle (*The Three Musketeers*)

Your Eyes (*The Three Musketeers*)

The He For Me (*The Three Musketeers*)

Donkey Serenade (*The Firefly*)

Biography

Rudolf Friml was born in Prague, Czechoslovakia, and studied piano and composition at the Prague Conservatory. Friml spent his twenties touring Europe and the United States as a pianist. Following the tour, in 1906, Friml moved to New York and began writing occasional pieces for shows. In 1912 when Herbert abandoned *The Firefly*, producer Arthur Hammerstein hired the unknown Friml to complete the score based on his classical training.

Friml contributed a great deal to American musical operettas until the Great Depression began encroaching on stage productions. In 1934 he moved to Hollywood to work on film musicals. Throughout the 1930s Friml's style of music became more and more out of date. Rather than adapt his style, Friml returned to his career as a concert pianist. Friml died in Los Angeles in 1972.

Resources

Friml's music has come to feel old-fashioned, and there is not much academic interest in his life. Few books are devoted to his life and works; the best sources are books such as Richard Traubner's *Operetta: A Theatrical History*.[13] As with the other composers in this section, much of Friml's work is available for viewing and listening online, in part because so many of his stage productions were adapted to film.

Sigmund Romberg (1887–1951)

Stylistic approach

Of the composers discussed in this chapter, Romberg spanned the greatest number of styles. Serving as a house composer for the Shubert Brothers, he was called on to write a diverse range of music. Romberg's music is rhythmically and metrically conservative. "Gentle syncopation may appear in his duple-meter songs, but nothing extravagant or pervasive. [Likewise his harmonic range, is] rooted in nineteenth-century diatonic-chromatic ("common practice") useage. Romberg employs a consistent tonal language with a conventional approach to non-harmonic tones and key relationships."[14] Romberg himself wrote about the straightforward way he went about creating atmosphere musically in a 1928 article in *Theatre Magazine*, "A Peep Into the Workshop of a Composer." "Music is in two keys, major and minor. Hungarian, Russian, and Balkan States, Persia and India take music in the minor key; Anglo-Saxon and Latin countries are written in major."[15]

His melodies were the driving mechanism behind his songs. Interesting and unexpected turns in melody leap out from Romberg's songs, but they ultimately make perfect sense by the time the end of the phrase is reached. This melodic gift requires the singer to allow the melody to soar, not to back off from it or to replace melodic integrity with dramatic integrity. With certain composers non-traditional phrasing can lead to interesting new interpretations; this is much less true of Romberg's music than many others'. Many recordings of Romberg's songs are available online and they are recommended listening.

Body of work

Romberg's stage musicals include:

The Whirl of the World (1914)
The Midnight Girl (1914)
The Passing Show of 1914 (1914)
Dancing Around (1914)
Maid in America (1915)
Hands Up! (1915)
The Blue Paradise (1915)
A World of Pleasure (1915)
Ruggles of Red Gap (1915)
Robinson Crusoe, Jr. (1916)
The Passing Show of 1916 (1916)
The Girl From Brazil (1916)
The Show of Wonders (1916)
Follow Me (1916)
Her Soldier Boy (1916)
The Passing Show of 1917 (1917)
Maytime (1917)
Doing Our Bit (1917)
Over the Top (1917)
Sinbad (1918)
Follow the Girl (1918)
The Passing Show of 1918 (1918)
The Melting of Molly (1918)
Monte Cristo, Jr. (1919)
The Passing Show of 1919 (1919)
The Magic Melody (1919)
Poor Little Ritz Girl (1920)
Love Birds (1921)
Blossom Time (1921)

Bombo (1921)
Blushing Bride (1922)
The Rose of Stamboul (1922)
Springtime of Youth (1922)
The Dancing Girl (1923)
The Passing Show of 1923 (1923)
Innocent Eyes (1924)
Marjorie (1924)
The Passing Show of 1924 (1924)
Artists and Models (1924)
The Student Prince (1924)
Louie the 14th (1925)
Artists and Models (1925)
Princess Flavia (1925)
The Desert Song (1926)
Cherry Blossoms (1927)
My Maryland (1927)
My Princess (1927)
The Love Call (1927)
Rosalie (1928)
The New Moon (1928)
Nina Rosa (1930)
East Wind (1931)
Melody (1933)
May Wine (1935)
Forbidden Melody (1936)
Sunny River (1941)
Up in Central Park (1945)
My Romance (1948)
The Girl in Pink Tights (produced posthumously in 1954)

Like so many other Broadway composers, Romberg reestablished his roots in Hollywood during 1930s. Some of Romberg's full-length films were adaptations of his stage pieces, while others were written specifically for the screen. These include:

Viennese Nights (1930)
New Moon (1930)
Children of Dreams (1931)
The Night is Young (1935)
Annapolis Farewell (1935)
Maytime (1937)
They Gave Him a Gun (1937)
The Girl of the Golden West (1938)

New Moon (1940)
The Desert Song (1943)
Up in Central Park (1948)

Posthumously:

The Desert Song (1953)
The Student Prince (1954)
Deep in My Heart (1954)

Some of Herbert's best remembered and most often performed songs include:

Soprano

Lover Come Back to Me (*The New Moon*)
One Kiss (*The New Moon*)
Wanting You (*The New Moon*)
Romance (*The Desert Song*)
Why Must We Always Be Dreaming (*Rosalie*)
I Bring a Love Song (film *Vienna Nights*)

Mother (*My Maryland*)
Silver Moon (*My Maryland*)
The Song of Love (*Blossom Time*)
Deep in My Heart, Dear (*The Student Prince*)
Close As Pages In a Book (*Up in Central Park*)

Mezzo

You Will Remember Vienna (film *Vienna Nights*)
One Alone (*The Desert Song*)

Will You Remember (*Maytime*)
Lover Come Back to Me (*The New Moon*)

Tenor

Mother (*Her Soldier Boy*)
Marianne (*The New Moon*)
When I Grow Too Old To Dream (*The Night is Young*)

Serenade (Overhead the Moon is Beaming, *The Student Prince*)
Golden Days (*The Student Prince*)

The Drinking Song (Drink, Drink, Drink) (*The Student Prince*)
One Alone (*The Desert Song*)
Will You Remember (*Maytime*)

I Bring a Love Song (film, *Vienna Nights*)
Deep in My Heart, Dear (*The Student Prince*)

Baritone

Serenade (*The Student Prince*)
Golden Days (*The Student Prince*)
The Riff Song (*The Desert Song*)
One Alone (*The Desert Song*)
Softly, As in a Morning Sunrise (*The New Moon*)
Stout-hearted Men (*The New Moon*)

Lover Come Back to Me (*The New Moon*)
Wanting You (*The New Moon*)
The Song of Love (*Blossom Time*)
The Desert Song (*The Desert Song*)
Close As Pages In a Book (*Up in Central Park*)
My Heart Won't Say Goodbye (*Up in Central Park*

Biography

Sigmund Romberg was born to a Jewish family in Gross-Kanizsa in the Austro-Hungarian Empire and raised in Belisce, Hungary. He studied engineering and musical composition in Vienna. Five years after his arrival in the United States, in 1909, he was working alternately as a pianist, an orchestra leader and occasional composer when the Shubert Brothers offered him a contract writing for them. His first assignment was a revue, *The Whirl of the World*, followed by a series of American adaptations of Viennese operettas. Romberg continued as a staff writer for the Shubert Brothers, taking all assignments he was given. Since the featured aspect of Shubert shows of the time was the chorus of beautiful women rather than the score, Romberg's scores were not required to be brilliant, and yet they always fulfilled expectations and frequently rose above them. The pieces at which Romberg excelled tended to be the operettas.

Romberg remained active professionally up until his death in 1951 in New York City. In fact, his final Broadway musical, *The Girl in Pink Tights*, was not produced until three years after his death, and his musical sketches for this work were completed after his death by orchestrator Don Walker.

Resources

William A. Everett's book *Sigmund Romberg*[16] provides a detailed analysis of Romberg's life and works. A Hollywood version of Romberg's life was told in the film *Deep in My Heart*, in 1954.

In summary

Operetta has traditionally suffered from an identity crisis; in defining it, music and theatre historians have been reduced to referring to operetta as "a convenient in-between label for things that are not quite musical theatre or opera."[17] Although sometimes viewed as opera's lesser sibling, operetta traditionally called for a classically trained voice of a lighter quality than traditional operas. Operetta singers have tended to come from the world of opera and used placements and tone that afforded them a lighter sound, affecting the qualities of floating or spinning. The true stars of operetta were the composers, and in deference to the composers, the vocal quality was most important.

With the advent of Gilbert and Sullivan, and much to Sullivan's chagrin, W.S. Gilbert became the first star lyricist and lyrics took precedence over vocal quality. Hearing Gilbert's clever rhymes and wordplay and following his topsy-turvy storylines became more important than the music. While a solid classical vocal technique is still important for singers, clarity and diction become essential.

The songs of Herbert, Romberg and Friml also require strong classical technique, but with attention to lyrical content. So many of their songs have highly poetic lyrics, requiring clarity of thought and articulation to allow listeners to follow the sometimes fanciful imagery. Seek out recordings of Richard Tauber, dubbed by some as the greatest operetta tenor of the twentieth century; he is able to spin out a full-bodied sound that never overwhelms the material or takes on the weight of a dramatic opera vocal style.

Singers of operetta were notoriously temperamental. Diva Emma Trentini incited Victor Herbert to storm off the podium in the middle of a performance of his *Naughty Marietta*, which he was also conducting. The ensuing argument caused Herbert to abandon his next writing project, *The Firefly*, for which Trentini had already been contracted, thus creating an opportunity for newcomer Rudolf Friml. These singers lived highly dramatic lives and performed in a highly dramatic style, in which the drama expressed itself in an intensely dynamic musical style.

Notes

1 K.E. Querns Langley, "K.E. Querns Langley: Bel Canto Vocal Studio," *A World of Art – A World of Entertainment*, www.belcantovocalstudio.co.uk/bel-canto-history, accessed May 5, 2016.
2 Robert Toft, *Bel Canto: A Performer's Guide*, Oxford, UK: Oxford University Press, 2013.
3 Chris Tondreau, "Welcome to The Bel Canto Technique," *The Bel Canto Technique*, http://thebelcantotechnique.com, accessed March 10, 2015.
4 Ethan Mordden, *Opera Anecdotes*, New York, NY: Oxford University Press, 1985, p. 133.
5 Uncredited, "Strauss, II, J. Orchestral edition," *Naxos Classical*, www.naxos.com/catalogue/item.asp?item_code=8.505226, accessed March 7, 2015.
6 David Ewen, *Wine, Women and Waltz: A Romantic Biography of Johann Strauss, Son and Father*, Whitefish, MT: Kessinger Publishing, LLC, 2007.
7 H.E. Jacobs, *Johann Strauss – Father and Son – A Century of Light Music*, New York, NY: Greystone, 1940.
8 François Cellier, *Gilbert and Sullivan and Their Operas; With Recollections and Anecdotes of D'Oyly Carte & Other Famous Savoyards*, Boston, MA: Little, Brown and Company, 1914.
9 Michael Ainger, *Gilbert and Sullivan: A Dual Biography*, New York, NY: Oxford University Press, 2002.
10 Harold Orel, *Gilbert and Sullivan: Interviews and Recollections*, Iowa City, IA: University of Iowa Press, 1994.
11 Bernard Grun, *Gold and Silver: The Life and Times of Franz Lehár*, London, UK: W.H. Auden/Virgin Books, 1970.
12 Neil Gould, *Victor Herbert: A Theatrical Life*, New York, NY: Fordham University Press, 2008.
13 Richard Traubner, *Operetta: A Theatrical History*, London, UK: Routledge, 2003.
14 William A. Everett, *Sigmund Romberg*, New Haven, CT: Yale University Press, 2007, p. 28.
15 Sigmund Romberg, "A Peep into the Workshop of a Composer," *Theatre Magazine*, xlvii/6 (1928), p. 72.
16 Everett, *Sigmund Romberg*.
17 Ilana Walder-Biesanz, "Opera, Operetta, or Musical Theatre? – Blog," *Opera Vivrà*, www.operavivra.com/blog/opera-operetta-or-musical-theatre/, accessed October 20, 2015.

Chapter 2

Popular musical theatre songs of the early 1900s

George M. Cohan, Irving Berlin, and
Jerome Kern

In the mid-nineteenth century, operetta was the reigning stage musical form throughout Europe, being popular with people of all classes, as opposed to opera, which tended to be accessible mostly to the upper classes. At the same time English-language opera had been firmly established by the work of Gilbert and Sullivan. Those who followed in their footsteps include Edward German, Ivan Caryll and Sydney James in England and Reginald De Koven and John Phillip Sousa in America. Whether dramatic plays or musicals, most theatrical entertainments in American were either imported from Europe or imitations of European theatre or musical theatre. The only exceptions were the variety entertainments. But shortly after the turn of the century that was about to change.

Just as *bel canto* had given way to *verismo*, as new American songwriters began writing for American voices, vocal production on the American musical theatre stage was shifting as well. There would always be a place for the "beautiful voice," but a new musical vocabulary was coming into vogue. As a nation, the United States was young, energetic, enthusiastic and, above all, optimistic. This youthful and edgy American spirit was reflected in the arts of America, particularly in the songs of the musical theatre, how they were written and how they were performed.

Three songwriters from this period are of particular interest in this regard. Each of them responded to this new American sound in different ways, the songs of all three continue to be popular today, and all three have heavily influenced the songwriters who came after them. These three songwriters are composer and lyricist George M. Cohan, composer and lyricist Irving Berlin and composer Jerome Kern.

George M. Cohan (1878–1942): The Yankee Doodle Boy

Stylistic approach

Composer and lyricist George M. Cohan's stage persona was the brash, energetic, cocky, young American. A complete entertainer, Cohan was known not only for his singing but for his dancing as well. He was reported to have been a strong, aggressive and masculine dancer. James Cagney's portrayal of Cohan in the 1942 biographic film, *Yankee Doodle Dandy*, is said to be quite accurate

Cohan's personal singing style was as aggressive and masculine as his dancing. Known for his unique vocal style, he would bark out lyrics on the pitch, making every single syllable clear while maintaining a sense of the melodic line. Rick Benjamin in *You're a Grand Old Rag: The Music of George M. Cohan* wrote:

> The first striking characteristic was his manner of *speaking* rather than actually *singing* many of the words to the songs he was performing. He used this technique intermittently, reciting a few words, and then singing a few, and then lapsing back to speech. He sometimes slurred these two deliveries together. In this process, Cohan often ignored the written melodies and rhythms of his own songs (and it should be noted that Cohan, with very few exceptions, performed *only* his own songs). But the effect was one of thrilling insouciance. To audiences it seemed as though he was making it all up off the top of his head – while the orchestra underscored him with jaunty Cohan melodies.[1]

Even Cohan's ballads were written for a plainer, simpler sound than had previously been popular. Cohan wrote for simple, clear voices able to make every word of his lyrics understood; added grace notes or ornamentation, admired in older styles, were not a part of the vocal aesthetic of a Cohan song.

Cohan's vocal style closely mirrors that of Tony Pastor, the creator of vaudeville. Cohan and his family had worked for Pastor early in their careers, and Cohan had adopted both Pastor's vocal style and his penchant for writing rousing patriotic tunes.

Body of work

Almost all of the shows that Cohan wrote are forgotten, while so many of his greatest songs are well remembered today. Nonetheless, Cohan, who also wrote the librettos, directed, produced and starred in most of his shows, wrote the following stage shows:

The Governor's Son (1901)
Running for Office (1903)
Mother Goose (only wrote
   additional songs, 1903)
*A Little Bit of
   Everything* (1904)
Little Johnny Jones (1905)
*Forty-five Minutes From
   Broadway* (1906)
Gallops (additional songs
   only, 1906)
George Washington, Jr., (1906)
Popularity (1906)
The Honeymooners (1907)
The Talk of New York (1907)
Fifty Miles From Boston (1908)
The Yankee Prince (1908)
*Cohan and Harris
   Minstrels* (1908)
The American Idea (1908)
The House Next Door (1909)
*Cohan and Harris
   Minstrels* (1909)
The Fortune Hunter (1909)
*The Man Who Owns
   Broadway* (1909)
*Get-Rich-Quick
   Wallingford* (1910)
The Aviator (1910)
The Little Millionaires (1911)
Vera Violetta (1911)
Broadway Jones (1912)

Seven Keys to Baldpate (1913)
The Miracle Man (1914)
Hello Broadway (1914)
Hit-the-Trail-Holiday (1915)
Cohan Revue of 1915 (1915)
Cohan Revue of 1918 (1917)
A Prince There Was (1918)
The Voice of McConnell
   (1918)
The Royal Vagabond (addi-
   tional songs only, 1919)
The Night Boat (additional
   songs only, 1920)
*Madeline and the
   Movies* (1922)
Little Nelly Kelly (1922)
*The Rise of Rosie
   O'Reilly* (1923)
*The Song and Dance
   Man* (1923)
American Born (1925)
The Home Owners (1926)
Baby Cyclone (1927)
The Merry Malones (1927)
Billie (1928)
Gambling (1929)
Friendship (1931)
Pigeons and People (1933)
Dear Old Darling (1936)
Fulton of Oak Falls (1937)
*The Return of the
   Vagabond* (1940)

None of Cohan's musicals has received a major first-class production since 1940, and yet so many of his songs are still very familiar to us. Among Cohan's most well-remembered songs are:

Forty-Five Minutes From Broadway
Give My Regards to Broadway
Harrigan
Mary
Mary Is a Grand Old Name
Molly Malone
Musical Comedy Man
Over There
Push Me Along in My Pushcart
Rose
So Long Mary
The Yankee Doodle Boy
Yankee Doodle Dandy
You're A Grand Old Flag

Biography

Composer, lyricist, librettist, star, director and producer George Michael Cohan was born into a theatrical family in Providence, Rhode Island. Although he was supposedly born on the 4th of July in 1878, records show that he was born on July 3rd. He joined his mother and sister onstage at the age of nine, and began writing comic sketches for his family's act in both vaudeville and minstrel shows when he was in his teens. By age 23 he had written, produced and starred in his first Broadway musical, *The Governor's Son*. By 27 he had had his first smash hit in *Little Johnny Jones*. A very popular composer, he published more than 300 songs in his life. Cohan ruled Broadway with the number of shows he created and in which he starred. He never stopped working from age nine until two years before his death at 64. He had been given the nickname, "the man who owned Broadway," and many consider him the father of musical comedy. To this day a statue of Cohan stands in Times Square in New York, on 45th Street, where Broadway crosses 7th Avenue.

Cohan embodied the spirit of the times, the *zeitgeist*. He was awarded the Congressional Medal of Honor for contributing the song "Over There" to the morale of the country during World War I.

Resources

Cohan's 1925 autobiography, *Twenty Years on Broadway and the Years it Took to Get There: The True Story of a Trouper's Life from the Cradle to the Closed Shop*,[2] is tough to find, but an invaluable, if biased, resource.

Irving Berlin (1888–1989)

Stylistic approach

Of Irving Berlin, Jerome Kern wrote, "Irving Berlin has no place in American music, he *is* American music." Berlin wrote his first song "Marie of Sunny Italy" in 1907 at age 19. As he was coming of age, the cakewalk was the popular dance and ragtime music had just started to spread from the brothels into more mainstream venues. Berlin took the popular European-based song forms of the nineteenth century, joined them with this new popular music and with the music that he heard in the synagogue where his father had been a cantor. Fusing these three disparate styles, Berlin found his own sound, a sound that would become the popular music for much of the twentieth century. Many of Berlin's early songs were waltzes, but they were waltzes with a distinctly American sound.

Berlin was a composer and lyricist of the people; he captured the ear and heart of the average American. That is not to say that his songs lack sophistication; they simply lack pretense. Famous for his patriotic songs, Berlin once said, "a patriotic song is an emotion, and you must not embarrass an audience with it, or they will hate your guts."[3] This aphorism applies directly to all of Berlin's songs: if the singer gets "arty" or pretentious with Berlin's songs they fail to hit their mark. This applies to singing technique as well as to dramatic lyric interpretation. While there were occasional soprano roles in Berlin shows, he tended to write best for belters.

Belting might be considered a controlled yell or shout on the pitch. The singer unused to belting will find that there are plenty of texts and teachers and texts to consult. Chapter 9 of Elisabeth Howard's *Sing!: The Vocal Power Method Male and Female Voices All Styles*[4] presents a detailed description of how to belt in a healthy manner. Berlin's songs don't require belting in extreme registers, but that bright, resonant "shouted" sound is part of what came to define this music as an American sound. One of the first stars to embrace Berlin's songs was Al Jolson, the greatest entertainer of his time; Jolson would prowl the stage and belt out songs at his audience. Other stars who embraced Berlin's songs, like Ethel Merman, also followed in this tradition.

These songs not only allow the personality of the singer to rise to the surface, they demand it. The melodies are catchy, tending to be short repetitive phrases, usually in an AABA structure. These songs ultimately charm, and their ability to soar lies in their enthusiasm (in the case of the up-tempo songs) or earnestness (in the ballads). While Offenbach or Strauss songs "star" the melody and Gilbert and Sullivan "star" the lyrics, Berlin's songs "star" the singer.

Many great singers in just about every genre of music have successfully interpreted Berlin's songs. Ella Fitzgerald's *Ella Fitzgerald Sings the Irving Berlin Songbook* is only one of many highly successful jazz renderings of Berlin's songs. Jazz artists from the styles of swing, scat, crooning, be-bop, R&B, fusion and just about every other sub-genre love singing Berlin's songs. The songs make room for the singers. Willie Nelson and countless other country singers have taken on Berlin's "Blue Skies," "What'll I Do," "Always" and many other Berlin songs. Of course Berlin has always been popular with singers in cabarets and supper clubs. Each one of these singers has approached Berlin's songs from a different perspective of vocal production, yet so many of them have found the truth of Berlin's songs by keeping it simple, essential and truthful.

Body of work

Berlin's career as a writer of Broadway musicals spanned 52 years, 1910–1962. The great majority of his shows are either revues or book musicals in which the book primarily acts as the connective tissue between musical numbers. His shows after 1943 (the opening of Rogers and Hammerstein's *Oklahoma!*) tend to be driven more by their librettos. The songs from the earlier musicals tend to be stand-alone songs, self-contained songs for which little or no context is needed. The songs from the later shows more often than not follow the Rodgers and Hammerstein model in which songs either reveal character or advance plot.

The Broadway musicals for which Irving Berlin was the primary songwriter include:

Ziegfeld Follies of 1910 (1910)
Peggy (1911)
Hokey Pokey/Bunty, Bulls and Strings (1912)
A Night With the Pierrots/ Sesostra/The Whirl of Society (1912)
The Passing Show of 1912 (1912)
Hanky Panky (1912)
The Sun Doctors (1912)
All Aboard (1913)
Watch Your Step (1914)
Ziegfeld Follies of 1915 (1915)
Stop! Look! Listen! (1915)
Ziegfeld Follies of 1916 (1916)
The Century Girl (1916)
Dance and Grow Thin (1917)
Jack O'Lantern (1917)
The Cohan Revue of 1918 (1917)
Ziegfeld Follies of 1918 (1918)
Yip Yip Yaphank (1918)
Everything (1918)
The Canary (1918)

Ziegfeld Follies of 1919 (1919)
Greenwich Village Follies of 1919 (1919)
Ziegfeld Follies of 1920 (1920)
Music Box Revue of 1921 (1921)
Music Box Revue of 1922 (1922)
Music Box Revue of 1923 (1923)
Music Box Revue of 1924 (1924)
George White's Scandals of 1925 (1925)
The Cocoanuts (1925)
Ziegfeld Follies of 1927 (1927)
Shoot the Works (1931)
Face the Music (1932)
As Thousands Cheer (1933)
Louisiana Purchase (1940)
This is the Army (1942)
Annie Get Your Gun (1946)
Miss Liberty (1949)
Call Me Madam (1950)
Mr. President (1962)

Hundreds of films have used Berlin songs; the Internet Movie Database (IMDB.com) lists 609 separate credits. A short list of full-length films for which Berlin made substantial contributions include:

The Jazz Singer (1927)
The Cocoanuts (1929)
Hallelujah (1929)
Puttin' on the Ritz (1930)
Mammy (1930)
Reaching For the Moon (1930)
Smart Money (1931)
Merrily We Go To Hell (1932)
Lilly Turner (1933)

Ticket or Leave It (1935)
Top Hat (1935)
Follow the Fleet (1936)
On the Avenue (1937)
Alexander's Ragtime Band (1938)
Carefree (1938)
Second Fiddle (1939)
Louisiana Purchase (1941)

Holiday Inn (1942)
This is the Army (1943)
Blue Skies (1946)
Easter Parade (1948)
Annie Get Your Gun (1950)

Call Me Madam (1953)
White Christmas (1954)
There's No Business Like Show Business (1954)

The majority of Berlin's scores were written prior to the advent of *Oklahoma!*. Very few of those shows have received any major revivals, and those shows remain relatively unfamiliar to us while many of the songs from them remain popular. Many of Berlin's most popular and long-lasting songs, listed below, have been performed in various vocal ranges. Most of these songs can be readily purchased in a variety of keys. And those not published are available in alternate keys through musicnotes. com and other online services. Of the more than 1,000 songs in Berlin's catalog, some of the most lasting and popular songs include:

Alexander's Ragtime Band
All Alone
All by Myself
Always
Anything You Can Do, I Can
    Do Better
Be Careful It's My Heart
The Best Things Happen While
    You're Dancing
Better Luck Next Time
Blue Skies
Change Partners
Cheek to Cheek
Count Your Blessings (Instead
    of Sheep)
Doin' What Comes Natur'lly
Easter Parade
Falling Out of Love
    Can Be Fun
The Girl That I Marry
Give Me Your Tired, Your Poor
God Bless America

Heat Wave
Hostess With the Mostest On
    the Ball
How Deep is the Ocean?
I Got Lost in His Arms
I Got the Sun in the Mornin'
    (and the Moon at Night)
I'm Putting All My Eggs in
    One Basket
I've Got My Love to Keep
    Me Warm
I Love a Piano
Isn't This a Lovely Day to Be
    Caught in the Rain
It's a Lovely Day Today
Let Me Sing and I'm Happy
Let Yourself Go
Let's Face the Music and Dance
Let's Have Another Cup
    of Coffee
Let's Take an Old
    Fashioned Walk

Mandy
Marie
Moonshine Lullaby
Mr. Monotony
My Defenses Are Down
My Walking Stick
No Strings (I'm Fancy Free)
Not for All the Rice in China
Old Fashioned Wedding
Oh! How I Hate to Get Up in
    the Morning
Pack Up Your Sins and Go To
    the Devil!
Play a Simple Melody/
    Musical Demon
A Pretty Girl is Like a Melody
Puttin' on the Ritz
Remember
Say It Isn't So
Shakin' the Blues Away
Sisters

Snookey Ookums
The Song is Ended (But the
    Melody Lingers On)
Steppin' Out with My Baby
Supper Time
There's No Business Like Show
    Business
They Say it's Wonderful
This Is the Army
Top Hat, White Tie and Tails
We're a Couple of Swells
What'll I Do
When the Midnight Choo
    Choo Leaves for Alabam'
White Christmas
Who
You Can Have Him
You Can't Get a Man
    with a Gun
You'd Be Surprised
You're just in Love

Biography

Berlin was born in Russia with the name Israel Baline, the son of
a Jewish cantor, in 1888. The Balines emigrated to New York in
1893. A love of America would always be a defining characteris-
tic of Berlin's catalog of songs. Israel's father struggled, working
in a kosher meat market and giving Hebrew lessons. The young
Baline had to quit school at age eight to sell newspapers and do
whatever else he could to bring in money for the family, leaving
home at age 14 so as not to be a financial burden to his family. Berlin had no education, no formal training, never learned
to read or write music and could only play the piano in the key
of F-sharp (all the black keys). A job as a singing waiter in a
Chinatown café led to him co-authoring a song with the house
pianist. An error on the sheet music of that song, "Marie From
Sunny Italy," changed his name from Baline to Berlin, and Irving
Berlin was born.
    In 1911, Berlin's song "Alexander's Ragtime Band" was a mas-
sive hit, selling one million copies of sheet music in the US and half

a million copies in the UK alone. Berlin bought his mother a house from the royalties of this one song. It made Berlin's reputation and sparked a rage for ragtime. Berlin's career was on solid ground, and he wrote hit after hit in a string of Broadway shows, many of them revues. Writing for a revue requires that the song functions fully without the support of character or situation. Some of Berlin's other massive hit songs are "God Bless America," "White Christmas" and "Easter Parade."

When asked by producers Rodgers and Hammerstein to write the score for *Annie Get Your Gun*, Berlin initially declined, saying that he couldn't write hillbilly music. Historians have speculated that he was afraid of writing in the new style of integrated musical. However, after having been convinced to accept the commission, *Annie Get Your Gun* turned out to be one of the biggest hits of his life. Berlin died in his sleep in New York City at the age of 101.

Resources

There are many excellent biographies on Berlin including Laurence Bergreen's *As Thousands Cheer: The Life of Irving Berlin*[5] and Jeffrey Magee's *Irving Berlin's American Musical Theatre*.[6] Also, there are audio and/or video recordings of a great majority of Berlin's work available online.

Jerome Kern (1885–1945)

Stylistic approach

While Berlin was the songwriter of the people, Kern was a more elite composer. Infused with elegance and intellectual sophistication not found in many other composers, Kern's work offers the sophisticated singer tremendous possibilities.

Kern's melodies and harmonic progressions surprise singers and audiences in wonderful ways. They are elegant and seem inevitable after the fact, but the harmonic and melodic journeys of his songs take unexpected turns along the way. Singers attempting to sing Kern for the first time are often surprised at how tricky some of his melodies are. They hear the song and think that they know the melody until they first attempt to sing it, at which point all of the little passing tones that seemed so obvious on listening are a struggle.

Whereas Cohan and Berlin practically abandoned the European traditions in arriving at their uniquely American sound, Kern embraced the older European model and styles. He used them as something to be built upon rather than put aside and replaced. Among Kern's innovations was the use of harmonic jazz progressions, syncopations and other jazz rhythms, and dance music written in 4/4 time. The other great innovation of Kern's, and perhaps the one most salient to the singer, is Kern's emphasis on using song (music as well as lyrics) to either reveal character or advance plot.

Take, for example, Kern's song "Thirteen Collar" from *Very Good Eddie*. This song is written for a diminutive, downtrodden man, wondering at his state in life, struggling to come to terms with his place in the world. The melody appears to wander randomly until one realizes that it is the character's thoughts that are meandering – the music merely echoes this.

The singer's job is to reflect the revelations of character in each song. Many of Kern's songs soar and require substantial technique. Songs like "All The Things You Are," "The Way You Look Tonight," "One Moment Alone," need to be clearly mapped out in terms of vocal production so that the singer can comfortably put technique aside and take the journey of the song. Compare Kristen Chenowith's, Maureen McGovern's, Billy Eckstein's and Frank Sinatra's recordings of "All the Things You Are," or any three or four recordings of this song, (there are many to choose from), and you will hear a great variation in inflection, phrasing and placement. But each of the singers arrives at different solutions to the musical difficulties of the song.

Kern's songs are sophisticated, musically and dramatically, and so do best when given a sophisticated interpretation. Jazz singers have had great success with Kern's songs, despite the fact that he hated jazz renderings of his songs. Mel Tormé, Ella Fitzgerald, Sarah Vaughan, and many others adore singing Kern. Opera singers looking to cross over into popular music have also had great success with Kern, and many opera or light opera companies have put together evenings of Kern as fundraisers over the years.

Body of work

Kern began his career writing songs to be interpolated into other shows that were transferring from the London stage or American-written musicals for which other composers had written the bulk of the score. The Broadway musicals for which Jerome Kern contributed additional songs include:

An English Diary (1904)
Mr. Wix of Wickham (1904)
The Catch of the Season (1905)
The Earl and the Girl (1905)
The Little Cherub (1906)
My Lady's Maid (1906)
The Rich Mr.
    Hoggenheimer (1906)
The Orchid (1907)
Fascinating Flora (1907)
The Dairymaids (1907)
The Girls of Gottenberg (1908)
Kitty Grey (1908)
The Girl and the Wizard (1909)
The Echo (1910)
Our Miss Gibbs (1910)
The Hen-Pecks (1911)
Ziegfeld Follies of 1911 (1911)
The Kiss Waltz (1911)

The Opera Ball (1912)
A Winsome Widow (1912)
The Girl From Montmartre
    (1912)
The "Mind-the-Paint"
    Girl (1912)
The Woman Haters (1912)
The Doll Girls (1913)
The Marriage Market (1913)
The Girl From Utah (1914)
To-Night's the Night (1914)
Fads and Fancies (1915)
A Modern Eve (1915)
Ziegfeld Follies of 1916 (1916)
Miss Springtime (1916)
Ziegfeld Follies of 1917 (1917)
The Canary (1918)
On, My Dear! (1918)

The Broadway musicals for which Kern was the primary composer include:

Fluffy Ruffles (1908)
The King of Cadonia (1910)
La Belle Paree/Bow-Sing/
    Tortajada (1911)
The Red Petticoat (1912)
Oh, I Say! (1913)
90 in the Shade (1915)
Nobody Home (1915)
Cousin Lucy (1915)
Miss Information (1915)
Very Good Eddie (1915)
Love o' Mike (1917)
Oh, Boy (1917)
Leave it to Jane (1917)
Miss 1917 (1917)

Oh, Lady! Lady! (1918)
Toot-Toot! (1918)
Rock-a-bye Baby (1918)
Head over Heels (1918)
She's a Good Fellow (1919)
The Night Boat (1920)
Hitchy-Koo of 1920 (1920)
Sally (1920)
Good Morning Dearie (1921)
The Bunch and Judy (1922)
Stepping Stones (1923)
Sitting Pretty (1924)
Dear Sir (1924)
Sunny (1925)
The City Chap (1925)

Criss Cross (1926)
Lucky (1927)
Show Boat (1927)
Sweet Adeline (1929)
The Cat and the Fiddle (1931)

Music in the Air (1932)
Roberta (1933)
Mamba's Daughter (1939)
Very Warm for May (1939)
Music in the Air (1951)

Like Berlin, hundreds of films have used Kern's songs. A short list of full-length films to which Kern personally made substantial contributions include:

Show Boat (1929)
Sally (1929)
The Three Sisters (1930)
Sunny (1930)
The Cat and The Fiddle (1934)
Music in the Air (1934)
Sweet Adeline (1934)
Robert (1935)
I Dream Too Much (1935)
Show Boat (1936)
Swing Time (1936)

High, Wide and Handsome
   (1937)
Joy of Living (1938)
One Night in the Tropics (1940)
You Were Never Lovelier (1942)
Cover Girl (1944)
Can't Help Singing (1944)
Centennial Summer (1946)
Till the Clouds Roll By (1946)
Show Boat (1951)
Lovely to Look at (1952)

Below are listed some of Kern's most popular and long-lasting songs. Most have been sung and recorded in several different vocal ranges. Many of these songs have been published in several keys and more are available in alternate keys through musicnotes.com and other online services.

All the Things You Are *
Bill **
Can't Help Lovin' Dat Man *
Cleopatterer **
Dearly Beloved ***
A Fine Romance ****
I Won't Dance * / ****
I'll Be Hard to Handle †
I'm Old Fashioned ***
I've Told Every Little Star *
The Last Time I Saw Paris *
Life Upon the Wicked Stage **
Long Ago and Far Away ††

Look for the Silver
   Lining †††
Lovely to Look at ****
Make Believe*
Never Gonna Dance ****
Ol' Man River *
Pick Yourself Up ****
Smoke Gets in Your
   Eyes ††††
The Song is You *
The Folks who Live on
   the Hill *
They Didn't Believe Me

The Way You Look Tonight ****   Why Do I Love You? Why Was
Thirteen Collar **   I Born? *
Who? ††††   You Couldn't Be Cuter ****

* lyrics by Oscar Hammerstein II
** lyrics by P.G. Wodehouse
*** lyrics by Johnny Mercer
**** lyrics by Dorothy Fields
† lyrics by Bernard Dougall
†† lyrics by Ira Gershwin
††† lyrics by Buddy DeSylva
†††† lyrics by Otto Harbach

Biography

Kern was born in New York in 1885 to German-Jewish immigrant parents; he was taught to play the piano and organ by his mother. When Kern was 12 the family moved to Newark, New Jersey, where he began writing shows for his new school. His father insisted that Kern leave high school before graduating to join in his business, but when Kern mistakenly ordered 200 pianos instead of two, his father realized his mistake. Kern studied piano and harmony at the New York College of Music and later in Heidelberg, Germany.

Returning from his studies in Germany to New York, Kern stopped in London, where he made the acquaintance of Charles Frohman, an American producer looking to import British successes. Frohman felt that many of these shows needed an American sounding song or two, and hired Kern to write songs for interpolation into the Broadway productions. Kern was active from 1904 to 1915 contributing one or more songs to other people's shows, working as a pianist on Broadway and song-plugger for Tin Pan Alley publishers. The first musical for which Kern supplied the full score was *The Red Petticoat* in 1912.

In 1915, Kern and Guy Bolton were asked to create a musical for the 299-seat Princess Theatre. With so few seats the box office could only generate a small weekly income, and the theatre could only support a show with low weekly expenses and a minimal initial production cost. Musicals at the time were defined by their opulence – large, spectacular scenery, a hundred or more performers onstage, large orchestras – none of which Kern and Bolton could afford. Stripped of everything that made a musical a musical, Kern and Bolton looked back to the Gilbert and Sullivan operettas and used story and characters as the driving mechanism rather than scenic spectacle. The characters were recognizable people one might meet on the street, speaking and singing the contemporary language of the day. The first Princess musical, *Nobody Home*, was such a big success that a string of small musicals written for the Princess Theatre followed.

Throughout the 1910s and 1920s, Kern was a constant presence on Broadway, regularly writing some of the biggest hit musicals. In 1927, Kern made another great leap forward composing the score to the landmark musical *Show Boat* with lyricist/librettist Oscar Hammerstein II. *Show Boat* represents a shift in the paradigm in many ways. The topics and subject matter were serious, it had full African American and white choruses sharing the stage, the sprawling story spanned 40 years and the length of the Mississippi River. But the continuity throughout Kern's career was that his music either revealed character or moved the plot forward.

As with many Broadway people, Kern moved to Hollywood in the 1930s to continue making a living during the Depression. While visiting New York in 1945 to supervise a revival of *Show Boat* and begin writing the score for *Annie Get Your Gun,* Kern suffered a cerebral hemorrhage crossing the street.

Resources

Kern has been the subject of several excellent biographies and critical analyses. Among them are Stephen Banfield's *Jerome Kern*,[7] which offers an in-depth analysis, and Thomas Hischak's *The Jerome Kern Encyclopedia*,[8] which offers a complete cataloguing of Kern's work. An older but still excellent biography and analysis of Kern is Gerald Bordman's *Jerome Kern: His Life and Music*.[9]

In summary

While today Cohan's popular songs remain somewhere on the periphery of our cultural awareness, both Berlin's and Kern's continue to hold their place front and center. Almost a century since many of these songs were written, Berlin's and Kern's songs are recorded by musical artists performing in a wide range of styles, and they continue to touch contemporary listeners through their keen observation and reflection on the human condition. Although

Berlin's songs represent the sentimental populist and Kern's the intellectual aesthete, both also partake of the other's domain. Berlin's clever rhymes and rhythms bespeak his intelligence, wit and verbal dexterity; and the essential beauty and simplicity of some of Kern's more simple and essential melodies, like "Old Man River," display his ability to cut to the heart of the matter. Together these two writers bookended the foundation of the American popular song.

Notes

1 Rick Benjamin, *You're a Grand Old Rag: The Music of George M. Cohan*, notes accompanying the world-premiere recording of original period orchestrations, at www.newworldrecords.org/uploads/file-JGsEj.pdf, accessed March 17, 2015.
2 George M. Cohan, *Twenty Years on Broadway and the Years It Took to Get There. The True Story of a Trouper's Life from the Cradle to the Closed Shop*, New York, NY: Harper and Brothers Publishers, 1925.
3 Irving Berlin quoted by Seymour Brody, *Jewish Heroes and Heroines of America: 150 True Stories of American Jewish Heritage*, New York, NY: Lifetime Books, 1996. Available online in the Jewish Virtual Library, www.jewishvirtuallibrary.org/jsource/biography/berlin.html, accessed March 17, 2015.
4 Elisabeth Howard, *Sing!: The Vocal Power Method Male and Female Voice All Styles*, Van Nuys, CA: Alfred Publishing, 2006.
5 Laurence Bergreen, *As Thousands Cheer: The Life of Irving Berlin*, New York, NY: Da Capo Press, 1996.
6 Jeffrey Magee, *Irving Berlin's American Musical Theatre*, New York, NY: Oxford University Press, 2012.
7 Stephen Banfield, *Jerome Kern*, New Haven, CT: Yale University Press, 2006.
8 Thomas Hischak, *The Jerome Kern Encyclopedia*, Plymouth, UK: Scarecrow Press, 2013.
9 Gerald Bordman, *Jerome Kern: His Life and Music*, New York, NY: Oxford University Press, 1980.

Chapter 3

The great songwriters of Tin Pan Alley

Harry Warren, Jimmy McHugh, Buddy DeSylva, Lew Brown, Ray Henderson, George Gershwin, Ira Gershwin, Arthur Schwartz, Howard Dietz, and Harold Arlen

Fueled by the illegal hooch served at speakeasies during Prohibition and underscored by hot new urban rhythms, the 1920s were the Jazz Age. The economy was booming, and money for all sorts of entertainments and activities flowed. There was plenty of money for producers to produce musicals and for theatregoers to buy theatre tickets – all entertainments including popular music and the musical theatre flourished; the number of Broadway shows produced exploded.

The area radiating from West 28th Street between 5th and 6th Avenues in New York was known as "Tin Pan Alley" because the sound of so many pianos playing different music through all the open windows created a tinny cacophony. This area was the heart of the music-publishing industry, the hub of activity for songwriters, publishers, musicians, song "pluggers," vaudevillians, Broadway stars and producers. At a time when every family had a piano in their parlor as their primary source of music, the sale of sheet music offered songwriters huge potential profits. With rising production of musicals and the financial rewards of profitable publishing, the musical theatre of the 1920s saw the flowering of a period of great songwriters. Most of the songs they wrote outlived the shows in which they originally appeared. The most important and prolific of these composers and lyricists continued writing well into the 1950s, adding to the body of work that ultimately became known as "The Great American Songbook."

These songwriters saw their early successes in the 1920s, but the Depression affected the kinds of songs they wrote and where they wrote them. The popular songs of the 1930s tended to be upbeat and hopeful – that was what people wanted to hear when they looked to popular culture to be cheered up. The locus of songwriting and publishing in the 1920s was New York. However as the money to produce Broadway musicals dried up during the Depression, many songwriters migrated to Hollywood, where talking movies needed songs for the newest rage, the movie musical. Hollywood musicals supported a great many of these songwriters. It allowed them to continue to add to the "American Songbook," while it sent their songs out into the world, traveling from screen to screen across the nation and the world. These songs have stood the test of time. Many of these songs, now nearing 100 years old, continue to be enjoyed by audiences, sung and recorded by cabaret and jazz artists, used in movies and put into jukebox musicals.

When these composers were born, between 1893 and 1909, the popular music of America was predominantly European or imitation-European. However, in their formative listening years, their teens, American sounds had begun to take hold. The music of Herbert, Romberg and Friml Americanized operetta, Berlin and Kern Americanized the musical theatre and popular songs and Joplin and others had popularized ragtime, paving the way for jazz. All of the composers in this chapter took these traditional forms and further Americanized them, infusing them with the pulse and rhythm of the jazz age. They applied the jagged rhythms of ragtime and the altered tones of the blues scale to traditional European song structure. Many of these composers also had the sounds of Jewish prayer, chanting and folk music in their ears, as so many of them were Jewish. These influences came together to make up the sound of the popular music of the 1920s and 1930s.

Vocal style

These songs overwhelmingly call for a bright sound. Traditional performances of these songs frequently have what might be considered a nasal quality associated with them, which makes sense considering the forward placement called for by these songs. Instrumental accompaniments that supported these songs leaned much more heavily on brass instruments than in previous periods. Also, in the woodwind section, the saxophone, invented in 1840 by Adolphe Sax, became much more predominant. The saxophone, with its range of tones in various registers, became a key component in the formation of early jazz. Microphone technology had not reached the point where they could be effectively used onstage in the theatre, although they were used in the recording studio and on the bandstand. Both saxophones and brass instruments, even when muted, have a weight to their tone, which requires more vocal power to overcome, and the nasal resonance helped to do just that.[1] To get the voice heard above these more piercing instruments a more nasal placement was adopted, as was the brighter, more "pingy" belt for women. Today we can overcome such hurdles electronically, but we still associate that vocal style with these songs.

Prior to this period, singers sought to attack each note exactly on the center of the pitch. With jazz beginning to enter the vocabulary of vocal music, however, the way singers attacked notes or moved between pitches changed. Sliding up or down to a note, moving from one pitch to another using a portamento, became important to vocal styles of the time.

Also in the songs of this time the singers use of rhythm became much more important, as did percussive aspects of the voice. In much of the music that had come earlier, the singer floated the melody above the accompaniment, staying in time but riding above the pulse. The songs of this period express the urge and energy of the cities, particularly New York, where Tin Pan Alley informed their urgent and driving rhythms. It naturally follows that the singer of these songs needs to be more aware of the rhythm of the melody and the groove of the song than singers of earlier songs. These writers wrote beautiful melodies, but there is a substantial shift in the singers' need to allow the rhythm and groove inform the vocal performance. Additionally, contemporary singers of these songs should pay particular attention to such lyric-writing devices as alliteration and use of plosive consonants in creating and sustaining the sense of rhythm and urgency.

As so many of the songs cited in this chapter are available in a range of keys, voice types are not indicated by the song titles. Since all of these writers spent substantial time working in Hollywood, lists of their major movie musicals are included in the descriptions of their body of work. Hopefully, the interested reader will seek out these movies to research these writers further and to see their work firsthand.

Harry Warren (1893–1981): Great character songs

Stylistic approach

Many of us know the songs of composer Harry Warren without knowing the name or knowing that he wrote them. Most of

Warren's work was in the movies, making it relatively easy to scour his old movies for some of his hidden gems.

Warren's songs have been recorded by many great jazz vocalists: Rosemary Clooney, Louis Armstrong, Nat "King" Cole, Bing Crosby, Al Jolson, Chet Baker, Dinah Shore, Dean Martin and more. Above all else, Warren's songs are highly melodic and imbued with an unrelenting spirit of optimism. Through the years, some singers have offered new interpretations while others have offered more faithful renditions. But in most successful instances, the newer interpretations have begun with a deep appreciation of the melodic nature of these songs as well as their upbeat and quirky qualities. These are, at heart, personality songs and intensely optimistic; they offer the singer a chance to let their personality (or the persona of a character they are playing) shine forth.

The unrelenting optimism and cheer of Warren's songs are genuine; they are without guile or irony. They lend themselves particularly well to jazz interpretation because of their strong rhythmic sense – even the ballads – and their sense of fun and play. For the same reason they stand up very well to being applied to what we might call character singing. Warren songs like "Shuffle Off to Buffalo," "Lulu's Back in Town," "You're getting to Be a Habit with Me" ask for more than *simply* a strong vocal instrument offering a heartfelt performance. They call for a personality; both in musical terms and acting terms they offer the performer a great opportunity to display him or herself.

The best period performances of Warren's songs are in the movie musicals making them readily viewable online. A 1933 documentary titled, *Harry Warren: America's Foremost Composer*, lets us watch and listen to Warren at the piano with a variety of guest artists, performing in a variety of styles. Each one of these singers provides the bright, forward-placed sound so essential in 1933 for the singer to be heard over the orchestra. Each of the performers in this filmed performance, among others, show how vitally important it is to use Harry Warren songs as a vehicle for showing personality. These kinds of performances were brought to the stage in the 1980s Broadway version of *42nd Street*, featuring many of Warren's greatest hits. Listening to Wanda Richert, Jerry Orbach, Tammy Grimes and the rest of the original cast also clarifies this aspect of Warren's songs.

Body of work

Warren personally worked on over 300 movies from 1926 until his death in 1981, and his songs have appeared in hundreds more. A short list of his most important or successful movies includes:

His Pastimes (1926)
Spring is Here (1930)
Blessed Event (1932)
Three on a Match (1932)
42nd Street (1933)
Gold Diggers of 1933 (1933)
Footlight Parade (1933)
Roman Scandals (1933)
Moulin Rouge (1934)
Wonder Bar (1934)
Dames (1934)
St. Louis Kid (1934)
Gold Diggers of 1935 (1935)
Go into Your Dance (1935)
Broadway Gondolier (1935)
Shipmates Forever (1935)
Cain and Mabel (1936)
Sing Me a Love Song (1936)
Gold Diggers of 1937 (1936)
The Singing Marine (1937)
Mr. Dodd Takes the Air (1937)
Gold Diggers in Paris (1938)
Hard to Get (1938)

Naughty but Nice (1939)
Down Argentine Way (1940)
That Night in Rio (1941)
The Great American Broadcast (1941)
Springtime in the Rockies (1942)
Sweet Rosie O'Grady (1943)
The Gang's All Here (1943)
Wing and a Prayer (1944)
Diamond Horseshoe (1945)
The Harvey Girls (1946)
Summer Holiday (1948)
The Barkleys of Broadway (1949)
Summer Stock (1950)
The Belle of New York (1952)
Skirts Ahoy (1952)
The Caddy (1953)
Artists and Models (1955)
An Affair to Remember (1957)
Rock-A-Bye Baby (1958)
Cinderfella (1960)

Predominantly a movie writer, Warren only wrote complete scores for two Broadway musicals:

The Laugh Parade (1931)
Shangri-La (1956)

He had individual songs featured in the Broadway musicals:

Sweet and Lowdown (1930)
Chamberlain Brown's Scrapbook (1932)
Swingin' the Dream (1939)

Warren's biggest Broadway success was the 1980 stage adaptation of *42nd Street*, directed and choreographed by Gower Champion, produced by David Merrick one year before Warren's death.

Warren wrote over 800 songs and published over 500. These are a few of the better-known titles; although, the lesser-known titles offer some terrific opportunities for the singer looking for a unique audition song or cabaret piece.

About a Quarter to Nine
An Affair to Remember ††
The Boulevard of
    Broken Dreams
By the River Sainte Marie *
Chattanooga Choo Choo ††
Cheerful Little Earful
Chica Chica Boom Chic
Dames
Down Argentine Way ††
Forty-Second Street *
Go into Your Dance
Honeymoon Hotel
I Got a Gal in Kalamazoo ††
I Found a Million
    Dollar Baby *
I Had the Craziest Dream *
I Love My Baby
I Only Have Eyes for You
I, Yi, Yi, Yi, Yi
I'll Sing You a Thousand Love
    Songs *
I'll String Along with You *
Jeepers Creepers ††
Lullaby of Broadway † *
Lulu's Back in Town

The More I See You *
My Heart Tells Me *
Nagasaki
On the Atchison Topeka and
    the Santa Fe †
Remember Me ††
September in the Rain *
Shadow Waltz *
She's a Latin from
    Manhattan *
Shuffle Off to Buffalo
The Stanley Steamer
That's Amore ††
Too Many Tears *
We're in the Money
With Plenty of Money
    and You *
Would You Like to Take
    a Walk
You Must Have Been a
    Beautiful Baby *
You'll Never Know † *
You're Getting to Be a Habit
    with Me *
Young and Healthy
Zing a Little Zong ††

* Indicates #1 hit
† Indicates Academy Award
†† Indicates Academy Award Nomination

Biography

Harry Warren, born Salvatore Guaragna to Italian immigrant parents in Brooklyn in 1893, began his career as a drummer at the age of 15. After working as a musician, stagehand, props man and assistant director in carnivals, vaudeville and for early silent movies, and serving in the Navy in World War I, his first published song appeared in 1922, at age 29. In the 1920s and early 1930s, Warren contributed songs to several Broadway musicals and early sound films. But in 1932 he moved to Hollywood to begin a six-year contract with Warner Brothers, who had hired him to write with Al Dubin. Warren wrote 32 movie musicals for Warner Brothers, 20 of them with Dubin, and 18 with director/choreographer Busby Berkeley. Some of Warren's Warner Brothers movies include *42nd Street*, *Gold Diggers of 1933*, *Footlight Parade*, *Dames*, *Go Into Your Dance* and *Gold Diggers of 1935*. Warren was the first American songwriter whose primary focus was the movies, and he was arguably the most prolific and most successful of the Hollywood songwriters of his time. With eleven nominations, he won three Academy Awards for Best Song.

In 1933 producer Leon Schlesinger created a division of Warner Brothers to produce animated short films. Schlesinger Studios produced two "lines" of animated short subjects, Looney Tunes and Merrie Melodies, featuring Bugs Bunny, Porky Pig, Speedy Gonzales, Wile E. Coyote and their friends. Warren's contract with Warner Brothers gave the studio the right to use Warren's material in any manner they saw fit without additional compensation or royalties. The need for the cartoons to sing and the catalog of Warren songs were a perfect fit. And so today, other than the stage musical *42nd Street*, many people know Warren's songs best from these cartoons.

By 1936 Warner Brothers decided that the national thirst for movie musicals had abated and they let the contracts of their musical talents lapse. Although Warren spent the rest of his life until 1980 writing music for other studios and independent producers, many of his greatest successes were those made famous in the Warner Brothers movie musicals of the Depression. Not surprisingly, these songs tend to embody a hopeful, optimistic outlook.

Warren's most frequent and most successful collaborations were with lyricists Al Dubin and Mack Gordon. The Warren and Dubin team produced most of the songs for Warner Brothers in the late 1920s and early 1930s. Other lyricists who worked with Warren regularly include Harold Adamson, Ralph Blane, Johnny Burke, Sammy Cahn, Arthur Freed, Ira Gershwin, Johnny Mercer and Dorothy Fields.

Resources

Harry Warren: American Songbook Series is a sound recording released by the Smithsonian Collection in 1995. It features twenty-two recordings of Warren songs by original artists like Ginger Rogers, Dick Powell, Fred Astaire and Judy Garland, and some jazz artists including The Hi-Los, Mel Tormé and Maureen McGovern.

Many DVD collections of Warren's movies are available, including two collections of the Busby Berkeley movies released by Warner Home Video.

Jimmy McHugh (1894–1969): Some of the best of "Jazz Age" jazz

Stylistic approach

More than anything else, composer Jimmy McHugh's music swings. Songs like "Digga Digga Do" and "Doin' the New Lowdown" and even his ballads like "Don't Blame Me" are defined by their solid grooves. Not surprisingly, the definitive recordings of McHugh's songs are by artists with great rhythmic sensitivity such as Frank Sinatra, Dinah Washington, Dean Martin, Billie Holiday, Fats Waller, Bill "Bojangles" Robinson and Judy Garland. Pulse is vital to these songs; they call for a vocal approach that references swing and big band music. McHugh songs stand up well to all different kinds of individualized phrasing and embellishment, but always with a strong sense of the pulse.

Such recordings as the Everly Brothers, "Don't Blame Me" and Aretha Franklin's "Exactly Like You" attest to McHugh's songs' continuing popularity into the time of rock and roll. Rock, blues and gospel singers looking for a good melody built overtop of a strong groove have found gold in McHugh's songs.

McHugh never pushed the genre forward like Kern, Berlin, Gershwin or Porter, but his songs are the backbone of the "American Songbook," and staples of the American jazz repertoire. McHugh published over 500 songs in the first half of the twentieth century. Applying legitimate vocal styling to McHugh's work is not recommended. His melodies require styling in any of the many sub-genres of popular music – jazz, pop, rock, blues or gospel. As the Jimmy McHugh page of the Songwriter's Hall of Fame claims, "Jimmy McHugh's most popular songs have an infectiously swinging quality that instantly endears them to the listener."[2] To deny McHugh's songs this quality is to do them a disservice.

Body of work

In addition to nine editions of the Cotton Club Revue and various other nightclub revues in New York in Chicago, McHugh wrote the following Broadway musicals:

Blackbirds of 1928 (1928) *	*The Vanderbilt Revue* (1930) *
Hello, Daddy (1928) *	*Shoot the Works* (1931) *
Ziegfeld Midnight Frolics	*Singin' the Blues* (1931) *
(1929) *	*Streets of Paris* (1939) **
The International Revue	*Keep Off the Grass* (1940) ***
(1930) *	*As the Girls Go* (1948) ****

* lyrics by Dorothy Fields
** lyrics by Al Dubin
*** lyrics by Al Dubin and Howard Dietz
**** lyrics by Harold Adamson

McHugh and Dorothy Fields wrote songs together for the following movies:

The Time, the Place, and the Girl (1929)	*The Cuban Love Song* (1931)
Glorifying the American Girl (1929)	*Red-Headed Woman* (1932)
Estree Calling (1930)	*Hold Your Man* (1933)
Love in the Rough (1930)	*Penthouse* (1933)
Flying High (1931)	*Plane Nuts* (1933)
	Meet the Baron (1933)

The Prizefighter and the
Lady (1933)
Dancing Lady (1933)
Fugitive Lovers (1934)

Manhattan Melodrama (1934)
Hooray for Love (1935)
Every Night at Eight (1935)
Wife vs. Secretary (1936)

The best known of the McHugh and Fields songs are:

Bandana Babies
Collegiana
Cuban Love Song
Diga Diga Doo
Doin' the New Low Down
Don't Blame Me
Every Night at Eight
Exactly like You
Full of the Devil
Hooray for Love
Hot Feet

I Can't Give You Anything but
    Love
I Feel a Song Coming On
I Must Have That Man
I'm in the Mood for Love
Lovely to Look At
My Dancing Lady
On the Sunny Side of the Street
Palsy Walsy
Shuffle Your Feet

McHugh never found a lyricist who made his music sing as well as Fields. His many collaborations in his later career never had the longevity of this earlier one. There is some speculation that several of the McHugh songs popularized by Thomas "Fats" Waller were, in fact, written by Waller, who sold them to McHugh. But those speculations have not been substantiated.

Popular McHugh songs with lyricists other than Dorothy Fields include:

Comin' in on a Wing and a Prayer †††
Dream, Dream, Dream *
I Couldn't Sleep a Wink Last Night †††
I Just Found Out About Love †††
I'd Know You Anywhere †††
I'm Shooting High **
It's a Most Unusual Day †††
I've Got My Fingers Crossed †††
Let's Get Lost †
Like the Fella Once Said ****
Lovely Way to Spend an Evening †††
Murder, He Says †
My Own †††
South American Way †

Spreadin' Rhythm Around * *
Too Young to Go Steady †††
When My Sugar Walks Down the Street ††
* Lyrics by Mitchell Parrish
** Lyrics by Ted Koehler
*** Lyrics by Johnny Mercer
**** Lyrics by Sammy Cahn
† Lyrics by Frank Loesser
†† Lyrics by Al Dubin
††† Lyrics by Harold Adamson

Biography

Jimmy McHugh was born and raised in Boston, the son of a plumber and a piano teacher. After working as a rehearsal pianist for the Boston Opera House, he took a job as a song plugger in Boston. In 1921 he moved to New York where began writing songs for nine different editions of the Cotton Club revues in Harlem. In 1927 McHugh and lyricist Dorothy Fields had three substantial hit songs in the Broadway revue, *Blackbirds of 1928*: "I Can't Give You Anything but Love," "Digga Digga Do" and "I Must Have That Man." The team had great success with their revue songs until 1930 when the Depression drove them to Hollywood where they began writing songs for movies.

In 1935, Fields began writing more and more with Jerome Kern, and McHugh worked mostly with Harold Adamson. Although he remained prolific through the 1950s, the collaboration with Fields yielded most of McHugh's most popular and successful songs.

Resources

The first biography of Jimmy McHugh, *I Feel a Song Coming On: The Life of Jimmy McHugh (Music in American Life)*[3] by Alyn Shipton, was published in 2009. Columbia House Music Collection released *The Great American Composers: Jimmy McHugh* containing 42 of the best recordings of Jimmy McHugh songs. Faber Edition, an imprint of the Alfred Music publishing company, offers an anthology of sheet music titled, *Jimmy McHugh – On the Sunny Side of the Street: The Jimmy McHugh Songbook*, which offers 15 of the more popular McHugh titles. Many others are readily available in other anthologies or as single sheets.

Buddy DeSylva (1895–1950), Lew Brown (1893–1958) and Ray Henderson (1896–1970): Personality songs – great songs for entertainers

Stylistic approach

Like so many of the other songs from this era, the songs of B.G. "Buddy" DeSylva, Lew Brown and Ray Henderson are steeped in the rhythms and harmonies of 1920s jazz. They may not have advanced the genre, but they do represent some of the best popular songs of the time; their songs made people feel good. William Zinsser writes, "The mindless optimism of the twenties had its perfect symbol in the songs written by [DeSylva, Brown and Henderson. They were] a household name, and no wonder – just the titles of the songs written by that trio made people feel better: 'The Best Things in Life Are Free', 'You're the Cream in My Coffee', 'Life is Just a Bowl of Cherries', [...] Even their classic 'Birth of the Blues' bubbles with major notes, blue only in its account of what got born."[4] Their songs are effervescent, optimistic and without a hint of irony or guile. Two of their songs, "The Black Bottom" and "The Varsity Drag," started two of the biggest dance crazes of the 1920s.

Their up-tempo songs, bright, cheery and catchy, are driven as much by their lyrics as by their melodies. The ballads have simple, lovely melodies; they are not challenging in range, structure or harmonic construction, but they are pleasant to the ear. In the same way that Harry Warren songs seem tailor-made for character performances, DeSylva, Brown and Henderson songs seem to be created for entertainers. Ballads and charm songs like "The Best Things in Life Are Free" and "Button Up Your Overcoat" are made to let the performer shine through, as are the up-tempos like "(Keep Your) Sunnyside Up" and "I'm Sitting on Top of the World." It only makes sense that Al Jolson, the greatest entertainer of the 1920s, discovered young Buddy DeSylva and brought him to Broadway.

There is a free-wheeling, rambunctious quality to DySylva, Brown and Henderson's songs. Listen to the throaty, braying quality that Zelma O'Neal brings to their songs "I Wanna Be Bad" and "The Varsity Drag." O'Neal respects every note on the page, but seems to throw the phrases away with a sense of good-natured fun and a modicum of flirtation. Broadway star Ruth Etting's hit recording of "Button Up Your Overcoat" offers the same qualities. Songs like "The Black Bottom," "Good News" and "Life is Just a

Bowl of Cherries" are not difficult to sing, but require a youthful enthusiasm and a genuine sense of hopefulness. There is no weary ennui in DeSylva, Brown and Henderson's songs. In terms of vocal styles, they ask for sliding into notes, back or front-phrasing and a bright, frontally-placed vocal quality.

Body of work

DeSylva, Brown and Henderson wrote four revues and six book musicals, but even the songs in their book musicals were great stand-alone songs, not terribly specific to plot or characters. These shows include:

George White's Scandals (1925)	*George White's Scandals* (1928)
George White's Scandals (1926)	*Hold Everything* (1928)
Good News (1927)	*Follow Through* (1929)
Manhattan Mary (1927)	*George White's Scandals* (1929)
Excess Baggage (1927)	*Flying High* (1930)

Brown and Henderson, without DeSylva, wrote the Broadway musicals:

George White's Scandals (1931)	*Strike Me Pink* (1933)
Hot Cha! (1932)	

Buddy DeSylva's Broadway musicals without Brown and Henderson include:

Sinbad (1918)	*Little Miss Bluebeard* (1923)
Follow the Girl (1918)	*Nifties of 1923* (1923)
Ziegfeld Follies of 1918 (1918)	*Sweet Little Devil* (1924)
La, La Lucille (1919)	*George White's Scandals* (1924)
Morrie Gest's "Midnight Whirl" (1919)	*Big Boy* (1925)
The Broadway Whirl (1921)	*Tell Me More* (1925)
Ziegfeld Follies of 1921 (1921)	*Captain Jinx* (1926)
George White's Scandals (1922)	*Queen High* (1926)
Orange Blossoms (1922)	*Take a Chance* (1932)
The Yankee Princess (1922)	*Du Barry Was a Lady* (book) (1939)
George White's Scandals (1923)	*Panama Hattie* (book) (1940)

Lew Brown wrote three Broadway musicals without DeSylva or Brown: *Piggy* (1927), *Calling All Stars* (1934) and *Yokel Boy* (1939). Ray Henderson wrote three Broadway musicals without DeSylva and Brown: *Say When* (1934), *George White's Scandals* (1936) and *Ziegfeld Follies of 1943* (1943).

The movies that DeSylva, Brown and Henderson wrote together include:

The Singing Fool (1928)	*Just Imagine* (1930)
Say It with Songs (1921)	*Hold Everything* (1930)
Sunny Side Up (1929)	*Good News* (1930)
Follow Through (1930)	*Indiscreet* (1931)

The biggest hits in the DeSylva, Brown and Henderson catalog include:

The Best Things in Life Are Free	Life is Just a Bowl of Cherries
The Birth of the Blues	Lucky Day
The Black Bottom	Magnolia
Button Up Your Overcoat	My Lucky Star
Don't Bring Lulu	One More Time
Good News	Sonny Boy
I Want to Be Bad	Sunnyside Up
If I Had a Talking Picture of You	The Thrill Is Gone
I'm a Dreamer (Aren't We All)	Together
I'm Flying High	Tweet Tweet
I'm Sitting on Top of the World	The Varsity Drag
It All Depends on You	Used to You
Just Imagine	Without Love
(I Want a) Loveable Baby	You're the Cream in My Coffee

Important songs with lyrics by DeSylva not written with Brown or Henderson include:

April Showers	I'll Say She Does
Avalon	If You Knew Susie
Blue Monday	Kickin' the Clouds Away
California Here I Come	Look for the Silver Lining
Do It Again	Orange Blossoms
I'll Build a Stairway to Paradise	

Biography

Lyricist Buddy DeSylva was born in New York and raised in California. Shortly after graduating from the University of Southern California, DeSylva met Broadway star Al Jolson, who brought DeSylva back to New York with him in 1917 to write the score for his new Broadway musical, *Sinbad*. In 1925, he joined forces with lyricist Lew Brown and composer Ray Henderson. They were the most successful songwriting trio throughout the rest of the decade. In 1929 they accepted an offer to write for the Fox movie studio and moved to Hollywood. In 1931 DeSylva struck out on his own, ultimately becoming an executive producer at Paramount.

Lyricist Lew Brown was born in Odessa, Russia (now Ukraine) in 1893 and emigrated to the US, settling in the Bronx in 1989. He began writing songs, both parodies of popular songs and original songs, in his teens. His first hit was "I'm the Lonesomest Girl in Town," which he wrote with Albert Tilzer in 1912. Brown continued writing with Tilzer and had several more hits, before meeting and teaming up with Ray Henderson in 1922. After DeSylva had left the team, Brown and Henderson continued to write together and with others. Brown died in New York in 1958.

Composer Ray Henderson was born in Buffalo, New York in 1896. After studying composition at the Chicago Conservatory, he moved to New York where he began arranging songs for vaudeville acts and publishing companies until he met Brown in 1922. After DeSylva's departure, Henderson continued writing until his death in 1970 in Greenwich, Connecticut.

Resources

Although Michael Curtiz's 1956 biographical movie musical about DeSylva, Brown and Henderson, *The Best Things in Life Are Free*, used their songs to tell their story, the accuracy of the details is questionable.

Several excellent CD compilations of their music include: *Birth of the Blues – Songwriters Series*, from the Pearl label, and *DeSylva, Brown and Henderson Revisited* and *DeSylva Brown and Henderson Revisited II* produced by Ben Bagley on his Painted Smiles label.

George Gershwin (1898–1937) and Ira Gershwin (1896–1983): The preeminent popular songs of the 1920s and 1930s

Stylistic approach

In 1994 George Martin produced an album of rock artists covering Gershwin songs, featuring Peter Gabriel, Sting, Elton John, Cher, Jon Bon Jovi, and others. At the other end of the spectrum, the opera diva, Dame Kiri Te Kanawa, recorded an album titled *Kiri sings Gershwin*. Gershwin's songs have been performed in more genres and styles than any other composer from this period. Gershwin has been a favorite of crooners, jazz artists, Broadway singers, concert artists, opera singers and rock artists.

Gershwin's melodies, rhythms, and harmonizations are unparalleled and soar in any genre or interpretation. As Warren songs are "personality" songs and DeSylva, Brown and Henderson songs are "entertainer" songs; Gershwin songs practically dare singers to display their musicality. The lyrics display wit and verbal dexterity (as in Ira's whimsical use of "not" and "knot" in the final stanza of "But Not for Me") without ever becoming cloying or overly optimistic. The wit never calls attention to the lyricist, but places focus on the poignancy of the singer. George Gershwin makes use of the rhythms of ragtime and comfortably combines classical styles, the blues scale and the melodic minor scale of Jewish music. Gershwin songs work as written, and a jazz interpretation of one asks for a faithful performance of the melody in the first A section before becoming freer with melody and rhythm in subsequent sections.

George Gershwin's songs have been recorded by most major recording artist of the twentieth century. Kiri Te Kanawa's excellent 1987 CD of Gershwin songs shows how wonderful these songs can be with a strictly legitimate interpretation. Te Kanawa respects every note value, phrasing and dynamic mark on the page, making them all feel organic to her performance. Major jazz singers or instrumentalists in all areas of jazz have recorded Gershwin, as well as many artists in different genres. Brian Wilson, in his CD, *Brian Wilson Reimagines Gershwin*, fuses jazz, rock and thick vocal harmonies to shed new light on Gershwin's songs. In all of the successful recordings, the essential human truths in the Gershwin songs come through, seen through the many different lenses of many different styles. Contemporary renderings of Gershwin songs have been particularly successful.

Body of work

George Gershwin contributed single songs to many Broadway musical revues. The Broadway musicals for which George wrote full scores include lyrics by Ira Gershwin except where otherwise noted:

La, La Lucille (1919) *
Morris Gest's Midnight Whirl (1919) *
George White's Scandals of 1920 (1920) **
The Broadway Whirl (1921) *
George White's Scandals of 1921 (1921) **
The French Doll (1922) *
George White's Scandals of 1922 (1922) *
Our Nell (1922) ***
George White's Scandals of 1923 (1923) *
Sweet Little Devil (1924) *
George White's Scandals of 1924 (1924) *
Lady Be Good! (1924)

Tell Me More (1925) †
Top-Toes (1925)
Song of the Flame (1925) ††
George White's Scandals of 1926 (1926) *
Oh, Kay! (1926)
Funny Face (1927)
Rosalie (1928)
Treasure Girl (1928)
Show Girl (1929)
Strike Up the Band (1930)
Girl Crazy (1930)
Of Thee I Sing (1931)
Pardon My English (1933)
Let 'Em Eat Cake (1933)
Porgy and Bess (1935)

* Lyrics by Buddy DeSylva
** Lyrics by Arthur Jackson
*** Lyrics by A.E. Thomas and Brian Hooker

† Lyrics by Buddy DeSylva and Ira Gershwin
†† Lyrics by Otto Harbach and Oscar Hammerstein II

The Gershwins' songs have appeared in hundreds of movies; the movies for which they were contracted to write music include:

The Song of the Flame (1930)
Delicious (1931)
Girl Crazy (1932)

Shall We Dance (1937)
A Damsel in Distress (1937)
The Goldwyn Follies (1938)

George Gershwin's first successful song was "Swannee," which he wrote at the age of 19. The song held the number one position in sales for 18 straight weeks, sold over one million copies of sheet music and over two million copies of the Al Jolson recording. It made Gershwin an overnight international star and earned him more money than any other single song in his career. Gershwin songs are second to none in the American Songbook; there is no such thing as a "bad" one. The catalog of Gershwin songs includes:

Bess, You Is My Woman	Love Is Here To Stay
Bidin' My Time	Love Is Sweeping the Country
Blah, Blah, Blah	Love Walked In
Boy Wanted	The Man I Love
But Not for Me	Mine
By Strauss	My Man's Gone Now
Do, Do, Do	Naughty Baby
Embraceable You	Nice Work if You Can Get It
Fascinating Rhythm	Of Thee I Sing
Foggy Day	S'Wonderful
Funny Face	Slap That Bass
He Loves and She Loves	Somebody Loves Me
How Long Has This Been	Someone to Watch over Me
Going On	Soon
I Can't Be Bothered Now	Strike Up The Band
I Got Plenty O' Nuttin'	Summertime
I Got Rhythm	Swannee
I Loves You Porgy	Sweet and Lowdown
I've Got a Crush on You	There's a Boat Dat's Leavin'
I've Got Beginners Luck	Soon for New York
Isn't It a Pity?	They All Laughed
It Ain't Necessarily So	They Can't Take That Away
Just Another Rhumba	from Me
Lady Be Good	Things Are Looking Up
Let's Call the Whole Thing Off	Who Cares
Little Jazz Bird	A Woman Is a Sometimes
Liza	Thing

Biography

Ira Gershwin was born Israel Gershowitz in 1896 in Brooklyn, the son of Russian-Jewish immigrants, Rosa Bruskin and Morris

Gershovitz. George Gershwin (born Jacob Gershovitz) was the younger brother by two years. When Ira was 11 years old, the family bought a piano for him to take lessons, but it was George who could not be pulled away from it. At 14 George began piano studies with Charles Hambitzer; at 15 he dropped out of school and took jobs playing in nightclubs and as a Tin Pan Alley song plugger. By age 19 George was an international sensation as the composer of the hit song "Swannee."

Ira dropped out of the City College of New York after completing two years. He tried a variety of jobs, not staying with any of them: steam room attendant, photographer's assistant, carnival business manager, theatre reviewer and others. At George's urging Ira tried writing lyrics and found success with his first Broadway show, *Two Little Girls in Blue*, with composer Vincent Youmans. In 1922, the brothers began working together, writing the song "I'll Build a Stairway to Paradise."

George's groundbreaking "Rhapsody in Blue" debuted in 1925 at an evening of new and innovative music produced and conducted by Paul Whiteman. The Gershwins moved the musical theatre forward towards the integrated musical in their political satire trilogy, *Strike Up the Band*, the Pulitzer Prize-winning *Of Thee I Sing* and *Let 'Em Eat Cake*. George stood simultaneously in the worlds of popular, jazz and classical music. The best example of this is his folk opera, *Porgy and Bess*, which partook of all three worlds and remains one of the greatest artistic achievements of the 1930s.

George died in 1937 during surgery to remove a brain tumor; he was 38 years old. Ira spent years championing the work of his late brother. Returning to writing lyrics later in life, he collaborated with Jerome Kern, Harold Arlen, Kurt Weill, Vernon Duke and Harry Warren.

Resources

Singer Michael Feinstein has written *The Gershwins and Me: A Personal History in Twelve Songs*.[5] Other excellent biographies include *Fascinating Rhythm: Collaboration of George and Ira Gershwin*[6] by Deena Rosenberg and *Gershwin: A Biography*[7] by Edward Jablonski. A search for Gershwin recordings on Amazon. com yields just shy of 5,000 – take your pick. If you listen to anything and everything you can and you learn how others have interpreted these songs, you can build your interpretations.

Arthur Schwartz (1900–1984) and Howard Dietz (1896–1983): Sophisticated songs

Stylistic approach

Of Howard Dietz's music, Zinsser writes, "Nobody wrote melodies as sensuous as 'Alone Together' and 'You and the Night and the Music,' with their rich minor-key coloring, or 'Dancing in the Dark' and 'I See Your Face Before Me.' They are grandly constructed songs, soaring at exactly the moment when they need to take flight and then returning to earth, all musical issues resolved."[8] Schwartz was a substantially more sophisticated composer than most others of the era: lush, romantic and sophisticated melodically, harmonically and structurally.

The Dietz and Schwartz songs are perfectly constructed, with beginnings, middles and ends that arc together beautifully; one feels a sense of having taken a journey after listening to a Dietz and Schwartz song. The majority of their successful shows were revues, where songs had to stand on their own without character or plot. The stand-alone nature of their songs helps explain why cabaret performers, chanteuses, and chanteurs favor Dietz and Schwartz; their songs allow them to marry intense musical values with strong interpretive skills. Perhaps these songs are too substantially developed, too sophisticated, to stand up under too much jazz re-interpretation. Maureen McGovern's version of "Confession" and Nancy Lamott's or Michael Feinstein's versions of "Rhode Island Is Famous For You" are terrific examples of these kinds of successful cabaret performances.

Body of work

Dietz and Schwartz's 11 Broadway shows include:

The Little Show (1929)	*At Home Abroad* (1935)
The Second Little Show (1930)	*Between the Devil* (1937)
Three's A Crowd (1930)	*Inside U.S.A.* (1948)
The Band Wagon (1931)	*The Gay Life* (1961)
Flying Colors (1932)	*Jennie* (1963)
Revenge with Music (1934)	

The catalog of Dietz and Schwartz songs includes:

Alone Together
By Myself (I'll Go My Way)
Confession
Dancing in the Dark
Get Yourself a Geisha Girl
Hammacher Schlemmer,
    I Love You
Haunted Heart
High and Low
Hoops
Hottentot Potentate
I Guess I'll Have to Change
    My Plan
I Love Louisa
I See Your Face Before Me
Louisiana Hayride
Love Is a Dancing Thing
Magic Moment
New Sun in the Sky

Oh, but I Do
Rainy Night in Rio
Rhode Island Is Famous For
    You
A Shine on Your Shoes
Sleigh Bells
Something to
    Remember You By
Something You Never
    Had Before
That's Entertainment
That's not Cricket
Triplets
What a Wonderful World
Why Go Anywhere at All
You and the Night and
    the Music
You Will Never Be Lovelier

Biography

Lyricist Howard Dietz was born and raised in New York, where he attended Townsend Harris High School. He began working at 15 as a newspaper copy boy, entered Columbia University as a journalism major, and in his junior year quit college to take a job in advertising. In 1919, after serving in the Navy during World War I, he became publicity director for MGM; by 1924 he was director of advertising and publicity. In 1929, Dietz and Schwartz began a collaboration that would last for thirty years. Dietz died in 1983 in New York City.

Composer Arthur Schwartz, born and raised in Brooklyn, New York, began earning pocket money by accompanying silent films at the age of 14. After completing his undergraduate degree at NYU and his Masters of Law at Columbia University, he passed the bar exam in 1924. However, he put aside the law in 1928 to write songs full-time. When Schwartz died in 1984, his obituary in the *The New York Times* referred to him as, "a composer who helped bring a new sophistication to Broadway songwriting in the 1930s, with such tunes as 'Dancing in the Dark,' and 'You and the Night and the Music'."[9]

Dietz also wrote lyrics for Jerome Kern, Kurt Weill, Vernon Duke, Jimmy McHugh and others, while Schwartz wrote music for Ira Gershwin, Frank Loesser, Dorothy Fields, Johnny Mercer, E.Y. "Yip" Harburg and others. Throughout their collaboration Dietz continued to serve in his capacity for MGM, and Schwartz continued to work as an attorney and producer for Columbia Pictures.

Resources

Howard Dietz's autobiography, *Dancing in the Dark*,[10] was published in 1974. There are several excellent sheet music anthologies including *All Time Favorite Dietz & Schwartz Songs Featuring Dancing in The Dark* and *That's Entertainment, The Great Songs of Dietz and Schwartz*. Original Broadway cast recordings are available of *Inside U.S.A.*, *The Gay Life*, and *Jennie*. The movie version of *The Band Wagon* is available as audio or video. Many artists have recorded these songs; most of these recordings are available.

Harold Arlen (1905–1986): Composer of the number one song of the twentieth century

Stylistic approach

Composer Harold Arlen's songs are the most melodically, harmonically and structurally complex of any of the Tin Pan Alley composers. Many of the other composers took from various jazz idioms, but Arlen's music infuses the popular song with the blues and with the aching minor sounds of the synagogue in which he grew up. Ben Sidran refers to it as a "minor-key-within-a-major key duality," and goes on to say that "Harold Arlen is the bridge between the blues and the Talmud. The Talmud itself pours scorn on anyone who reads without melody and studies without a tune."[11]

This helps explain why Arlen's songs have been so popular with jazz and blues singers, but they are so well crafted that for the more legitimate singer these songs can speak for themselves. The singer needs to be true to their nature, tell the stories honestly and allow Arlen's rich writing to speak for itself. Crooners, belters, swingers,

blues singers all love Arlen songs – these are songs are most successfully performed with tremendous stylistic commitment.

Body of work

Harold Arlen's Broadway scores include:

Earl Carroll's Vanities (1930)	*Life Begins at 8:40* (1934)
You Said It (1931)	*Hooray for What!* (1937)
Earl Carroll's Vanities (1932)	*Bloomer Girl* (1944)
Americana (1932)	*St. Louis Woman* (1946)
George White's Music Hall	*House of Flowers* (1954)
Varieties (1932)	*Jamaica* (1957)
George White's Music Hall	*Saratoga* (1959)
Varieties (1933)	

Harold Arlen's movies include:

Let's Fall in Love (1933)	*Up in Arms* (1944)
Strike Me Pink (1936)	*Here Come the Waves* (1944)
The Singing Kid (1936)	*Casbah* (1948)
Stage Struck (1936)	*My Blue Heaven* (1950)
Gold Diggers of 1937 (1937)	*Down Among the Sheltering*
The Wizard of Oz (1939)	*Palms* (1953)
At the Circus (1939)	*The Farmer Takes a*
Blues in the Night (1941)	*Wife* (1953)
Rio Rita (1942)	*A Star Is Born* (1954)
Star Spangled Rhythm (1942)	*The Country Girl* (1954)
Cabin in the Sky (1943)	*Gay Purr-ee* (1962)
The Sky's the Limit (1943)	

Of the over 500 songs that Arlen wrote, the following are just
some of the most important and well remembered:

Ac-cent-tchu-ate the Positive	Blues in the Night
Any Place I Hang My Hat Is	Buds Won't Bud
Home	Come Rain or Come Shine
Between the Devil and the Deep	Ding Dong! The Witch is Dead
Blue Sea	Down with Love
Black Magic (That Old)	The Eagle and Me

Easy Street
Evalina
Follow the Yellow Brick Road
Get Happy
Happiness Is a Thing Called Joe
Hooray for Love
I Got a Right to Sing the Blues
I Had Myself a True Love
I Love a Parade
I Love to Sing-a
I Never Has Seen Snow
I Wonder What Became of Me
If I Only Had a Brain (A Heart; The Nerve)
If I Were King of the Forest
I've Got a Right to Sing the Blues
I've Got the World on a String

Last Night when We Were Young
Let's Fall in Love
Lydia the Tattooed Lady
The Man that Got Away
Munchkinland
My Shining Hour
One for My Baby (and One More for the Road)
Over the Rainbow
Push De Button
Right as the Rain
A Sleepin' Bee
Stormy Weather
Sweet and Hot
This Time the Dream's on Me
We're Off to See the Wizard
You're a Builder Upper

Biography

Born Hymen Arluck, son of a synagogue cantor in Buffalo New York, Arlen "emerged as one of the greatest of all American [...] songwriters, writing extraordinarily complex melodies and harmonies that somehow remained accessible to a broad popular audience."[12] By age seven, he was singing in the synagogue choir and by 15 he was performing professionally in nightclubs, on lake boats and in vaudeville, where he was immensely popular. "Arlen's unique singing style, influenced by liturgical singing and the techniques of black vocalists, led to jobs in vaudeville."[13]

Veering from his career as a performer, Arlen accepted a contract to compose in 1929. That year Arlen wrote his first hit, "Get Happy." The hits kept coming for nightclub shows, revues and variety artists. Broadway and Hollywood hits yielded hit song after hit song. In 2000, Arlen's "Somewhere Over the Rainbow" was recognized as the number one song of the twentieth century.

Arlen's career was slowed substantially by the advent of rock and roll in the 1960s, but he did write "over 50 songs between 1961 and 1976 and continued to enjoy a successful career."[14] After his wife Anya's death in 1970 Arlen lost interest in everything. He died in New York in 1986.

Resources

Edward Jablonski has written two biographies of Harold Arlen, *Harold Arlen, Happy With the Blues*[15] and *Harold Arlen: Rhythm, Rainbows and Blues*.[16] Original cast recordings of Arlen's later Broadway shows, *Bloomer Girl, St. Louis Woman, House of Flowers, Jamaica* and *Saratoga* are available. Compilation albums by most major jazz or blues artists abound, as do albums by cabaret and popular artists like Ella Fitzgerald, Frank Sinatra, Maureen McGovern, Tom Wopat, Michael Bublé, Rufus Wainwright and many more.

In summary

Taken together, these songwriters' output represents a great part of the enduring musical legacy of the 1920s and 1930s. Frequently they wrote for singers with great style and personality. Performers like Al Jolson, Fanny Brice, Eddie Cantor, Beatrice Lillie, Marilyn Miller and Fred and Adele Astaire did not necessarily bring the most highly trained vocal instruments to the stage. Nonetheless, they thrilled audiences nightly, singing this material. While so many of these songs have been reinterpreted time and again over the intervening years, a contemporary singer approaching songs from this era would be well served to find a *joie de vivre*, a larger than life quality and an identifiable persona to give these songs context. Listen to the great jazz artists who have reinvented so many of these songs time and time again, or the numerous revivals, stage adaptations and jukebox musicals that have used these songs so successfully. Use those performances as models, not to copy or imitate, but rather to distil and define essential qualities.

Notes

1 Uncredited, "Instruments in Depth – The Saxophone," *Bloomingdale School of Music*, www.bsmny.org/exploring-music/features/iid/saxophone/2.php, accessed February 12, 2015.
2 "Jimmy McHugh Biography," *Songwriters Hall of Fame*, www.songwritershalloffame.org/exhibits/C51, accessed July 26, 2015.
3 Alyn Shipton, *I Feel a Song Coming On: The Life of Jimmy McHugh (Music in American Life)*, Champaign, IL: University of Illinois Press, 2009.
4 William Zinsser, *Easy To Remember: The Great American Songwriters and Their Songs*, Jaffrey, NH: David R. Godine, 2006, p. 55.

5 Michael Feinstein, *The Gershwins and Me: A Personal History in Twelve Songs*, New York, NY: Simon and Schuster, 2012.

6 Deena Ruth Rosenberg, *Fascinating Rhythm: The Collaboration of George and Ira Gershwin*, Ann Arbor, MI: University of Michigan Press, 1998.

7 Edward Jablonski, *Gershwin A Biography*, Lebanon, NH: Northeastern Press, 1990.

8 William Zinsser, *Easy to Remember: The Great American Songwriters and Their Songs*, Jaffrey, NH: David R. Godine, 2006, p. 67.

9 John Pareles, "Arthur Schwartz, Composer of Broadway Shows, is Dead," *The New York Times*, September 5, 1984. www.nytimes.com/1984/09/05/obituaries/arthur-schwartz-composer-of-broadway-shows-is-dead.html, accessed May 19, 2014.

10 Howard Dietz, *Dancing in the Dark: Words by Howard Dietz*, New York, NY: Quadrangle, 1974.

11 Jesse Hamlin, "Ben Sidran Revisits Jewish Influence on American Music," *SFGate*, March 26, 2014, www.sfgate.com/movies/article/Ben-Sidran-revisits-Jewish-influence-on-American-5351966.php accessed May 20, 2104.

12 "Harold Arlen Biography," *Songwriters Hall of Fame*, www.songwritershalloffame.org/exhibits/bio/C53, accessed May 18, 2014.

13 Michael Feinstein, "Harold Arlen," *Michael Feinstein's American Songbook*, www.michaelfeinsteinsamericansongbook.org/songwriter.html?p=45, accessed May 20, 2014.

14 Sharon Zak Marotta, "Harold Arlen – Biography – Last Night When We Were Young," *The Official Harold Arlen Website*, www.haroldarlen.com/bio-9.html, accessed May 19, 2014.

15 Edward Jablonski, *Harold Arlen: Happy With the Blues*, New York, NY: Da Capo Press, 1986.

16 Jablonski, *Harold Arlen: Rhythm, Rainbows and Blues*, Lebanon, NH: Northeastern University Press, 1996.

Chapter 4

The great wits and sophisticates

Cole Porter, Richard Rodgers, and Lorenz Hart, E.Y. "Yip" Harburg, Johnny Mercer, Dorothy Fields and Vernon Duke

The late 1920s and early 1930s saw a wave of great wits and sophisticates writing for musical theatre. Much of this is evident in the wordplay and verbal dexterity displayed in these artists' lyrics, but sometimes this wit and sophistication is also present in the music. Cole Porter and Johnny Mercer wrote both music and lyrics. Vernon Duke and Richard Rodgers wrote music only, Duke with a variety of lyricists and Rodgers with Lorenz Hart at this stage of his career. This chapter also looks at the work of lyricists Lorenz Hart, E.Y. "Yip" Harburg, and Dorothy Fields.

A great many of the songs mentioned in this chapter intentionally call attention to themselves and their cleverness – this is part of their fun. Anyone listening to practically any performance of Cole Porter's "Friendship" or Lorenz Hart's "Manhattan," marvels at Porter and Hart's wit, rather than the singer's.

These writers' careers and works came to define the era of the star songwriters. Audiences went to the theatre to see what "the boys" (Rodgers and Hart) were up to now, they were the name attraction even more than the title of the show or a particular star. Musicals were considered successful if they ran through a season, and much of a composer's income was derived through the sale of recordings of their songs covered by popular artists. The most popular artists of the day were jazz artists, so the most successful songwriters tended to be those who wrote in either a jazz idiom or those whose work transferred easily to jazz.

The musical theatre writers covered in this chapter had many of their songs, certainly their greatest hits, recorded by many jazz artists. Their melodies are some of the most popular ever written, but they are led by their lyrics, and as such require verbal dexterity. Not only do the words need to be clearly articulated, but more importantly, the thoughts underlying the words need to be clear to the singer, who then needs to make them clear to the listener. In other words, clarity and specificity of thought are required of the singer of these songs.

These writers were of the same era as the songs in Chapter 3, and as such partake in the same vocal aesthetic. Bright "pingy" sound with a frontal resonance (nasality) helps these songs to be sung out from the stage over the pit orchestras of the time. The frontal placement, sharp articulation and clarity of what is being communicated should be of primary importance to the singer of these songs. Jazz styles will explored in the next chapter and could also certainly be applied to the songs in this chapter.

In today's post-literate world, we receive the bulk of our information through visual images. But audiences and listeners of the 1920s and 1930s were highly literate, used to getting the bulk of their information through words. These songs place great importance on the wit and wordplay of these lyricists. Because of this cultural shift in how we receive and process information, we need to attend to these songs lyrically more than singers of earlier generations did.

Cole Porter (1891–1964): One of America's greatest wits and sophisticates

Stylistic approach

Some of the very best and most lasting songs of the 1930s and 1940s are Cole Porter songs. Porter was one of the few popular American songwriters to have written both music and lyrics. Lyrically, he is best known for clever, sophisticated and often ribald list songs like "Let's Do It, Let's Fall in Love" and "Let's Misbehave," and heartfelt ballads which express a deep ennui like "What Is This Thing Called Love," "Love for Sale," "Night and Day," "All Through the Night," "Begin the Beguine" and "I Love Paris."

Porter was born to great wealth and educated in a way that such wealth could provide. His songs – and the characters who sing them – are well educated, articulate and sophisticated, and they frequently use their intelligence and sense of irony as weapons against the vagaries of the world. Porter had a long-term marriage to his female best friend, but there was a distinct break between his marriage and his love life. He was a closet homosexual at a time when homosexuality was neither accepted socially nor even legal. John Kenrick writes, "Porter limited his sex life to emotionless encounters with sailors and prostitutes. He found that sex, like other pleasures, could be far less complicated when it was purchased."[1] So many of his ballads seem to express a deep yearning to find lasting and total love. As such, many of Porter's songs are filled with double meanings, one for the larger audience, and a second one for the audience who is "in the know." This double set of meanings is a great source of what we consider the "wit" of Porter, and the singer of Porter's songs would be well advised to take this into account.

Porter's songs are also intensely sophisticated musically. Frequently writing in minor keys, or modally shifting between major and minor keys, the lone non-Jewish successful songwriter at the time borrowed heavily from his Jewish colleagues. Porter admitted to both Richard Rodgers and Sammy Cahn that he considered his successful songs to be Jewish tunes. "I laughed at what I took to be a joke," Rodgers wrote. "But [...] Cole [was] dead serious, [...]. Just hum the melody that goes with 'Only you beneath the moon or under the sun' from 'Night and Day,' or any of 'Begin the Beguine,' or 'Love for Sale,' or 'My Heart Belongs to Daddy,' or 'I Love Paris.' These minor-key melodies are unmistakably eastern Mediterranean."[2] William Zinsser writes, "Unlike Jerome Kern, whose melodies had their roots in Viennese operetta, or Gershwin and Harold Arlen, whose music grew out of their Jewish heritage and the black jazz they grafted onto it, Porter seems to be self-invented, an American original. Most of his songs are built of short bursts of melody, which almost demand a beguine accompaniment, and many have the further exoticism of being in a minor key, nearer to Russia than Indiana. The resulting sound is unlike anybody else's."[3]

Porter's songs have been successfully interpreted by musicians from all genres, and stand up well to traditionally classical interpretations, more spoken-sung character interpretations, or jazz or even rock interpretations. The greatest common denominator in successful interpretations of Porter is the sense of the witty sophisticate, deeply regretful that he or she is too smart or effete to connect truly with others.

Porter has always been a favorite of jazz artists. "Singers love his lyrics, which contain great wit, amazing rhymes and beautiful imagery. Instrumentalists love his elegant melodies and sophisticated song structures. During the three decades of Porter's greatest productivity – the late 1920s through the late '50s – jazz musicians would latch on to the latest Porter songs from his Broadway shows or Hollywood musicals and turn them into jazz standards almost immediately. Jazz artists are still exploring Cole Porter today."[4] To begin listening to jazz interpretations of Porter's songs, listen to any of the various recordings by Ella Fitzgerald, Bobby Short or Frank Sinatra. In addition to these, there are hundreds of others, each with their own stylistic spin. Porter's songs tend to stand up well to interpretation and stylization. Not only jazz performers, but also rock performers love Cole Porter songs. Rock singers who have successfully recorded Cole Porter songs include k.d. lang, Sinead O'Connor, David Byrne, Tom Waits, U2 and Rod Stewart.

Porter songs thrive under the embellishments of almost any style – rock, jazz, country, punk, legitimate. The songs work perfectly well sung completely straight, without embellishment, but they seem completed, given context, personalization, when the singer provides stylistic choices. Listen to early recordings of Danny Kaye singing Porter songs and you will hear a range of styles, mostly jazz and swing.

Body of work

While Porter loved visiting and living in Hollywood, the overwhelming majority of his work was done for the stage. Much of his film work consisted of adapting his stage musicals for the screen, or rewriting his stage songs to fit into movie musicals. His stage musicals include:

Hands Up (additional lyrics, 1915)	Hitchy-Koo of 1922 (1922)
Miss Information (additional lyrics, 1915)	Greenwich Village Follies (1924)
See American First (1916)	La Revue des Ambassadeurs (Paris nightclub revue, 1928)
Hitchy-Koo of 1919 (1919)	
A Night Out (London, 1920)	Paris (1928)
As You Were (1920)	Wake Up and Dream (1929)
Mayfair and Montmartre (London, 1922)	Fifty Million Frenchmen (1929)
	The New Yorkers (1930)

Gay Divorce (1932)
Nymph Errant (London, 1933)
Anything Goes (1934)
Jubilee (1935)
Red, Hot and Blue (1936)
You Never Know (1938)
Leave It to Me! (1938)
Dubarry Was a Lady (1939)
Panama Hattie (1940)

Let's Face It (1941)
Something for the Boys (1943)
Mexican Hayride (1944)
Seven Lively Arts (1944)
Around the World (1946)
Kiss Me Kate (1948)
Out of This World (1950)
Can-Can (1953)
Silk Stockings (1955)

Porter spent substantial time living in Hollywood and contributing to hundreds of movie musicals; however, many of these were screen adaptations of his Broadway successes or movies to which he contributed pre-existing songs. Movie musicals for which Porter did substantial hands-on work include:

Fifty Million Frenchmen (1931)
Paree, Paree (1934)
The Gay Divorcee (1934)
Anything Goes (1936)
Born to Dance (1936)
Rosalie (1937)
Broadway Melody of
    1940 (1940)
You'll Never Get Rich (1941)

Panama Hattie (1942)
Something to Shout
    About (1943)
Dubarry Was a Lady (1943)
Let's Face It (1943)
The Pirate (1948)
Mexican Hayride (1948)
Kiss Me Kate (1953)

Listed below are some of the most successful and well known of Porter's almost 1,000 songs. Although Porter songs tend to be available in a variety of keys for a variety of vocal types, in cases where these songs are traditionally particular to a voice type, they are indicated.

All of You
All Through the Night ** †
Always True to You in My
    Fashion ††
Another Op'nin', Another
    Show ** ††
Anything Goes
At Long Last Love ** ††

Be a Clown*,**
Begin the Beguine
Blow Gabriel, Blow ††
Brush Up Your
    Shakespeare * **
Buddie, Beware ††
C'est Magnifique ††
Can-Can ††

Cherry Pies Ought To Be You
Don't Fence Me In ** ††
Down in the Depths (on the
   90th Floor) ††
Easy to Love
Ev'ry Time We Say Goodbye
Find Me a Primitive Man ††
Friendship
From This Moment On
Get out of Town
Give Him the Oo-La-La
I Concentrate on You
I Get a Kick Out of You
I Happen to Like New York *
I Hate Men †
I Love Paris
I'm in Love Again
In the Still of the Night
It's All Right with Me
It's De-Lovely
I've Got You Under My Skin
Just One of Those Things
Let's Do It
Let's Misbehave
Let's Not Talk About Love
Let's Step Out
Love for Sale ††
Miss Otis Regrets

Most Gentlemen Don't
   Like Love
My Heart Belongs to Daddy ††
Night and Day
Ridin' High
So in Love
Take Me Back to Manhattan
Thank You So Much, Mrs.
   Lowsborough-Goodby
The Heaven Hop ††
The Laziest Gal in Town ††
The Leader of a Big-time Band
Too Darn Hot
True Love
Well, Did You Evah?
Were Thine That Special
   Face **
What Is This Thing
   Called Love?
Where, Oh Where? †
Why Can't You Behave? †
Wunderbar
You Do Something to Me
You Don't Know Paree
You'd Be So Nice to Come
   Home To
You're the Top
You've Got That Thing

† soprano
†† mezzo
* tenor
** baritone

Biography

Porter was born in Peru, Indiana, grandson of the wealthiest man in the state, J.O. Cole. His mother, Kate, saw to his artistic education, including violin lessons starting at age six and piano starting at age eight. His grandfather sent Cole back East to study at the Worcester Academy at age 14, and sent him on a grand tour of Europe after high school, followed by an undergraduate degree from Yale University. Having brought an upright piano with him to Yale, Cole found himself successful socially thanks to his ability to entertain. He wrote over 30 songs while he was at Yale, including several football fight songs still sung at Yale today. After graduation, Cole was enrolled at Harvard Law School by his grandfather but switched to a graduate program in music. He dropped out shortly after his grandfather discovered the transfer.

Cole had a few songs placed in Broadway shows in 1916, and his first full show, *See America First*, opened in 1917, to horrific reviews. Healing from this defeat, Cole moved to Paris, where he claimed to have worked with the French Foreign Legion during World War I, although no record of his involvement with the legion exists. He lived a lavish lifestyle, renting extravagant villas and throwing wild parties, which "were marked by much gay and bisexual activity, Italian nobility, cross-dressing, international musicians, and a large surplus of recreational drugs."[5] At this time, Porter met Linda Lee, an older divorcee; the two became inseparable and married in 1919. During this time Porter continued to study and write, all the while maintaining his lifestyle.

Finally, at age 36, Porter returned to Broadway with the musical *Paris* (1928), which initially was supposed to have been written by Rodgers and Hart. The success of *Paris* marked Porter's acceptance as one of the top songwriters. Broadway producers and Hollywood movie studios vied for him. The Depression was Porter's most prolific and successful period. He wrote sophisticated songs for witty, urbane, characters who belonged to the upper class – he wrote of a world of wealth and privilege, just the kind of world people wanted to escape into during the Depression.

In 1937, a horse-riding accident damaged both of Porter's legs and left him in constant pain. Despite being crippled and in great pain for the rest of his life, Porter came back with his biggest hit ever, *Kiss Me Kate* (1948), followed by *Out of This World* (1950) and the highly successful *Can-Can* (1952) and *Silk Stockings* (1955). Following the 1958 amputation of his right leg, Porter allowed his vanity to turn him into a recluse. In 1964, Porter died of kidney failure in Santa Monica, California.

Resources

Of the many biographies of Porter, William McBrien's book, *Cole Porter: A Biography*[6] is an excellent place to start, as is Stephen Citron's double biography of Porter and Noel Coward, *Noel and*

Cole: The Sophisticates.[7] The Cole Wide Web, www.coleporter.org is an excellent online source.

Richard Rodgers (1902–1979) and Lorenz Hart (1895–1943): America's most popular songwriting team of the 1920s and 1930s

Stylistic approach

The songs of Rodgers and Hart exemplify their era; they offered swinging melodies, contemporary jazz harmonies and lyrics that spoke in the readily recognizable patois of everyday people. There is an artful self-consciousness to Rodgers and Hart songs. The listener is constantly aware of the verbal and musical wit and sophistication and always waiting for the next clever couplet, rhyme, catchy turn of phrase, or intensely personal revelation about the human condition.

Hart's lyrics frequently manage to transition from sentimental to cynical easily and with great facility. Informed by the Jewish music of his upbringing and the sounds of African American music (jazz), Rodgers' music during this period of his career was contemporary and youthful. Between 1935 and 1942 Rodgers and Hart were at the peak of their artistic powers. The ten musicals they wrote in these seven years contained some of their greatest songs including: "My Romance," "Little Girl Blue," "There's a Small Hotel," "My Funny Valentine," "The Lady is a Tramp," "Where or When," "Have You Met Miss Jones," "Falling In Love With Love" and "Bewitched, Bothered and Bewildered."

Like Porter, Rodgers and Hart songs have always been very popular with jazz artists. Still popular today with cabaret artists, Rodgers and Hart songs remain at the center of the world of the standard song. Rodgers and Hart wrote during the time when swing music was all the rage, and many of the early artists to sing their work came from that tradition.

For traditional jazz renderings of Rodgers and Hart songs, a vast amount of recorded material is available. A good place to start encountering this material is with Ella Fitzgerald, Dawn Upshaw or Tony Bennett. As with Porter, these songs are cornerstones of the American Songbook, so they have received different interpretations in many different styles. Rock singer Rod Stewart shows a great understanding of phrasing and respect for the swing origins inherent in the Rodgers and Hart ballad "My Heart Stood Still" on his album, "The Complete Great American Songbook." As with Porter's songs, and those of other writers in this chapter, these songs do best when the singer brings their musical personality to the table in whatever style they are most comfortable. For the musical-theatre singer with a variety of styles at their fingertips this leaves a wide range of possibilities.

Body of work

Rodgers and Hart's stage musicals include:

You'd Be Surprised (1920)	*Chee-Chee* (1928)
Fly with Me (1920)	*Spring Is Here* (1929)
Poor Little Ritz Girl (1920)	*Head's Up!* (1929)
You'll Never Know (1921)	*Lady Fingers* (1929)
The Melody Man (1924)	*Ever Green* (1930)
The Garrick Gaieties (1925)	*Simple Simon* (1930)
June Days (1925)	*America's Sweetheart* (1931)
Dearest Enemy (1925)	*Jumbo* (1935)
Fifth Avenue Follies (1926)	*On Your Toes* (1936)
The Girl Friend (1926)	*The Show Is On* (1936)
The Garrick Gaieties (2nd	*Babes in Arms* (1937)
Edition) (1926)	*I'd Rather Be Right* (1937)
Lido Lady (1926)	*I Married an Angel* (1938)
Peggy-Ann (1926)	*The Boys from Syracuse* (1938)
Betsy (1926)	*Too Many Girls* (1939)
A Connecticut Yankee (1927)	*Higher and Higher* (1940)
One Damn Thing After	*Pal Joey* (1940)
Another (1927)	*By Jupiter* (1942)
She's My Baby (1928)	*A Connecticut Yankee*
Present Arms (1928)	*(revised)* (1943)

Rodgers and Hart also contributed to Hollywood movie musicals, including:

Spring is Here (1930)	*Evergreen* (1934)
Love Me Tonight (1932)	*Mississippi* (1935)
The Phantom President (1932)	*The Boys from Syracuse* (1940)
Hallelujah! I'm a Bum (1933)	*Too Many Girls* (1940)
Yours Sincerely (1933)	*They Met in Argentina* (1941)

Listed below are some of the most successful and well known of Rodgers and Hart's songs. These songs tend to be available in a variety of keys for a variety of vocal types. In cases where these songs are traditionally particular to a voice type, they are indicated.

Babes in Arms
Bewitched, Bothered and
    Bewildered
Blue Moon
The Blue Room
Dancing on the Ceiling
Falling in Love with Love
Glad to Be Unhappy
Have You Met Miss Jones?
He and She ††
He Was Too Good to Me
I Could Write a Book **
I Didn't Know What
    Time it Was
I Wish I Were in Love Again
It Never Entered My Mind
I've Got Five Dollars
Johnny One Note ††
The Lady Is a Tramp
Little Girl Blue
Love Me Tonight
Manhattan

Mimi
The Most Beautiful Girl in
    the World
Mountain Greenery
My Funny Valentine
My Heart Stood Still
My Romance
A Ship Without a Sail
Sing for Your Supper
Ten Cents a Dance ††
There's a Small Hotel †/*
This Can't Be Love †/*
Thou Swell†/*
To Keep My Love Alive †
Wait Till You See Her *
What Can You Do with
    a Man ††
Where or When
With a Song in My Heart
You Took Advantage of Me
Zip ††

† soprano
†† mezzo
* tenor
** baritone

Biography

Richard Rodgers and Lorenz Hart were both born to German Jewish immigrant parents within a few blocks of Mount Morris Park in what is now Harlem in New York City. Rodgers' father was an eminent physician and Hart's was "a real estate broker and con artist, a stout 'voluptuary' whose West 119th Street brownstone teemed with characters of all stripes."[8]

Rodgers was a student at Columbia University where Hart had studied journalism when a mutual friend introduced them. After collaborating on several amateur productions, they had a song included in the Broadway musical *A Lonely Romeo* less than a year later, in 1919. After six years of struggle, failure and near-failure, their big break came in *The Garrick Gaieties*, produced by the prestigious Theatre Guild as a fundraising event. *The Garrick Gaieties* was supposed to run for one performance, but it proved so successful that the guild ran the show for almost a year and a half and 211 performances.

The success and popularity of their song "Manhattan" put Rodgers and Hart in great demand almost immediately. From 1925 to 1931 the two wrote 20 musicals. As the Depression ravaged Broadway, they spent several years in Hollywood, writing for the movies. They returned to Broadway in 1935 and began the most productive seven years of their collaboration, creating many of the greatest songs of the American Songbook.

Throughout their collaboration Rodgers was the level-headed one, the businessman. Hart suffered from a form of dwarfism, never growing beyond five feet tall, and spent his life feeling awkward and uncomfortable about his looks. He was a tormented soul, an alcoholic, and a closet gay man in a time when there was no tolerance for homosexuality. Ultimately Hart's lifestyle took its toll on his health and their collaboration. His alcoholism incapacitated him, forcing Rodgers to seek another collaborator. Hart passed away in 1943, and Rodgers found another long-term partner in Oscar Hammerstein II. Rodgers lived until 1979.

Resources

There are various biographies of Hart as there are of Rodgers. Samuel Marx and Jan Clayton's *Rodgers and Hart: Bewitched, Bothered and Bedeviled, an Anecdotal Account*[9] offers a great look at their collaboration.

E.Y. "Yip" Harburg (1896–1981): Socialist, dreamer and master of whimsy

Stylistic approach

Lyricist E.Y. "Yip" Harburg's eyes were open to the injustices of the world. That's what led him to write lyrics such as the Depression-era anthem "Brother, Can You Spare a Dime?" Harburg always maintained his belief in the ability of people to stand up and do what should be done, and always held hope for the possibilities of a brighter future, as evidenced by his lyric to "Somewhere Over the Rainbow." Harburg's lyrics are drenched in wit, whimsy and wordplay.

For Glocca Morra, the hometown in Ireland of characters Sharon and Finian in *Finian's Rainbow*, Harburg took the German *gluck*, meaning luck, and the Scottish *morra*, meaning tomorrow. The implied suggestion of a lucky tomorrow gives the song "How Are Things in Glocca Morra?" its "Harburgian" aura of hope, on a sub-conscious level. This one example shows how Harburg used words for more than their literal meaning, but for their implied meaning and even for the quality of their sounds. In speaking about James Joyce, Leonard Bernstein said that his, "repetition of elementary sounds gives us 'the whole range of poetic assonance .... We can see poetry born of the repetition of actual words, not just sounds, that it is repetition, modified in one way or another that gives poetry its musical qualities."[10] Harburg was very aware of Joyce and whether consciously or not, used similar techniques in his own writing.

The singer of a Harburg song must embrace and enjoy the lyricist's supple wordplay. Harburg songs from "How Are Things in Glocca Morra" to "If I Were King of the Forest" to "Right as the Rain" and hundreds of others call for good-hearted warmth and humor. Harburg's lyrics do more than just land well on the notes with the best sounding consonants and vowels; they resonate on various levels at once. There is simplicity and ease to a Harburg lyric, but that simplicity gently folded back usually reveals great depth. Listen to the clear and unadorned performance of Judy Garland's original recording of "Over the Rainbow," or the way that Burt Lahr, Ray Bolger and Jack Haley allow the cleverness of the lyric to override the melody as the Lion, Scarecrow and Tin Woodsman in Harburg's "If I Only Had the Nerve," "If I Only Had a Brain" and "If I Only Had a Heart" in *The Wizard of Oz*. This respect for the cleverness and simple emotional honesty of the words is essential to an interpretation of Harburg's songs.

Body of work

Harburg's Broadway scores include:

Earl Carroll's Sketch Book (1929) *	*Earl Carroll's Vanities* (1930) **

Shoot the Works (1931) * * *
Ballyhoo of 1932 (1932) * * * *
Americana (1932) * *
Walk A Little Faster
   (1932) * * * * *
Ziegfeld Follies of 1934
   (1934) †
Life Begins at 8:40 (1934) ††
The Show is On
   (1936/1937) ††
Hooray for What! (1937) ††

Hold on to Your Hats
   (1940) †††
Bloomer Girl (1944) ††
Finian's Rainbow (1947) ††
Flahooley (1951) ††††
Jamaica (1957) ††
The Happiest Girl in the World
   (1961) †††††
Darling of the Day
   (1968) ††††††

* music by Jay Gorney
* * music by Jay Gorney and Harold Arlen
* * * music by Jay Gorney and Vernon Duke
* * * * music by Lewis E. Gensler
* * * * * music by Vernon Duke
† music by various
†† music by Harold Arlen
††† music by Burton Lane
†††† music by Sammy Fain
††††† music by Jacques Offenbach
†††††† music by Jule Styne

   Harburg's film scores include:

Moonlight and Pretzels (1933)
The Singing Kid (1936)
Golddiggers of 1937 (1936)
The Wizard of Oz (1939)
At the Circus (1939)

Babes on Broadway (1941)
Ship Ahoy (1942)
Can't Help Singing (1944)
Gay Purr-ee (1962)
Finian's Rainbow (1968)

   A list of Harburg's most well-known songs would include:

April in Paris*
Brother, Can You Spare a
   Dime * *
Ding Dong the Witch is
   Dead * * *
Down with Love * * *
The Eagle and Me * * *

Evelina * * *
Follow the Yellow Brick
   Road * * *
Happiness Is a Thing Called
   Joe * * *
How Are Things in Glocca
   Morra * * * *

I Like the Likes of You *
I Love to Sing-a ***
If I Only Had a Brain (A Heart;
   The Nerve) ***
If I Were King of the Forest ***
If This Isn't Love ****
It's Only a Paper Moon ***
Look to the Rainbow ****
Lydia the Tattooed Lady ***

Necessity ****
Old Devil Moon ****
Over the Rainbow ***
Right as the Rain ***
That Great Come and Get It
   Day ****
We're Off to See the
   Wizard ***
You're a Builder Upper ***

* music by Vernon Duke
** music by Jay Gorney
*** music by Harold Arlen
**** music by Burton Lane

Biography

Born Isidore Hochberg to desperately poor, Orthodox Jewish, Russian immigrant parents on New York's Lower East Side, the lyricist would later take on the name Edgar Yipsel, E.Y. "Yip" Harburg. At Townsend Harris High School, Harburg and classmate Ira Gershwin shared their deep admiration for the lyrics of W.S. Gilbert and the social consciousness of dramatist George Bernard Shaw.

After serving in World War I, Harburg began writing light verse for local newspapers and began writing lyrics at Ira Gershwin's urging. Gershwin introduced Harburg to his first collaborator, composer Jay Gorney. Together the two contributed songs to a variety of Broadway revues including *Americana* (1932), for which they wrote "Brother, Can You Spare a Dime?,' the song that became the anthem of the Great Depression. The success of this song led to a contract to write for Hollywood movies, where Harburg began working with other composers such as Vernon Duke, Jerome Kern, Jule Styne, Burton Lane and especially Harold Arlen. Harburg wrote most of his greatest successes with Arlen, including the score for the film *The Wizard of Oz* (1939).

Throughout the 1940s, Harburg continued to write lyrics for both screen and stage musicals. Harburg's stage musicals took a strong socialist position on social issues, ultimately causing him to be a victim of Red Scare. While being blacklisted from working in film, radio or television, Harburg's passport was revoked from

1950 to 1962. Tragically, Harburg's career never recovered. In 1981, Harburg died of a heart attack in Hollywood.

Resources

Harold Meyerson and Harburg's son, Ernie Harburg, wrote an excellent biography, *Who Put the Rainbow in The Wizard of Oz?: Yip Harburg, Lyricist*.[11] Harriet Hyman Alonso's book *Yip Harburg: Legendary Lyricist and Human Rights Advocate*[12] uses a great deal of primary material, interviews, broadcasts, speeches, and so on, to discuss Harburg's life, work and political beliefs.

Johnny Mercer (1909–1976)

Stylistic approach

Johnny Mercer is primarily thought of as a lyricist, although he did write music as well from time to time. Mercer wrote lyrics for composers Frank Loesser, Hoagy Carmichael, Richard Whiting, Harry Warren, Arthur Schwartz, Jerome Kern, Harold Arlen, Jimmy Van Heusen, Duke Ellington, Lionel Hampton and Henry Mancini among others. Mercer's writing defines a whimsical, fun and gracious world. His lyrics reflect a Southern gentility, a great love of nature and natural things. Southern black culture and the blues heavily influenced Mercer. His words bounce, they are informed by the rhythms and the groove of swing, and when singing a Johnny Mercer song, one would do well to embrace that world. Mercer's grounding in the jazz and blues of his native Savannah, and his deep association with swing music informs his writing heavily.

Early in his career, Johnny Mercer aspired to be one of the era's great popular swing singers. He and Bing Crosby began their careers as friendly professional rivals; Crosby became the crooner and Mercer the writer (lyrics and music) who also performed on the side. Mercer also co-founded Capitol Records (with Buddy DeSylva), which he used to promote the careers of jazz artists, many of whom came from African American and Southern cultural roots. Capitol featured artists like Nat "King" Cole, Margaret Whiting, Peggy Lee, Billie Holiday, Les Paul, Stan Kenton, Miles Davis, Judy Garland, Frank Sinatra, Harry James and others. Mercer's lyrics, even the great ballads like "Skylark" and "Moon River," have a strong pulse to them. With his natural inclination towards jazz, his songs easily lend themselves to all kinds of different jazz styles.

Body of work

In addition to the lyrics he wrote to other composers' music, he sometimes also wrote his own music as well for songs like "Dream" and "Something's Gotta Give." Many of his important songs are looked at in the next chapter, in examining the great jazz composers. But Mercer is too important in both worlds not to be included here.

Johnny Mercer's Broadway musicals include:

Garrick Gaieties (1930)	Texas Li'l Darlin' (1949)
Lew Leslie's Blackbirds of	Top Banana (1951)
1939 (1939)	Li'l Abner (1956)
Walk With Music (1940)	Saratoga (1959)
St. Louis Woman (1946)	Foxy (1964)

An abbreviated list of Mercer's Hollywood musicals includes:

Old Man Rhythm (1935)	Star Spangled Rhythm (1942)
To Beat the Band (1935)	Here Come the Waves (1944)
Ready, Willing and Able (1937)	The Harvey Girls (1946)
Varsity Show (1937)	The Belle of New York (1952)
Hollywood Hotel (1937)	Top Banana (1954)
Garden of the Moon (1938)	Seven Brides for Seven
Going Places (1938)	Brothers (1954)
Naughty but Nice (1939)	Daddy Long Legs (1955)
You'll Find Out (1940)	You Can't Run Away from It
You're the One (1941)	(1956)
Navy Blues (1941)	Merry Andrew (1958)
Blues in the Night (1941)	Li'l Abner (1959)
The Fleet's In (1942)	Not with My Wife, You Don't!
You Were Never	(1966)
Lovelier (1942)	Darling Lili (1970)

Among Mercer's most well-known songs are:

Accentuate the Positive **
And the Angels Sing ***
Any Place I Hang My Hat is
    Home **
Autumn Leaves *††††††
Blues in the Night **
Bob White *****
Bye Bye Baby **
Charade †
Come Rain or Come Shine **
The Days of Wine and
    Roses †
Day In, Day Out ††
Dream *
Easy Street **
Everything Happens to Me †††
Fools Rush In ††
G.I. Jive *
Glow Worm ††††
Goody Goody †††††
Hooray for Hollywood ******
I Had Myself a True Love **
I Remember You ††††††
I Wonder What Became
    of Me **
I'm an Old Cowhand *

I'm Old Fashioned *†
In the Cool Cool Cool of the
    Evening **
Indian Summer *††
Jeepers Creepers **
Laura *†††
Lazy Bones**
Moon River †
My Shining Hour **
On the Atchison Topeka and
    the Santa Fe *††††
One for My Baby (and One
    More for the Road) **
Out of This World **
Pardon My Southern
    Accent †††††
Satin Doll *†††††
Skylark †††
Something's Gotta Give *
Tangerine ††††††
That Old Black Magic **
Too Marvelous for
    Words ******
You Must Have Been a
    Beautiful Baby *††††
You Were Never Lovelier *†

* Music by Johnny Mercer
** Music by Harold Arlen
*** Music by Ziggy Elman
**** Music by André Previn
***** Music by Bernard
    Hanighen
****** Music by Richard
    Whiting
† Music by Henry Mancini
†† Music by Rube Bloom
††† Music by Hoagy
    Carmichael
†††† Music by Paul Lincke

††††† Music by Matt Melnick
†††††† Music by Victor
    Schertzinger
*† Music by Jerome Kern
*†† Music by Peter Tinturin
*††† Music by David Raskin
*†††† Music by Harry Warren
*††††† Music by Duke
    Ellington
*†††††† Music by Joseph
    Kosma

Mercer received Academy Award nominations for Best Song for the following:

Jeepers Creepers (1939)
I'd Know You Anywhere (1941)
Love of My Life (1941)
Blues in the Night (1942)
Dearly Beloved (1943)
My Shining Hour (1944)
That Old Black Magic
  (1944)
Welcome Egg Head (1946)
On the Atchison Topeka and
  the Santa Fe (1947) *

In the Cool, Cool, Cool of the
  Evening (1951) *
Something's Gotta Give (1956)
Facts of Life (1956)
Moon River (1962) *
Days of Wine and Roses
  (1963) *
Charade (1964)
Sweetheart Tree (1966)
Darling Lili (1971)
Whistling Away the Dark (1971)

* indicates Academy Award winner

Biography

Mercer, born in Savannah, Georgia, was the Southern gentleman of Tin Pan Alley. Mercer was exposed to African American music from a young age, having black playmates and servants, attending black churches and listening to the fishermen and vendors of Savannah, Gullah people who spoke a dialect called Geechee. His musical influences as a teenager included Ma Rainey, Bessie Smith and Louis Armstrong. Ultimately Mercer would write lyrics to over 1,500 songs.

Mercer started performing and writing songs at 15, and at 19 he moved to New York to pursue an acting career. Mercer's first song to appear on Broadway was in *Garrick Gaieties of 1930*, and his first big hit came in 1933 with "Lazy Bones." Also in 1933 he moved to Hollywood and began writing for and performing in movies. In 1942, he co-founded Capitol Records with Buddy DeSylva. Capitol took off and "by 1946 Capitol produced one-sixth of all records sold in the U.S."[13] Mercer wrote consistently excellent songs (both as lyricist and composer) and died in Los Angeles in 1976.

Resources

Skylark: The Life and Times of Johnny Mercer,[14] is an excellent biography, as is *Johnny Mercer: Southern Songwriter for the World*.[15] Authors and historians Robert Kimball, Barry Day, Miles Krueger and Eric Davis have compiled *The Complete Lyrics of Johnny Mercer*. Original Broadway cast recordings exist for *St. Louis Woman*, *Texas Li'l Darlin'*, *Top Banana*, *Li'l Abner* and *Saratoga*, although many of the best recordings of Mercer's songs are by popular and jazz singers like Judy Garland, Frank Sinatra and Margaret Whiting.

Dorothy Fields (1905–1974): One of very few female lyricists

Stylistic approach

Lyricist Dorothy Fields contributed more than 400 songs to the American Songbook over five decades. Her success with a variety of composers, including Jerome Kern, Sigmund Romberg, Harold Arlen, Arthur Schwartz, Burton Lane, Jimmy McHugh, Harry Warren and Cy Coleman is a testament to her range and versatility.

While Fields' lyrics spoke the contemporary slang of everyday people, she was able to stay current and up to date through the decades without ever sounding affected or like someone from another time. She wrote directly from the heart and without any irony or artifice. William Zinsser says that her lyrics, "say what someone in love should say – no inversion, no allusion, no poetic effects." Citing as an example Fields' lyric to "I Can't Give You Anything but Love," he continues, "this is the English language at its most declarative – a writer making her feelings available to us."[16] Her colleague Betty Comden echoed this sentiment, saying, "The marvelous thing about the way Dorothy wrote is that her lyrics were inventive without being tricky."[17]

With this in mind, the singer of a Dorothy Fields song would be well advised to keep the performance simple, genuine and without comment. Recorded by many artists, two good places to begin listening to Fields' work, other then the original cast recordings, are Barbara Cook's *Dorothy Fields: Close as Pages in a Book*, and Sally Mayes' *The Dorothy Fields Songbook*. Both singers bring their personality, their style, to Fields' songs without ever getting in their way. Cook offers an up-tempo version of "Don't Tell Me," which Mayes performs in its traditional ballad form; and Mayes offers a very contemporary version of "Make the Man Love Me," which Cook gives a traditional ballad performance. Listening to these two great singers give their own voice to the same material offers a great lesson in just how far a singer can go in applying style to these songs while remaining true to them.

Body of work

Dorothy Fields' stage musical credits include:

Blackbirds of 1928 (1928) *
Hello, Daddy (1928) *
Ziegfeld Midnight Frolic
  (1929) *
International Review (1930) *
Vanderbilt Revue (1930) *
Shoot the Works (1931) *
Singing the Blues (1931) *
Stars in Your Eyes (1939) **

Up in Central Park (1945) ***
Arms and the Girl (1950) ****
A Tree Grows in Brooklyn
  (1951) **
By the Beautiful Sea (1954) **
Redhead (1959) *****
Sweet Charity (1966) †
Seesaw (1973) †

* music by Jimmy McHugh
** music by Arthur Schwartz
*** music by Sigmund
    Romberg

**** music by Morton Gould
***** music by Albert Hague
† music by Cy Coleman

Fields' most successful songs include:

Big Spender *
Close as Pages in a Book ****
Digga, Digga, Doo **
Doin' the New Lowdown **
Don't Blame Me **
Exactly Like You **
A Fine Romance ***
I Can't Give You Anything but
  Love **
I Feel a Song Coming On **
I Won't Dance **
I'm in the Mood for Love
If My Friends Could See
  Me Now *
It's Not Where You Start *
Lovely to Look At **

Make the Man Love Me ****
Never Gonna Dance ***
Nobody Does It Like Me *
On the Sunny Side of the
  Street **
Pick Yourself Up ***
The Rhythm of Life *
Remind Me ***
There's Gotta Be Something
  Better Than This *
Too Many Tomorrows *
The Way You Look
  Tonight ***
Welcome to Holiday Inn *
Where Am I Going? *
You Couldn't Be Cuter ***

* music by Cy Coleman
** music by Jimmy McHugh
*** music by Jerome Kern
**** music by Arthur Schwartz

Biography

Dorothy Fields was one of the very few successful female Tin Pan Alley or Hollywood songwriters, and her unusually long career spanned from the 1920s through the 1970s. Fields was the daughter of Lew Fields, a Polish Jewish immigrant, and one of the most successful Broadway entertainers of the late nineteenth century. He was one-half of the comedy team of Weber and Fields. They had been the most prolific producers on Broadway, running Weber and Fields' Broadway Music Hall on Broadway and 29th Street, where they produced well over 50 musicals between 1896 and 1913.

Dorothy was born in Allenhurst, New Jersey, and raised in New York. Discouraged from an acting career by her father, she tried her hand at writing poetry and teaching drama after high school until she met composer Jimmy McHugh. Together they began writing songs for revues at the Cotton Club in Harlem. In 1928, they had their first hit with the song "I Can't Give You Anything but Love," in the Broadway revue *Blackbirds of 1928*. Their next smash hit was "On the Sunny Side of the Street," written for *The International Show* (1930).

Moving to Hollywood movies, Dorothy began working with a slew of other major composers, including Jerome Kern, Sigmund Romberg, Harold Arlen, Arthur Schwartz and Cy Coleman. She also wrote musical theatre librettos and movie screenplays, often in collaboration with her brothers Herbert and Joseph Fields

Resources

Two exceptionally good biographies are Deborah Grace Winder's book, *On the Sunny Side of the Street: The Life and Lyrics of Dorothy Fields*,[18] and Charlotte Greenspan's *Pick Yourself Up: Dorothy Fields and the American Musical*.[19]

Vernon Duke (1903–1969): One foot in two worlds

Stylistic approach

Duke's firm rooting in classical music is apparent in his popular songs and musicals. Duke's melodic sense is rich, which requires that the singer of his songs pay attention to accuracy of pitch; it is easy to go out of tune in a Vernon Duke song. Duke was comfortable in the worlds of both popular and classical music. Friends and supporters of Duke included Serge Koussevitzky and George Gershwin. Like Gershwin, Duke wrote both popular songs and symphonic works. Although few of Duke's songs are in print and few have been recorded, his catalog is a source of top-drawer, lesser known material. There is a gentility and an elegance to Duke's songs, even the jazzier ones like "Taking a Chance on Love." Duke's melodies are beautifully crafted and seem right – they give the feeling that those notes "have" to be in that configuration. And yet, when singing them, many of the passing tones can be elusive until the singer takes the time to clarify and nail each pitch down. For this reason his songs are deceptively simple, but well worth the effort of the time put in on them.

Body of work

Vernon Duke's stage musical credits include:

Garrick Gaieties (1930) *	*Cabin in the Sky* (1940)****
Walk a Little Faster (1932) *	*Banjo Eyes* (1941) ****
Ziegfeld Follies of 1934 (1934) *	*The Lady Comes Across*
Thumbs Up! (1934) **	(1942) ****
Ziegfeld Follies of 1936	*Jackpot* (1944) ****
(1936) **	*Sadie Thompson* (1944) †
The Show is On	*Two's Company* (1952) ††
(1936/1937) ***	*The Littlest Revue* (1956) ††
It Happens on Ice	
(1940/1941) ****	

* lyrics by E.Y. "Yip" Harburg	***** lyrics by John Latouche
** lyrics by Ira Gershwin	† lyrics by Howard Dietz
*** lyrics by Ted Fetter	†† lyrics by Ogden Nash
**** lyrics by Albert Stillman	
and Mitchell Parish	

Duke's list of successful songs may be shorter than others included in this chapter, but his importance lies in the fact that he expanded the melodic and harmonic range of popular music of his time. His most popular songs include.:

April in Paris *	He Hasn't a Thing Except
Autumn in New York **	Me ****
Cabin in the Sky ***	I Can't Get Started ****

I Like the Likes of You *   Taking a Chance on Love ***
A Penny for Your Thoughts *   What is There to Say *

* lyrics by E.Y. Harburg
** lyrics by Vernon Duke
*** lyrics by John LaTouche
**** lrycis by Ira Gershwin

Biography

Vernon Duke was born Vladimir Dukelsy in 1920 in a train sta-
tion in Minsk, when his parents, who lived in Kiev, were travelling by train. By age 11, Dukelsky was studying composition and
music theory at the Kiev Conservatory. Duke's grandmother was
a princess, a direct descendant of the kings of Georgia. In 1919,
the family fled the Russian Civil War and spent a year and a half
in Constantinople until they could obtain proper travel docu-
ments to emigrate to America in 1921. In 1922, George Gershwin
befriended Dukelsky and suggested he Americanize his name.
Throughout his career, Duke wrote his popular songs under
the name Vernon Duke and signed his classical works Vladimir
Dukelsky.

From 1924 to 1929 Duke left America and split his time between
writing classical works in Paris and musical comedies in London.
By 1929 he had returned to New York where he continued to divide
his time between the worlds of popular and classical music, finding great success in both. His biggest success on Broadway was
Cabin in the Sky (1940), directed and choreographed by George
Balanchine. Although he moved to California in 1948, he continued
to write for the Broadway stage and Hollywood films as well as
classical works. Duke died in California in 1969.

Resources

While biographies of Duke are hard to come by, there are plenty of
good articles, like Cynthia J. Miller, " 'Don't Be Scared About Going
Lowbrow:' Vernon Duke and the American Musical on Screen."[20]

In summary

If the writers encountered in the previous chapter represent the
stalwarts of the American musical popular songs of the 1920s and

1930s, the writers in this chapter represent the wits, sophisticates and poets. Their songs seem to hold up quite well in a vast range of styles from legitimate to jazz and even rock interpretations; however, they absolutely glow when the singer is able to bring out the poetic qualities in both music and lyrics. In so many instances, the singer of these songs is aware that they are being particularly insightful, witty or verbally (or musically) dexterous, and this self-knowledge allows the material to sparkle. Where the songs were written for characters, the characters often take on the qualities of intelligence and wit of their authors. Just simply having an emotional "connection" to this text is not necessarily enough; the singer becomes the vehicle for the wit and sophistication of Rodgers and Hart, Porter, Harburg, Fields and the like.

Notes

1 John Kenrick, "Musical Closets: Gay Songwriters," *Musicals101. com: The Cyber Encyclopedia of Musical Theatre, Film & Television*, www.musicals101.com/gay5.htm, accessed March 21, 2015.
2 Richard Rodgers, quoted by Howard Reich in "Joan Curto Celebrates the Genius of Cole Porter," *Chicago Tribune*, February 7, 2013, http://articles.chicagotribune.com/2013-02-07/entertainment/ct-ott-0208-jazz-scene-20130207_1_cole-porter-jewish-music-words-and-music, accessed December 1, 2014.
3 William Zinsser, *Easy to Remember: The Great American Songwriters and Their Songs*, Jaffrey, NH: David R. Godine, 2006, p. 90.
4 Nick Morrison, "Get To Know: The Cole Porter Songbook." *NPR*, www.npr.org/2011/02/09/105032124/get-to-know-the-cole-porter-songbook, accessed July 26, 2015.
5 J.X. Bell, "Cole Porter Biography," *The Cole Porter Resource Site*, www.coleporter.org/bio.html, accessed December 1, 2014.
6 William McBrien, *Cole Porter*, New York, NY: Vintage Press, 2000.
7 Stephen Citron, *Noel and Cole: The Sophisticates*, New York, NY: Oxford University Press, 1993.
8 Marion Rosenberg, "Lorenz Hart, Inside Out," *Capital New York*, July 3, 2012, www.capitalnewyork.com/article/culture/2012/07/6132084/lorenz-hart-inside-out, accessed December 6, 2014.
9 Samuel Marx and Jan Clayton, *Rodgers and Hart: Bewitched, Bothered and Bedeviled, an Anecdotal Account*, New York, NY: G.P. Putnam's Sons, 1976.
10 Leonard Bernstein quoted in Jimmy Webb, *Tunesmith: Inside the Art of Songwriting*, New York, NY: Hachette Books, 1999.
11 Harold Meyerson and Ernie Harburg, *Who Put the Rainbow in the Wizard of Oz?: Lyricist, Yip Harburg*, Ann Arbor, MI: University of Michigan Press,1995.

12 Harriet Hyman Alonso, *Yip Harburg: Legendary Lyricist and Human Rights Advocate*, Middletown, CT: Wesleyan Press, 2012.
13 "Johnny Mercer Biography," *Songwriters Hall of Fame*, www.songwritershalloffame.org/exhibits/bio/C18, accessed May 21, 2014.
14 Furia, Phillip, *Skylark: The Life and Times of Johnny Mercer*, New York, NY: St. Martin's Press, 2004.
15 Eskew, Glenn, *Johnny Mercer: Southern Songwriter for the World*, Athens, GA: University of Georgia Press, 2013.
16 William Zinsser, *Easy to Remember*.
17 Betty Comden, *On the Sunny Side of the Street: The Life and Lyrics of Dorothy Fields*, Foreword, New York, NY: Schirmer Books, 1997, p. IX.
18 Deborah Grace Winer, *On the Sunny Side of the Street: The Life and Lyrics of Dorothy Fields*, New York, NY: Schirmer Books, 1997.
19 Charlotte Greenspan, *Pick Yourself Up: Dorothy Fields and the American Musical*, New York, NY: Oxford University Press, 2010.
20 Cynthia J. Miller, "'Don't Be Scared About Going Lowbrow': Vernon Duke and the American Musical on Screen," Paper read at the conference *Popular Music in the Mercer Era, 1910–1970*, November 13–14, 2009, http://scholarworks.gsu.edu/cgi/viewcontent.cgi?article=1017&context=popular_music, accessed December 11, 2014.

Chapter 5

The great jazz composers

Eubie Blake, Jelly Roll Morton, Duke Ellington,
Hoagy Carmichael, and Fats Waller, and the
great jazz singers

Jazz was born in the United States, of African and European roots. As the first genuinely native American art form, it is absolutely central to the evolution of the rest of American popular culture in the twentieth century and therefore to the American Songbook. A great many jazz composers contributed to this canon, creating the music of their time and inspiring the jazz composers of later generations. This chapter briefly examines five of the most prolific of these composers.

Almost more important and more musically identifiable than these composers are the great jazz singers who interpreted these composers' work, jazz being essentially an interpretive art. To jazz musicians, the notes on the page are frequently viewed as a framework, the template on which they construct their artistry through interpretation and embellishment. In the mid-seventeenth century, opera singers were judged on the vocal ornamentation with which they embellished their arias. Similarly, the expectation of twentieth-century jazz artists is that they transcend the notes on the page, offering variations on the composer's rhythms, melodic lines, phrasings and so on. There is a wide range of jazz styles, including gospel and blues, crooners and band singers, scat singers, be-bop and more recent jazz vocalists following a range of jazz styles.

Jazz singers like Ma Rainey, Bessie Smith, Billie Holiday, Nina Simone, Dinah Washington and Ray Charles are just a handful of the hundreds of gospel- and blues-based jazz singers. This category of jazz singers has its roots in religious gospel music, and in the music created by African American communities in the American deep South in the late nineteenth century. Blues is an agglomeration of religious spirituals, work songs, field hollers and European folk music. Vocally blues singers use:

- a highly melismatic improvisation based on the written melody;
- rhythmic variations, particularly highly syncopated rhythms;
- microtonal tuning, sitting ever so slightly below or above the pitch and tuning into the pitch while sustaining;
- a call and response structure;
- imitation of the sounds of a guitar or harmonica, the primary instruments of blues accompaniment (which were themselves modeled on an imitation of the voice).

Most of the greatest crooners, like Frank Sinatra, Tony Bennett, Nat "King" Cole, Louis Prima, Billy Eckstein, Harry Connick and Michael Bublé, came from the bandstand. Big bands, like those of Tommy and Jimmy Dorsey, Louis Armstrong, Count Basie, Duke Ellington and Cab Calloway, frequently featured singers to establish the melodies before the instrumental soloists could then improvise on them. The introduction of microphones made it possible for these singers to explore more intimacy and a greater emotional and dynamic range by taking away the need to shout out over the band.

In scat singing the singer improvises on the melody using nonsense syllables and sounds, not words. Quite often in scatting the singer will imitate the sound of an instrumental soloist, frequently a trumpet, trombone or saxophone, playing an improvised melody over chord changes. Scatting is one of the purest forms of using the voice as an instrument. Some of the greatest scat singers include Adelaide Hall, Louis Armstrong, Ella Fitzgerald, Mel Tormé, Cab Calloway, Sarah Vaughan and Jon Hendricks.

In the 1960s and 1970s new sounds entered the jazz lexicon as Latin, Afro-Cuban, Brazilian, new forms of be-bop, wider uses of African rhythms and scales, and jazz/rock and jazz/funk fusions gained popularity. Some of the major artists who explored these newer jazz styles include Sarah Vaughan, Al Jarreau, Carmen McRae, George Benson, Bobby McFerrin, Diana Krall and Amy Winehouse.

No written material can replace listening to these singers' vocal styles, phrasings, and techniques. One apocryphal story tells of a jazz saxophonist hired to teach a jazz class at a major university. On the first day of class he handed out his list of the 100 most important jazz recordings and told the students to listen to all 100 albums, and then come back for their A's.

There is vast vocal diversity within the world of jazz singing, and so many wonderful stylistic devices that have found wild success in being applied to the musical theatre repertoire. Listening to as many jazz artists as possible will give the widest array of tricks, techniques and styles to borrow from. Finding that a singer slides in a particular way from one particular note to another may lead the listener to try a similar portamento in their jazz performance. This chapter will briefly discuss these singers' vocal jazz styles. Since jazz vocal styles are associated more with jazz singers than with the songwriters, biographical information will be given for the composers, but equal time and attention will be given to exploring the styles of these singers.

THE COMPOSERS

Eubie Blake (1887–1983): Popularizing ragtime and stride piano

Stylistic approach

Blake was one of the greatest composers and pianists of ragtime and stride piano, introducing ragtime to Broadway musical and popular music. This music is highly rhythmic, being based on syncopated (i.e. "ragged") rhythms. It began as a highly sexually charged music, starting in the parlors of the brothels and bordellos.

Body of work

Broadway musicals that Blake wrote scores for include:

Shuffle Along (1921)
Elsie (1923)
Andre Charlot's Revue of 1924 (1924)
The Chocolate Dandies (1924)
Lew Leslie's Blackbirds (1930)
Chamberlain Brown's Scrap Book (1932)
Shuffle Along (1933 version) (1923)
Swing It (1937)

Other Broadway musicals that used Blake's songs include:

Shuffle Along (2016 and 1952 revivals)
Doctor Jazz (1975)
Bubbling Brown Sugar (1976)
Eubie! (1978)
Big Deal (1986)
Black and Blue (1989)
Sally Marr ... and Her Escorts (1994)

Except for ragtime aficionados, Blake's songs are not widely known today, aside from "I'm Just Wild About Harry," but among the hundreds of songs he published are:

Baltimore Buzz	I'm Just Wild About Harry
Bandana Days	In Honeysuckle Time
Boll Weevil Blues	It's All Your Fault
Charleston Rag	Love Will Find a Way
Good Night Angeline	Memories of You
Hot Feet	Shuffle Along
I'm Just Simply Full of Jazz	

Biography

Blake claims he wrote his first composition, "The Charleston Rag" at age 12 but was unable to notate music until 16 years later. At age 15 Blake began his career as a ragtime pianist, playing in a Baltimore bordello. He teamed with Noble Sissle to form a vaudeville team that went on to write the musical *Shuffle Along*, the first African American blockbuster Broadway hit. *Shuffle Along* included the songs "I'm Just Wild About Harry" and "Love Will Find a Way." Although Blake's career began to wind down after World War II, the 1973 film *The Sting* used the music of ragtime artist Scott Joplin for its soundtrack, sparking a resurgence of interest in ragtime. This surge of interest ultimately led to the 1979 Broadway revue *Eubie!*, featuring Blake's music. When Blake died at age 97, he was still writing and performing.

Resources

Blake claimed to have been born in 1883 and to have lived to 100, although his birth papers and census materials show that he was born in 1887 and lived to 96. He remained an active musician and music historian until the final days of his life. With such longevity, there are many audio and video clips of Blake available online, as well as many interviews with Blake. Robert Kimball and William Bolcom crafted a series of interviews with Blake and Sissle into a book, *Reminiscing With Nobel Sissle and Eubie Blake*,[1] published in 2000, and Al Rose wrote a biography, *Eubie Blake*,[2] in 1979.

Jelly Roll Morton (1890–1941): Pivotal in forming modern jazz in the 1920s

Stylistic approach

Morton blended the ragtime and dance rhythms he learned playing piano in the bordellos of New Orleans with the music of the minstrel shows, and was the first to create written musical arrangements for what had been a primarily improvised form. Known for his arrogance, as much as for his music, Morton claimed to have invented jazz, which he did not. But Morton's contribution to the development of jazz cannot be diminished. Starting primarily as a ragtime pianist, Morton evolved into one of the great stride and barrelhouse pianists. Indicative of his piano style is playing the melody with the thumb of the right hand while harmonizing above it. He also preferred a bass-line that moved in parallel sixths rather than octaves or tenths.

Body of work

Some of Morton's most popular and successful compositions include:

Black Bottom Stomp	Kansas City Stomp
Boogaboo	King Porter Stomp
Burnin' the Iceberg	Mint Julep
Creole Boy	Mr. Jelly Lord
The Creole Way	New Orleans Bump
Dead Man Blues	The Original Jelly Roll
Doctor Jazz Stomp	Pacific Rag
Finger Buster	Pontchartrain
Frog-I-More Rag	Red Hot Peppers
Hyena Stomp	Shreveport Stomp
Jelly Roll	Wild Man Blues
Jungle Blues	Wolverine Blues

Biography

Born and raised in New Orleans, Morton began his career at 14 years old playing ragtime and dance piano in a brothel. Within the year, he had left home to tour the South as a pianist for several minstrel shows, using his down time to compose and gamble. Touring ultimately took him to the North, from New York to Vancouver. He settled in Chicago for several years where he was influential in shaping the sound of Chicago jazz, and then New York, all the while continuing to compose, play and record jazz. With the Depression, Morton's fortunes shifted, and he moved to Washington, DC where historian Alan Lomax recorded a series of interviews with Morton for the Library of Congress, discussing the evolution of jazz.

Resources

Lomax's recordings for the Library of Congress,[3] finally released in 2005, are the greatest resource for Morton. The University of California Press published Lomax's book on Morton, *Mister Jelly Roll: The Fortunes of Jelly Roll Morton, New Orleans Creole and Inventor of Jazz*,[4] in 2001. Howard Reich and William M. Gaines also have an excellent book about Morton, *Jelly's Blues: The Life, Music and Redemption of Jelly Roll Morton*.[5]

Duke Ellington (1899–1974): The largest body of work of any jazz composer

Stylistic approach

Ellington did not consider his music to be jazz, but just American music. He not only wrote more than any other jazz composer, well over 1,000 compositions, but he also wrote some of the greatest and most lasting of the jazz repertoire. His catalog of compositions makes up a great majority of the essential jazz tunes of the 1940s and 1950s. Ellington was a great collaborator and editor; a good many of his songs began as instrumental works and later had lyrics added. The music from each period of his life was strongly influenced by the musicians who were playing for him and his other collaborators. An idea would be thrown out onto the bandstand, developed and evolved in performance and then later committed to paper. His three-decade long collaboration with composer and arranger Billy Strayhorn yielded the richest of his compositions, as well as the largest and most symphonic in scope.

Body of work

Some of Ellington's most popular and successful compositions include:

Azure
Black and Tan Fantasy
Bli-Blip
Caravan
Demi-Tasse
Do Nothin' till You Hear
    from Me
Don't Get Around Much
    Anymore
Drop Me Off in Harlem
Hit Me with a Hot Note and
    Watch Me Bounce
I Ain't Got Nothin' but
    the Blues
I Got It Bad (and That
    Ain't Good)
I Let a Song Go Out of
    My Heart

I'm Beginning to See the Light
I'm Just a Lucky So-and-So
In a Mellow Tone
In a Sentimental Mood
It Don't Mean a Thing (If It
    Ain't Got That Swing)
Love You Madly
The Mooche
Mood Indigo
Perdido
Prelude to a Kiss
Rocks in My Bed
Satin Doll
Solitude
Something to Live For
Sophisticated Lady
Take the "A" Train

Biography

Born and raised in Washington, DC, Ellington made his home in New York, beginning as bandleader for the Cotton Club in Harlem in the 1930s. Ellington excelled in bringing out the best in musicians, and in getting some of the greatest musicians to play as ensemble members in jazz orchestras where the orchestra was the star, rather than the soloists. In 1938, Ellington met Billy Strayhorn, a young composer, arranger and pianist; Strayhorn had aspirations to a career as a classical composer, but at the time that goal was not accessible to a young African American. For the next 25 years, according to Ellington, "Billy Strayhorn was my right arm, my left arm, all the eyes in the back of my head, my brain waves in his head, and his in mine."[6] Strayhorn was able to add symphonic elements and scope to Ellington's work. With Strayhorn's collaboration Ellington adapted Tchaikovsky's *Nutcracker Suite* and Greig's *Peer Gynt Suites* for jazz band.

In 1965, 1968 and 1973 Ellington turned towards religion and premiered three concerts of "sacred" compositions. Following Ellington's death in 1974 his son Mercer took over leadership of the Duke Ellington Orchestra, which he maintained until his death in 1996.

Resources

Recordings of Ellington from every period of his career are widely available. Terry Teachout's 2014 biography, *Duke: A Life of Duke Ellington,*[7] captures many of the contradictions of Ellington.

Hoagy Carmichael (1899–1981): Songwriter, singer, pianist and actor

Stylistic approach

Carmichael was weaned on "hot" ragtime, and the new Chicago style of jazz becoming popular in the late 1910s. Carmichael wrote jazz songs, but his most successful songs tended to be the popular songs. They tend to be straightforward musically, sometimes even folksy, but they leave enough room for jazz styling and solos, and many have made their way into the canon of great jazz standards.

Body of work

Carmichael was a prolific songwriter, but not a Broadway regular, nor a Hollywood insider. For Broadway, Carmichael composed the score to *Walk With Music* (1940).

Some of Carmichael's most popular songs include:

Baltimore Oriole	In the Still of the Night
College Swing	Lazy Bones
(In the) Cool, Cool, Cool of the Evening	The Nearness of You
	Rhumba Jumps
Cranky Old Yank	Rocking Chair
Doctor, Lawyer, Indian Chief	Skylark
Georgia on My Mind	Small Fry
Heart and Soul	Stardust
Hong Kong Blues	Two Sleepy People
I Get Along Without You Very Well	Up a Lazy River
	Washboard Blues

Biography

Carmichael's jazz credentials are impressive. Born and raised in relative poverty in Bloomington, Indiana, Carmichael befriended Reg DuValle, one of the leading jazz musicians in the state, who became his mentor. Carmichael received a Bachelors degree in 1925 and a law degree in 1926, both from Indiana University, supporting his schooling by playing piano and leading a college ensemble. Cornetist Bix Beiderbecke, who he met while at college, introduced him to Louis Armstrong on a trip to Chicago.

Carmichael attempted a career in law, but after failing to pass the bar in Miami and finally passing it back in Indiana, he found his attention firmly placed on music. One of his biggest hits, and one of the greatest jazz tunes ever, "Stardust," was recorded in 1927. Shortly after, Paul Whiteman, who had debuted Gershwin's "Rhapsody in Blue," recorded his song, "Washboard Blues."

Carmichael moved to New York in 1929, where he turned out hits like "Georgia on My Mind," "Up a Lazy River" and "Lazy Bones." By 1935, Carmichael had signed a contract with Paramount and moved to Hollywood, where he turned out hit-after-hit jazz standards, and occasionally appeared in films – always as a singing pianist.

Carmichael's career peaked in the late 1950s just before rock and roll eclipsed all other forms of popular music and the need for jazz songs diminished. He passed away in California in 1981.

Resources

Hoagy Carmichael's autobiography, *The Stardust Road & Sometimes I Wonder: The Autobiography of Hoagy Carmichael*,[8] is a great place to start researching his life and work. For a more objective look at his life, Richard Sudhalter's *Stardust Melody: The Life and Music of Hoagy Carmichael*,[9] is a great reference.

Fats Waller (1904–1943): Master of stride

Stylistic approach

So much of Waller's compositional technique rises out of his extraordinary technique as a pianist; he was a consummate stride pianist. Stride piano uses "a standard left hand pattern, the beat-by-beat alternation between the interval of a tenth struck deep in the bass register of the keyboard and a complex, three- or four-pitch chord struck in the tenor or alto range (the center of the keyboard). Simultaneously, the right-hand plays a highly embellished and syncopated version of the melody, often so completely altered as to be lost amidst the complex cascade of notes."[10]

Writer Murray Horowitz considers Waller and his songs to be simultaneously jazz and comedy. "He is, after all, the point where those two art forms meet: he is the greatest jazz pianist who ever tried to make people laugh, and the greatest comedian who ever played jazz."[11] Waller, as both songwriter and singer was a funny, engaging entertainer; his songs exude his sense of fun and humor.

Body of work

In addition to Waller's credited songs, it is rumored, but not proven, that he wrote and sold songs to white composers who would then publish them under their own names. There is a rumor that Waller and his frequent lyricist Andy Razaf wrote "I Can't Give You Anything but Love" and sold it to Jimmy McHugh for $500 when they were in need of money. The same has been said of "Spreadin' Rhythm Around" and "On the Sunny Side of the Street."

Although Waller primarily wrote popular songs, he composed the scores to three Broadway musicals, *Keep Shufflin'* (1928), *Hot Chocolates* (1929) and *Early to Bed* (1943). *Ain't Misbehavin'*, a 1978 revue, featured music written by or made popular by Waller.

Waller's best-remembered compositions today include:

Ain't Misbehavin'
Black and Blue
Blue Turning Gray over You
Concentratin' on You
Find Out What They Like and How They Like It
Get Some Cash for Your Trash
Handful of Keys
Honeysuckle Rose
I'm Crazy 'bout My Baby
I've Got a Feeling I'm Fallin'
The Joint Is Jumpin'
Keepin' Out of Mischief Now
Ladies Who Sing With the Band
Lounging at the Waldorf
My Fate is in Your Hands
Squeeze Me
Take it From Me
Willow Tree
You're My Ideal

Biography

Born in New York, Waller began playing piano and organ at age six at the Abyssinia Baptist Church, where his father served as pastor. Against his father's wishes, he began playing piano professionally at age 15. At 16 he became a protégé of James P. Johnson, the great ragtime pianist. Through the 1920s, Waller regularly played in the nightclubs of Harlem as well as clubs in Chicago and Philadelphia, where his extraordinary talent and his gregarious personality made him a regular fixture. In the 1930s, he had two regular radio shows: "Paramount on Parade" (1930–1931, from WABC in New York), and "Fats Waller's Rhythm Club" (1932–1934, from WLW in Cincinnati). The success of these radio shows resulted in RCA Victor placing Waller under contract in 1934; he put together a five-piece jazz band with the name "Fats Waller and his Rhythm" and they toured, recorded over 400 songs and appeared in countless radio broadcasts and two movies. Waller died of bronchial pneumonia in 1943, at age 39.

Resources

There are several excellent biographies of Fats Waller available, including Alyn Shipton's *Fats Waller: The Cheerful Little Earful*[12] Maurice Waller and Anthony Calabrese's *Fats Waller*[13] and Ed Kirby's *Ain't Misbehavin': The Story of Fats Waller*.[14]

THE SINGERS

Jazz singers play with rhythm in different ways – but whether back-phrasing or front-phrasing there needs to be a clear sense of where the downbeat sits; jazz singers refer to that as knowing where "one" is. Some singers stretch written rhythms until they are almost unrecognizable, while others stick closer to the composer's written rhythms. Frequently in jazz, the journey from one note to the next is as important as the notes themselves; leaning, sliding, hitting a note slightly under pitch and grinding up to pitch, turns or trills between notes – these are all stylistic devices used by jazz singers. Ultimately it is the singer's personal sense of taste that determines what is enough and what is too much. Many of the great jazz singers were also instrumentalists, and those that were not spent considerable time studying the great jazz instrumentalists and their solos in an effort to affect their styles, tones, timbres, phrasings and breathing.

Around the world there have been hundreds of great jazz singers throughout the twentieth and into the twenty-first centuries. Below are several who are considered among the finest, representing as wide a range of jazz styles as possible. For the greatest understanding of jazz singing, listen to as many and as much as possible. Many jazz singers emulate great jazz instrumentalists, so an understanding and knowledge of the great players can only deepen a singer's mastery of the genre.

Ma Rainey (1886–1939)

Born Gertrude Pridgett in Columbus, Georgia, she is considered to be the mother of the blues; she is reported to be the first female entertainer to have integrated genuine blues songs into her repertoire. Rainey was "a contralto with a rural blues feel, and an almost male delivery."[15] Rainey's style was firmly rooted in the country blues tradition.

Bessie Smith (1894–1937)

Born in Chattanooga, Tennessee, Bessie was dubbed "Empress of the Blues" by a publicity agent at Columbia Records. Smith, who was "a soprano with [an] urban, polished style,"[16] became Columbia's biggest star and was the highest paid black entertainer of her time. While many of Smith's great hits were traditional blues, she also had hit recordings of popular songs like "After You've Gone," "I Ain't Got Nobody" and "Alexander's Ragtime Band."

Adelaide Hall (1901–1993)

Hall had a career that lasted for eight decades, from 1921 to 1993, beginning as a Broadway performer and establishing a wordless style of singing that ultimately evolved into scat singing. Hall introduced the songs "Digga, Digga Do" and "I Can't Give You Anything but Love."

Louis Armstrong (1901–1971)

A trumpet player turned singer, Armstrong was nicknamed "Satchmo" and "Pops." In addition to the jazz he grew up listening to in New Orleans, Armstrong's gravelly sounding tenor voice was influenced by the Yiddish melodies he heard working in the household of the Karnofshys, a Russian Jewish immigrant family, and the great singers he listened to on his phonograph, including jazz artists like Bessie Smith, Irish tenor John McCormack and Italian opera tenor Enrico Caruso. It is reported that at an early recording session Armstrong dropped the lyric sheet for a song called "Heebie Jeebies" and began singing nonsense syllables, beginning the tradition of scat singing.[17] One of the most widely popular jazz musicians ever, Armstrong existed simultaneously in the worlds of jazz and popular music. A very abbreviated list of his most popular recordings includes: "What a Wonderful World," "Hello, Dolly!," "When the Saints Go Marching In," "Mack the Knife" and "Ain't Misbehavin'."

Cab Calloway (1907–1994)

Calloway was a bandleader and highly energized scat singer, frequently enlisting his audience in participatory call-and-response. His most popular recordings include "St. James Infirmary" and "Minnie the Moocher." A "hepster" in the 1940s, Calloway wrote *The New Cab Calloway's Hepsters Dictionary: Language of Jive* translating the slang of current slang for the less "enlightened."

Billy Eckstein (1914–1993)

Eckstein's smooth, warm baritone and suave sensuality helped him become one of the first African American jazz singers to cross over and become popular not simply as a "race" singer, but as a popular jazz singer. His sound was romantic and silky, and his persona was that of a matinee idol. He has been described as being a cross between Frank Sinatra and Billy Dee Williams.

Billie Holiday (1915–1959)

Holiday was born Eleanora Harris in Philadelphia. She began recording in 1933 for bandleader Benny Goodman, and her career peaked from 1936 to 1942. Holiday's unique vocal style is known primarily for her dramatic intensity and the songs most closely associated with her include "Strange Fruit," "God Bless the Child" and "The Man I Love." Holiday claimed that she strove for the "style" of Louis Armstrong and the "feeling" of Bessie Smith.[18]

Frank Sinatra (1915–1998)

Sinatra was the biggest of the crooners. Francis Albert Sinatra, variously nicknamed "The Voice," "The Sultan of Swoon," "Old Blue Eyes" and "The Chairman of the Board," began his career as a big band singer, working with bandleaders Harry James and Tommy Dorsey. The development of the microphone allowed Sinatra to introduce *bel canto* singing to the big band bandstand, bringing the crooning style initiated by Bing Crosby to full fruition. Dr. Tom Benjamin has distilled the Sinatra style down to the following list of tips to the singer:

> **Range** voice is like a saxophone – a brassy reed
> **Open throat** on high and low notes
> **Phrasing** deliberately diverging from the expected timing
> **Research** study clarinet, trumpet and sax solos
> **Breathing** hold and taper out long notes without breath
> **Hoboken twang** a bouncy, lilting club style of sing-song
> **Hoboken accent** particularly avoiding harsh "r" sounds
> **Swing era croon** but don't shout, notes in time with rhythm
> **Later years** a harsh, abrupt, staccato barking sound
> **Radio era** ballads Quiet, seductive notes
> **Flat sound** no yodel or falsetto [minimal vibrato]
> **Lack of echo or effects** except some warmth (valve) and bass[19]

Ella Fitzgerald (1917–1996)

Fitzgerald's three-octave voice and impeccable musicality helped her sustain a career that spanned six decades. Her *New York Times* obituary said that her: "sweet, silvery voice and endlessly inventive vocal improvisations made her the most celebrated jazz singer of her generation. ... [and] won the sobriquet 'first lady of song.' ... Her material became a springboard for ever-changing, ebullient vocal inventions, delivered in a sweet, girlish voice that could leap, slide or growl anywhere within a range of nearly three octaves. ... She was sometimes criticized for a lack of bluesiness and emotional depth. But her perfect intonation, vocal acrobatics, clear diction and endless store of melodic improvisations – all driven by powerful rhythmic undercurrents – brought her nearly universal acclaim."[20] Fitzgerald recorded a series of albums celebrating the American Songbook, including *Ella Fitzgerald Sings the Cole Porter*

Songbook, Ella Fitzgerald Sings the Rodgers and Hart Songbook, Ella Fitzgerald Sings the Duke Ellington Songbook, Ella Fitzgerald Sings the Irving Berlin Songbook, Ella Fitzgerald Sings the George and Ira Gershwin Songbook, Ella Fitzgerald Sings the Harold Arlen Songbook, Ella Fitzgerald Sings the Jerome Kern Songbook, and *Ella Fitzgerald Sings the Johnny Mercer Songbook.*

Nat "King" Cole (1919–1965)

Originally a jazz pianist, Nat "King" Cole is known for his velvety baritone voice, exquisite phrasing, absolutely perfect pitch and impeccable diction. Cole's greatest hits include: "Mona Lisa," "Nature Boy," "Rambling Rose," "L-O-V-E" and "Walking My Baby back Home."

Jon Hendricks (1921)

Hendricks created the vocal style known as "vocalese," taking famous jazz instrumental solos and crafting lyrics that allow singers to perform these instrumentals. He is most well known for the work he did with David Lambert and Annie Ross in their jazz vocal group, Lambert, Hendricks and Ross from 1957 to 1962.

Carmen McRae (1922–1994)

McRae was also known as "The Singer's Singer," moving fluidly between traditional jazz, bebop and pop music. Phrasing and interpretation of lyrics were McRae's forte. As a young performer she worked closely with Benny Carter, Count Basie, Earl "Fatha" Hines and Mercer Ellington, as well as with her mentor, Billie Holiday. Phrasing that sat behind the beat was stock-in-trade for McRae, as was great technical control, an ability to swing and to scat better than almost every other jazz great, and an ability to create spectacular languid long lines in ballads.

Sarah Vaughan (1924–1990)

Known as "The Diving One," Vaughan was a pianist as well as a singer. Beginning her career at age 18 with Earl "Fatha" Hine's band after winning a talent contest at Harlem's Apollo Theatre, she was comfortable scatting, crooning and singing bebop and popular music. "Vaughan was a contralto who gloried in displaying the distinctive instrumental qualities of a voice that had a comfortable three-octave range and was marked by a voluptuous, heavy vibrato. Known for her dazzling vocal leaps and swoops, she was equally adept at be-bop improvisation and singing theater songs with a symphony orchestra."[21] Some of her great recordings include "Misty," "My Man is Gone Now," "Black Coffee," "Summertime" and "Spring Will Be a Little Late This Year."

Dinah Washington (1924–1963)

Born Ruth Lee Jones in Tuscaloosa, Alabama, Washington's technical control of her instrument enabled her to perform jazz, blues, R&B, gospel and pop music. Of Washington, Quincy Jones wrote: "Every single melody she sang she made hers. Once she put her soulful trademark on a song, she owned it and it was never the same. She was complete, original and magnificent."[22] Although she died at age 39, she released 31 long-playing albums and 56 of her singles hit the charts. Her hits to reach number one in the charts include "Am I Asking Too Much," "Baby Get Lost," and "This Bitter Earth."

Mel Tormé (1925–1999)

Tormé, whose voice earned him the nickname "The Velvet Fog," was as accomplished as a drummer, pianist, songwriter, arranger and orchestrator as he was a singer. His technical facility was impeccable, and he ranged stylistically from "cool jazz" (an offshoot of crooning) to scatting, the most popular to the most experimental jazz. Will Friedwald wrote, "Tormé works with the most beautiful voice a man is allowed to have, and he combines it with a flawless sense of pitch ... As an improviser he shames all but two or three other scat singers and quite a few horn players as well."[23] Some of Tormé's most lasting recordings include "The Christmas Song (Chestnuts Roasting on an Open Fire)," (which he also wrote), "Mountain Greenery," "What Are You Doing the Rest of Your Life," "Harlem Nocturne" and "A Nightingale Sang in Berkeley Square."

Tony Bennett (b. 1926)

Like Frank Sinatra, Bennett steeped himself in the study of the great jazz instrumentalists, rather than other vocalists, giving him a wide repertoire of sounds and jazz styles to call on. Bennett has had a longer successful career than any other jazz singer, starting with his first recording in 1950 and continuing today. His biggest hits include: "I Left My Heart in San Francisco," "Fly Me to The Moon," "Rags to Riches" and "I Wanna Be Around (To Pick Up the Pieces)."

Ray Charles (1930–2004)

Also referred to as "the Genius," Charles integrated soul, R&B, gospel and the blues and was one of the most popular and successful African American performers across the spectrum of popular music genres and styles, including country music, jazz and mainstream popular music. Charles' greatest hits include: "I Can't Stop Loving You," "Hit the Road Jack," "Georgia on My Mind," "I Got a Woman" and "Unchain My Heart."

Nina Simone (1933–2003)

Born Eunice Kathleen Waymon in Tryon, North Carolina, the eclectic Simone was not only a singer, but also a songwriter, pianist, arranger and civil rights activist. Simone borrowed from classical, jazz, blues, jazz, folk, R&B, gospel and pop. Simone's hits include "I Loves You Porgy," "My Baby Just Cares for Me" and "Feeling Good," Simone's title was the High Priestess of Soul, and her vocal style comes from her strong classical roots and her vocal range, which ranged from a low alto to tenor and even baritone notes, giving her an androgynous quality at times.

Al Jarreau (b. 1940)

Jarreau's popular hits include songs like "We're in This Love Together," "So Good," "Moonlighting (Theme)" and "Mornin'." Jarreau is adept, in his scat singing, at imitating percussion instruments, basses and guitars. He remains a popular artist and continues to record and tour.

George Benson (b. 1943)

Benson began his professional career as a guitarist at the age of 21, in 1964. In 1976 he saw his first hit single as a vocalist in "This Masquerade" on his *Breezin'* album. Benson is comfortable moving his smooth tenor voice facilely between the musical worlds of jazz, pop, R&B singing and scat singing, winning 10 Grammy Awards to date. Benson has developed a style of scat singing an octave above his improvised guitar lines.

Bobby McFerrin (b. 1950)

McFerrin's unique control over his extraordinary instrument allows him to sing "fluidly but with quick and considerable jumps in pitch – most famously, for example, sustaining a legato melody while also rapidly alternating with arpeggios and harmonies – as well as scat singing, polyphonic overtone singing, and improvisational vocal percussion."[24] According Jeff Tamarkin, on Bobbymcferrin.com,

> McFerrin's four-octave vocal abilities and capacity for constant invention are on par with those of the greatest improvising instrumentalists, yet simultaneously the power, sophistication and soulfulness of his singing place him in a class of its own. Bobby is at once funky and smooth, meticulous and carefree, elegant and feisty. It's almost as if the liberties of Miles Davis and John Coltrane, the grace and class of Duke Ellington and Mozart, the funk of James Brown and Sly Stone, the cool of Bob Marley and the silky soul of Marvin Gaye, the miraculous command and range of Aretha Franklin and Ella Fitzgerald, and the ethereal, other-worldliness of African field hollers, austere chants and primal blues, were all put into a blender. [… Bobby] incorporates dense rhythms, extraordinary scales, tricky intervals and such.[25]

Ironically McFerrin's most well known recording is the novelty hit, "Don't Worry, Be Happy."

Contemporary singers like Canadian pianist and contralto **Diana Krall (b. 1964)**, pianist, singer, songwriter, arranger **Harry Connick (b. 1967)** and **Michael Bublé (b. 1975)** carry the traditions of the velvety baritone crooner forward. Other contemporary jazz greats like **Janis Segal (b. 1952)**, a singer, arranger and founding member of the jazz vocal ensemble The Manhattan Transfer continue to strike out in directions in vocal jazz.

In summary

The stylistic range of jazz expands almost daily as jazz artists merge older styles in new ways and explore new boundaries; the broadest possible range of listening will yield the deepest possible grasp of styles and nuances. The oft quoted "talent imitates, genius steals," has been attributed to Picasso and Oscar Wilde among others. In *The Sacred Wood*, T.S. Eliot built on this sentiment, writing "Immature poets imitate; mature poets steal; bad poets deface what they take, and good poets make it into something better, or at least something different."[26] The exact same sentiment can be applied to singing styles. Nothing, especially art in any form, is created in a vacuum – the key to a singer bringing themselves to new material and putting their own "stamp" on it is to listen, borrow, rethink and reconsider. In no style is listening to a wide range of artists as important as it is in jazz.

Notes

1 Robert Kimball and William Bolcolm, *Reminiscing with Noble Sissle and Eubie Blake*, New York, NY: Cooper Square Press, 2000.

2 Al Rose, *Eubie Blake*, New York, NY: Macmillan, 1979.

3 Jelly Roll Morton and Alan Lomax, *Jelly Roll Morton: Library of Congress Recordings*, Washington, DC: Rounder, 2005.

4 Alan Lomax, *Mister Jelly Roll: The Fortunes of Jelly Roll Morton, New Orleans Creole and Inventor of Jazz*, Oakland, CA: University of California Press, 2001.

5 Howard Reich and William M. Gaines, *Jelly's Blues: The Life, Music and Redemption of Jelly Roll Morton*, New York, NY: Da Capo Press, 2004.

6 Duke Ellington, *Music Is My Mistress*, New York, NY: Da Capo Press, 1976, p. 167.

7 Terry Teachout, *Duke: A Life of Duke Ellington*, New York, NY: Gotham, 2014.

8 Hoagy Carmichael, Stephen Longstreet and John Edward Hasse, *The Stardust Road & Sometimes I Wonder: The Autobiography of Hoagy Carmichael*, New York, NY: Da Capo Press, 1999.

9 Richard Sudhalter, *Stardust Melody: The Life and Music of Hoagy Carmichael*, New York, NY: Oxford University Press, 2003.

10 Paul Machlin, "The Music of Fats Waller," *Institute of Jazz Studies: Dana Library: Rutgers University Library*, http://newarkwww.rutgers.edu/ijs/fw/music.htm, accessed December 30, 2014.

11 Murray Horowitz, "Fats Waller Now, Fats Waller Forever," *Institute of Jazz Studies: Dana Library: Rutgers University Library*, http://newark-www.rutgers.edu/ijs/fw/contemp.htm accessed December 30, 2014.

12 Alyn Shipton, *Fats Waller: The Cheerful Little Earful*, London, UK: Bloomsbury Academic, 2005.

13 Maurice Waller and Anthony Calabrese, *Fats Waller*, New York, NY: Macmillan Publishing Company, 1979.

14 Ed Kirby, *Ain't Misbehavin': The Story of Fats Waller*, New York, NY: Da Capo Press, 1975.

15 Roanna Forman, "Smith Bessie," *Encyclopedia of Jazz Musicians*, www. jazz.com/encyclopedia/smith-bessie, accessed December 25, 2014.

16 Forman, "Smith Bessie,", accessed December 25, 2014.

17 Jim Luce and Dick Golden, producers, "Louis Armstrong: the Singer," *Jazz Profiles from NPR*, www.npr.org/programs/jazzprofiles/archive/armstrong_singer.html, accessed December 27, 2014.

18 Leslie Gourse, *The Billie Holiday Companion: Seven Decades of Commentary*, New York: Schirmer, 1997, p. 76.

19 Tom Benjamin, *How to Sound Like Sinatra*, www.tom.com.au/karaoke/sinatra.pdf, accessed December 27, 2014.

20 Stephen Holden, "Ella Fitzgerald, the Voice of Jazz, Dies at 79," *The New York Times*, June 16, 1996, www.nytimes.com/1996/06/16/nyregion/ella-fitzgerald-the-voice-of-jazz-dies-at-79.html, accessed December 27, 2014.

21 Stephen Holden, "Sarah Vaughan, 'Divine One' of Jazz Singing, Is Dead at 66," *The New York Times*, April 5, 1990, www. nytimes.com/1990/04/05/obituaries/sarah-vaughan-divine-one-of-jazz-singing-is-dead-at-66.html, accessed December 27, 2014.

22 Quincy Jones, *Q: The Autobiography of Quincy Jones*, New York, NY: Three Rivers Press, 2002.

23 Will Friedwald, *Jazz Singing: America's Greatest Voices: From Bessie Smith to Bebop and Beyond*. New York, NY: Da Capo Press, 1996.

24 Uncredited blurb, "Bobby McFerrin" on *Google Play*, https://play. google.com/store/music/artist/Bobby_McFerrin?id=Ahooqdruubnd4ee 76yq7grr4ju4&hl=en, accessed December 28, 2014.

25 Jeff Tamarkin, "Extended Bio," *Bobby McFerrin Home*, http://bobbymcferrin.com/whos-bobby/press-kit/extended-bio/, accessed December 28, 2014.

26 T.S. Eliot, "The Sacred Wood." *Goodreads*, www.goodreads.com/work/best_book/442581-the-sacred-wood, accessed October 28, 2015.

Chapter 6

The Golden Age – the integrated musical

Richard Rodgers and Oscar Hammerstein II,
Alan Jay Lerner and Fredrick Loewe,
Frank Loesser, Kurt Weill, Burton Lane,
Leonard Bernstein, Betty Comden and
Adolph Green, and Jule Styne

Beginning in 1943 with *Oklahoma!*, all elements of a musical were integrated into the telling of the story. Songs were no longer ornamental; they were a means of developing character or advancing the plot. Although prior to 1943 successful composers and lyricists were great songwriters and after 1943 they were great musical dramatists, some songwriters who had established their careers in earlier times had their biggest successes in this period. Cole Porter's most enduring score was *Kiss Me Kate* (1948), and Irving Berlin's was *Annie Get Your Gun* (1946). But for the most part, this period ushered in a new breed of musical theatre writers.

This period represents a golden age not just for the musical theatre stage, but for the material of the musical theatre beyond the stage as well. This time predated the arrival of rock and roll when, in popular music, the rock and roll singer/songwriter would displace the swing-singers and crooners. During this period, much of the literature of America's popular music came from the musical theatre, recorded by popular musical artists. Singers like Frank Sinatra, Tony Bennett, Ella Fitzgerald, Louis Armstrong, Rosemary Clooney, Bing Crosby, all recorded and popularized the songs from Broadway musicals and other songs by the writers of musicals.

A singer preparing to sing these songs needs to understand their original theatrical context, whether or not they are choosing to remain faithful to that context. These songs can be interpreted in new and interesting ways, but knowledge of the musicals, characters and situations these songs were written for is important for understanding how these songs might work in other settings.

All of the writers examined in this chapter wrote for legitimate voices. Some make more use than others of belting for women, but underlying this is the need for a strong classical technique. The songs of Rodgers and Hammerstein, Lerner and Loewe and Leonard Bernstein are overwhelmingly legitimate, requiring a strong classical technique. But the songs of Kurt Weill, Frank Loesser and Jule Styne use the same technical vocabulary. Weill, Loesser and Styne make more use of belting, Loesser and Styne use various swing and jazz styles, and Weill makes much use of *Sprechstimme*, a vocal technique midway between talking and singing. But for the most part, the songs of these composers seem most appropriate and most at home in the voice of singers with legitimate training.

While the musical theatre song lists in this chapter indicate voice type, the popular song lists do not, since most of these songs have been published in a range of keys for different vocal ranges. The composers examined in this chapter wrote their songs in vocal registers that allowed singers to perform them over full orchestras without amplification. For the most part, these songs call for a legitimate sound, a bright "pingy" frontal placement and full resonance. Of all the composers examined in this chapter, Jule Styne is the most rooted in swing and jazz music, but even Styne's music calls for the same strong traditional vocal technique. These songs tend to have great shapes, melodic lines that require substantial breath control and musicianship to execute admirably.

Richard Rodgers (1902–1979) and Oscar Hammerstein II (1895–1960): Setting the bar

Stylistic approach

The characters in the Rodgers and Hammerstein musicals tend to fall neatly into vocal type. Leading ladies tended to be light sopranos or mezzo-sopranos like Laurey Williams in *Oklahoma!* and Julie Jordan in *Carousel*. The leading men are baritones like Curly McLane in *Oklahoma!*, Billy Bigelow in *Carousel* and Emile de Becque in *South Pacific*. Soubrettes, comic females like Ado Annie or Bloody Mary, are altos. Secondary male leads are entertaining in some way, either by being comics or dancers, and were usually tenors or bari-tenors like Will Parker and Luther Billis. Rodgers' musical approach to these characters tends to be legitimate, particularly in light of his jazzier writing with Hart. These songs call for a strong, legitimate classical vocal style. Although performed and recorded by singers in many diverse genres, they are essentially character art songs and are best served by a classical approach. A lifted palate, spun resonance, and a strong understanding of musical line (classical phrasing) serve these songs well. These songs are tremendously accessible and can be sung by anyone, but to be sung well they require a great deal of support and technique.

Prior to *Oklahoma!*, the stars of the show were just that, the stars of the show, whether it was a singer like Ethel Merman, a dancer like Fred Astaire, or a comedian like Ed Wynn. Beginning with Rodgers and Hammerstein's *Oklahoma!*, the story, songs and dances were the star. So, for the first time people were not flocking to the theatre to see star personalities, they were flocking to see actors portraying characters. Originally these roles were sung with a legitimate sound that we find old-fashioned today; to compensate, many revivals opt for a more contemporary sound. These songs first and foremost need to be well acted, but they also need to be well sung.

Body of work

Rodgers and Hammerstein's nine musicals between 1943 and 1960 established the model for the Golden Age of the musical theatre. Essentially romantic, and informed by a strong sense of social justice, this model includes paralleling a plot and subplot, one serious and one comic, which reflect and amplify each other. The Rodgers and Hammerstein model also includes a scene structure in which scenes build up to the song, and the climax of the song acts as the climax of the scene. Each Rodgers and Hammerstein songs is like a one-act play in miniature, with a clear progression from beginning to middle to the end.

The musicals they wrote together are:

Oklahoma! (1943) Curly McLane, baritone; Laurey Williams, soprano; Ado Annie, alto; Will Parker, tenor; Jud Fry, baritone.

Carousel (1945) Julie Jordan, soprano; Carrie Pipperidge, soprano; Billy Bigelow, baritone; Nettie Fowler, mezzo-soprano, Enoch Snow, tenor.

State Fair (film, 1945) Mary Frake, mezzo-soprano; Wayne Frake, baritone; Emily Arden, mezzo-soprano; Pat Gilbert, tenor.

Allegro (1947) Joseph Taylor, Jr., tenor; Emily, alto; Jenny, alto; Dr. Taylor, baritone; Marjorie Taylor, soprano.

South Pacific (1949) Nellie Forbush, mezzo-soprano; Emile De Becque, baritone; Lt. Joe Cable, tenor; Bloody Mary, alto.

The King and I (1951) Anna Leonowens, soprano; King of Siam, baritone; Lady Thiang, mezzo-soprano; Lun Tha, tenor, Tuptim, soprano.

Me and Juliet (1953) Jeanie, soprano; Bob, tenor; Larry, tenor.

Pipe Dream (1955) Doc, baritone; Suzy, soprano; Hazel, bass; Mac, tenor; Fauna, soprano; Jim Blaikey, baritone.

Cinderella (television musical, 1957) Cinderella, soprano; Stepmother, mezzo-soprano, Prince Charming, baritone; Step-sisters, mezzo-soprano, Fairy Godmother, soprano.

Flower Drum Song (1958) Sammy Fong, baritone; Linda Low, mezzo-soprano; Mei-Li, soprano; Madam Liang, mezzo-soprano, Wang Ta, baritone; Helen Chao, soprano; Frankie Wing, baritone.

Sound of Music (1960) Maria Rainer, soprano; Mother Abbess, soprano; Captain von Trapp, baritone; Liesel, mezzo-soprano; Rolf, baritone.

The Rodgers and Hammerstein songs are some of the best known in the musical theatre canon. Some of these include:

Oklahoma!
Oh, What a Beautiful
  Mornin' ††
Surrey With the Fringe
  on Top ††
Kansas City †
I Cain't Say No **
Many a New Day *
People Will Say We're In Love
  */††
Pore Jud is Daid ††
Out of My Dreams *
All Er Nuthin' †/**
Carousel
If I Loved You */††
June Is Busting Out All Over **
When the Children Are Asleep †

Soliloquy ††
What's the Use of Wond'rin'? *
You'll Never Walk Alone **
South Pacific
Cockeyed Optimist **
Some Enchanted Evening ††
Bali Ha'i **
I'm Gonna Wash That Man
  Right Outa My Hair **
I'm In Love with a Wonderful
  Guy **
Younger Than Springtime †
Happy Talk **
You've Got To Be Taught †
This Nearly Was Mine ††
The King and I
I Whistle a Happy Tune *

My Lord and Master *
Hello Young Lovers *
Getting to Know You *
We Kiss in a Shadow †
Something Wonderful *
I Have Dreamed †
Shall We Dance */††
Sound of Music

The Sound of Music *
My Favorite Things *
Do-Re-Mi *
Sixteen Going on
  Seventeen **/††
Climb Every Mountain *
Edelweiss ††

Biography

By 1943 composer Richard Rodgers and lyricist/librettist Oscar Hammerstein II both appeared to be on the declining side of meteoric careers. By age 41, Rodgers collaboration with Hart had yielded some of the greatest swingy, jazzy, sophisticated hits of the 1920s and 1930s, hit shows including: *On Your Toes, Babes in Arms, The Boys from Syracuse* and *Pal Joey*. Hammerstein had been a great lyricist/librettist of operettas with composers Otto Harbach, Jerome Kern, Vincent Youmans, Rudolf Friml and Sigmund Romberg. Hammerstein's hit shows included *Very Warm for May, Rose-Marie, The Desert Song, The New Moon* and *Show Boat*. Rodgers and Hammerstein seemed unlikely collaborators, but in their own way, each had been working towards a new kind of musical theatre.

Resources

Rodgers' *Musical Stages: An Autobiography*,[1] is a good place to start learning about Rodgers, but is limited to his perspective. Meryl Secrest's *Somewhere For Me – a Biography of Richard Rodgers*[2] offers a good contrast. Hugh Fordin's *Getting to Know Him: A Biography of Oscar Hammerstein, II*[3] is an excellent place to start exploring Hammerstein's life. Frederick Nolan has written about them as collaborators in *The Sound of Their Music: The Story of Rodgers and Hammerstein*.[4]

Alan Jay Lerner (1918–1986) and Fredrick Loewe (1901–1988): intensely act-able

Stylistic approach

Like Rodgers and Hammerstein, Lerner and Loewe's songs are firmly rooted in a classical, legitimate sound as a result of Loewe's

European training and Lerner's strong background in the classics. The majority of the Lerner and Loewe material calls for a warm resonance, a raised palate, and strong sense of musical line. And yet they also wrote perfectly for the non-singer; they developed the concept of speak-singing for Rex Harrison, the original Henry Higgins in *My Fair Lady*. Listen to one of the various available recordings of Harrison speaking most of his songs in rhythm while the melody played beneath him in the orchestra. Melodically, harmonically and orchestrally Loewe's music is classical and lush; somehow Harrison's spoken delivery does not diminish these qualities. Lerner and Loewe contrasted this with beautiful soprano pieces like "I Could Have Danced All Night," sung by Julie Andrews in the original production and the glorious tenor song "On The Street Where You Live." The role of King Arthur in *Camelot* was also created for a non-singing actor, Richard Burton. They frequently reference other styles such as English music hall traditions in the songs sung by Alfred Doolittle in *My Fair Lady*, Scottish folk music in *Brigadoon* and so on. Knowledge of these styles is useful to the singer. Aside from their non-singing lead males, Lerner and Loewe's songs are known for their gorgeous, soaring melodies.

Body of work

Lerner and Loewe's musicals are:

The Life of the Party (1942)	*My Fair Lady* (1957)
What's Up (1943)	*Gigi* (1958, film)
The Day Before Spring (1945)	*Camelot* (1960)
Brigadoon (1947)	*Gigi* (1973, stage)
Paint Your Wagon (1951)	*The Little Prince* (1974, film)

Lerner's projects without Loewe include:

Love Life (1948, with Kurt Weill)	*On a Clear Day You Can See Forever* (1965, with Burton Lane)
Royal Wedding (1951, screenplay)	*Coco* (1969, with André Previn)
An American in Paris (1951, screenplay)	*Lolita, My Love* (1971, with John Barry)
The Adventures of Huckleberry Finn (1960, screenplay)	

1600 Pennsylvania Avenue
　(1976, with Leonard
　Bernstein)

Carmelina (1979, with
　Burton Lane)
Dance a Little Closer (1983,
　with Charles Strouse)

Some of the most successful Lerner and Loewe shows and songs include:

Brigadoon (Tommy Albright, tenor; Fiona MacLaren, soprano; Andrew MacLaren, baritone; Jean MacLaren, mezzo-soprano; Meg Brockie, alto; Charley Dalrymple, tenor)

Waitin' For My Dearie *
I'll Go Home With Bonnie
　Jean ††
The Heather on the Hill */††

Come to Me, Bend to Me †
Almost Like Being in Love ††
There but for You Go I †
My Mother's Wedding Day * *

Paint Your Wagon (Ben Rumson, baritone; Jennie Rumson, mezzo-soprano; Julio Valveras, tenor; Jacob Woodling, baritone; Elizabeth Woodling, mezzo-soprano)

I Talk to the Trees ††

They Call the Wind Maria ††

My Fair Lady (Eliza Doolittle, soprano; Henry Higgins, baritone, Alfred Doolittle, baritone, Freddy Eynsford-Hill, tenor)

Why Can't the English ††
Wouldn't It Be Loverly *
I'm an Ordinary Man ††
Just You Wait *
I Could Have Danced All
　Night *

On the Street Where You Live †
Show Me *
Without You *
I've Grown Accustomed to Her
　Face ††

Gigi (Honoré Lachaille, baritone; Mamita, mezzo-soprano; Gaston Lachailles, tenor; Gigi, soprano)

Thank Heaven For Little
　Girls ††
I Remember It Well ††/**

Gigi ††
I'm Glad I'm Not Young
　Anymore ††

Camelot (Arthur, baritone; Guenevere, soprano; Lancelot, baritone, Mordred, baritone; Morgan Le Faye, soprano)

I Wonder What the King is
  Doing Tonight ††
Where Are the Simple Joys of
  Maidenhood? *
Camelot ††
Follow Me *

C'est Moi ††
How to Handle a Woman ††
Before I Gaze at You Again *
If Ever I Would Leave You ††
The Seven Deadly Virtues ††
I Loved You Once in Silence *

Biography

Born and raised in New York City in a Jewish upper-middle class family, Lerner received his education at the Choate School and Harvard; at both he was a classmate of John F. Kennedy. Lerner's theatrical career began in college theatre as a contributor to Harvard's Hasty Pudding Shows. Having lost the sight in his left eye in a boxing accident, he was not accepted by the Army during World War II. Lerner met Loewe at the Lamb's Club in New York.

Loewe was born and raised in Berlin, the son of a Jewish operetta star. He began composing at age seven and made his premiere as a concert pianist with the Berlin Philharmonic at age 13. In 1924 Loewe moved with his father to New York. After New York he spent a year travelling through the American West, where he took a series of odd jobs including postal delivery, cattle punching and professional boxer, before returning to New York and meeting Lerner.

Lerner and Loewe's first collaboration, *Life of the Party*, played for nine weeks at a summer theatre in Detroit. They followed this up with *What's Up?* (1943) and *The Day Before Spring* (1945). In 1947, their first hit *Brigadoon* opened, followed by 1951's *Paint Your Wagon* and 1956's *My Fair Lady*. *Gigi*, their 1958 film musical, was followed by 1960's *Camelot* on Broadway. Loewe retired to Palm Springs until Lerner coaxed him out of retirement to adapt *Gigi* for the stage and then to write the film musical *The Little Prince* (1974). Although Loewe stopped writing, Lerner continued to write for the rest of his life, never finding the success he had found with Loewe. Lerner had just begun work on *Phantom of the Opera* with Andrew Lloyd Webber when he died of lung cancer at age 67.

Lerner and Hammerstein were two of the few writers who wrote librettos and lyrics; this probably helped them to integrate the songs they wrote into the forward motion of their plots. As staid and traditional as Loewe's life was, Lerner's was equally tumultuous. He struggled with an addiction to amphetamines for more than twenty years and was married eight times.

Resources

Lerner's autobiography, *The Street Where I Live*,[5] is an excellent place to start further research. Edward Jablonski's, *Alan Jay Lerner: A Biography*,[6] and Dominic McHugh's *Alan Jay Lerner: A Lyricist's Letters*[7] offer excellent contrasting perspectives on Lerner. Very little biographical material has been devoted solely to Loewe.

Frank Loesser (1910–1969)

Stylistic approach

Frank Loesser came to the musical theatre from great success as a popular songwriter for movies just at the time when music theatre songwriters were becoming musical dramatists. He began his career as a lyricist, writing lyrics for a number of other composers and later writing both the music and lyrics for his own songs. In some ways, his training in the movies stood him in good stead – some of Loesser's biggest successes in Hollywood were written for actors like Betty Hutton and Danny Kaye, who had strong personas. Loesser "wanted 'to create situations' rather than songs: 'Songwriting is a little thing, and I settled for a big thing.' The 'big thing' was the Broadway musical, and Loesser never again wrote single songs."[8]

Listening to Loesser sing his material in recordings like *An Evening with Frank Loesser*, one gets a clear sense of Loesser's persona. Loesser was an inveterate New Yorker, a little coarse, a little street-wise and slangy in a 1950s/1960s "*Mad Men*" sense, and yet that comically tough exterior frequently revealed the good-natured romantic heart inside. "Even as a child Frank was aggressively lowbrow: his first lyrics were set to the rhythms of the elevated trains, and he took pride in winning third prize in a citywide harmonica contest."[9]

The glib, wisecracking New Yorker was such an integral part of Loesser's personal persona, and he wrote great up-tempo songs for these kinds of characters, but his greatest achievements are his more lyrical pieces. *Guys and Dolls* is a bright, up-beat, energetic musical, and yet the musical highlights are ballads like, "I'll Know," "If I Were A Bell," "My Time of Day," "I've Never Been in Love Before" and "More I Cannot Wish You." *The Most Happy Fella* contains the comic character song "Ooh, My Feet," and up-tempos like "Standing on the Corner" and "Big D," but the ballads "Joey, Joey, Joey," "Somebody Somewhere," "Don't Cry" and "My Heart Is So Full of You" are the heart of the score.

Perhaps the most interesting fact about Loesser's scores is that they each have their own unique sound. *Greenwillow* sounds nothing like *Guys and Dolls*; songs from *How To Succeed in Business Without Really Trying* could never be confused with those from *The Most Happy Fella*. He wrote for character men, like Ray Bolger and Sam Levene and also for operatic baritone Robert Weede. The character voice of Adelaide in *Guys and Dolls* is contrasted with the legitimate voice of Miss Sarah Brown. These contradictions make Loesser hard to pin down stylistically, and the singer must take each of his songs on its own.

Body of work

Loesser's career as lyricist and composer can be divided into three sections: the popular songs from the Hollywood period, the Army songs and the Broadway shows. Included in the list below are not only songs for which he wrote the music, but also those for which he served as lyricist for another composer. The popular/Hollywood period started in 1934. These songs have not been categorized by vocal range since most of them are available in a range of keys. Some of the best known of these songs include:

Baby, It's Cold Outside *	I Go for That ††
Bloop-Bleep *	I Hear Music * * * *
(See What the) Boys in the Back Room Will Have * *	I Wish I Didn't Love You So *
	Jingle, Jangle, Jingle †††
Can't Stop Talking *	Let's Get Lost ††††
College Swing * * *	Moon of Mankoora †††††
Dancing on a Dime * * * *	Murder, He Says ††††
Heart and Soul * * *	On a Slow Boat to China *
Howd'ja Like to Love Me? * * * *	Rumble, Rumble, Rumble *
	Sand in my Shoes * * * * *
I Don't Want to Walk Without You †	Small Fry * * *
	Snug as a Bug in a Rug ††

Spring Will Be a Little Late This
    Year *
Two Sleepy People ***

What Are You Doing New
    Year's Eve? *

* music by Frank Loesser
** music by Freidrich
    Hollander
*** music by Hoagy
    Carmichael
**** music by Burton Lane
***** music by Victor
    Schertzinger

† music by Jule Styne
†† music by Matt Malneck
††† music by Joseph Lilley
†††† music by Jimmy McHugh
††††† music by
    Alfred Newman

Of his Hollywood movies, the 1952 movie musical *Hans Christian Andersen* yielded the songs written for bari-tenor, Danny Kaye:

The King's New Clothes
Inch Worm
Wonderful Copenhagen
Thumbelina

The Ugly Duckling
Anywhere I Wander
No Two People

Some of Loesser's Army songs include:

First Class Private Mary Brown
Kiss the Boys Goodbye
Praise the Lord and Pass the
    Ammunition
(The Ballad of) Roger Young

They're Either Too Young or
    Too Old
What Do You Do in the
    Infantry?
What Do They Call a Private

Loesser's Broadway scores contain some of the great songs from this period.

Where's Charley? (1948) (Jack Chesney, tenor; Charley Wykeham, baritone; Kitty Verdun, soprano; Amy Spettigue, mezzo-soprano; Mr. Spettigue, bass; Donna Lucia D'Alvadorez, soprano)

My Darling, My Darling *
Make a Miracle **

Once in Love with Amy ††

Guys and Dolls (1950) (Sarah Brown, soprano, Sky Masterson, baritone, Nathan Detroit, baritone, Miss Adelaide, mezzo-soprano, Nicely Nicely Johnson, tenor)

I'll Know *
A Bushel and a Peck * *
Adelaide's Lament * *
If I Were a Bell *
My Time of Day ††
I've Never Been in Love
   Before */††

Take Back Your Mink * *
More I Cannot Wish
   You †
Luck Be a Lady ††
Sit Down, You're Rocking
   the Boat †

The Most Happy Fella (1956) (Tony Esposito, baritone; Rosabella, soprano, Cleo, mezzo-soprano; Herman tenor; Joe, baritone)

Ooh, My Feet! * *
Somebody Somewhere *
Standing on the Corner †/††
Joey, Joey, Joey ††
Don't Cry ††

Big D * */†
Warm All Over *
My Heart is So Full of
   You ††
Song of a Summer Night †

Greenwillow (1960) (Gideon Briggs, baritone; Dorrie Whitbred, soprano; Clara Clegg, mezzo-soprano)

The Music of Home ††
Summertime Love ††

Walking Away Whistling *
Never Will I Marry ††

How to Succeed in Business Without Really Trying (1961) (J. Pierpont Finch, baritone, Rosemary Pilkington, mezzo-soprano; Bud Frump, baritone; Bert Bratt, baritone; J.B. Biggley, baritone; Hedy La Rue, mezzo-soprano)

Happy To Keep His Dinner
   Warm * *
Been a Long Day ††/* *
Grand Old Ivy ††

Rosemary ††
Love From a Heart of
   Gold ††/* *
I Believe in You ††

Biography

Frank Loesser's father was a distinguished German emigré who taught classical piano, and his brother, Arthur, was a concert pianist, musicologist and music critic. Despite never having formal musical training, Frank wrote his first song "The Mad Party" at age four and taught himself to play the harmonica and the piano. Born and raised in New York, Loesser graduated from Townsend Harris High School and dropped out of New York's City College, supporting himself by selling newspaper advertising, working as a process server, serving as city editor to a local New Rochelle newspaper and other jobs, finally ending up writing songs, sketches and radio scripts.

Loesser found great success writing lyrics for Hollywood movies, through the 1930s, and by 1939 he had begun writing music as well. While serving in World War II he provided songs for camp shows for the Special Services. Following a huge string of popular hits in the movies and the army songs, producers Cy Feuer and Ernest Martin lured Loesser back to New York to write the score for his first Broadway musical, *Where's Charley?*. Six other Broadway musicals followed, including three huge successes: *Guys and Dolls*, *The Most Happy Fella* and *How to Succeed in Business Without Really Trying*. His last produced musical, *Pleasures and Palaces*, directed and choreographed by Bob Fosse, closed out of town before reaching Broadway. Loesser died at age 59 of lung cancer in New York. At the time of his death, Loesser left an unfinished musical titled "Señor Discretion Himself," which was ultimately produced by Musical Theatre Works in New York (1985) and Arena Stage in Washington DC (2004).

Resources

An excellent place to begin learning more about Loesser is the biography, *A Most Remarkable Fella: Frank Loesser and the Guys and Dolls in His Life: A Portrait by His Daughter*, by his daughter Susan.[10] The corporation that manages the Loesser estate, Frank Loesser Enterprises, maintains the website frankloesser.com. Both of these sources offer great places to begin researching and exploring the life and works of Frank Loesser

Kurt Weill (1900–1950): A stranger here myself

Stylistic approach

Composer Weill's writing is firmly rooted in his classical composition training, in the music of the synagogue, the avant-garde art songs and operas of Berlin, and the multitudinous American sounds that influenced him. These wide-ranging influences make him more eclectic than any other composer examined so far in this text. The end of the twentieth century saw a trend towards "recycled" culture, but Weill had anticipated this trend by more than 50 years. His work began much earlier than many of the other writers in this section but was so driven by dramatic necessity that his work fits into this chapter more than any other. His music is more harmonically dense than other composers of this era, and his songs test the singers' sense of pitch. Frequently, young singers just beginning to work with Weill's music underestimate how difficult his melodic lines can be, missing important passing tones in a phrase.

The ultimate interpreter of Weill's music was his wife, Lotte Lenya, known for her speak-singing and the intensity of her dramatic connection to the material. Weill's songs have also received more "singerly" performances, including recordings by opera star, soprano Teresa Stratas. Stratas' recordings combine a spectacular instrument, a strong acting technique and a deep connection to the material.

The style most often associated with Weill, the one used by his wife, Lenya, is *Sprechstimme*, which "combines elements of song and speech. [I]nstead of singing the pitches, the performer recites them."[11] Rhythms are followed strictly, but the words are said on spoken approximation of the pitches. Weill made great use of this device in many of his earlier works in Berlin in collaboration with playwright and director Berthold Brecht. By the late 1930s, Weill had adopted a substantially more melodic style. His later works like *Knickerbocker Holiday*, *Lady In the Dark*, *Street Scene* and *Lost In the Stars* offer some of the most beautiful and haunting melodies ever heard on Broadway.

The key to doing Weill justice is making sure every note is correct. Once you have done this, almost any style can be imposed on his songs without diminishing them. Weill has been extensively recorded by Lenya and other theatre/cabaret artists as well as opera singers. In 1985, Hal Willner produced an album of Kurt Weill songs featuring rock artists like Sting, Marianne Faithful, Lou Reed and Tom Waits. This album is well worth a listen, as these recordings only tend to illuminate the songs in new ways.

Body of work

Weill's German (and European) musicals include:

Zriny (opera, 1916)
Ninon von Lenclos
   (opera, 1920)
Zaubernacht (ballet with
   song, 1922) *
Der Protagonist (opera,
   1926) **
Royal Palace (opera, 1927) ***
Na und? (1927) ****
Mahagonny-Songspiel
   (1927) †
*Der Zar last sich photograph-
   ieren* (opera, 1928)**
Die Dreigroschenoper (*The
   Threepenny Opera*)
   (1928) †
Happy End (1929) †

*Aufstieg und Fall der Stadt
   Mahagonny* (*The Rise
   and Fall of the City of
   Mahagonny*) (opera, 1930) †
Der Jasager (1930) †
Die Bürgschaft (opera,
   1932) ††
Die sieben Todsünden (sung
   ballet, 1933) †
Der Silbersee (1933) **
Marie Galante (1934) †††
Der Kuhhandel (operetta,
   1934) ††††
A Kingdom for a Cow
   (1935) †††††
Der Weg der Verheissung
   (1935) ††††††

* libretto by Wladimir Boritsch
** libretto by George Kaiser
*** libretto by Yvan Goll
**** libretto by Felix
   Joachimson
† libretto by Bertolt Brecht
†† libretto by Caspar Neher

††† libretto by Jacques Deval
†††† libretto by Robert
   Vambrey
††††† libretto by Reginald
   Arkell and D. Carter
†††††† libretto by
   Franz Werfel

Weill's American stage musicals include:

Johnny Johnson (1936) *
The Eternal Road (1938) **

Knickerbocker Holiday
   (1938) ***

Davy Crockett (1938) ****
Railroads on Parade (A
   Fantasy on Rail Transport)
   (1939) *****
Ulysses Africanus (1939) ***
Lady in the Dark (1941) †
One Touch of Venus
   (1943) ††

The Firebrand of Florence
   (1944) †††
Street Scene (1947) ††††
Down in the Valley
   (1948) †††††
Love Life (1948) *†
Lost in the Stars (1949) ***
Huckleberry Finn (1950) ***

* libretto/lyrics by Paul Green
** libretto/lyrics by
   Franz Werfel
*** libretto/lyrics by Maxwell
   Anderson
**** libretto/lyrics by
   H.R. Hays
***** libretto/lyrics by Edward
   Hungerford
† libretto/lyrics by Moss Hart
   and Ira Gershwin

†† libretto/lyrics by
   Ogden Nash
††† libretto/lyrics by Ira
   Gershwin
†††† libretto/lyrics by Elmer
   Rice and Langston
   Hughes
††††† libretto/lyrics by Arnold
   Sundgaard
*† libretto/lyrics by Alan
   Jay Lerner

Weill's most successful songs include:

The Alabama Song
The Bilbao Song
Economics
Foolish Heart
Here I'll Stay
It Never Was You
Lost in the Stars
Mack the Knife
Mandalay Song
Moon-Faced, Starry-Eyed
My Ship
A Rhyme for Angela
The Saga of Jenny
September Song
Speak Low
(I'm a) Stranger Here Myself
Surabaya Johnny
What Good Would the Moon Be?

In addition to these, he wrote songs setting lyric texts by Walt Whitman, Howard Dietz, Oscar Hammerstein II, Robert Frost, Rainer Maria Rilke, Berthold Brecht, Jean Cocteau, and others.

Biography

Weill is the hardest composer in this chapter to pin down, having flourished in so many different worlds simultaneously. A German Jew deeply steeped in religious music, he was trained as a Post-Romantic classical composer, was quickly integrated into the avant-garde arts scene of Berlin in the 1920s, and fled Germany in the 1930s. He continued to write "serious" works at the same time that he found success in the popular arts (such as the musical theatre). Upon his arrival in America in 1935, he quickly fell in love with all things American. Gregg Wager writes, "Many who unconditionally praise Weill's output typically pick only one of his musical 'person-alities' and contrive ways of dismissing whatever other body of his work might offend them."[12] To come to terms with Weill as a whole is a daunting task.

The son of a Jewish cantor in Dessau, Germany, at 18 Weill moved to Berlin to study classical composition and began writing instrumental works, art songs and an opera. But by the age of 20 he found himself in the center of the avant-garde classical musi-cal world of Berlin. His association with the Novembergruppe, a group of progressive artists, and his strong left-wing political beliefs led him to turn his efforts to the more popular artform of musical theatre. Brecht's most fruitful collaboration in Germany, with the playwright Berthold Brecht, resulted in musicals *The Threepenny Opera*, *Happy End* and *The Rise and Fall of the City of Mahagonny*. Fleeing Germany in 1933, "with little more than a suitcase,"[13] Weill stopped in Paris for two years, before finally settling in New York. Weill was passionate about American music and theatre, and embraced the commercial theatre. Scholars and critics frequently attempt to separate Weill into the German period and the American period, or the classical works and the popular works, but the body of his work comprises an important part of this material. "Michael Feingold, drama critic for *The Village Voice*, calls Weill 'the most influential composer of the [20th] century' […] Feingold uses Weill to articulate the view […] that, in the 20th century, American pop culture became the heir of European 'classical' music of the 18th and 19th centuries within a universal musical language that resonates with and within important historical events."[14] Weill anticipated what Andy Warhol would do in the art world, embracing popular culture and elevating it to high culture.

Resources

There is a wealth of biographical and scholarly writing about Weill, including many exceptionally good websites. One of the best to use as a starting place for further research is The Kurt Weill Foundation for Music (www.kwf.org/). Many excellent books are available, including Ethan Morrden's *Love Song: The Lives of Kurt Weill and Lotte Lenya*,[15] and Foster Hirsch's *Kurt Weill On Stage: From Berlin to Broadway*.[16] Singers from many different genres from opera to avant-garde contemporary have recorded Weill's songs; his music stands up exceptionally well to re-examination and new interpretations.

Leonard Bernstein (1918–1990): Straddling the worlds of classical music and musical theatre

Stylistic approach

Bernstein employs a vast range of styles in his writing, and yet his music is squarely rooted in the classical mode. While some of the other material we have explored has been accessible to a less trained voice, Bernstein's music calls for serious classical technique. His music expresses character and is plot driven, but one should not attempt to sing "Maria" or "Glitter and Be Gay" without being able to comfortably float the high notes of the obbligato. While other composer's songs can be transposed so that a baritone can sing a tenor song for example, Bernstein writes so specifically for the singer's instrument that it is very difficult to shift his vocal music from one register to another successfully.

Bernstein's musical magnetism stemmed from his ability to find the humanity and humility in whatever music he was writing, to take the "stuffiness" out of classical music. When Bernstein was coaching jazz singer Bobby McFerrin who was preparing to conduct Beethoven's Seventh, Bernstein got McFerrin to access the music by reminding him, "You know, it's all jazz."[17] Bernstein is best sung with a strong classical technique, ease, fluidity and a great sense of the humanity of the character singing. Listen to any good recording of *Candide*, and there are many, and you will begin to understand Bernstein's brilliance. Every bit of "ink on the page" in a Bernstein song is an important piece of information. Note durations, dynamics, phrasing indications, indications of accompaniment dynamics, all inform the singer, and following them all leads to a much stronger performance. Many composers write songs that need to be interpreted. Bernstein has done a great deal of that work for the singer, and following his roadmap can lead to a spectacular performance. Bernstein himself was one of the most charismatic conductors of the twentieth century, and finding his insatiable energy in his songs will also lead the singer to great performances. When singing Bernstein, be present and trust the maestro.

Body of work

Bernstein's ballets include:

Conch Town (1941)   Facsimile (1946)
Fancy Free (1944)   Dybbuk (1974)

Bernstein's operas and theatre pieces include:

The Birds (1939,   The Firstborn (1958, incidental
   incidental music)   music) †
The Peace (1941,   The Race to Urga (1969,
   incidental music)   abandoned during
On the Town (1944) *   auditions, but received a
Peter Pan (1950) **   presentation in 1987, also
Trouble in Tahiti (1952) **   known as A Pray
Wonderful Town (1953) *   by Blecht) *
The Lark (1955,   Mass: A Theatre Piece for
   incidental music)   Singers, Players and
Salomé (1955, incidental music)   Dancers (1971) ††
Candide (1956, 1973, 1982,   1600 Pennsylvania Avenue
   1988) ***   (1976) †††
West Side Story (1957) ****   A Quiet Place (1983, opera)

* lyrics by Betty Comden and Adolph Green
** lyrics by Leonard Bernstein
*** lyrics by Richard Wilbur, John LaTouche, Dorothy Parker,
    Lillian Hellman, Leonard Bernstein, Stephen Sondheim
**** lyrics by Stephen Sondheim
† lyrics by Christopher Fry and Leonard Bernstein
†† lyrics by Leonard Bernstein and Stephen Schwartz
††† lyrics by Alan Jay Lerner
†††† lyrics by Stephen Wadsworth and Leonard Bernstein

The songs from some of Bernstein's more popular theatre pieces
include:

On the Town (1944) (Ozzie, baritone; Chip, baritone; Gabey,
  baritone; Hildy Esterhazy, mezzo-soprano; Claire DeLoone,
  mezzo-soprano)

New York, New York ††	I Can Cook Too **
Carried Away **	Lucky to Be Me ††
Lonely Town ††	Some Other Time **

Wonderful Town (1953) (Ruth Sherwood, alto; Eileen Sherwood,
  soprano; Bob Baker, baritone; Frank Lippencott, tenor; Chick
  Clark, baritone; Wreck, baritone)

Ohio **	A Quiet Girl ††
One Hundred Easy Ways to Lose a Man **	Swing **
	It's Love ††
A Little Bit in Love *	Wrong Note Rag **
Pass the Football ††	

Candide (1956) (Candide, tenor; Cunneganda, soprano; Paquette,
  alto; Pangloss/Voltaire, baritone; Maximillian, baritone; Old
  Lady, mezzo-soprano

It Must Be So ††	Make Our Garden Grow
Glitter and Be Gay *	

West Side Story (1957) (Tony, tenor; Maria, soprano; Anita, mezzo-soprano, Riff, tenor)

Something's Coming †	I Feel Pretty *
Maria †	Somewhere *
Cool †	A Boy Like That/I Have a
One Hand, One Heart †/*	Love **/*
Tonight †/*	

Mass (1971)
Simple Song (soprano or baritone)

Other various choral pieces, songs and vocal pieces include:

Psalm 148 (1935)	*Get Hep!* (1955) *
I Hate Music: A cycle of Five	*Harvard Choruses* (1957) †
Kid Songs for Soprano and	*Canon in Five Parts (from*
Piano (1943) *	*"Kaddish")* (1963)
Big Stuff (1944) *	*Chichester Psalms* (1965)
Hashiveinu (1945)	*Haiku Souvenirs* (1967) ††
Simhi Na (1947)	*So Pretty* (1968) ****
Re'ena (1947)	*Warm-Up* (1970) *
La Bonne Cuisine: Four	*'if you can't eat you got to'*
Recipes for Voice and	(1973) †††
Piano (1948) **	*White House Cantata* (1976) †
Two Love Songs on Poems	*My New Friend* (1979) *
by Rainer Maria Rilke	*Piccola Serenata* (1972) *
(1949) ***	*Arias and Barcarolles* (1980) *
Yigdal (1950)	*Screwed on Wrong* (1980) *
Silhouete (Gallilee) (1951) *	*Olympic Hymn* (1981) *
The Story of My Life	*Opening Prayer* (1986)
(1952) ****	*Missa Brevis* (1988)
On the Waterfront (1954)	*My Twelve Tone Melody* (1988) *

Where no lyricist is indicated, lyrics pre-existed the musical setting
* lyrics by Leonard Bernstein
** lyrics by Emile Dutoit and Leonard Bernstein
*** Ranier Maria Rilke and Leonard Bernstein
**** lyrics by Betty Comden and Adolph Green
† lyrics by Alan Jay Lerner
†† lyrics by Jack Gottlieb
††† lyrics by e e cummings

Orchestral and chamber works include:

Piano Trio (1937)
Violin Sonata (1939)
Four Studies for two Clarinets,
  two Bassoons and
  Piano (1940)
Sonata for Violin and
  Piano (1940)
Sonata for Clarinet (1942)
Sonata for Clarinet and
  Piano (1942)
Symphony No.
  1: Jeremiah (1942)
Afterthought (1945)
Facsimile: Three Dance
  Variations from "Fancy
  Free" (1946)
Three Dance Episodes from
  "On The Town" (1947)
Fanfare for Bima (1948)
Elegy for Mippy I & II (1948)
Waltz for Mippy III (1948)
Rondo for Lifey (1948)
Symphony No 2: The Age of
  Anxiety (1949)
Prelude, Fugue, and
  Riffs (1949)
Serenade for Solo Violin,
  Strings, Harp and
  Percussion (1954)
Symphonic Suite from "On The
  Waterfront" (1955)
Overture to "Candide" (1956)
Brass Music (1959)

Symphonic Dances from "West
  Side Story" (1961)
Fanfare I: For the inauguration
  of John F. Kennedy
  (1961)
Fanfare II: For the 25th
  Anniversary of the High
  School of Music and Art,
  NYC (1961)
Symphony No.
  3: Kaddish (1963)
Shivaree: A Fanfare (1969)
Three Meditations from
  "Mass" (1971)
Dybbuk Suites No. 1 and
  2 (1974)
Songfest: A Cycle of American
  Poems for Six Singers and
  Orchestra (1977)
Two Meditations from
  "Mass" (1977)
Slava! A Political
  Overture (1977)
CBS Music (1977)
Divertimento for
  Orchestra (1980)
Halil (1981)
Concerto for
  Orchestra: "Jubilee
  Games" (1986)
Dance Suite (1988)
Variations of an Octatonic
  Scale (1989)

Biography

One of the captivating musical figures of the twentieth century, Leonard Bernstein was a composer of serious and popular music, a conductor, an author, music lecturer and pianist. He was also one of the first musicians to use his charismatic nature and good looks to exploit the new media of television, in a series of televised concerts designed to introduce young people to classical music. As a classical conductor, he was beloved by orchestras around the world and was associated with the New York Philharmonic from 1943 to 1990. His obituary in *The New York Times* referred to him as "one of the most prodigally talented and successful musicians in American history."[18]

Born Louis Bernstein in Lawrence, Massachusetts to Ukrainian Jewish parents, Bernstein attended Garrison Grammar School and Boston Latin School, and Harvard University. Following Harvard, Bernstein did his graduate work studying conducting at the Curtis Institute of Music. On November 14, 1943, the 25-year old assistant conductor for the New York Philharmonic was called in at 9:00 a.m. and told that he would be stepping in for that evening's guest conductor, Bruno Walter, who had become ill. Bernstein created such a sensation that *The New York Times* reviewed his conducting premiere in a front-page article. Never content to limit his world, Bernstein embraced all styles and genres of music. As with Weill, classical scholars alternately claim him as one of their brightest stars and excoriate him for wasting his time in the musical theatre. His classical compositions referenced jazz, Latin music, rock and Jewish folk music among other styles; and his popular music reflected all of those styles plus his strong classical background. His earliest pieces include vocal pieces, piano pieces, chamber music, orchestral and choral works, ballets, operas and musicals.

Resources

The Bernstein estate maintains a terrific website, www.leonardbernstein.com/lb.htm, which is an excellent place to begin researching Bernstein and his work. Bernstein himself wrote several wonderful books including *The Joy of Music*,[19] a collection of his essays. There are several good biographies. A documentary on the making of the 1985 studio cast recording of *West Side Story* allows singers to watch Bernstein working with the singers and the orchestra and coaching the songs himself.

Betty Comden (1917–2006) and Adolph Green (1914–2002): Creators of wonderful larger-than-life characters

Stylistic Approach

Betty Comden and Adolph Green's 54-year collaboration as lyricists, librettists and screenwriters yielded some of the funniest and most poignant moments in the musical theatre. Of the composers most associated with Comden and Green, Leonard Bernstein was a close life-long friend with whom they wrote *On the Town* and *Wonderful Town*. Jule Styne collaborated with Comden and Green more than any other composer, writing: *Two on the Aisle*, *Peter Pan*, *Bells Are Ringing*, *Say Darling*, *Do-Re-Mi*, *Subways Are for Sleeping*, *Fade Out – Fade In*, *Hallelujah, Baby!* and *Lorelei*.

The immediacy and exuberance in their writing are matched only by their craft. Initially performers, Comden and Green frequently wrote characters for themselves to play (like Claire and Ozzie in *On The Town*) or characters based on themselves (like Lester and Lily in the movie *The Band Wagon*). The wisecracking, over-the-top, scenery-chewing types of characters they wrote best for include Captain Hook in *Peter Pan*, Oscar Jaffe, Lily Garland, Letitia Primrose and Bruce Granite in *On the Twentieth Century*. Stylistically, their characters are larger than life and gregarious.

In 1958, Betty Comden and Adolph Green compiled and performed an evening of their songs, performing them all themselves. This evening, *A Party With Betty Comden and Adolph Green*, was revived and recorded in 1977. For the singer preparing to work on songs by Comden and Green, there is no better record of the gregariousness of their characters. Listening to this recording will help the singer find the larger-than-life quality that the lyrics embrace.

Body of work

Betty Comden and Adolph Green provided lyrics and librettos for:

On the Town (1944) *   *Wonderful Town* (1953) *
Billion Dollar Baby (1945) **   *Peter Pan* (1954) ***
Two on the Aisle (1951) ***   *Bells Are Ringing* (1956) ***

Say Darling (1958) ***
Do Re Mi (1960) ***
Subways Are for Sleeping
    (1961) ***
Fade Out – Fade In (1964) ***
Hallelujah, Baby! (1967) ***
Applause (1970) ****

Lorelei (1974) ***
On the Twentieth Century
    (1978) †
A Doll's Life (1982) ††
Singing in the Rain (1985) †††
The Will Rogers Follies
    (1991) †

* music by Leonard Bernstein
** music by Morton Gould
*** music by Jules Styne
**** music by Charles Strouse, lyrics by Lee Adams
† music by Cy Coleman
†† music by Larry Grossman
††† music by Herb Nacio Brown and Arthur Freed, lyrics by
    Arthur Freed

Their screenplays include:

Good News (1947)
The Barkleys of Broadway
    (1949)
On the Town (1949)
Singing in the Rain (1952)

The Band Wagon (1953)
Auntie Mame (1958)
Bells Are Ringing (1960)
What a Way to Go (1964)

The songs from some of Comden and Green's more popular theatre pieces include:

On the Town (1944) (Ozzie, baritone; Chip, baritone; Gabey, baritone; Hildy Esterhazy, mezzo-soprano; Claire DeLoone, mezzo-soprano)

New York, New York ††
Carried Away **
Lonely Town ††

I Can Cook Too **
Lucky to Be Me ††
Some Other Time **

Wonderful Town (1953) (Ruth Sherwood, alto; Eileen Sherwood, soprano; Bob Baker, baritone; Frank Lippencott, tenor; Chick Clark, baritone; Wreck, baritone)

Ohio **
One Hundred Easy Ways to
   Lose a Man **
A Little Bit in Love *
Pass the Football ††

A Quiet Girl ††
Swing **
It's Love ††
Wrong Note Rag **

Peter Pan (1954) (Pater Pan, soprano/mezzo-soprano; Captain Hook, baritone)

Neverland **

Captain Hook's Waltz ††

Bells Are Ringing (1956) (Ella Peterson, mezzo-soprano; Jeff Moss, baritone; Sandor, baritone, Sue, mezzo-soprano)

It's a Perfect Relationship **
Long Before I Knew You **/††
Just in Time **/††

The Party's Over **
I'm Going Back **

Do Re Mi (1960) (Hubert Cram, baritone; Kay Cram, mezzo-soprano; Brains Berman, baritone; John Henry Wheeler, baritone; Tilda Mullen, soprano)

I Know About Love ††
Fireworks **/††

Make Someone Happy ††

On the Twentieth Century (1978) (Lily Garland, soprano; Oscar Jaffe, baritone; Letitia Primrose, alto; Bruce Granit, baritone)

Never *
Our Private World */††

Repent **
Babbette *

Will Rogers Follies (1991) (Will Rogers, baritone; Betty Blake, mezzo-soprano)

Give a Man Enough Rope ††
My Unknown Someone **

Never Met a Man I Didn't
   Like ††

Biography

Adolph Green was born in the Bronx to Hungarian Jewish immigrants. After high school, he took a job on Wall Street to support his budding career as an actor. Mutual friends introduced Comden and Green in 1938, and they formed a performance group, The Revuers, which performed ever-changing topical material in a late-night cabaret in the Village Vanguard, a jazz club in Greenwich Village. Judy Holliday, who would go on to star in their *Bells Are Ringing*, was also a member. The budding young conductor Leonard Bernstein was a fan and sometimes ad hoc accompanist.

Their first Broadway musical was the smash *On the Town*, with Bernstein writing the score. Their next two musicals failed fairly dismally, *Billion Dollar Baby* (1945), and *Bonanza Bound* (1947 – it closed out of town and never made it to New York). Trying their hand at screenwriting in Hollywood, they worked for MGM and wrote the scripts for *Good News* (1947), *The Barkleys of Broadway* (1949), *On the Town* (1949), *Singing in the Rain* (1952), *The Band Wagon* (1953) and more.

In 1951 they wrote the Broadway revue *Two on the Aisle* for Bert Lahr and Dolores Gray which was the first of many scores with composer Jule Styne. Nominated for 12 Tony Awards, they won seven.

Resources

Betty Comden's autobiography, *Off Stage*,[20] offers Comden's perspective on their careers and their work.

Jule Styne (1905–1994): the peak of the Golden Age of the American musical

Stylistic approach

Composer Jule Styne reigned at the end of the Golden Age as a songwriter whose theatre work was the popular music of the day, and his work came to comprise a substantial niche in the American songbook. Discussing his great stylistic range, his *New York Times* obituary quotes him speaking to the fact that he let his lyricists set the stylistic tone of the score or song. "I had 15 No. 1 songs with Sammy Cahn. He loved that big-band sound, so every song had that

big-band sound. Then I read lyrics by Yip Harburg and Leo Robin and I thought, 'I'd like to write to those kinds of words.' Yip's syllables and sounds tingle with music. Leo had a wonderful edge, a suave and very sophisticated way of comedy."[21]
  Styne's eclectic background mirrors his stylistic diversity. Putting aside his classical career as a child prodigy, at age 13 he started his own dance band which played at burlesque houses and in jazz clubs. He spent the 1920s primarily working with jazz bands. The 1930s were spent mostly as a vocal coach in New York and Hollywood, and by the 1940s his composing career had taken off writing songs for movies produced by Twentieth Century Fox and Paramount Pictures.
  Jule Styne's songs have been successfully sung by singers from many areas – jazz, swing, pop, legitimate, country. The melodies are beautiful and open to interpretation. While Styne's songs are very specific to the characters who sing them, they are highly musical. And the dramatic moment is most often found through the musicality of the song, rather than in spite of it. Listen to Barbra Streisand singing both "Who Are You Now" and "The Music That Makes Me Dance," to say nothing of "People," from the original Broadway cast recording of *Funny Girl*, and you will understand how the character uses the melody to seek an answer to their dilemma. The dramatic moment is activated by the melody.

Body of work

Styne wrote music for hundreds of movies; a small sampling of these include:

Sing, Dance, Plenty Hot (1940)	*Carolina Blues* (1944)
Melody and Moonlight (1940)	*Follow the Boys* (1944) *
Hit Parade of 1941 (1940) *	*Tonight and Every Night*
Melody Ranch (1940)	(1945) *
Sailors on Leave (1941)	*Anchors Aweigh* (1945) *
Sweater Girl (1942)	*Cinderella Jones* (1946)
Priorities on Parade (1942)	*The Kid from Brooklyn*
Youth Parade (1942) *	(1946)
Hit Parade of 1943 (1943) *	*It Happened in*
Step Lively (1944)	*Brooklyn* (1947)

Romance on the High Seas
(1948) *
Two Guys from Texas (1948)
It's a Great Feeling (1949) *
The West Point Story (1950)
Meet Me After the Show (1951)
Two Tickets to Broadway
(1951)

Three Coins in the
Fountain (1954)
Mister Magoo's Christmas Carol
(1962 – television special)
The Dangerous Christmas of
Red Riding Hood (1965 –
television special)
Funny Girl (1968) *

* Academy Award nomination

His musical theatre scores include:

High Button Shoes (1947) *
Gentlemen Prefer Blondes
(1949) **
Two on the Aisle (1951) ***
Hazel Flagg (1953) ****
Peter Pan (1954) ***
Bells Are Ringing (1956) ***
Say Darling (1958) ***
Gypsy (1959) *****
Do Re Mi (1960) ***
Subways Are for Sleeping
(1961) ***
Funny Girl (1964) †
Fade Out – Fade In (1964) ***
Hallelujah, Baby! (1967) ***
Darling of the Day (1968) ††
Look to the Lilies (1970) *

Prettybelle (1971 – closed prior
to Broadway) †
Sugar (1972) ††
Lorelei (1974) ***
Hellzapoppin' (1976 –
closed prior to
Broadway)
Serafina (1976 – never
produced) †
Bar Mitzvah Boy (1978 –
London, West End)
One Night Stand (1980 –
closed prior to
Broadway) †††
Pieces of Eight
(1985 – Edmunton)††††
The Red Shoes (1993) †††††

* lyrics by Sammy Cahn
** lyrics by Leo Robin
*** lyrics by Betty Comden
  and Adolph Green
**** lyrics by Bob Hilliard
***** lyrics by Stephen
  Sondheim

† lyrics by Bob Merrill
†† lyrics by E.Y. "Yip" Harburg
†††† lyrics by Herb Gardner
†††† lyrics by Susan
  Birkenhead
††††† lyrics by Marsha
  Norman and Paul Stryker

The songs from some of Styne's more popular stage musicals
include:

Gentlemen Prefer Blondes (1949) (Lorelei Lee, mezzo-soprano; Gus Esmond, baritone; Dorothy Shaw, mezzo-soprano)

Bye Bye Baby ††
A Little Girl from Little
  Rock **
I Love What I'm Doin' **
Diamonds Are a Girl's Best
  Friend **

Two on the Aisle (1951)
(starring Bert Lahr and
  Dolores Gray)
Hold Me Tight **
If (You Hadn't, but You
  Did) **

Peter Pan (1954) (Peter Pan, soprano/mezzo-soprano; Captain Hook, baritone)

Neverland **   Captain Hook's Waltz ††

Bells Are Ringing (1956) (Ella Peterson, mezzo-soprano; Jeff Moss, baritone; Sandor, baritone, Sue, mezzo-soprano)

It's A Perfect Relationship **   The Party's Over **
Long Before I Knew You **/††   I'm Going Back **
Just in Time **/††

Gypsy (1959) (Mama Rose, mezzo-soprano; Herbie, baritone; June, mezzo-soprano, Louise, mezzo-soprano, Tulsa, tenor)

Let Me Entertain You **
Some People **
Small World **
Little Lamb **
You'll Never Get Away from
  Me **/††
If Momma Was Married **

All I Need Is the Girl ††
Everything's Coming Up
  Roses **
Together Wherever We
  Go **/††
You Gotta Get a Gimmick **

Do Re Mi (1960) (Hubert Cram, baritone; Kay Cram, mezzo-soprano; Brains Berman, baritone; John Henry Wheeler, baritone; Tilda Mullen, soprano)

I Know About Love ††   Make Someone Happy ††
Fireworks **/††

Funny Girl (1964) (Fanny Brice, mezzo-soprano, Nick Arnstein, baritone, Eddie Ryan, baritone, Mrs. Brice, alto)

I'm the Greatest Star * *	Don't Rain on My Parade * *
People * *	Who Are You Now * *
You Are Woman (I Am	The Music That Makes Me
Man) ††/* *	Dance * *

Here is a very abbreviated list of some of Styne's over 1,500 published songs not from Broadway musicals. Since most of these songs have been published in various keys to accommodate different voices, vocal types are not indicated here.

All the Way
And the Angels Sing
Anywhere
As Long as There's Music
Change of Heart
Christmas Waltz
Down Mexico Way
Every Street's a Boulevard in Old New York
Five Minutes More
Guess I'll Hang My Tears Out to Dry
I Don't Want to Walk Without You
I Fall in Love Too Easily
In the Cool of the Evening
It Seems I Heard That Song Before
It's a Great Feeling
It's Been a Long, Long Time
It's Magic
I've Heard That Song Before
Let it Snow! Let it Snow! Let it Snow!
Put 'em in a Box, Tie 'em with a Ribbon (And Throw 'em in
      the Deep Blue Sea)
Saturday Night (is the Loneliest Night of the Week)
The Seven Year Itch
Some Other Time
Three Coins in the Fountain
Time After Time
Who Am I?

Biography

Jule Styne was born in 1905 in London as Julius Kerwin Stein, the son of Jewish Ukrainian immigrants, Isadore and Anna Stein, who ran a butter-and-egg store. In 1913, the Steins moved to Chicago, where his father struggled to come up with money for a second-hand piano and piano lessons for Julius, who quickly proved to be a prodigy. Julius was performing with the Chicago, Detroit and St. Louis symphony orchestras by the age of 10. Three years later, when pianist Harold Bauer told Julius that his hands were too small for him to be a successful concert pianist, Julius gave up classical music in favor of playing in dance bands, burlesque houses and jazz clubs.

On the advice that Stein sounded too Jewish, Julius became Jule Styne and moved to New York to become a vocal coach and conductor for Broadway star Harry Richman. His early New York work brought him to the attention of Hollywood, where he began work in 1938 for Twentieth Century Fox, coaching their stars and writing occasional songs. Moving to Republic Pictures and Paramount he began his prolific career as a composer, working with lyricists like Sammy Cahn and Frank Loesser. Through the 1940s and well into the 1950s Styne scored tens of Hollywood movies every year; his output was extraordinary in both quantity and quality.

High Button Shoes, Styne's first Broadway show, opened in 1947 with lyrics by Sammy Cahn. In addition to Cahn, Styne's most frequent Broadway collaborators were Betty Comden and Adolph Green. Others included Stephen Sondheim, Bob Merrill, Leo Robin and E.Y. "Yip" Harburg. Some of the highlights of Styne's Broadway career include: *Gentlemen Prefer Blondes* (1949), *Two on the Aisle* (1951), *Peter Pan* (1954), *Bells Are Ringing* (1956) and *Do Re Mi* (1960). The Golden Age and Styne's career both peaked with *Gypsy* (1959) and *Funny Girl* (1964). Following Styne's 1967 musical *Hallelujah, Baby!*, he failed to find the success that had come so plentifully to him earlier. The times had changed, the kinds of shows and songs that audiences expected changed and Styne's post-1967 career was comprised of revivals and shows that closed quickly or prior to reaching Broadway. He continued writing until his death in 1994 but never found the kind of success he had experienced earlier in his career.

Resources

Theodore Taylor's 1979 *Jule: The Story of Composer Jule Styne* is the one biography of Styne available.[22] The website www.julestyne.com/ offers a good online source to begin researching Styne further.

In summary

On Broadway in the Golden Age, voices tended to return to classical training. Roger Pines describes this sound as follows: "generally not quite operatic in scale, offered full but smooth-textured tone, wide range, easy access to head tone, and clear, unfussy shaping of text – in effect, 'Broadway bel canto'."[23] In addition to tone and vocal quality, these shows and the songs from them embrace a unique cultural ethos. In his theatre article in *The New York Times*, on January 24, 1993, Stephen Holden wrote about this cultural and moral universe, saying:

> Once upon a time, America dreamed of itself as a singing fairy tale for grown-ups, with a happy ending. Norman Rockwell painted this storybook country, and Richard Rodgers and Oscar Hammerstein 2d wrote its songs. More than just pop confections, they added up to a kind of secular catechism that sweetly but firmly instructed people on the rules of behavior in a world where America knew best and good triumphed over evil. Certainly, Rodgers and Hammerstein didn't invent the code of values that their songs taught. With their stern, semi-operatic melodies and know-it-all lyrics, they offered an idealized mirror image of American middle-class morality in the heady afterglow of Hitler's defeat. At a moment when everyone understood what was meant by terms like "maturity," "good citizenship" and "mental hygiene," they helped define the notion of a national culture. In this wholesome, cheery land, nothing could be more desirable than to be as corny as Kansas in August and as normal as blueberry pie. If you kept on whistling a happy tune, you would never walk alone. And on some enchanted evening, you might even find your true love. Those who climbed every mountain, beginning with foothills that were alive with the sound of music, would surely find their dreams.[24]

Understanding the world as it was reflected on the stages of the American musicals in the 1940s and 1950s helps the singer enter that world and perform these songs without any of the irony or cynicism that so defines our own times.

Notes

1 Richard Rodgers, *Musical Stages: An Autobiography*, New York, NY: Random House, 1975.
2 Meryl Secrest, *Somewhere For Me – A Biography of Richard Rodgers*, New York, NY: Applause Theatre & Cinema Books, 2002.
3 Hugh Fordin, *Getting to Know Him – A Biography of Oscar Hammerstein, II*, New York, NY: Da Capo Press, 1995.
4 Fredrick Nolan, *The Sound of Their Music: The Story of Rodgers & Hammerstein*, New York, NY: Applause Theatre & Cinema Books, 2002.
5 Alan Jay Lerner, *The Street Where I Live*, New York, NY: W.W. Norton, 1978.
6 Edward Jablonski, *Alan Jay Lerner: A Biography*, New York, NY: Henry Holt & Co, 1996.
7 McHugh, Dominic, *Alan Jay Lerner: A Lyricist's Letters*, Oxford, UK: Oxford University Press, 2014.
8 John D. Shout, "Frank Loesser," *Broadway: The American Musical*, www.pbs.org/wnet/broadway/stars/frank-loesser/, accessed August 25, 2014.
9 Shout, "Frank Loesser."
10 Susan Loesser, *A Most Remarkable Fella: Frank Loesser and the Guys and Dolls in His Life: A Portrait by His Daughter*, Milwaukee, WI: Hal Leonard, 2000.
11 "Sprechstimme," Columbia University Sonic Glossary, http://ccnmtl.columbia.edu/projects/sonicg/terms/sprechstimme.html, accessed July 25, 2015.
12 Gregg Wager, "Kurt Weill," *The Orel Foundation\Kurt Weill\Biography*, http://orelfoundation.org/index.php/composers/article/kurt_weill/, accessed August 30, 2014.
13 Wager, "Kurt Weill," accessed August 28, 2014.
14 Wager, "Kurt Weill," accessed August 30, 2014.
15 Ethan Mordden, *Love Song: The Lives of Kurt Weill and Lotte Lenya*, New York, NY: St. Martin's Press, 2012.
16 Foster Hirsch, *Kurt Weill Onstage: From Berlin to Broadway*, New York, NY: Knopf, 2002.
17 Bobby McFerrin, quoted by Susan Kepecs in "Bobby McFerrin and the Simplest Form of Expression," *Isthmus*, www.isthmus.com/isthmus/article.php?article=24851, accessed September 1, 2014.
18 Donald Henahan, "Leonard Bernstein, 72, Music's Monarch, Dies," *The New York Times*, October 15, 1990, www.nytimes.com/learning/general/onthisday/bday/0825.html, accessed August 30, 2014.

19 Leonard Bernstein, *The Joy of Music*, New York, NY: Amadeus Press, 2014.
20 Betty Comden, *Off Stage*, Milwaukee, WI: Limelight Editions, 2004.
21 Eleanor Blau, "Jule Styne, Bountiful Creator of Song Favorites, Dies at 88," *The New York Times*, September 21, 1994, www.nytimes.com/1994/09/21/obituaries/jule-styne-bountiful-creator-of-song-favorites-dies-at-88.html, accessed November 17, 2014.
22 Theodore Taylor, *Jule: The Story of Composer Jule Styne*, New York, NY: Random House, 1979.
23 Roger Pines, "That Broadway Sound," *Opera*, www.opera.co.uk/view-review.php?reviewID=87&PHPSESSID=cd8435ec4e79e48fc5f90 18e9f7900c3, accessed October 28, 2015.
24 Stephen Holden, "Their Songs Were America's Happy Talk," *The New York Times*, January 4, 1993, www.nytimes.com/1993/01/24/theater/theater-their-songs-were-america-s-happy-talk.html, accessed October 28, 2015.

Chapter 7

The culmination of the Golden Age of the American musical

Jerry Herman, Charles Strouse, Tom
Jones and Harvey Schmidt, Jerry Bock
and Sheldon Harnick, Cy Coleman, and
John Kander and Fred Ebb

In the 1920s and 1930s, musical theatre songs were written with the intent that they could change placement in a show, or be removed from a show completely and stand on their own. Whether written as popular songs, or for revues or book musicals, the popular songs far outlasted the shows in which they first appeared. With the advent of the integrated musicals of Rodgers and Hammerstein in 1943, songs were used to advance either character or plot. But the music of the musical theatre still crossed over to be recorded by popular singers like Eddie Fisher, Doris Day, Rosemary Clooney and Louis Armstrong. Financial rewards were high for Broadway composers and lyricists who wrote songs for their shows that became hits. For a song to cross over in this way, it needed to be less specific to the character and situation, and roughly two and a half to three minutes long. Song structure was frequently A-A-B-A, sometimes with a repeat of the B section as an instrumental and a final sung A section with a coda. Of course other structures existed, but composers had to keep in mind that the song had to adapt to this kind of structure for the popular recordings that could bring in so much money.

But by the mid-1960s rock and roll had overtaken all other popular music, edging out the pop singers who had been recording cover versions of the musical theatre repertoire. Since the rock singers were predominantly singer-songwriters who provided their own songs, musical theatre songs no longer had much life beyond their shows. No longer driven by cover recordings and sheet music sales, musical theatre composers and lyricists of the 1960s and 1970s focused more heavily on dramaturgy; more than ever, their songs advanced the plot and helped to develop the character.

The writers examined in this chapter established themselves at a time before every actor had a microphone, when the unamplified voice was the rule on Broadway. Their songs were written in registers that allowed the singers to be heard acoustically over a live orchestra. The vocal style they wrote for is bright and "pingy," the placement is frontal; belting and a mix which favored belt qualities was very much the norm. In 1968's *Promises, Promises* for the first time ever, every singer on-stage and every musician in the pit had a microphone, and the sound that the audience heard was primarily in the hands of the soundboard operator. This trend didn't fully overtake acoustic sound until the mid-1970s. But by then, all of these writers had established themselves and their sounds.

Freed from the constraints of the popular music form, writers of the 1960s and 1970s began moving musical theatre songwriting forward, to find new forms and structures. It was a time of heavy experimentation with both form and content. These writers' songs tend to call for singers who are also strong actors. Whereas musicals of the 1940s and 1950s called for strong singers with personas that fit particular types (leading man, ingénue, juvenile, and so on), musicals of the 1960s and later called for performers to integrate their singing and acting techniques.

This is the era of the big Broadway belt. While all of these writers contributed some extraordinary legitimate songs, these writers also are responsible for some of the biggest and best belt numbers for women, and songs that require other "screaming-on-pitch" techniques. Belting had been tremendously popular in the 1920s and 1930s but had been eclipsed by the more classical compositional styles of the 1940s. But belting made a strong comeback with these writers in the 1960s.

This chapter presents a brief examination of the vocal style most appropriate to each writer, an overview of the body of their work, a brief biographical sketch and a short list of further biographical resources. For additional research resources for these writers and specific songs, the Internet is an invaluable tool. Performances of practically every song these writers wrote can be found online, as can much of their sheet music. The body of work includes a list of songs of note and in many cases a voice type is identified, although transpositions make many of these songs available to other voice types.

Jerry Herman (b. 1931): Larger than life and intensely emotional

Stylistic approach

More than anything else, composer and lyricist Jerry Herman writes wonderfully catchy melodies. In his acceptance speech for the Best Score Tony Award for *La Cage Aux Folles*, Herman said, "There's been a rumor around for a couple of years that the simple, hummable show tune was no longer welcome on Broadway. Well, it's alive and well at the Palace [Theatre]."[1] Although some took this as a snub of Sondheim's more sophisticated and less accessible *Sunday in the Park with George*, which *La Cage* bested for the award, Herman was right; his songs are catchy and immensely hummable.

Additionally, for the most part Herman's songs are deeply felt; other writers can be more cerebral, but Herman's songs are extremely visceral. Frequently they are moments in time that the composer/lyricist has frozen so that the character can revel in and express their feelings; this calls for intense emotional engagement on the singers' part. Herman's songs tend to explore the extreme moments of larger-than-life characters, but even the smaller more intimate songs like "Ribbons Down My Back" are intensely personal and deeply felt. These songs call as much for excellent technical vocal production, as for emotional immediacy. In Jerry Herman shows, even the songs for the more sedate or staid characters like Irene in *Hello, Dolly!*, Gooch in *Mame* and Jean-Michel in *La Cage* are heightened emotionally.

Herman writes tuneful songs that celebrate life and extol the listener to live life to the fullest. In *Hello, Dolly!* Cornelius and Barnaby sing exuberantly about heading out on an adventure and not coming home "until we kiss a girl." In "It Takes A Woman," Horace Vandergeller extols womanhood, even if it is from his unique, antiquated perspective. Whether they are celebrating the small moments or the life-changing ones, these songs are positive and contain humor. Herman's songs work very well as written; they are rarely reinterpreted in contemporary styles. These tend to be big songs for big voices and big personalities.

Herman's bigger-than-life ladies have been created by Carol Channing, Angela Lansbury, Bernadette Peters and George Hearn. Carol Channing's replacements in the original Broadway production of *Hello, Dolly!* included Pearl Bailey, Phyllis Diller, Betty Grable and Ethel Merman, all of whom are defined by their oversized personalities. The smaller characters who surround them yearn to live life that fully. Listen, for instance, to the yearning in Eileen Brennan's "Ribbons Down My Back," or Charles Nelson Reilly's "It Only Takes a Moment." Listen to Jane Connell busting to live life to the fullest in "Gooch's Song" on the original cast recordings. All of Herman's characters have great size or great needs that drive their vocal style. He is the last of the great writers of the Golden Age of the American musical, as can be heard in Robert Weede's performance in *Milk and Honey*. Weede was a great opera star from 1937 to 1956, when he transitioned into the musical theatre. In his performance in *Milk and Honey* he finds all the yearning and need of the character in the beauty of the melodic line.

Body of work

Jerry Herman is the one writer in this chapter who wrote both music and lyrics. Herman's writing was almost exclusively for the theatre; his theatre scores include:

I Feel Wonderful
    (off-Broadway, 1954)
Nightcap (off-Broadway, 1957)
Parade (off-Broadway, 1960)
From A to Z (contributed one
    song, 1960)
Madame Aphrodite
    (off-Broadway, 1961)
Milk and Honey (1961)

Hello Dolly! (1964)
Mame (1966)
Dear World (1969)
Mack and Mabel (1974)
The Grand Tour (1979)
La Cage Aux Folles (1983)
Miss Spectacular
    (unproduced, 2003)

Herman also contributed additional songs to:

Ben Franklin in Paris (1964)
A Day in Hollywood/A Night in the Ukraine (1980).

Herman's best-known songs, and some that are lesser-known but may be well worth exploring include:

Milk and Honey (1961) (Phil, baritone; Ruth, mezzo-soprano; Mrs.
    Weiss, mezzo-soprano; David, tenor)

There's No Reason in the
World ††
Let's Not Waste a Moment ††

Like a Young Man ††
I Will Follow You †

Hello, Dolly! (1964) (Dolly Levi, mezzo-soprano; Horace Vandergelder, baritone; Irene Molloy, soprano; Minnie Fay, mezzo-soprano; Barnaby Tucker, baritone; Cornelius Hackl, baritone)

Before the Parade Passes By * *
Hello, Dolly!
It Only Takes a Moment †

Put On Your Sunday Clothes
Ribbons Down My Back *

Mame (1966) (Mame Dennis, mezzo-soprano; Vera Charles, mezzo-soprano; Agnes Gooch, mezzo-soprano; Beaureguard Burnside, baritone; Patrick Dennis, baritone)

Bosom Buddies * *
Gooch's Song (soprano)
If he Walked Into My Life * *
It's Today * *

My Best Girl ††
Open a New Window * *
That's How Young I Feel * *
We Need a Little Christmas

Dear World (1969) (Countess Aurelia, mezzo-soprano; Nina, soprano; Julian, tenor)

I Don't Want to Know * *
I Never Said I Love You *

Kiss Her Now * *

Mack and Mabel (1974) (Mack Sennett, baritone; Mabel Normand, mezzo-soprano; Lottie Ames, mezzo-soprano)

Look What Happened to
Mabel * *
I Won't Send Roses ††

Tap Your Troubles Away * *
Wherever He Ain't * *
Time Heals Everything * *

The Grand Tour (1979) (S.L. Jacobowsky, baritone; Colonel Tadeusz Boleslav Stjerbinsky, baritone; Marianne, soprano)

I'll Be Here Tomorrow †
I Belong Here *

Marianne †

La Cage Aux Folles (1983) (Albin, baritone; Georges, baritone; Jean-Michel, baritone; Jacqueline, mezzo-soprano)

I Am What I Am ††	The Best of Times **
Song in the Sand ††	Look Over There ††
With Anne on My Arm ††	

Biography

Born in 1931, Herman was raised in a Jewish middle-class home in Jersey City, New Jersey, surrounded by two strong nurturing women, his mother Ruth and grandmother Pauline. A self-taught pianist, Herman became active in the theatre at the summer camp run by his parents. Early in his college career Ruth arranged a meeting between her son and Frank Loesser. Loesser was supportive and encouraging of Herman's songs, and Herman abandoned his plans to study at the Parsons School of Design to enroll in the theatre department at the University of Miami. As an undergraduate Herman wrote, directed and produced a highly successful musical revue, *Sketchbook*.

Upon graduation Herman moved to New York and created an off-Broadway revue, *I Feel Wonderful,* primarily from the material that he had written in college. Herman's beloved mother passed away from cancer shortly after *I Feel Wonderful* opened. The loss of his mother had a tremendous impact on Herman, who built his career on writing songs for strong, life-affirming female characters.

After three more revues, two off-Broadway and one on Broadway, Herman received an offer to write the score to a book musical about the state of Israel. *Milk and Honey* was a wild success and led to Herman's next show. *Hello, Dolly!*, one of the biggest hits ever, ran for 2,844 performances, becoming, for a while, the longest running Broadway musical, and won Herman his first two Tony Awards.

Dolly Levi was the first in a string of Herman's strong leading female characters; the list includes Mame, Countess Aurelia, Mabel Normand, Marianne and Zaza. The larger-than-life woman who is the bearer of the life force, the big Broadway belt, big choral sound with each vocal section straining at the top of their ranges, all of these help define a Jerry Herman musical.

Resources

Two excellent biographical sources for Jerry Herman are his auto-biography, *Showtune: A Memoir By Jerry Herman*[2] and Stephen Citron's *Jerry Herman: Poet of the Show tune*,[3] published by Yale University Press in 2004.

Charles Strouse (b. 1928): A paean to positivity

Stylistic approach

Many of composer Charles Strouse's most successful songs tend to be upbeat, like "Tomorrow" and "Put on a Happy Face." These songs rarely allow a character to bemoan their fate; rather they take an optimistic stance. But Strouse's body of work goes deeper than this. A skillful composer who uses all the tools at his disposal, his songs take advantage of all registers of the voice; he writes adeptly for the middle and lower registers as well as the upper register.

That Strouse writes strong melodies with good hooks, sometimes belies the fact that there is a fierce intelligence underlying his writing. Although his songs may at first appear simple and straightforward, they are carefully and professionally crafted. *Bye Bye Birdie* was the first Broadway show to use rock and roll as the native musical idiom of the teenage characters. Strouse's handling of this genre and his integration of rock music into a standard "Broadway" score reveals his compositional sophistication and depth. The songs from more serious Strouse musicals, like *Rags* or *An American Tragedy*, readily make apparent Strouse's range as a composer.

Stylistically, Strouse's songs do not tend to hold up well to interpretations that overlay ornamental stylings like jazz, rock, pop or gospel. But there are classical, pop, pastiche, jazz, gospel, rock and roll and country songs within his body of work.

Golden Boy gave Strouse the chance to compose a score for entertainment dynamo and pop song stylist Sammy Davis Jr. Strouse's score includes songs like "Night Song," "Stick Around," "While The City Sleeps" and "I Want to Be With You," which cry out for embellishment and stylization, unlike much of the rest of Strouse's canon. In addition to writing for Sammy Davis, Jr. for *Golden Boy*, Strouse's writing for stars includes *Applause* for non-singing movie star Lauren Bacall and *Rags* for opera diva Teresa Stratas; all of these scores were very successful. He moves fluidly from one idiom to another.

Strouse and collaborator Martin Charnin have asserted that *Annie*, which won Strouse his third Tony Award, is not a children's musical, but rather a family musical that children can take their parents to see. Following *Annie*, Strouse worked on a great number of musicals in which his songs and scores tend to be more successful than the shows that contained them; many of the songs from these shows are hidden treasures. While they tend toward a traditional "Broadway" sound, Strouse's music is always well fitted to the show in terms of period, style and tone.

Body of work

Strouse's career was predominantly in the theatre. His theatre scores include:[4]

Shoestring Revue (1955)
Shoestring '57 (1956)
The Littlest Revue (1956)
Kaleidoscope (1957)
Bye Bye Birdie (1960)
Medium Rare (1960, Chicago)
All American (1962)
Golden Boy (1964)
It's a Bird, It's a Plane, It's Superman (1966)
Applause (1970)
Six (1971, off-Broadway) *
I and Albert (1972, London)
Charlotte's Web (1973) *
Annie (1977) **
A Broadway Musical (1978)
Charlie and Algernon (1979 London, 1981 Broadway) ***
Bring Back Birdie (1981)
Nightingale (1982, London)
Dance a Little Closer (1983) †
Mayor (1985) *

Rags (1986) ††
Annie 2: Miss Hannigan's Revenge (1989, off-Broadway) ***
Bojangles (1993, Barksdale Theatre, Richmond, VA) ****
Nick and Nora (1993) †††
Annie Warbucks (1993, off-Broadway)
An American Tragedy (1995)
Alexander and the Terrible, Horrible, No Good, Very Bad Day (1998, Kennedy Center)
Marty (2002, Huntington Theatre, Boston, MA)
The Future of the American Musical Theatre (2004, opera)
Real Men (2005, Coconut Grove Playhouse, Miami, FL) *
Studio (2006)

Minsky's (2009, Ahmanson
   Theatre, Los Angeles,
   CA) ††††
Dancing With Time (in
   development) *

Marjorie Morningstar (in
   development)
North and South (in
   development) †††
The Truth About Cinderella (in
   development) * * *

Lyrics by Lee Adams
   unless noted
* Lyrics by Charles Strouse
* * Lyrics by Martin Charnin
* * * Lyrics by David Rogers
* * * * Lyrics by Sammy Cahn

† Lyrics by Alan Jay Lerner
†† Lyrics by Stephen Schwartz
††† Lyrics by Richard
   Maltby Jr.
†††† Lyrics by Susan
   Birkenhead

Strouse's film and television works include:

Bye Bye Birdie (1963, movie
   version)
Alice in Wonderland (What's
   A Nice Girl Like You
   Doing in a Place Like
   This?) (1966)
Bonnie and Clyde (1967)
The Night They Raided
   Minsky's (1968)
All In the Family (1971–1979,
   television theme song)
Just Tell Me What You
   Want (1980)
Annie (1982, movie version)
Lyle, Lyle, Crocodile (1984)

All Dogs Go to Heaven
   (1980)
Alexander and the Terrible,
   Horrible, No Good, Very
   Bad Day (1990, animated
   television musical)
A Children's Garden of Verses
   (1992, television musical)
Bye Bye Birdie (1995, television
   version)
Annie (1999, television version)
Sherlock Holmes and the Case
   of the Missing Santa Claus
   (unproduced television
   musical)

Strouse's songs meld smart and dramatically effective with bright
and brassy – what one thinks of as quintessentially "Broadway style"
songs. Strouse's lesser-known shows contain a wealth of wonderful
material. Most of these songs are unknown because they are so closely
integrated with character and plot. But many could stand on their own
and offer the singer looking for great "Broadway style" songs material
that is well written both musically and dramatically. The well-known
songs and lesser-known songs that might be of interest include:

The Littlest Show
I Lost The Rhythm (bari-tenor)

Bye Bye Birdie (1960) (Albert Peterson, baritone; Rose Grant, mezzo-soprano; Kim Macafee, soprano; Conrad Birdie, baritone)

How Lovely to be a Woman **	A Lot of Livin' to Do ††
Put on a Happy Face ††	Kids ††
One Boy **	Baby, Talk to Me ††
One Last Kiss ††	Rosie ††

Golden Boy (1964) (Joe Wellington, tenor; Eddie Satin, baritone; Lorna Moon, mezzo-soprano; Ronnie, baritone)

Night Song †	While the City Sleeps ††
Stick Around †	I Want to Be With You †
Lorna's Here *	

It's a Bird, It's a Plane, It's Superman (1966) (Superman/Clark Kent, baritone; Max Mencken, baritone; Lois Lane, mezzo-soprano; Dr. Abner Sedgewick, baritone; Sydney, mezzo-soprano)

We Don't Matter at All **	What I've Always Wanted **
Revenge ††	The Strongest Man in the
The Woman for the Man††	World ††
You've Got Possibilities **	Ooh, Do You Love You! **

Applause (1970) (Margo Channing, alto; Eve Harrington, mezzo-soprano; Bonnie, mezzo-soprano; Bill Sampson, baritone)

The Best Night of My Life **	Welcome to the Theatre **
Who's That Girl? **	One Hallowe'en **
Hurry Back **	Something Greater **

Annie (1977) (Daddy Warbucks, baritone; Grace Farrell, soprano; Annie, mezzo-soprano; Miss Hannigan, alto; Rooster Hannigan, tenor; Lily St. Regis, mezzo-soprano)

Maybe **
The Hard Knock Life **
Tomorrow **
Little Girls **
Easy Street **/†

You're Never Fully Dressed
Without a Smile †
Something Was Missing ††
I Don't Need Anything but
You ††/**

Rags (1986) (Rebecca Hershkowitz, soprano; Saul, baritone; Bella Cohen, mezzo-soprano; Nathan Hershkowitz, baritone; Ben, tenor)

Blame It on the Summer
Night *
Brand New World *
Children of the Wind *
Easy For You ††
For My Mary †

I Remember *
Rags *
The Sounds of Love †
Three Sunny Rooms **
Wanting *

Biography

Born and raised on West 70th Street in New York, Charles Strouse is known more than anything for the sunny optimism of his songs. He grew up as a "pudgy adolescent spending an inordinate amount of energy trying to make his clinically depressed mother happy. 'I was dedicated to making her feel better, to make her smile.' [Ultimately, his] music became his means of putting a happy face on millions."[5]

Unusually talented and precociously smart, he began college at the Eastman School of Music at the age of 15. At the age of 18 he won two scholarships, allowing him to study composition, first with Aaron Copland at Tanglewood and later with Nadia Boulanger in Paris. A list of Boulanger's students reads like a "Who's Who" of twentieth-century serious composers, including: Daniel Barenboim, Robert Russell Bennett, Leonard Bernstein, Marc Blitzstein, Aaron Copland, Philip Glass, Quincy Jones, Michel Legrand, Gian Carlo Menotti, Walter Piston and Virgil Thomson. Following his Paris studies, he returned to the US, where he resumed his studies with Copland.

A chance meeting with lyricist Lee Adams at a party in 1949 began a long collaboration. They began contributing material to revues at the Green Mansions summer resort, special material for Kaye Ballard, Carol Burnett, Jane Morgan and Dick Shawn, and

Broadway revues *Shoestring Revue* (1955), *Shoestring '57* (1956), *The Littlest Revue* (1956) and *Kaleidoscope* (1957). In 1958 Adams and Strouse were paid $100 per week to write the score for *Bye Bye Birdie*, the show for which they won their first Tony Award.

Strouse has never stopped writing musicals to this day, many with Adams. While *Bye Bye Birdie* and *Annie* were massive hits and *Applause* and *Golden Boy* were moderate successes, many of his shows closed very quickly. *Charlie and Algernon* ran for 17 performances, *Bring Back Birdie* ran for four performances, and *Rags* ran for four performances. Despite these failures, the level of Strouse's writing is consistently high, and his less successful shows contain some wonderful material waiting to be discovered by the enterprising singer.

In addition to Strouse's writing, he has been very active helping to train the next generation of musical theatre writers. In 1977, he founded the ASCAP Musical Theatre Workshop in New York, in which generations of aspiring musical theatre writers have developed their material and honed their craft.

Resources

Charles Strouse's autobiography *Put On a Happy Face: A Broadway Memoir*[6] was published in 2008.

Tom Jones (b. 1928) and Harvey Schmidt (b. 1929): Mythic and experimental

Stylistic approach

Lyricist Tom Jones and composer Harvey Schmidt's material is adventurous and spare. Schmidt favors an expansive sound frequently using open fourths or fifths, or other open chord voicing. Schmidt's harmonizations and accompaniments lean heavily on the added tones of jazz chords, ninths, elevenths, thirteenths of various kinds. Creating musical tension, he sustains dissonances longer than other composers before finally resolving them. Jones' lyrics are highly poetic, metaphoric, filled with imagery of nature, the seasons and time – winter versus summer, age versus youth. The sense of ritual is strong in their musicals, giving them a Greek theatre feeling.

Their songs are essential, simple. The more that a singer can respect and honor that simplicity, the more successful the rendition will be. That being said, their material has been performed by all manner of singers. For instance, popular singers, jazz singers, country singers, folk groups, rock artists, reggae singers and more have recorded "Try to Remember." Greek singer Nana Mouskouri recorded it in three languages (German, French and Italian). There are some country sounds in Schmidt's music; Schmidt also tips his hat to jazz in his harmonies and some of his extended dissonances. But singers are strongly urged to avoid going too far towards country or jazz stylings.

Body of work

Jones and Schmidt's shows include:

Shoestring '57 (1957)	*The Bone Room* (1969)
Demi-Dozen (1958)	*Colette* (1970)
The Fantasticks (1960)	*Philemon* (1973)
New York Scrapbook (television special 1961)	*Colette Collage* (1982)
	Grover's Corners (1987)
110 in the Shade (1963)	*Mirette* (1996)
I Do! I Do! (1966)	*Roadside* (2001)
Celebration (1969)	

Their better known songs and songs that might be of interest include:

The Fantasticks (1960) (Matt, baritone; Louisa, soprano; Huckleby, baritone; Bellamy, baritone; El Gallo, baritone)

Try to Remember ††	Soon It's Gonna Rain */††
Much More *	I Can See It ††
Metaphor ††	Plant a Radish ††
Never Say No ††	They Were You */††

110 in the Shade (1963) (Lizzy Curry, mezzo-soprano; Bill Starbuck, baritone; File, baritone; Snookie Updegraff, mezzo-soprano)

A Man and a Woman	Is It Really Me? **
Everything Beautiful Happens at Night	Little Red Hat **
	Love Don't Turn Away **

A Man and a Woman **/††   Rain Song ††
Melisande ††   Raunchy **
Old Maid **   Simple Little Things **

I Do! I Do! (1966) (Agnes, mezzo-soprano; Michael, baritone)

Together Forever ††/**   The Honeymoon is Over ††/**
I Love My Wife ††   Where are the Snows? ††/**
My Cup Runneth Over ††   What Is a Woman? **
Flaming Agnes **

Celebration (1969) (Angel, mezzo-soprano; Mr. Rich, baritone;
   Orphan, tenor; Potemkin, baritone)

Orphan in the Storm ††   I'm Glad to See You Got What
Somebody **   You Want **/†
Where Did It Go ††   Fifty Million Years Ago ††
Love Song **/†   Under the Tree **

Philemon (1973) (Cockian, tenor; Marcus, baritone; Kiki, soprano)

I'd Do Almost Anything to   I Love Order ††
   Get Out of Here †   I Love His Face *

Colette Collage (1982) (Collette, soprano; Willy, baritone; Maurice,
   tenor)

Claudine *   The Room is Filled with You *
La Vagabonde *   Growing Older *
Decorate the Human Face *

Biography

Lyricist and librettist Tom Jones was born in Littlefield, Texas, and composer Harvey Schmidt was born in Dallas, Texas. They met as undergraduates at the University of Texas where they began collaborating. They continued collaborating during their time in the Army, stationed across the country from each other. After the Army they moved to New York, Schmidt to pursue a career as a graphic artist, and Jones to take a job working in a bookstore and teaching a drama group. Their songs began being used in various revues, including Julius Monk's *Upstairs at the Downstairs* and the *Shoestring Revue*.

In 1959 a friend from college, director Word Baker, was hired to direct three one-act plays for a summer theatre at Barnard College. He asked Jones and Schmidt if they could revise a piece that they had been working on as a one-act musical and get it done in three weeks. Tom Jones has said they figured it was never going to reach the stage anyway, "so we did all the things we liked in the theatre – all the presentation things, the *commedia dell'arte*, the Shakespeare, the Oriental theatre, the invisible prop man sprinkling snow – everything that used the imagination, a celebration of theatricality. [...] It took eight months to raise the $15,000 that it took to put on the show."[7] That piece, ultimately expanded to two acts, became *The Fantasticks*, Jones and Schmidt's biggest hit and the longest running show ever, ultimately running over 17,000 performances in the 42 years of its original off-Broadway production.

With the longest run in the history of the American theatre, *The Fantasticks* gave Jones and Schmidt a secure enough source of income to write only what they wanted to write. In 1969, they opened the Portfolio Studio, which they used as a workshop to develop small-scale musicals in new forms and styles such as primal theatre. These included *Celebration*, *Philemon* and *The Bone Room*.

Jones and Schmidt's output of shows is smaller than the others examined in this chapter, but their work is important, especially as their work was so experimental. They continually pushed the envelope. For many of their shows they have written substantially more songs for each show, and then cut and replaced as the show developed. This is why there are so many cut songs, many of which are of exceptionally high quality.

Resources

There is very little biographical material available on Tom Jones and Harvey Schmidt.

Jerry Bock (1928–2010) and Sheldon Harnick (b 1924): Intensely act-able

Stylistic approach

Bock and Harnick's songs are extremely act-able; they tend to be perfect little musical scenes or character studies in musical monologue form. They are not driven by emotion like Jerry Herman's songs, although they are certainly informed by the characters' emotions. Written not only for specific characters but also the specific actors who created those characters, their songs have varying vocal requirements. "Ice Cream" from *She Loves Me* was written for Barbara Cook and calls for melding exceptional soprano vocal technique and acting. "Far from the Home I Love" from *Fiddler on the Roof* was written for the young soprano Julia Migenes and also provides the challenge of combining strong vocal technique, an excellent sense of musical line and strong acting choices. These songs call for legitimate singing, for big Broadway voices. Other of their songs have less rigorous vocal requirements, but every song in their canon is an actor's song.

Some writers' songs are difficult to learn, but not Bock and Harnick's. Even their longer story-songs like "I Love a Cop" or "A Trip to the Library" make so much sense in their trajectory and storytelling, that they are relatively easily memorized. Bock melodies lay well in the voice and make musical as well as dramatic sense. Harnick's lyrics are clever, literate and witty – in some ways he is an artistic descendant of E.Y. "Yip" Harburg – but the cleverness manages to draw attention to the character who is singing, not the lyricist. A song like "A Trip to the Library" pulls the listener into the story and the character. The clever rhymes and double-meanings are written to feel natural and inevitable. In addition to their wit and literacy, Bock and Harnick's songs speak directly to the heart. A song like "Far from the Home I Love," "Sunrise, Sunset" or "When Did I Fall in Love" are emotionally compelling without becoming indulgent.

Body of work

Bock and Harnick's theatre scores include:[8]

The Body Beautiful (1958)	*She Loves Me* (1963)
Fiorello! (1959)	*Fiddler on the Roof* (1964)
Tenderloin (1960)	*The Apple Tree* (1966)
Man in the Moon (1963)	*The Rothschilds* (1970)

Harnick's theatre scores without Bock include:

Leonard Sillman's New Faces of 1952 (1952) *	*Two's Company* (1952) *
	The Littlest Revue (1956) *

Portofino (1958) *
Vintage '60 (1960) **
Pinnochio (1973) ***
Rex (1976) ****
The Umbrellas of Cherbourg
  (1979) †

Sutter's Gold (1980) ††
A Christmas Carol (1981) †
Dragons (1984) *
A Wonderful Life (1986) ††
Cyrano – The Musical
  (1993) †††

* Music by Sheldon Harnick
** Music by David Baker
*** Music by Mary Rodgers
**** Music by Richard Rogers

†Music by Michel Legrand
†† Music by Joe Raposo
††† Music by Ad Van Dijk

Harnick has also written the operas *Captain Jinx of the Horse Marines* (1975), *Love in Two Countries* (1991) and *The Phantom Tollbooth* (1995) and provided translations for classical operas including *The Merry Widow* (1977), *The Umbrellas of Cherbourg* (1979), *Carmen* (1981) and *La Tragedie De Carmen* (1984).

Bock and Harnick's most well-known songs and lesser known songs that are worth a listen include:

Fiorello! (1959) (Fiorello LaGuardia, tenor; Maria Fischer, mezzo-soprano; Thea LaGuardia, soprano; Dora, alto

Marie's Law *
When Did I Fall In Love *
Gentleman Jimmy **

The Very Next Man *
I Love a Cop **

Tenderloin (1960) (Reverend Brock, baritone; Tommy Howatt, baritone; Laura, soprano; Nita, mezzo-soprano)

Artificial Flowers ††
Tommy, Tommy *

My Gentle Young Johnny **

She Loves Me (1963) (Georg Nowack, baritone; Amalia Balash, soprano; Arpad Laszlo, baritone; Ilona Ritter, mezzo-soprano; Steven Kodaly, tenor)

Days Gone By ††
Tonight At Eight ††
Will He Like Me? *

Ilona †
Romantic Atmosphere *
Dear Friend *

Try Me ††   A Trip to the Library **
Ice Cream *   Grand Knowing You †
She Loves Me ††

Fiddler on the Roof (1964) (Tevye, baritone; Golde, mezzo-soprano;
   Tzeitel, mezzo-soprano; Hodel, soprano; Motel, tenor)

Matchmaker **   Sunrise, Sunset ††/**
If I Were a Rich Man ††   Do You Love Me? ††/**
To Life ††   Far from the Home I Love *
Miracle of Miracles †

The Apple Tree (1966) (Adam/Sanjar/Flip, tenor; Eve/Barbara/Ella,
   mezzo-soprano; Snake/Balladeer/Narrator, baritone)

Feelings **   What Makes Me Love Him **
Friends **   I've Got What You Want **
It's a Fish †   Tiger, Tiger **
Go to Sleep, Whoever   Oh, To Be a Movie Star **
   You Are **   Gorgeous **

The Rothschilds (1970) (Mayer Rothschild, baritone; Nathan
   Rothschild, baritone; Hannah Cohen, mezzo-soprano)

He Tossed a Coin ††   I'm In Love! I'm In Love! ††
Sons ††   In My Own Lifetime ††

Biography

Born in New Haven, Connecticut and raised in Flushing, Queens,
New York, composer Jerry Bock attended the University of
Wisconsin at Madison, where he met and began a collabora-
tion with Larry Holofcener. Together they wrote a musical *Big
As Life,* about Paul Bunyan, and spent their summers writing at
the Tamiment Playhouse in the Pocono Mountains. After college
Bock and Holofcener wrote songs for Sid Caesar's *Your Show of
Shows,* contributed three songs to the Broadway revue, *Catch
a Star,* and wrote the score to the Sammy Davis Jr. vehicle, *Mr.
Wonderful.* Bock and lyricist Harnick began working together
two years later.

Sheldon Harnick was born and raised in Chicago and was a violin major at Northwestern University. During his college years Harnick also honed his skills writing comedy sketches, songs and parody lyrics, and ultimately decided to test the waters in New York. He contributed songs to many Broadway revues, including *New Faces of 1952, John Murray Anderson's Almanac, The Shoestring Revue* and *The Littlest Revue.*

Bock and Harnick began writing together beginning with 1958's *The Body Beautiful.* Bock and Harnick won the Best Musical Tony Award and the Pulitzer Prize for *Fiorello!,* their second musical, and changed musical theatre with their longest-running show, *Fiddler on the Roof,* which also won many Tony Awards. Together they wrote eight musicals until the strain of working on *The Rothschilds* drove a wedge between them. They went their separate ways – Bock went into semi-retirement, and Harnick has continued to work through the rest of his life with a range of collaborators, never finding the success he found with Bock.

Resources

Phillip Lambert's dual biography of Bock and Harnick, *To Broadway, To Life!: The Musical Theater of Bock and Harnick,*[9] was published in 2010.

Cy Coleman (1929–2004): Eclectic scores rooted in jazz

Stylistic approach

Cy Coleman's songs are fun to sing – they are jazzy, sexy and they swing. His sense of harmony is impeccable, and his music is deeply rooted in jazz. His stylistic range is wide. He has written in styles from operetta to R&B, but no matter the style, every Coleman score is infused with various forms of jazz, from different periods.

Coleman's first two shows were written to service stars. In *Wildcat,* which offered a fairly standard "Broadway" sound, he successfully created a score for the non-singing television star Lucille Ball. *Little Me* featured another television star, Sid Caesar, as the seven different men in the life of the fictitious Belle Poitrine. Coleman's score offered a diverse array of styles including straight-ahead Broadway belt numbers, mock-operetta, French chanson, country two-step, swingy jazz tunes, to underscore Caesar's character differences.

Bob Fosse, who had choreographed *Little Me*, conceived, directed and choreographed *Sweet Charity*, the show with which Coleman came into his own. Although Coleman's score was not praised when the show opened, it has become a classic. It includes "Big Spender," "If My Friends Could See Me Now," "I'm a Brass Band" and "Where Am I Going." *Sweet Charity* is highly jazz infused – sexy and fun. In *Charity*, the jazz is in the accompaniment, not the vocal line. The singing is traditional Broadway belting, but Ralph Burns' orchestration makes it all feel like jazz. Coleman excels and seems to feel very at home in this "Broadway jazz," a style that served as the basis for both *Seesaw* and *I Love My Wife*. *Seesaw* even included some contemporary rock and Latin rhythms, and *I Love My Wife* replaced the pit orchestra with an onstage jazz quartet, who also played all of the smaller acting roles.

In his next two shows, Coleman explored new sounds. *On the Twentieth Century* is an operetta, an extension of the show's hyperbolic acting style. *Barnum* uses circus music, early ragtime, and other musical styles of the late 1800s. With his next show, the failed *Welcome to the Club*, Coleman returned to his jazz roots, where he remained for the rest of his career. Even the country-tinged *The Will Rogers Follies* included "No Man Left for Me" and other jazz-infused songs.

Columnist Roger Whitaker articulates the feeling of braggadocio and swagger present in so much of Coleman's music, "Pepper and salt and Tabasco sauce are the customary ingredients of a Coleman ballad ... whether the words that go with these songs are the effect of the Coleman music or whether it is the other way round doesn't matter; the end product is the entertaining spectacle of the American swain bragging about his magnificence to his damsel and then conceding that perhaps she is just as smart as he is."[10]

Coleman's songs stand up extremely well to jazz, rock and gospel stylings. The noir musical *City of Angels* features great jazz ballads "With Every Breath I Take" and "Lost and Found," and up-tempo numbers like "You Can Always Count on Me," an updated version of "Nobody Does It Like Me" from *Seesaw*. His final show, *The Life*, was his most contemporary, employing a range of rock, R&B and gospel styles.

Music notation can record a melody, but all of the highly individualized choices that we call style cannot be notated; they have to be applied singer by singer, and listening to what has been done before is the best place to start forming your own interpretation or sense of style. Coleman's inherent sense of fun makes his songs an invaluable resource for the singer looking for a song in almost any jazz style. For a great sense of Coleman's facility with jazz, listen to the "Overture" from *City of Angels*, which features a four-singer scat ensemble. Also from *City of Angels*, listen to Kay McClelland's "With Every Breath I Take." Or Rachel York's "Lost and Found." Among some of the many great jazz performances of Coleman songs are Sammy Davis Jr. as Big Daddy, singing "The Rhythm of Life," Sam Harris singing "Use What You Got" and Lillias White singing "The Oldest Profession," both from *The Life*.

Body of work

Coleman is known primarily for his theatre scores, although his early successes were with popular individual songs. Both male and female recording artists have recorded these songs in a variety of keys. While many of his popular songs may have passed on to obscurity, among those that remain popular are:

The Best Is Yet to Come *	She's Too Hip to Be
Firefly *	Happy ***
I'm Gonna Laugh You Out of	When in Rome (I Do as the
My Life **	Romans Do) *
It Amazes Me *	Why Try to Change
Pass Me By *	Me Now **
The Riviera **	Witchcraft *
The Rules of the Road *	You Fascinate Me So *

* Lyrics by Carolyn Leigh
** Lyrics by Joe McCarthy
*** Lyrics by Peggy Lee

Coleman's theatre scores each have their own unique sound. Although his jazz background is always present, there is great range to his theatre scores. These include:

Wildcat (1960)*	*Sweet Charity* (1966) **
Little Me (1962)*	*Seesaw* (1973) **

I Love My Wife (1977) * * *
On the Twentieth Century
   (1978) * * * *
Barnum (1980) * * *.
Welcome to the Club (1989) †

City of Angels (1989) ††
The Will Rogers Follies
   (1991) * * * *
The Life (1997) †††

* Lyrics by Carolyn Leigh
* * Lyrics by Dorothy Fields
* * * Lyrics by Michael Stewart
* * * * Lyrics by Betty Comden
   and Adolph Green

† Lyrics by Cy Coleman and
   A.E. Hotchner
†† Lyrics by David Zippel
††† Lyrics by Ira Gasman

Coleman's theatre songs that are worth exploring include:

Wildcat (1960) (Wildcat Jackson, alto; Joe Dynamite, baritone; Janie Jackson, mezzo-soprano)

Hey, Look Me Over * *

Little Me (1962) (Noble Eggleston/Mr. Pinchley/Val du Val/Fred Poitrine/Otto Schnitzler/Prince Cherney/Noble Junior, baritone; Older Belle, mezzo-soprano; Younger Belle, mezzo-soprano)

The Other Side of the
   Tracks * *
Dimples * *
Boom-Boom ††

Real Live Girl ††
Poor Little Hollywood
   Star * *
I've Got Your Number ††

Sweet Charity (1966) (Charity Hope Valentine, mezzo-soprano; Vittorio Vidal, baritone; Nikki, mezzo-soprano; Helene, mezzo-soprano; Oscar Lindquist, baritone; Daddy Johann Sebastian Brubeck, baritone; Herman, tenor)

Big Spender * *
If My Friends Could See Me
   Now * *
Too Many Tomorrows ††

I Love to Cry at Weddings †
Where Am I Going * *
I'm a Brass Band * *

Seesaw (1973) (Gittel Mosca, mezzo-soprano; Jerry Ryan, baritone; David, baritone)

Nobody Does It Like Me ** 　　Poor Everybody Else **
Welcome to Holiday Inn ** 　　It's Not Where You Start, It's
He's Good for Me ** 　　　　　Where You Finish ††

I Love My Wife (1977) (Alvin, baritone; Wally, baritone; Cleo, mezzo-soprano; Monica, mezzo-soprano)

Love Revolution ** 　　　　　Hey There Good Times ††
Someone Wonderful 　　　　　Lovers on Christmas Eve ††
I Missed ** 　　　　　　　　　I Love My Wife ††

On The Twentieth Century (1978) (Lily Garland, soprano; Oscar Jaffe, baritone; Bruce Granit, tenor; Letitia Primrose, mezzo-soprano)

I Rise Again †† 　　　　　　　Babette *
Our Private World †† 　　　　　Repent **
Never * 　　　　　　　　　　　The Legacy ††

Barnum (1980) (Phineas Taylor Barnum, baritone; Charity Barnum, mezzo-soprano; Joyce Heth, alto; Tom Thumb, tenor; Jenny Lind, soprano)

There Is a Sucker Born Every 　Bigger Isn't Better †
　Minute †† 　　　　　　　　Love Makes Such Fools of
Thank God I'm Old ** 　　　　　Us All *
The Colors of My Life ††/** 　Out There ††
Museum Song †† 　　　　　　The Prince of Humbug ††
I Like Your Style ††/**

City of Angels (1989) (Stine, baritone; Stone, baritone; Buddy Fidler, baritone; Jimmy Powers, tenor; Oolie/Donna, mezzo-soprano; Alaura Kingsley/Carla Haywood, mezzo-soprano; Bobby, mezzo-soprano)

What You Don't Know About 　You Can Always Count
　Women ** 　　　　　　　　on Me **
With Every Breath I Take ** 　It Needs Work **
Lost and Found ** 　　　　　　Funny ††
You're Nothing Without Me †† 　I'm Nothing Without You ††

The Will Rogers Follies (1990) (Will Rogers, baritone; Betty Blake, mezzo-soprano; Clem Rogers, baritone)

Never Met a Man I Didn't   Look Around ††
     Like ††   No Man Left For Me **
Give a Man Enough Rope ††

The Life (1997) (Jojo, tenor; Sonja, mezzo-soprano; Memphis, baritone; Queen, mezzo-soprano)

Use What You Got †
The Oldest Profession **
Don't Take Too Much ††
He's No Good **
I'm Leaving You **
My Friend **

Biography

Born Seymour Kaufman, Coleman was raised in the Bronx, New York. He began playing piano at the age of four, on a piano abandoned by deadbeat tenants of his parents. A child prodigy, Coleman was giving piano recitals at Steinway Hall, Town Hall and Carnegie Hall from the age of six. After studying composition, conducting and orchestration at New York City's High School of the Performing Arts, Coleman abandoned the classical world to become a jazz musician. He found great success in nightclubs and recordings with his jazz ensemble, the Cy Coleman Trio.

By the 1950s he was composing jazz standards, which were recorded by artists like Mabel Mercer, Nat "King" Cole, and Frank Sinatra. These included such popular standards as "Witchcraft," "Firefly" and "The Best is Yet to Come." Coleman's solid classical grounding brought surety to his jazz and popular compositions. One can hear in Coleman's music a sense of swaggering machismo, which made them perfect for singers like Tony Bennett, Dean Martin and Frank Sinatra. In fact, Coleman wrote the theme to *Playboy After Dark*, a 1960s television show produced by Hugh Hefner.

His great early collaboration was with lyricist Carolyn Leigh, with whom he transitioned into musical theatre, writing his first two shows, *Wildcat* and *Little Me*. After Coleman and Leigh parted ways, Coleman joined forces with Dorothy Fields, twenty-four years his senior, to write *Sweet Charity* and *Seesaw*.

Resources

While there are no biographies devoted to the life of Cy Coleman, he is referenced in most books about the Broadway musicals of the latter half of the twentieth century, and the biographies of Bob Fosse.

John Kander (b. 1927) and Fred Ebb (1928–2004): Moving the musical theatre forward

Stylistic approach

John Kander and Fred Ebb were more instrumental in moving the musical forward than any of the other writers of the 1960s. *Flora, The Red Menace*, their first show, was relatively traditional. But by their second show, *Cabaret*, their writing was highly experimental. Half of the songs in *Cabaret* were traditional book songs while the ones that took place in the Kit Kat Klub reflected and commented on the main action.

Kander and Ebb are smart writers who pull from many different styles. A singer who is looking to perform their material would be well advised to start with an understanding of what style they are referencing or evoking. One of their favorite sources is American entertainment from the nineteenth and early twentieth century. They used the structures and vocabulary of minstrel shows to create *The Scottsboro Boys*, the vocabulary of the great vaudeville entertainers in *Chicago*. They reference the sounds of Kurt Weill in *Cabaret*, and the songs of the Depression in *Steel Pier*. The score of *The Act* is written in the style of a Las Vegas nightclub act, whose songs reflect the life of the act's star, Michelle Craig. Their knowledge of these styles is deep; the songs in *Chicago*, for instance, are based on the songs of the great vaudeville entertainers, vaudeville being the central metaphor of the show. Amos Hart is based on Bert Williams, and his song "Mr. Cellophane" is based directly on Bert Williams' signature song "Nobody." Matron "Mama" Morton is based on Sophie Tucker, and so on.

Two of Kander and Ebb's muses are Chita Rivera and Liza Minnelli, two strong performers with big Broadway belt voices. They are also both known for playing theatrically large characters who are fully fleshed; an ability to play that size is helpful in performing Kander and Ebbs songs. One sees these qualities in many of the other actors who have created roles in Kander and Ebb musicals including Joel Grey, Robert Goulet, Gwen Verdon, Lauren Bacall, Karen Ziemba and Debra Monk – all have great theatrical size and powerful vocal instruments. Listen to these singers singing the music of Kander and Ebb to start developing a sense of the range of styles one could reasonably apply to their songs.

Body of work

Kander and Ebb's musicals include:

Flora, The Red Menace (1965)	*Kiss of the*
Cabaret (1966)	*Spiderwoman* (1992)
The Happy Time (1968)	*Steel Pier* (1997)
Zorba (1968)	*Over and Over* (a.k.a. *All*
70, Girls, 70 (1971)	*About Us*, a.k.a. *The Skin*
Chicago (1975)	*of Our Teeth*, 1999)
The Act (1978)	*The Visit* (2001)
Woman of the Year (1981)	*Curtains* (2006)
The Rink (1984)	*The Scottsboro Boys* (2010)

In addition to the film versions of *Cabaret* and *Chicago*, they wrote the scores to two movie musicals, the sequel to *Funny Girl*, titled *Funny Lady*, (1975) and *New York, New York* (1977).

Some of the more familiar songs and some that are less familiar but well worth a look include:

Flora, The Red Menace (1965) (Flora Meszaros, mezzo-soprano; Harry Toukarian, baritone)

All I Need Is One Good Break **	Dear Love **
A Quiet Thing **	Sing Happy **

Cabaret (1966) (Sally Bowles, mezzo-soprano; Emcee, tenor; Cliff Bradshaw, baritone; Fraulein Schneider, alto; Herr Schultz, baritone)

Wilkommen †	Why Should I Wake Up ††
Don't Tell Mama **	The Money Song †

If You Could See Her †   Mein Herr * *
What Would You Do? * *   Maybe This Time * *
Cabaret * *

The Happy Time (1968) (Jacques Bonnard, baritone; Grandpere
Bonnard, baritone; Bibi Bonnard, baritone)

I Don't Remember You ††   Seeing Things ††
Walking Among My   The Happy Time ††
  Yesterdays ††

Zorba (1968) (Zorba, baritone; Mikos, tenor; The Widow, mezzo-
soprano; Mme. Hortense; mezzo-soprano; Leader, alto)

The Butterfly * *   Why Can't I Speak * *
Only Love * *

70, Girls, 70 (1971) (Ida Dodd, mezzo-soprano; Walter, baritone;
Eunice, mezzo-soprano)

Broadway, My Street * *   The Elephant Song * *
Coffee in a Cardboard Cup * *   Yes * *
Go Visit Your Grandmother †

Chicago (1975) (Roxie Hart, mezzo-soprano; Velma Kelly, alto;
Amos Hart, baritone; Billy Flynn, baritone; Matron "Mama"
Morton, alto; Mary Sunshine, countertenor)

All That Jazz * *   I Can't Do It Alone * *
All I Care About ††   My Own Best Friend * *
A Little Bit of Good †   Me and My Baby * *
Razzle Dazzle ††   Mr. Cellophane ††
When You're Good to   Class * *
  Mama * *   Nowadays * *
Roxie * *

The Act (1978) (Michelle Craig, mezzo-soprano)

It's the Strangest Thing * *   Arthur in the Afternoon * *
Bobo's * *   The Money Tree * *

City Lights ** 　　　　　　 My Own Space **
There When I Need Him **

Woman of the Year (1981) (Tess Harding, alto; Sam Craig, baritone;
Jan Donovan, alto)

See You in the Funny Papers ††　　 The Grass Is Always
One of the Boys ** 　　　　　　　　　 Greener **
I Wrote the Book** 　　　　　　　 We're Gonna Work It
Sometimes a Day Goes By †† 　　　　 Out ††/**

The Rink (1984) (Angel, mezzo-soprano; Anna, mezzo-soprano;
Dino, tenor; Lenny, baritone)

Colored Lights ** 　　　　　　　　 We Can Make It **
Chief Cook and Bottle 　　　　　　 The Apple Doesn't Fall **
　　 Washer ** 　　　　　　　　　　 Marry Me ††
Blue Crystals † 　　　　　　　　　 Wallflower **

Kiss of the Spider Woman (1992) (Molina, tenor; Valentin, baritone; Spiderwoman, mezzo-soprano)

Dressing Them Up † 　　　　　　　 She's a Woman ††
Dear One ** 　　　　　　　　　　 Gimme Love **
Marta † 　　　　　　　　　　　　 Kiss of the Spider Woman **

Steel Pier (1997) (Mick Hamilton, baritone; Bill Kelly, baritone;
Rita Racine, mezzo-soprano; Shelby Stevens, mezzo-soprano;
Precious McGuire, soprano)

Willing to Ride ** 　　　　　　　 Lovebird **
Second Chance ††/** 　　　　　　 Somebody Older **
Everybody's Girl ** 　　　　　　 Running in Place **
Wet ††/**

Curtains (2006) (Lieutenany Frank Cloffi, baritone; Niki Harris,
soprano; Aaron Fox, baritone; Georgia Hendricks, mezzo-
soprano; Carmen Bernstein, alto; Bobby Pepper, baritone)

Thinking of Him ** 　　　　　　　 I Miss The Music **
Coffee Shop Nights ††

The Scottsboro Boys (2010) (Interlocutor/Judge/Governor/Bus Driver, baritone; Haywood Patterson, baritone; Mr. Bones/ Sheriff Bones/Lawyer Bones/Guard Bones/ Attorney General/ Clerk, baritone; Mr. Tambo/Deputy Tambo/Lawyer Tambo/ Guard Tambo/Samuel Leibowitz, baritone)

Nuthin' ††
Commencing in Chattanooga ††
Alabama Ladies ††
Go Back Home ††
Shout ††
Make Friends with the Truth ††
Never Too Late ††Financial Advice ††
It's Gonna Take Time ††

Biography

Composer John Kander was born and raised in Kansas City Missouri, in a house filled with music. He received his Bachelors degree from Oberlin College in 1951 and a Master of Arts degree from Columbia University in 1954. After seeing a pre-Broadway performance of *West Side Story* in Philadelphia, he ran into the show's pianist, who asked Kander to substitute for him when he went on vacation. *West Side Story*'s stage manager asked Kander to play the auditions for her next show, *Gypsy*. At the auditions, Kander met Jerome Robbins, who asked Kander to write the dance music for *Gypsy*. Kander's first Broadway musical as composer was *A Family Affair*, a flop which ran for only 65 performances.

Fred Ebb was born and raised in New York, in a home where music was very seldom played. After holding a range of jobs, including baby-shoe bronzer, credit office clerk and trucker's assistant, he received his Bachelors degree from New York University and his Masters from Columbia, both in English. Ebb began writing popular songs in the early 1950s with Phil Springer. His theatrical career began contributing lyrics to revues *Baker's Dozen* (1951), *Isn't America Fun* (1959) and *Put it in Writing* (1962). Ebb's first full book musical, *Morning Sun*, was a flop, running for only nine performances off-Broadway.

In 1962 (or 1963, depending on the source) Kander was introduced to Ebb by the music publisher, Tommy Valando. While their first musical, *Golden Gate*, never found a production, it did bring them to the attention of producer Harold Prince, who hired them to write the score for the George Abbott musical *Flora, The Red Menace*. *Flora* closed relatively quickly, but cemented the collaboration. Kander and Ebb wrote exclusively with each other from 1962 through 2004, when their collaboration was ended by Ebb's death.

Resources

Colored Lights: Forty Years of Words and Music, Show Biz, Collaboration and All That Jazz,[11] is an interview book; Greg Lawrence interviewed Kander and Ebb talking about their work and their collaboration and transcribed the sessions into this fascinating book. James Leve's *Kander and Ebb* (Yale Broadway Master Series)[12] is another very useful reference.

In summary

The songwriters examined in this chapter represent the culmination of the Golden Age of the American musical. Although each has their own unique voice, they all participate in the vocabulary of the traditional musical theatre; but more important than that is the fact that in all of their works, character and plot always come first. Herman rode the crest of the Golden Age musicals, continuing to write in that style through all of his career. Charles Strouse, Tom Jones, Harvey Schmidt and Cy Coleman used the model of the traditional musical to try to push dramaturgical boundries. Jerry Bock, Sheldon Harnick, John Kander and Fred Ebb's musicals pushed the traditional towards the concept musical in shows like *Fiddler on the Roof* and *Cabaret*.

Their songs are so deeply rooted in the characters for whom they were written that a comprehensive understanding of those characters is an important first step in preparing to perform these songs outside of that context. A deep understanding of what characters sang these songs and in what context is invaluable to the singer preparing these songs. In addition, a knowledge of the performers who originally sing these songs can be very useful. For instance, understanding that Lillias White originally sang "The Oldest Profession" in Cy Coleman's *The Life*, or that Sammy Davis Jr. sang "The Rhythm of Life" in the film version of Coleman's *Sweet Charity* gives the singer very useful information about the vocal stylization with which the composer intended these songs to be performed.

Some of these songs were written for great big glorious resonant voices, like "Walking Among My Yesterdays" from Kander and Ebb's *The Happy Time*, which was originally sung by baritone Robert Goulet; others were written with the expectation of a singing actor with a limited vocal range but strong acting skills, like Lauren Bacall's "I Wrote the Book" from Kander and Ebb's *Woman of the Year*. Look not only at the song, but the character, the story of the musical and some of the casting that has proven successful regarding the song you choose to sing from this period.

Notes

1 Jerry Herman. "Tony Awards Acceptance Speech: *La Cage Aux Folles*," Gershwin Theatre, New York, NY, June 3, 1984, www.youtube.com/watch?v=v4SGTEv1164, accessed June 12, 2014.

2 Jerry Herman, *Showtune: A Memoir by Jerry Herman*, New York, NY: Dutton, 1996.

3 Stephen Citron, *Jerry Herman, Poet of the Showtune*, New Haven, CT: Yale University Press, 2004.

4 "Shows," *Charles Strouse Website*, www.charlesstrouse.com/shows.php, accessed May 9, 2016.

5 Harry Haun, "Charles Strouse Shares the Music of His Life," *Playbill*, August 29, 2008, www.playbill.com/article/charles-strouse-shares-the-music-of-his-life-com-152893, accessed May 9, 2016.

6 Charles Strouse, *Put on a Happy Face: A Broadway Memoir*, New York, NY: Union Square Press, 2008.

7 Tom Jones interviewed by Nancy Rosati in "Spotlight on Tom Jones and Harvey Schmidt," www.talkinbroadway.com/spot/jonesschmidt1.html, accessed May 9, 2016.

8 "Shows," *Charles Strouse Website*.

9 Phillip Lambert, *To Broadway! To Life! The Musical Theatre of Bock and Harnick*, New York, NY: Oxford University Press, 2010.

10 Quoted in Christopher Hawtree, "Cy Coleman: Composer of Broadway Shows and Song Standards," *The Guardian*, November 22, 2004, www.theguardian.com/news/2004/nov/22/guardianobituaries.artsobituaries, accessed June 10, 2014.

11 Greg Lawrence, *Colored Lights: Forty Years of Words and Music Show Biz, Collaboration and All That Jazz*, London, UK, Faber & Faber, 2004.

12 James Leve, *Kander and Ebb*, Yale Broadway Masters Series, New Haven, CT: Yale University Press, 2009.

Chapter 8

Sui generis

Stephen Sondheim

Stephen Joshua Sondheim (b. 1930): *Sui Generis*

Stylistic approach

In a March 2010 article in *The Guardian*, Michael Ball asked, "Is Stephen Sondheim the Shakespeare of musical theatre?"[1] One point that Ball makes is that critical works allow Sondheim's score for *Sweeney Todd* often to overshadow his lyrics for *West Side Story* and *Gypsy*. Part of the difficulty in discussing Sondheim is that, not only is he unique unto himself as an artist, but each one of his works is unique – a genus of its own, *sui generis*.

For example, in looking for an appropriate audition song for a production of a Sondheim show, actors and singers will often look immediately towards another Sondheim show. The problem with this is that *Sweeney Todd* or *Pacific Overtures* or *Passion* have almost no stylistic commonality with *A Little Night Music* or *Sunday in the Park With George*. Each Sondheim work, it seems, is a unique and completely individual work unto itself. The connection between his scores is the brilliance with which the composer/lyricist connects character and material to the text. The intensity of Sondheim's craftsmanship, the brilliance of the intellect behind the words and music and the level of detail are what identify a Sondheim musical, rather than a particular musical or syntactic style. For that reason, each musical will be explored individually.

Taken as a whole, Sondheim's body of work comes out of the traditions of serious twentieth-century music and vaudeville. But he pulls heavily from a wide range of styles and genres as they are appropriate for each song, each character and each show. Sondheim has said that his most substantial classical influences are Rachmaninoff and Ravel. In *How Sondheim Found His Sound*, Steve Swayne catalogs Sondheim's personal musical library, going so far as to cite which recordings of certain pieces Sondheim has been said to prefer. According to Swayne, Sondheim's personal collection of recordings is weighed heavily in favor of the following:

Bartok (16)	Kodály (12)	Saint-Saëns (11)
J.S. Bach (14)	Liszt (13)	Schubert (12)
Beethoven (10)	Martinů (10)	Schumann (10)
Brahms (15)	Mendelssohn (10)	Strauss (10)
Britten (13)	Milhaud (15)	Stravinsky (17)
Chopin (18)	Mozart (11)	Tchaikovsky (12)
Copland (10)	Poulenc (13)	Vaughan
Debussy (16)	Prokofiev (18)	Williams (13)[2]
Hindemith (17)	Rachmaninoff (18)	
Ives (14)	Ravel (13)	

Swayne's book gives a full account of Sondheim's collection.

Additionally, Sondheim has shown an intimate knowledge of and passion for the great songwriters of Tin Pan Alley. He himself has admitted an affection and an indebtedness to the work of Kern, DeSylva, Brown and Henderson, and particularly Harold Arlen.

His knowledge of twentieth-century music is sprawling and includes popular, classical, theatrical and film music. Sondheim himself has said, "I was such a movie fan that I think I got into Romantic and tonal music first as opposed to classical – you know, pre-Beethoven – and as opposed to contemporary because of movies. All the movie scores were Strauss-influenced and influenced by later nineteenth-century Romanticism. I got into that kind of symphonic music, I think, unconsciously through listening to Korngold, Steiner and Waxman."[3] This intense knowledge of and affection for all of the music of the twentieth century has given Sondheim an extensive palette and helped him to find a unique musical vocabulary for each of his shows.

Body of work

Stephen Sondheim has written music and lyrics for the following works, except where other composers are indicated, in which cases he has written the lyrics.

By George (performed at the
  George School, 1946)
Phinney's Rainbow (produced
  at Williams College, 1948)
All That Glitters (performed at
  Williams College, 1949)
I Know My Love (Broadway
  play, single song, Christmas
  Carol, 1951)
Topper (wrote ten episodes of
  television show, 1953)
Saturday Night (1954, but
  unproduced until 1997)
A Mighty Man Is He (play,
  with single song, "Rag Me
  That Mendelssohn March,"
  1955)
The Girls of Summer (incidental
  music, 1956)
Take Five (off-Broadway
  revue, single song "Pour le
  Sport,"1957)
West Side Story (music by
  Leonard Bernstein, 1957)
Gypsy (music by Jule
  Styne, 1959)
Invitation to a March
  (Broadway play, incidental
  music, 1960)
The World of Jules Feiffer
  (closed out of town, one
  song and incidental music,
  "Truly Content," 1962)
*A Funny Thing Happened
  on the Way to the
  Forum* (1962)
Hot Spot (additional lyrics to
  "Don't Laugh" and "That's
  Good, That's Bad" music
  by Mary Rodgers, 1963)
Anyone Can Whistle (1964)

Do I Hear a Waltz? (music by
  Richard Rodgers, 1965)
Evening Primrose (made-for-
  television musical, 1966)
The Mad Show (off-Broadway,
  single song "The Boy
  From," 1966)
Company (1970)
Twigs (incidental music, 1971)
Follies (1971)
A Little Night Music (1973)
The Enclave (incidental
  music, 1973)
Stavisky (film score, 1974)
Candide (new/additional lyr-
  ics to music by Leonard
  Bernstein, 1974)
The Frogs (1974)
Pacific Overtures (1976)
The Seven Percent Solution
  (song, "I Never Do
  Anything Twice,"
  film, 1976)
Sweeney Todd (1979)
Reds (song, "Goodbye For
  Now," film, 1981)
Merrily We Roll Along
  (1981)
*Sunday in the Park with
  George* (1984)
Into the Woods (1987)
Assassins (1990)
Dick Tracy (film, 1990)
Passion (1994)
The Birdcage (film, 1996)
King Lear (off-Broadway, The
  Public Theatre, incidental
  music, 2007)
Bounce (2003)
Road Show (a revision of
  Bounce, 2008)

According to *The Stephen Sondheim Reference Guide*,[4] miscellaneous Sondheim songs, not connected to any theatrical or film project include:

"Birthday Prayer" (written for Leonard Bernstein)
"Christmas Island at Christmas Time" (co-written with Mary Rodgers)
"Come Over Here" (music by Jule Styne, written for Tony Bennett)
"Home Is the Place" (music by Jule Styne, recorded by Tony Bennett and Michael Feinstein)
"I Have the Funniest Feeling"
"Lenny" or "The Saga of Lenny" (new lyrics written to Kurt Weill's "The Saga of Jenny" to celebrate Leonard Bernstein's 70th birthday. Performed by Lauren Bacall, 1989)
"The Night is the Best Time of the Day" (written for Ginger Rogers' nightclub act, 1959)
"A Star is Born" (written for the birth of a friend's child, 1954)
"Ten Years Old"(co-written with Burt Shevelove, for CBS television special "The Fabulous Fifties," never used)
"The Two of You" (written for television program "Kukla, Fran and Ollie," but never used, 1952)
"You're Only as Old as You Look," (written for a friend's birthday, 1955)

In the lists of songs from Sondheim's major scores, original vocal ranges are indicated for songs when appropriate as solo audition, cabaret or concert material (see p. 10 for key to symbols). But many of these songs are available in different keys accommodating different vocal ranges, either from publishers, through independent notation software or online services such as musicnotes.com.

Saturday Night

Saturday Night was Sondheim's first show optioned for production. Sadly, the producer, Lemuel Ayers, died while still raising money for the production, so the show languished unproduced until 1997, when it was staged in London. The songs show great verbal dexterity and a sophisticated use of traditional Broadway musical comedy sounds. The singer of these songs needs to understand the style of the musical theatre classics, with occasional nods towards popular musical styles of the 1920s, the period in which the show is set.

Listen, for instance, to the pastiche song, "Love's a Bond," sung by Donald Corren, or the gently nostalgic "I Remember That," sung by Clarke Thorell and Andrea Burns on the original New York cast recording. (Artie, tenor; Bobby, baritone; Celeste, mezzo-soprano; Dino, baritone; Gene Gorman, tenor; Helen Fogel, soprano)

Saturday Night	Montana Chem
Class	So Many People */††
Delighted I'm Sure	One Wonderful Day
Love's a Bond ††	I Remember That */††
Isn't It? *	All for You *
In the Movies	That Kind of a Neighborhood
Exhibit A ††	What More Do I Need **
A Moment with You */††	

West Side Story *(music by Leonard Bernstein)*

Despite that fact that Sondheim has claimed to be embarrassed by some of the lyrics in *West Side Story*, it is one of the greatest musical theatre scores ever written. A dynamic tension has always existed between the need for the characters to be young and streetwise and the classical vocal requirements of the score. Compare the original cast recording, informed by the acting and characters, and Bernstein's 1985 recording featuring opera stars, which is superior musically but lacks so much of the dramatic urgency of the original. Sondheim has said that some of his lyrics to *West Side Story* are not his favorite. He cites "I Feel Pretty," as too clever for the character – giving Maria smart and clever triple rhymes and inner rhymes goes against the nature of the innocence and naiveté of the character. Nonetheless, this show remains one of the greatest and most popular ever produced. Vocally, Bernstein's score is divided between the legitimate singers, Tony and Maria, and the jazz singers. (Tony, tenor; Maria, soprano; Anita, mezzo-soprano, Riff, tenor)

Something's Coming †	I Feel Pretty *
Maria †	Somewhere *
Cool †	A Boy Like That/I Have a
One Hand, One Heart †/*	Love **/*
Tonight †/*	

Gypsy *(music by Jule Styne)*

Also considered one of the greatest musicals of the Golden Age of the American musical, the score of *Gypsy* musically and lyrically reflects the world of burlesque in which the story takes place. As with *Saturday Night*, the singer of these songs should be grounded in the style of the musical theatre classics, and in popular musical styles of the 1920s and 1930s. Jule Styne's music calls for big Broadway belting – this is no surprise, considering that the show was written to star the great Broadway belter Ethel Merman and that it lives in the world of vaudeville and burlesque. (Mama Rose, mezzo-soprano; Herbie, baritone; June, mezzo-soprano; Louise, mezzo-soprano; Tulsa, baritone)

Let Me Entertain You **	All I Need Is the Girl ††
Some People **	Everything's Coming up
Small World **	Roses **
Little Lamb **	Together Wherever We
You'll Never Get Away from	Go **/††
Me **/††	You Gotta Get a Gimmick **
If Momma Was Married **	

A Funny Thing Happened on the Way to the Forum

A Funny Thing Happened on the Way to the Forum is Sondheim's first produced score for which he wrote music and lyrics. *Forum* melds Roman comedy with vaudeville, and most of Sondheim's score feels vaudevillian, particularly "Comedy Tonight" and "Everybody Ought to Have a Maid." Philia's songs, "Lovely" and "That'll Show Him" call for a clear, unadorned, legitimate soprano voice; and Hero's "Love I Hear" calls for a light baritone or baritenor. The rest of the score, however, calls for character voices with a strong sense of vaudevillian style. (Pseudolus, baritone; Hero, tenor; Philia, soprano; Hysterium, baritone; Senex, baritone; Domina, mezzo-soprano)

Comedy Tonight	Lovely
Love, I Hear †	Pretty Little Picture
Free ††	Everybody Ought to Have a
Lovely */†	Maid ††
The House of Marcus Lycus	I'm Calm ††

Impossible †/††	That Dirty Old Man **
Bring Me My Bride ††	That'll Show Him *

Anyone Can Whistle

The score to *Anyone Can Whistle* uses the vocabulary of the 1960s musical theatre show tune, but turns it on its head. The show is an absurdist social satire that questions the nature and relationship of sanity to insanity – suggesting that those considered sane may be the maddest of all. The Sondheim website, Sondheim.com writes, "a deft takeoff of traditional show tunes to point up the insincerity and shallowness of some of the characters."[5] Singers who are looking to perform this material should be familiar with standard show tune styles, and their offshoot, the nightclub styles, to understand how to send them up. The song "Me and My Town," for instance, was based on the great musical numbers arranged by Kay Thompson. The singer performing "Me and My Town" will have a much greater understanding of it after listening to Ms. Thompson's work. (Cora Hoover Hooper, alto; Fay Apple, mezzo-soprano; J. Bowden Hapgood, baritone)

I'm Like the Bluebird	A Parade in Town **
Me and My Town **	Everybody Says Don't ††
Miracle Song	I've Got You to Lean On
There Won't Be Trumpets **	See What It Gets You **
Simple	With So Little To Be Sure
Come Play Wiz Me **/††	Of **/††
Anyone Can Whistle **	

Do I Hear a Waltz? *(music by Richard Rodgers)*

The combination of Richard Rodgers music and Stephen Sondheim's lyrics did not yield a hit musical, but many of the songs are very appealing individually. The Rodgers tunes are relatively standard musical theatre fare, but the wit and wordplay of Sondheim elevates them. Since the show originally starred popular tenor Sergio Franchi, this is a good source of material for a tenor. (Leona Samish, mezzo-soprano; Renato di Rossi, tenor; Signora Fioria, mezzo-soprano; Jennifer Yaeger, mezzo-soprano; Eddie Yaeger, baritone)

Someone Woke Up **	What Do We Do? We Fly!
This Week Americans	Someone Like You †

Bargaining †   Moon in My Window * *
Here We Are Again * *   We're Gonna Be Alright * */††
Thinking †/* *   Do I Hear a Waltz? * *
No Understand * */††   Stay ††
Take the Moment †   Thank You So Much * *'†

Evening Primrose

In this television musical, one can hear Sondheim beginning to find "his sound." Both melody and accompaniment take full advantage of suspensions and dissonances that only resolve at the last minute. The wordiness of "If You Can Find Me I'm Here" and the list song, "I Remember" foreshadow complicated songs to come later in Sondheim's mature works. These are songs that ask for no adornment or ornamentation. Few songwriters are so specific; every note duration, phrasing mark and dynamic should be adhered to, as in all Sondheim songs, as all of those elements inform the performance. (Charles Snell, baritone; Ella Harkins, mezzo-soprano)

If You Can Find Me I'm Here ††   When
I Remember *   Take Me To The World * *

Company

The score to the breakout 1970 Sondheim musical *Company*, in part an homage to New York City, is infused with pop and folk sounds of the 1970s. Sondheim takes popular folk feelings and bends them to his uses in songs like "Another Hundred People," "Someone Is Waiting," "and "Marry Me a Little." He uses different popular and folk feels in "The Little Things You Do Together," "Barcelona" and "Being Alive." An understanding of these styles will serve the singer well, particularly in terms of the relationship between the voice and the accompaniment. Back-phrasing and sitting just slightly ahead of the beat help define the drive of these songs. Revivals have reconsidered this show, but the score remains gloriously and unabashedly grounded in the music of 1970. While the vocal style of the show is fairly straightforward and legitimate, not inflected with pop styling, the accompaniments are – a fact that helps to inform the singer. (Robert, baritone; Joanne, mezzo-soprano; Harry, baritone; David, baritone; Larry, baritone; Kathy, soprano; April, mezzo-soprano; Marta, mezzo-soprano)

Company
The Little Things You Do
   Together **
Sorry-Grateful (trio)††
You Could Drive a Person
   Crazy (trio) */**
Have I Got a Girl for You
Someone Is Waiting †
Another Hundred People **

Getting Married Today */**/††
Marry Me a Little †
Barcelona **/†
Side by Side by Side
Poor Baby
Barcelona
The Ladies Who Lunch **
Being Alive †

Follies

Follies uses the great revues of the 1920s as a metaphor for the American Dream. Sondheim uses two different kinds of songs in this show: pastiche songs sung originally by the follies girls in their youth, and traditional book musical songs. The pastiche songs include "Beautiful Girls," "I'm Still Here," and "One More Kiss" and the book musical songs include "The Road You Didn't Take," "Too Many Mornings" and "Could I Leave You." For the pastiche songs, a clear understanding of vocal styles of the 1920s is particularly useful. These songs call for a clear, bright, forward sound production, in order to be heard at the back of the theatre over an orchestra without amplification, and a relatively legitimate sound free of stylistic embellishment. The traditional book songs in this show express great regret at the failure of dreams to come to fruition. It is important that the singer not allow the emotional content of these songs to stifle the breathing apparatus, impairing musical lines. The beauty and poignancy of these lines is what makes these songs work so well. (Sally Durant Plummer, soprano; Phyllis Rogers Stone, alto; Ben Stone, baritone; Buddy, baritone; Roscoe, tenor; Solange, mezzo-soprano; Hattie Walker, mezzo-soprano; Stella Deems, mezzo-soprano; Carlotta Campion, mezzo-soprano; Heidi Schiller, soprano)

Beautiful Girls †
Don't Look at Me */††
Waiting for the Girls Upstairs
Rain on the Roof
Ah, Paris!
Broadway Baby
The Road You Didn't Take ††
In Buddy's Eyes *

Who's That Woman **
I'm Still Here **
Too Many Mornings */††
The Right Girl ††
One More Kiss *
Could I Leave You? **
You're Gonna Love Tomorrow/
   Love Will See Us Through

The God-Why-Don't-You-Love-Me Blues ††	The Story of Lucy and Jessie **
Losing My Mind *	Live, Laugh, Love

A Little Night Music

Sondheim's score or *A Little Night Music* is written entirely in meters that are multiples of 3/4 time; the music swirls, waltz-like. Although the title is a nod to Mozart, the score is primarily evocative of Satie, Ravel and Rachmaninoff. Written for legitimate, classical voices, except for Desiree, who sings "The Glamorous Life" and "Send in the Clowns," the vocal style is distinctly lyric, as opposed to dramatic. And while the musical style is operatic, these are very clearly songs written for a musical, not operatic arias. (Desiree Armfeldt, mezzo-soprano; Fredrik Egerman, baritone; Henrik Egerman, tenor; Count Carl-Magnus Malcolm, baritone; Countess Charlotte Malcolm, mezzo-soprano; Anne Egerman, soprano; Madame Armfeldt, alto; Petra, mezzo-soprano)

Now/Later/Soon (trio) ††/†/*	Every Day a Little Death *
The Glamorous Life **	It Would Have Been Wonderful
You Must Meet My Wife **/††	(duet) ††
Liaisons **	Send in the Clowns **
In Praise of Women ††	The Miller's Son **

The Frogs

The Frogs is an adaptation of Aristophanes' play, written to be performed by Yale Repertory Theatre in the Yale swimming pool. Sondheim and Burt Shevelove wrote *The Frogs* in one month in 1974. In 2004, the Lincoln Center produced the piece with substantial revisions. Appropriately enough for a musical version of a Greek play, *The Frogs*' score makes great use of a range of Greek modes (scales). For such a broad and satiric comedy, it employs vaudevillian turns, witty and wicked lyrics and larger than life characterizations. The original production of *The Frogs*, starring Larry Blyden, was not recorded, but a pirated live recording has surfaced. In addition, there was a studio recording made in 2001 starring Nathan Lane and Brian Stokes Mitchell, featuring Davis Gaines singing "Fear No More." There was also a full cast recording made of the 2005 Lincoln Center revival starring Nathan Lane. (Zantias, baritone; Dionysos, baritone; Herakles, baritone)

Invocation and Instructions to the Audience ††	All Aboard ††
I Love to Travel ††	Ariadne ††
Dress Big ††	Fear No More ††

Pacific Overtures

Pacific Overtures melded traditional Broadway and Japanese Kabuki storytelling devices. In the same way, the score evokes the sounds of traditional Japanese music. A familiarity with traditional Japanese music will serve the singer of these songs well. Sondheim uses lyrical Japanese forms as well; the score abounds in the imagery of nature and use of haiku. When a more Western sound is called for, as in "Pretty Lady" or "Please Hello," it always seems to be as it might be heard and reinterpreted by a foreigner. Listening to just the opening strains of Mako performing the opening number "The Advantage of Floating in the Middle of the Sea," on the original cast recording, give a great clarity to the vocal style of this score. (Manjiro, baritone; Kayama Yesaemon, baritone; Reciter, baritone)

The Advantages of Floating in the Middle of the Sea ††	Welcome to Kanagawa
There is No Other Way †	Someone in a Tree ††
Four Black Dragons	Please Hello
Chrysanthemum Tea	A Bowler Hat ††
Poems (duet) †/††	Pretty Lady (trio) †/††
	Next

Sweeney Todd

The composer himself admitted that much of the score for *Sweeney Todd* is an homage to film composer Bernard Herrmann. Sondheim writes for actors, but in *Sweeney Todd*, many of the roles are written for exceptionally technically adept voices. Johanna, Anthony, Tobias, Pirelli, Beadle Bamford and Judge Turpin all need exceptional tone and resonance, and clear articulation to make complex and rapidly sung words clear and seemingly effortless. The characters of Sweeney Todd and Mrs. Lovett are written for serious actors, although Sweeney's "Epiphany" is an intense challenge. The songs from this show, more than most, require over-enunciated consonants, but the diction must come from a need to communicate the thought, not simply over-articulation. Listen to how Len Cariou venomously spits out consonants in "Epiphany" on the original cast recording. Final consonants are particularly important, and especially in sections with many words, like: "Because the lives of the wicked should be made brief, for the rest of us death will be a relief." Also listen to Angela Lansbury's articulation in her bravura performance of "The Worst Pies in London." (Sweeney Todd, baritone; Mrs. Lovett, alto; Anthony Hope, tenor; Johanna, soprano; Beggar Woman, mezzo-soprano; Judge Turpin, baritone; Beadle Bamford, tenor; Adolfo Pirelli, tenor; Tobias Ragg, tenor)

The Ballad of Sweeney Todd	Kiss Me */†
No Place Like London	Ladies in the Sensitivities †
The Barber and His Wife †	Pretty Women (duet) ††
Worst Pies in London **	Epiphany ††
Poor Thing **	A Little Priest **/††
My Friends ††	God, That's Good!
Green Finch and Linnet Bird *	By the Sea **
Ah, Miss	Not While I'm Around **/†
Johanna (Anthony's song) †	Sweet Polly Plunket
Pirelli's Miracle Elixir	Tower of Bray
Johanna – Mea Culpa (Judge's song) ††	City on Fire
Wait **	Beggar Woman's Lullaby

Merrily We Roll Along

Since the world of *Merrily We Roll Along* is the world of the successful/aspiring Broadway songwriters Franklin Shepard and Charley Kringas, Sondheim chose the musical vocabulary of the musical theatre as the sound of this score. This score calls for a big Broadway belt for most of the female material. A bright, pingy frontally placed sound is called for in the men's material. Even the beautiful ballads "Good Thing Going" and "Not a Day Goes By" require this sort of bright frontal placement. (Franklin Shepard, tenor; Charley Kringas, tenor; Mary Flynn, mezzo-soprano; Joe Josephson, baritone; Beth Spencer, mezzo-soprano; Gussie Carnegie, mezzo-soprano)

Merrily We Roll Along	Like It Was **
Rich and Happy	Franklin Shepard, Inc. †
That Frank (1994 revival)	Old Friends (trio) **/†/††

Growing Up (1994 revival)	Good Thing Going †
Not a Day Goes By ††	Bobby and Jackie and Jack
Now You Know	Opening Doors
It's a Hit!	Out Time
The Blob (1994 revival)	The Hills of Tomorrow

Sunday in the Park with George

Sondheim took his musical cue from the pointillist style of this musical's subject, painter Georges Seurat. Inspired by Seurat's masterpiece, "A Sunday Afternoon on the Island of La Grand Jatte," the musical examines the artist in the act of creation. Seurat was central to the artistic movement of Pointillism. In Pointillism, rather than mixing colors on his palette, the artist would place dots of pure, primary color next to each other which would be merged by the viewer's eye. Sondheim began writing this score attempting to place notes against each other in the same way but ultimately chose a more traditional approach. However, the motif of thousands of tiny dots making up the whole picture is carried through in his score. Singers of this music need to be aware of staccato passages contrasted by legato lines. The sharp, often percussive quality of the attack required by much of the score is intentionally used to evoke the painter's brush creating dots on the canvas over and over. (George Seurat/George, tenor; Dot/Marie, mezzo-soprano; Jules, baritone)

Color and Light **/†	Putting It Together †
Everybody Loves Louis **	Children and Art **
Finishing the Hat †	Move On †/**
We Do Not Belong Together **/†	

Into the Woods

The repetition and development of small motifs throughout are central to this score. The two-note "I Wish" theme and the repeated "Into the Woods" theme develop and return through the score. In *Into the Woods*, the action stops and characters step out of the play to address the audience, commenting on what they have learned or are thinking. The songs in this score, stepping outside the story as they do, require an urgent need to share the revelation and need to be completely without guile. The singer must make the lyrics, which are often intricate, seem comfortable and inevitable. This music and these lyrics must appear to be spontaneous and genuine. Listen to the original cast recording of songs like Red Riding Hood's "I Know Things Now," and Jack's "Giants in the Sky" and you will hear this quality for yourself. (The Baker, baritone; the Baker's Wife, mezzo-soprano; the Witch, mezzo-soprano; Cinderella, soprano; Jack, tenor; Little Red Riding Hood, mezzo-soprano; Jack's Mother, soprano)

Hello Little Girl ††	Stay with Me **
I Guess This is Goodbye †	On the Steps of the Palace *
Maybe They're Magic	Witch's Lament **
Our Little World	Any Moment
I Know Things Now **	Moments in the Woods **
A Very Nice Prince (duet) */**	Last Midnight **
Giants in the Sky †	No More †
Agony (duet) ††	No One Is Alone *
It Takes Two **/†	

Assassins

Originally opened off-Broadway at Playwrights Horizons, *Assassins* examines the American psyche through the phenomenon of attempted Presidential assassinations. Sondheim takes as his musical vocabulary traditional American music of the various eras in which these scenes take place. The Balladeer sings in a variety of traditional American folk styles. Sondheim presses "Hail to the Chief" into 3/4 time. Stephen Banfield identifies Sondheim's use of aspects of bluegrass music in "The Ballad of Booth," a hoe-down for "The Ballad of Czolgosz" and folk/pop music in "Unworthy of Your Love." Sondheim also references gospel hymns and the cakewalk in "The Ballad of Guiteau." An ability to embrace these styles is important to singing these songs well. (John Wilkes Booth, tenor; the Balladeer, tenor; Leon Czolgosz, baritone; Sara Jane Moore, alto; Lynette "Squeaky" Fromme, soprano; Samuel Byck, baritone)

Everybody's Got the Right	Unworthy of Your
Ballad of Booth ††	Love **/††
How I Saved Roosevelt	The Ballad of Guiteau
The Gun Song	Another National Anthem ††
The Ballad of Czolgosz	Something Just Broke

Dick Tracy

Sondheim contributed five songs to the 1990 film *Dick Tracy*. The film takes place in the 1930s, and all five songs are rooted in popular songs of the 1930s. But being written primarily for pop singer Madonna, they are an interesting amalgam of the 1930s and 1990s pop styles.

Sooner or Later **
More **
Live Alone and Like It ††

Back in Business **
What Can You Lose? **/†

Passion

The songs from *Passion* require exceptional classical technique to sing well. This score is much closer to opera than anything else in Sondheim's canon. Sondheim has adamantly insisted that he has no interest in writing opera; the flow of spoken scene into song interests him above all as a composer. While not an opera, the operatic nature of this music is at its heart. There are many songs that can be well performed without necessarily being well sung; these songs are not among them. (Clara, soprano; Giorgio Bachetti, baritone; Fosca, mezzo-soprano)

Happiness *
First Letter
Second Letter
Third Letter
Fourth Letter
I Read *
Transition #1
Garden Sequence
Transition #2
Trio
I Wish I Could Forget You *
Transition #4
Soldier's Gossip
Flashback

Sunrise Letter
Is This What You Call
Love? ††
Nightmare
Transition #5
Forty Days
Loving You */††
Transition #6
Christmas Carol
Farewell Letter
Just Another Love Story */††
No One Has Ever
Loved Me ††
The Duel

Bounce/Road Show

Sondheim had been working on a musical based on the life of the Mizner brothers for many years. In 1997 and 1998 this musical, then titled *Wise Guys*, received three readings in New York under the direction of Sam Mendes, which led to a workshop production in 1999. In 2003, after revision, the show, then retitled *Bounce,* was produced at the Goodman Theatre in Chicago and the Kennedy Center in Washington, DC under the direction of Harold Prince. While this production was scheduled to move to Broadway, that move never happened, although this production did result in an original cast recording. After further revisions, in 2008 the show opened off-Broadway under the direction of John Doyle with the title *Road Show.* This score represents a return to using the traditional sounds of the heyday of the American musical to comment on the characters and action. The same kind of sound production required by shows like *Gypsy* and *Merrily We Roll Along* is required of the singer of the songs from this score. (Addison Mizner, baritone; Wison Mizner, tenor)

Bounce	Alaska
Opportunity	Isn't He Something **
Gold!	The Game
What's Your Rush *	Talent ††
The Game ††	You
Next to You	Addison's City
Addison's Trip	Get Rich Quick
The Best Thing That Ever	Boca Raton
Happened (duet) ††	Last Fight
I Love This Town	

Songs that were written for *Road Show* (the revised version of *Bounce*) include:

Waste	Land Boom!
It's in Your Hands Now ††	Get Out †
Brotherly Love (duet) ††	Go
That Was a Year	

Biography

Born in New York City in 1930, Stephen Sondheim's parents divorced in 1942, and he moved with his mother to Doylestown, Pennsylvania. Sondheim became friendly with the son of the lyricist, librettist and producer Oscar Hammerstein II. It was Hammerstein who inspired the young Sondheim to pursue a career in the theatre. While attending The George School, a private Quaker boarding school near Doylestown, Sondheim offered a piece of his writing to Hammerstein for criticism. Hammerstein spent the day going through the entire piece with Sondheim, line by line, and then set up a program of study for his protégé. Hammerstein charged Sondheim with musicalizing a play that he admired, a play that he considered flawed, a novel or short story not in dramatic form and an original story.

Sondheim graduated magna cum laude from Williams College and went on to study with composer Milton Babbitt. After several years of struggle, writing television episodes in California, and sleeping on his father's sofa in New York, Sondheim had his first musical optioned, *Saturday Night.* Unfortunately the producer, Lemuel Ayers, passed away before getting the show to the stage. But *Saturday Night* led to two important jobs writing lyrics to other composers' work, *West Side Story,* with Leonard Bernstein, and *Gypsy,* with Jule Styne.

The catalog of Sondheim's shows is well known; there are many excellent biographies offering intense levels of detail and fascinating analysis of his life, career and the individual works.

Resources

There are library shelves filled with books about Sondheim's life and works. Sondheim has written two detailed analysis of his lyrics, *Look I Made a Hat* and *Finishing the Hat.* There is also *Sondheim on Music: Minor Details and Major Decisions,*[6] a series of interviews with Sondheim. Other writers analyzing Sondheim's work include: *How Sondheim Found His Sound,*[7] *Sondheim's Broadway Musicals*[8] and *Art Isn't Easy: The Theatre of Stephen Sondheim.*[9] It seems that practically every song of Sondheim's has been recorded multiple times; original cast albums, bonus tracks, recordings by cabaret artists, jazz artists, and others fill the CD racks. Four revues of Sondheim's works, *Side By Side By Sondheim* (1976), *Marry Me*

A Little (1980), *You're Gonna Love Tomorrow* (1983) and *Putting it Together* (2010) have been compiled. These created theatrical evenings around Sondheim's songs and have been recorded in multiple productions.

In summary

Sondheim has been called the greatest musical theatre dramatist in the history of the artform, the Shakespeare of the American musical theatre. While each show is unique, a style unto itself, each song and each score present the singer with so much information and so much clarity, that the answer to performing any Sondheim song always seems to be, dig deeper into the text. While other songwriters' material can call for the singer to bring something of themselves to the text, Sondheim's songs almost demand that the singer digs deeply into the text musically and lyrically. Digging deeply brings clarity of thought and intent, thereby allowing the singer to commit fully to each carefully crafted moment. In this clarity is the effectiveness of these songs.

Bernadette Peters, one of the premier interpreters of Sondheim's songs, spoke about singing his songs in an interview with Robert Sokol. "They just ring very true to me. His songs make so much sense. They have such depth. There are layers and layers and layers to his songs. You sing a song and the next time you sing it it can mean something else totally. It's like this beautiful Maui onion that you keep peeling and there's all these layers and layers and layers and layers."[10]

Notes

1 Michael Ball, "Is Stephen Sondheim the Shakespeare of Musical Theatre?," *The Guardian*, www.theguardian.com/stage/theatreblog/2010/mar/29/stephen-sondheim-musical-theatre, accessed February 8, 2015.
2 Steve Swayne, *How Sondheim Found His Sound*, Ann Arbor, MI: University of Michigan Press, 2007, pp. 8–9.
3 Stephen Sondheim, quoted in Swayne, *How Sondheim Found his Sound*, p. 10.
4 Uncredited, "The Songs," *The Stephen Sondheim Reference Guide*, www.sondheimguide.com/songs.html, accessed May 9, 2016.
5 Uncredited, "Anyone Can Whistle," *Sondheim.com*, www.sondheim.com/works/anyone_can_whistle/, accessed February 9, 2015.

6 Mark Eden Horowitz, *Sondheim on Music: Minor Details and Major Decisions*, New York, NY: Scarecrow Press, 2010

7 Swayne, *How Sondheim Found His Sound*.

8 Stephen Banfield, *Sondheim's Broadway Musicals*, Ann Arbor, MI: University of Michigan Press, 1995.

9 Joanne Gordon, *Art Isn't Easy: The Theatre of Stephen Sondheim*, New York, NY: Da Capo Press, 1992.

10 Quoted in Robert Sokol, "Rubbing Shoulders with Bernadette Peters," *Stephen Sondheim Stage*, www.sondheim.com/interview/sbswbp.html, accessed October 30, 2015.

Chapter 9

New sounds – the 1970s

Galt MacDermot, Stephen Schwartz,
Marvin Hamlisch, Maury Yeston, Howard Ashman
and Alan Menken, Richard Maltby Jr and
David Shire, and William Finn

The 1970s brought with them the successful integration of popular music into the repertoire of the musical theatre. Traditionally, the music of the theatre had been "covered" (re-recorded) by popular and jazz singers, becoming the popular music of the day. The ascension of the singer-songwriters concurrent with the advent of rock and roll made this no longer possible.

A new generation of writers, born mostly in the late 1930s through the early 1950s, were mostly teenagers when the popularity of rock and roll edged most other popular music off the market. They spent their formative years growing up to the rock and folk music of their adolescence; it became their natural idiom. As these composers and lyricists reached the age when they were writing for the musical theatre, it seemed natural that their characters expressed themselves in this idiom.

Just as belting, popular in the 1920s and 1930s and again in the 1960s, called for a technique of controlled screaming on pitch, so did a lot of the early rock and roll. New vocal placements offered singers new ways to produce sound. The scat singers had based their vocal improvisations on the sounds of other instruments of their era; in exactly that same way, the rock and roll singers frequently emulated the sounds of the electric guitar. Leaning or sliding into notes, a twangy tonal quality, high pitched screaming emulating an electric guitar lead-line solo all became part of the rock and roll singer's vocal vocabulary. Rhythm and groove were as important in singing rock as they had been in swing singing; it was simply a different groove or feel. Sometimes diction took a back seat to tonal quality.

Charles Strouse found great success in using rock and roll as the musical vocabulary for the teenagers in *Bye Bye Birdie*. *Hair* had great success having performers step forward out of the play and just wail out great rock songs. Most early experiments at using rock music in the musical theatre, however, were not so successful.

Early rock songs were based on an insistent unchanging rhythmic groove, were usually in AABA format, and usually limited to the roughly three or so minutes that fit onto one side of a 45rpm record. Composers found such a strict structure difficult to use to reveal character or advance plot. In early rock musicals, the plots would stop so that actors with rock star voices could just wail out great tunes. There was a great theatricality to stopping to belt out a great tune with contemporary inflections. Shows like *Viet Rock* (1966, Megan Terry), *Your Own Thing* (1968, Hal Hester and Danny Apolinar), *Salvation* (1969, Peter Link and C.C. Courtney), *The Last Sweet Days of Isaac* (1970, Gretchen Cryer and Nancy Ford) and *Inner City* (1971, Eve Merriam and Helen Miller) got audiences accustomed to hearing rock and roll in musicals, but didn't solve the dramaturgical problems. That would come later.

Rock singing is an incredibly individual pursuit; there are many sub-genres of rock and many stylistic devices at the singer's disposal. Wikipedia has almost 250 different kinds of rock music, not taking into account folk and pop genres. A solid vocal technique has to underlay any attempt to sing rock and roll to protect against vocal damage. That being said, pitched screams, vocal fry, hitting notes under pitch and sliding up into them, portamento (sliding from pitch to pitch), grunts, groans, inserted ad lib vocal licks, grace notes – all of these can be very effectively used in rock singing. As with jazz singing (discussed in Chapter 5) the best way to learn to sing these styles is to listen to them. The more different kinds of singers one listens to, the wider vocabulary one has at one's disposal. Listen to everything you can in any genre that you want to learn to sing and take inspiration from every source.

Galt MacDermot (b. 1928): The Age of Aquarius

Stylistic approach

Canadian composer MacDermot came to the musical theatre from the world of popular music, with an especially eclectic background and range of styles. After studying traditional Western music, he received a Bachelor of Music from Cape Town University in South Africa, where he specialized in African music. His piano teacher, Neil Chotem, is known for comingling disparate jazz and pop music styles. He received a Grammy Award in 1960 for Cannonball Adderley's recording of his composition "African Waltz." MacDermot's eclectic approach has incorporated aspects of jazz, funk, rap, hip-hop, traditional African and classical music. He has written rock musicals, ballet scores, chamber music, Anglican liturgy, orchestral music, popular instrumental music, single popular songs and opera.

Singing MacDermot's songs requires interpretation, and asks the singer to contribute their musical stylings. They are well suited to be adapted to many jazz, rock and world music styles, but without stylistic interpretation they tend to fall flat. Recently MacDermot's music has been sampled by rap artists, including Run DMC and Busta Rhymes, for use in their remixes.

Galt MacDermot theatre scores all need rock styling. *Hair*, *Dude*, *Via Galactica* and *The Human Comedy* are all rock scores. MacDermot's score for *Hair* pulls from areas of popular musical ranging from gentle folk to early pop/rock power ballads. Listen to Shelly Plimpton's folk-infused version of "Frank Mills," Diane Keaton and Melba Moore's Motown homage in "Black Boys/White Boys," Lynn Kellogg's throbbing rock ballad styling on "Easy To Be Hard," or the full company rocking out on "Let The Sun Shine," all on the original Broadway cast recording of *Hair*. MacDermot's songs need this degree of stylization or they fall quite flat.

Body of work

According to his website www.galtmacdermot.com,[1] MacDermot's theatre scores include:

My Fur Lady (McGill University, 1957)

Hamlet, Twelfth Night, Troilus and Cressida, The Tempest (New York Public Theatre, 1964–1967)

Hair (New York Public Theatre, 1967 and Broadway, 1968)

Two Gentlemen of Verona (Broadway, 1970)

Isabel's Jezebel (West End, 1972)

Who The Murderer Was (London, 1970)

Dude (Broadway, 1973)

Via Galactica (Broadway, 1973)

The Joke of Seville (Trinidad, 1976, Boston and Trinidad, 1994)

The Human Comedy
  (Broadway, 1984)
The Special
  (off-Broadway, 1985)
Blondie (New York, 1986)
The Prophets
  (New York, 1986)
Steel (Philadelphia, Boston,
  Trinidad, 1990)
Sun (New York, 1991)
Clown Woman (Guggenheim
  Museum, New York, 1993)

The Odyssey (Washington,
  DC, 1995)
Time and the Wind
  (off-Broadway, 1995)
To Take Arms (Los
  Angeles, 1997)
Concerto for Sung Harbor/
  The Legend of Joan of Arc
  (New York, 1997)
Sun (New York, 1998)
Corporation (New York,
  1999)

MacDermot's score for the musical *Hair* was tremendously successful: popular artists covered many of the songs, and the original cast recording received a Grammy Award. His score for the Afro-Caribbean treatment of *Two Gentlemen of Verona* won him a Tony Award and ran for over 600 performances. His other theatre scores were substantially less successful. His better-known songs include:

Abie Baby
Ain't Got No
Air
Aquarius
Black Boys/White Boys
Calla Lily Lady
Colored Spade
Donna
Don't Put It Down
Easy to be Hard
Flesh Failures
Frank Mills
Good Morning Starshine

Hair
Hashish
Hot Lover
I Got Life
I Love My Father
Let the Sun Shine In
Manchester England
Night Letter
Sodomy
Thurio's Samba
Walking in Space
What a Piece of Work is Man
Where Do I Go?

Biography

MacDermot was born in Montreal, Canada and raised in Montreal and Toronto. He studied with Canadian pianist Neil Chotem and received a Bachelor of Music at Cape Town University in South Africa. His majors were composition and organ, and he specialized in the rhythms of the native South African music he heard in the ghettos of Cape Town. From 1954 to 1961 he worked as a Baptist organist and choirmaster and jazz organist in Montreal. In 1961, his jazz composition "African Waltz," recorded by John Dankworth and Cannonball Adderley, won Grammy and Novello Awards for best jazz piece and best instrumental composition. This success prompted MacDermot to test the waters in London and eventually settle in New York, where his career shifted to playing studio gigs and in R&B bands. His greatest success, the tribal love-rock musical *Hair*, was written in 1967, at which point MacDermott put playing aside to focus on his writing. MacDermot has continued writing but since then he has never seen that degree of success.

Resources

Many books have chronicled the success of *Hair*, including Scott Miller's *Let the Sun Shine In: The Genius of Hair*,[2] Eric Grode's *Hair: The Story of the Show that Defined a Generation*,[3] and Jonathon Johnson's *Good Hair Days: A Personal Journey with the American Tribal Love-Rock Musical, Hair*.[4]

Stephen Schwartz (b. 1948): 1970s folk/rock influenced

Stylistic approach

In discussing his formative influences, Schwartz notes a wide stylistic range. He grew up in a musically literate home with a mother who loved contemporary 1950s folk music as well as classical, opera and the musical theatre repertoire. As a young piano student his favorite classical composers included, "Handel, Bach, Beethoven, Puccini, Mussorgsky, Rachmaninoff, Stravinsky, Copland and maybe Steve Reich and Philip Glass. [Musical theatre influences include] Richard Rodgers, Kern, Berlin, Loewe, Bock, and Sondheim."[5] By his college years the Motown sound had taken over college campuses as had the Beach Boys. Schwartz's favorites during his college years included Laura Nyro, James Taylor, Joni Mitchell, Carole King and The Mamas and The Papas. Many of these artists drew their inspiration from soul, jazz, blues, R&B and folk music, and many used the guitar as their writing instrument. One can hear in Schwartz's piano accompaniments guitar-sounding chord voicings and arpeggiation.

He cites influences on his lyrics as "for theatre: Sheldon Harnick, Larry Hart, Carolyn Leigh, Hammerstein, Sondheim of course [...] for pop: other than Joni Mitchell, who's the best, I would cite James Taylor and Don Henley, and more recently Sting and Mary Chapin Carpenter. [...] Paul Simon and Laura Nyro."

While his score for *The Baker's Wife* is a very traditional "legitimate" theatre score, all of Schwartz's other scores are heavily pop/rock/folk influenced. Deeply grounded in the pop sounds of the 1970s, much of Schwartz's work reveals these influences. The musical-theatre singer approaching Schwartz's songs would be well advised to take a pop approach to performing his songs. This style calls for addressing not only the length of a phrase but how one gets from one note to the next – scooping, sliding, leaning, squeezing. Also, the use of riffing or ad-libbing, not to change the notes of the melody, but to affect the journey from note to note or to begin or end phrases, is stylistically appropriate.

Stephen Schwartz fell in love with the sounds of Joni Mitchell, Paul Simon and Laura Nyro. Finding their inflections in Schwartz's songs will help anyone singing his songs. The role of the Leading Player in *Pippin* was originally conceived as an old man who led the troupe of players, intended as an old vaudevillian. But Ben Vereen's audition convinced Bob Fosse, Schwartz and the others at the audition table to cast the role differently. Vereen brought out all of the rock and Motown influences in Schwartz's score, embellishing and accentuating Schwartz's strongest suit, his tremendous ability to write great 1970s pop/rock music. Listen to Vereen's rock styling on the original cast recording, or Patina Miller's rock styling on the revival cast recording to get a great understanding of how this approach to Schwartz's writing makes it work. While the quality of Schwartz's writing has remained consistently high through the years, his sounds and style remain essentially rooted in 1970s pop/rock throughout his career.

Body of work

Schwartz wrote both music and lyrics except where indicated. His film, theatre and recorded scores include:

Godspell (off-Broadway, 1971)	*Pippin* (1972)
Mass (The Kennedy Center, lyrics only, 1972)	*The Magic Show* (1974)

The Baker's Wife (closed prior to Broadway 1976)
Working (1978)
The Trip (one-act children's musical, 1981
Personals (off-Broadway, three songs, 1985)
Captain Louie (children's show, 1986)
Rags (lyrics only, 1986)
Children of Eden (1991)
Pocahontas (film, lyrics only, 1995)

The Hunchback of Notre Dame (film, lyrics only, 1996)
Reluctant Pilgrim (CD, 1997)
The Prince of Egypt (film, 1998)
Geppetto (film, 2000)
Uncharted Territory (CD, 2001)
Wicked (2003)
Mit Eventyr/My Fairy Tale (Copenhagen, 2005)
Enchanted (film, lyrics only, 2007)
Séance on a Wet Afternoon (opera, 2009)

Listed below are some of Schwartz's better-known songs with indication of the vocal registers in which these songs were originally written, but they can be purchased and sung in many different keys (see p. 10 for key to symbols).

Godspell (1971) (Jesus, tenor; John the Baptist/Judas, baritone; Lamar, tenor; Herb, baritone; Jeffrey, tenor; Sonia, alto; Joanne, soprano)

Alas for You ††
All for the Best ††
All Good Gifts †
Beautiful City ††
Bless the Lord **
Day by Day **

Learn Your Lessons Well **
O Bless the Lord **
On the Willows ††
Save the People ††
Turn Back, O Man **

Pippin (1972) (Leading Player, tenor; Pippin, tenor; Charlemagne, baritone; Fastrada, mezzo-soprano; Berthe, alto; Catherine, mezzo-soprano)

Corner of the Sky †
Extraordinary †
I Guess I'll Miss the Man *
Kind of Woman *
Love Song †/*
Magic to Do †
Marking Time (cut) †

Morning Glow †
No Time At All **
On the Right Track †
Simple Joys †
Spread a Little Sunshine **
With You †

Mass (music by Leonard Bernstein) (1972)
A Simple Song ††

The Magic Show (1974) (Charmin, mezzo-soprano; Feldman, baritone; Cal, mezzo-soprano)

Charmin's Lament *	Style ††
Lion Tamer **	Two's Company **
Solid Silver Platform Shoes **	West End Avenue **

The Baker's Wife (1976) (Amiable Castagnet, tenor; Genevieve, mezzo-soprano; Dominique, baritone; Denise, soprano)

Chanson *	Merci, Madame ††
Gifts of Love ††	Proud Lady ††
If I Have to Live Alone ††	Where is the Warmth **
Meadowlark **	

Working (1978) (Mike Dillard, baritone; Al Calinda, tenor; Rose Hoffman, mezzo-soprano; Roberto, baritone; Grace Clements, alto; Anthony Coelho, tenor; Frank Decker, baritone; Dave, baritone)

Fathers and Sons ††	Neat to be a Newsboy †
It's an Art **	

Rags (1986) (music by Charles Strouse) (Rebecca Hershkowitz, soprano; Saul, baritone; Bella Cohen, mezzo-soprano; Nathan Hershkowitz, baritone; Ben, tenor)

Blame It on the Summer Night *	I Remember *
Brand New World *	Rags *
Children of the Wind *	The Sounds of Love †
Easy for You ††	Three Sunny Rooms **
For My Mary †	Wanting *

Children of Eden (1991) (Abel/Ham, tenor; Adam/Noah, tenor; Eve/Mama Noah, mezzo-soprano; Cain/Japheth, tenor; Father, baritone; Yonah, mezzo-soprano; Seth/Shem, tenor; Aphra, alto; Aysha, alto)

Children of Eden **   Lost in the Wilderness †
The Hardest Part of Love ††   The Spark of Creation **
In Whatever Time We   Stranger to the Rain **
     Have **/††   A World Without You †
Let There Be †

Pocahontas (music by Alan Menken) (1995)

Colors of the Wind **   Just Around the River Bend **

The Hunchback of Notre Dame (music by Alan Menken) (1996)

God Help the Outcasts **   Out There †

Wicked (2003) (Elphaba, mezzo-soprano; Glinda, soprano; The Wizard of Oz, baritone; Madame Morrible, alto; Fiyero, tenor; Nessarose, alto)

Dancing Through Life ††   A Sentimental Man ††
Defying Gravity **   The Wizard and I **
Popular *   Wonderful ††

Biography

Born in New York, Schwartz studied piano and composition at Juilliard while in high school. He received a B.F.A. in Drama from Carnegie Mellon University in 1968, at age 20.

His first produced full score was *Godspell*, a musical retelling of the Gospel according to St. Matthew, turning the disciples into actors/clowns/hippies. The piece was developed at Carnegie Mellon and had been given a prior off-off-Broadway production, but Schwartz was brought onboard to write music and some new lyrics to move the show to off-Broadway. *Godspell* was one of the smashes of the decade, running for more than five years off-Broadway, followed by a year and a half on Broadway.

The following year he wrote the lyrics for Leonard Bernstein's *Mass*, which had been commissioned to open the opera house at the Kennedy Center. *Pippin*, which had also begun as a college musical at Carnegie Mellon, opened on Broadway in 1972, and despite lukewarm reviews, was a massive success, running for just shy of five years.

The Magic Show had been running in Toronto when Schwartz was asked to write a score for its transfer to Broadway. In the matter of just a few weeks, Schwartz had finished his commission on time, and the show opened on Broadway. Once again the reviews were uniformly mediocre, but the performance of magician Doug Henning kept the show running for four and a half years. Schwartz had defied the critics, but his next four major shows would not be so lucky. Producer David Merrick shut down *The Baker's Wife* during its out-of-town preview period. *Working* and *Rags* were both eviscerated by the critics; *Working* lasted only three weeks before closing while *Rags* only lasted for four performances. *Children of Eden* opened in London to poor reviews on the eve of the 1991 Gulf War. People feared congregating in crowded places like theatres and it closed very quickly (although it did receive a successful production at Paper Mill Playhouse in Millburn, New Jersey in 1997).

Burned once too many times in the theatre, Schwartz headed to Hollywood, where he wrote lyrics to Alan Menken's music for several Disney musicals: *Pocahontas*, *The Hunchback of Notre Dame* and *Enchanted*. He also wrote music and lyrics for the movie *The Prince of Egypt* and the television special *Gepetto*.

Schwartz has had a triumphant return to Broadway with 2003's *Wicked*. Although *Wicked*, too, did not receive great critical acclaim, it has become one of the greatest Broadway hits ever.

Resources

Schwartz has a website of his own, www.stephenschwartz.com,[6] and there is an fan website, www.musicalschwartz.com,[7] with extensive and excellent links. Carol de Giere's 2008 book *Defying Gravity: The Creative Career of Stephen Schwartz from Godspell to Wicked*[8] is also an excellent source.

Marvin Hamlisch (1944–2012): What I Did For Love

Stylistic approach

Hamlisch comes from a traditional classical background; he began studying piano at the Juilliard School at age six. But his music is highly pop-infused. Leslie Gore's recording of "Sunshine, Lollipops and Rainbows" rose to #13 on the *Billboard* charts and became 19-year old Hamlisch's first hit in 1963. Many of the musical theatre scores of the 1980s and 1990s were infused with pop and disco stylings, and Hamlisch's theatre scores led the way. He wrote almost exclusively for pop and character voices. His earliest song hits were pop/rock songs like the aforementioned "Sunshine, Lollipops and Rainbows," or movie title songs like "The Way They Were," from the film of the same name, made famous by Barbra Streisand. Listening to the original cast recording of *A Chorus Line* reveals how deeply grounded Hamlisch's songs are in R&B, disco and the sounds of Motown. Listen particularly to Robert Klein or Lucie Arnaz on the original cast recording of *They're Playing Our Song*, Hamlisch's disco-infused score and you will hear the degree of styling that clearly identifies Hamlisch's songs.

Body of work

Composer Hamlisch had two major theatrical successes, *A Chorus Line* and *They're Playing Our Song*. He wrote more than 40 film scores and wrote orchestral arrangements for and conducted major pops orchestras and concerts for artists like Groucho Marx and Barbara Streisand. His theatre work includes:

A Chorus Line (1975)
They're Playing Our Song (1978)
Jean Seberg (London, 1983)
Smile (1986)
The Goodbye Girl (1993)
The Sweet Smell of Success (2002)
The Nutty Professor (regional, 2012)

Best remembered songs of Hamlisch's include:

A Chorus Line (1975) (Cassie Ferguson, mezzo-soprano; Maggie Winslow, soprano; Mike Costa, tenor; Sheila Bryant, alto; Richie Walters, tenor; Diana Morales, mezzo-soprano; Val Clark, mezzo-soprano)

I Can Do That ††

At the Ballet **

Sing!

Nothing **

Dance: Ten; Looks: Three **

The Music and the Mirror **

One

What I Did for Love **

They're Playing Our Song (1978) (Sonjia Walsk, mezzo-soprano; Vernon Gersch, baritone)

Fallin' ††

If He/She Really Knew Me **/††

They're Playing Our Song **/††

Just For Tonight **

I Still Believe in Love **/††

Smile (1986) (Doria Hudson, mezzo-soprano; Robin Gibson, mezzo-soprano; Ted Farley, baritone)

Disneyland **

The Sweet Smell of Success (2002) (J.J. Hunsecker, baritone; Sidney, baritone; Rita, mezzo-soprano; Dallas, tenor; Susan, soprano)

I Cannot Hear the City ††

For Susan ††

Biography

Hamlisch was born in Manhattan, to Viennese-born Jewish parents. He began studying piano at Juilliard at age six. His first job was as a rehearsal pianist for Jule Styne's *Funny Girl* with Barbra Streisand when he was 21. He scored his first Hollywood film in 1968 at age 24 and scored 14 films before his return to New York for *A Chorus Line*. *A Chorus Line* earned Hamlisch a Tony Award, a Drama Desk Award and a Pulitzer Prize. His next musical, *They're Playing Our Song*, ran for more than 1,000 performances. The later shows in his career failed to live up to the successes of the first two. *Jean Seberg* opened at the National Theatre in London to poor critical and audience response. *Smile*, with a book, lyrics and direction by Howard Ashman, failed to reach 50 performances on Broadway. *The Goodbye Girl* eked out 188 performances despite dire reviews, and *The Sweet Smell of Success* just topped 100 performances before closing. Shortly before Hamlisch passed away, the Tennesee Performing Arts Center produced his final musical, *The Nutty Professor*. The show received a tour, but never made it to Broadway.

Resources

Hamlisch's official website, http://marvinhamlisch.us/, offers a lot of links and much good information. Hamlisch also wrote an autobiography titled *The Way I Was.*[9]

Maury Yeston (b. 1945): The "other" *Phantom*

Stylistic approach

Composer and lyricist Yeston has a broad and deep understanding of musical styles, having played vibraphone with a jazz group, sung in a madrigal ensemble, played folk guitar and so on. But his music is more firmly rooted in a bravura classical sound than any of his contemporaries. His earliest musical training was classical and religious; his grandfather was a Jewish cantor in the synagogue. Yeston's material requires a great deal of technique; he often writes long legato lines, long and sustained crescendos, phrases that create interesting challenges of phrasing and placement. While Yeston's songs can certainly withstand some stylization, they do not require it. They stand on their own much more than most of the other composers examined in this chapter.

Body of work

Yeston has only seen Broadway productions of three of his musicals, but his body of work is much more extensive and interesting than the small number of Broadway productions might suggest. His works include:

Nine (1982)
In the Beginning (Manhattan Theatre Club under the title *1-2-3-4-5*, 1987)
Grand Hotel (1989)
Goya: A Life in Song (musical released as a concept album, 1989)
Phantom (produced regionally, withheld from Broadway due to Andrew Lloyd Webber's *The Phantom of the Opera*, 1991)
History Loves Company (Chicago production, 1991)
December Songs (a song cycle, 1991)
Titanic (1997)
An American Cantata (commissioned by the Kennedy Center, 2000)
Hans Christian Andersen (adaptation of Frank Loesser's film, London, 2000)

Tom Sawyer: A Ballet in Three Acts (2011)	*Death Takes a Holiday* (off-Broadway, 2011)

Some notable songs of Yeston's include:

Nine (1982) (Guido Contini, baritone; Luisa Contini, mezzo-soprano; Carla Albanese, alto; Claudia Nardi, mezzo-soprano; Liliane La Fleur, mezzo-soprano; Saraghina, mezzo-soprano)

Guido's Song ††	Unusual Way *
A Call from the Vatican *	Simple *
Only with You ††	Be on Your Own *
Folies Bergeres * *	I Can't Make This Movie ††
Nine *	Getting Tall †
The Bells of St. Sebastian ††	

In the Beginning (1987) (Avi, tenor; Arielle, soprano; Romer, baritone)

New Words

Grand Hotel (1989) (Doctor Otternschlag, baritone; Hermann Preysing, baritone; Felix von Gaigern, tenor; Flaemmchen, mezzo-soprano; Otto Kringelein, baritone)

I Want to Go to Hollywood * *	Til I Loved You †
Love Can't Happen †	Picture It * *

Goya: A Life In Song (1989)

Phantom (1991) (Phantom, baritone; Christine, soprano; Carlotta, mezzo-soprano; Gerard Carrier, baritone; Count de Chanton, tenor)

Where in the World ††	Who Ever Could Have
This Place Is Mine *	Dreamed Up You? ††/*
Home *	My True Love *
You Are Music ††/*	My Mother Bore Me ††

December Songs (1991)

Please Let's Not Even Say Hello * *	My Grandmother's Love Letters *
I Had a Dream About You * *	By the River *
Now and Then * *	

Titanic (1997) (Thomas Andrews, baritone; J. Bruce Ismay, baritone; E.J. Captain Smith, baritone; Murdoch, baritone; Harold Bride, tenor; Frederick Barrett, baritone; Henry Etches, tenor; Alice Beane, mezzo-soprano)

Barrett's Song ††   No Moon †
The Proposal ††

Biography

Yeston was born in Jersey City and raised in a home filled with music. His mother was a skilled pianist and his grandfather was a Jewish cantor. Yeston, noting that Berlin, Gershwin and Weill also had cantors in the family, commented, "When you take a young, impressionable child and put him at age three in the middle of a synagogue, and that child sees a man in a costume, dramatically raised up on a kind of stage, singing his heart out at the top of his lungs to a rapt congregation, it makes a lasting impression."[10]

Yeston's undergraduate degree was in theory and composition with a minor in French, German and Japanese literature. He completed his Masters degree at Cambridge University in England. Upon returning to the US, in 1972, Yeston accepted a teaching position at a small African American college in Pennsylvania where he taught music, art, philosophy, religion, western civilization and the history of black music. At the same time, he began working on his Ph.D. in musicology at Yale.

He developed his first musical, *Nine*, at the BMI workshop in New York and the O'Neill Center. Industry interest in his work on *Nine* let to an adaptation of *La Cage Aux Folles*, set in New Orleans and titled *The Queen of Basin Street*, a project that he ultimately left. Following *Nine*'s opening, Yeston began work on a musical adaptation of Gaston Leroux's *The Phantom of the Opera*. As money was being raised for Yeston's *Phantom*, Andrew Lloyd Webber's version became a smash in London's West End. Yeston's has been very successful regionally but has never appeared on Broadway.

1-2-3-4-5, Yeston's 1987 musical based on the first five books of the Bible, had been workshopped and revised at Manhattan Theatre Club and in 1998 saw a fully mounted production as *In The Beginning* at Maine State Theatre. *Goya: A Life in Song* saw life as a concept album starring opera star Placido Domingo. At the request of director/choreographer Tommy Tune, Yeston supplied additional songs for the Robert Wright and George Forest musical, *Grand Hotel*, in 1989. *Titanic* opened in 1997 to uniformly negative reviews but developed a following, won five major Tony Awards and managed to run for more than 800 performances. His most recent musical, *Death Takes a Holiday*, ran off-Broadway in 2011 garnering a number of Drama Desk and Outer Critics Circle Awards.

Resources

Yeston's website www.mauryyeston.com/about offers a great deal of useful information.

Alan Menken (b. 1949): From counter-culture to mainstream

Stylistic approach

Best known for his work at Walt Disney Pictures, many of composer Menken's film scores have been transferred to the stage by Disney Theatrical. Menken's sound is primarily an energized revival of the Golden Age musicals with occasional inclusion of various ethnic or pop styles as appropriate. He employed calypso stylings in *The Little Mermaid* in songs like "Under the Sea" and "Kiss the Girl." Some of his songs have received pop power ballad renditions like the Celine Dion and Peabo Bryson cover of "Beauty and the Beast" or the Peabo Bryson and Regina Belle cover of "A Whole New World." His score for *Little Shop of Horrors* evokes the light pop/rock of the early 1960s while his scores for *Hercules* and *Sister Act* are appropriately gospel infused. Overall, though, Menken's songs predominately evoke the sound of the Golden Age of Broadway, the old-fashioned show tune like "Beauty and the Beast," "Part of Your World" (*The Little Mermaid*), "Out There" (*The Hunchback of Notre Dame*) or "Proud of Your Boy" (*Aladdin*).

Much of the fun of Menken's work with Ashman is that he places the rock and pop styles inside traditional standard American show tunes. This is what has made his material work so well for animated films. Listen to the original cast recording of *Beauty and the*

Beast and you will hear the pop inflections of the standard songs sung by Belle, the Beast and others. Other scores, like *Sister Act*, are unabashedly pop based. Menken's music, for the most part, works best when given a pop/rock based interpretation. All of the performances on the original cast recording of *Little Shop of Horrors*, or Patina Miller in *Sister Act*, are just a few good examples of how to apply these kinds of stylistic devices to Menken's songs. Even Menken's more traditional musical comedy songs, like the vaudevillian "You Ain't Never Had a Friend Like Me," from *Aladdin*, or "King of New York," from *Newsies*, reflect Menken's pop/rock sensibility.

Body of work

Menken's film scores include:

Little Shop of Horrors (1986) *
The Little Mermaid (1989) *
Beauty and the Beast (1991) *
Aladdin (1992) ***
Newsies (1992) †††
Pocahontas (1995) †
The Hunchback of Notre Dame (1996) †
Hercules (1997) **
Home on the Range (2004) ††

A Christmas Carol (Hallmark Entertainment for NBC, 2004) ****
The Shaggy Dog (2006)
Enchanted (2007) †
Tangled (2010) ††
Galavant (ABC Television, 2015) ††
Lidsville (in production for DreamWorks Animation)

* lyrics by Howard Ashman
** lyrics by David Zippel
*** lyrics by Howard Ashman and Tim Rice

**** lyrics by Lyn Ahrens
† lyrics by Stephen Schwartz
†† lyrics by Glenn Slater
††† lyrics by Jack Feldman

His theatre scores include:

God Bless You, Mr. Rosewater (off-Broadway, 1979) *
Little Shop of Horrors (off-Broadway, 1982) *

Weird Romance (off-Broadway, 1992)
Beauty and the Beast (1994) ***

A Christmas Carol (Madison
Square Garden, 1994) * * * *
King David (written as an ora-
torio to celebrate the three-
thousandth anniversary of
the city of Jerusalem, it was
produced for nine perfor-
mances on Broadway in
1997) * * * * *
Der Glöckner von Notre Dame
(*The Hunchback of Notre
Dame*, German production,
1999) †
The Little Mermaid (2008) ††
Sister Act (London, 2009/
Broadway, 2011) †††

Leap of Faith (2012) †††
Newsies (2012) ††††
Aladdin (2014) †††††
*The Hunchback of Notre
Dame* (produced in
Berlin, La Jolla Playhouse,
Paper Mill Playhouse and
Tuacahn Center, Tokyo, no
Broadway production is
currently planned) †
*The Apprenticeship of Duddy
Kravitz* (Montreal, 2015) * *
A new musical based on
the film *Corinna, Corinna*
is currently being
written *†

* lyrics by Howard Ashman
* * lyrics by David Spencer
* * * lyrics by Howard Ashman
and Tim Rice
* * * * lyrics by Lyn Ahrens
* * * * * lyrics by Tim Rice
† lyrics by Stephen Schwartz

†† lyrics by Howard Ashman
and Glenn Slater
††† lyrics by Glenn Slater
†††† lyrics by Jack Feldman
††††† lyrics by Howard
Ashman and Chad Beguelin
*† lyrics by Brian Yorkey

Due in great part to his success with the Disney animated films,
Menken's work is extremely well known and beloved. Some of his
most popular songs include:

Little Shop of Horrors (1986) (Seymour Krelbourn, tenor; Audrey,
mezzo-soprano; Orin Scrivelle, D.D.S., baritone; Audrey II,
baritone)

Grow for Me †
Somewhere That's Green * *
Dentist! †/††

Feed Me ††
Suddenly Seymour †
Suppertime ††

Beauty and the Beast (1991) (Belle, mezzo-soprano; The Beast,
baritone; Gaston, baritone; Maurice, baritone; Lefou, baritone;
Lumiere, baritone; Mrs. Potts, mezzo-soprano)

Me ††   Beauty and the Beast **
Home *   A Change in Me *
Gaston ††

The Hunchback of Notre Dame (1999) (Quasimodo, tenor; Dom
   Claude Frollo, baritone; Esmeralda, mezzo-soprano)

Out There †

The Little Mermaid (2008) (Ariel, mezzo-soprano; Eric, tenor;
   Sebastian, baritone; Ursula, alto)

Part of Your World   Poor Unfortunate Souls **
Under the Sea †   Kiss the Girl †

Sister Act (2011) (Deloris Van Cartier, mezzo-soprano; Mother
   Superior, mezzo-soprano; Sister Mary Robert, mezzo-soprano;
   Sister Mary Patrick, mezzo-soprano; Curtis Jackson, baritone/
   tenor; Lt. Eddie Souther, baritone/tenor)

Here Within These Walls *   The Life I Never Lead *

Newsies (2012) (Jack Kelly, tenor; Katherine Plummer, mezzo-
   soprano; Medda Larkin, mezzo-soprano; Spot Conlon, tenor)

Santa Fe †   Watch What Happens **

Aladdin (2014) (Aladdin, baritone/tenor; Jafar, baritone; Genie,
   baritone; Jasmine, mezzo-soprano;

Proud of Your Boy †   A Whole New World */†
Friend Like Me ††

Pocahontas (film, 1995)

Just Around the River Bend *   Colors of the Wind *

Hercules (film, 1997)
Go the Distance *

Biography

Raised in New Rochelle, a suburb of New York City, in a home filled with the songs of the musical theatre, Menken entered NYU as a pre-med student before ultimately graduating with a degree in music. He worked on several early musicals in the BMI Lehman Engel Musical Theatre Workshop.

In 1978, in collaboration with librettist/lyricist/director Howard Ashman, Menken wrote the show that was their first big success, *Little Shop of Horrors* in 1982. *Little Shop's* five-year run at the Orpheum Theatre "set the box-office record for highest grossing Off-Broadway show of all time."[11] After working with other people, Ashman called in 1988, offering Menken the chance to write a new animated film musical for Disney, *The Little Mermaid*. Based on the success of *Mermaid*, Ashman and Menken began work on *Beauty and the Beast*, which Ashman completed and *Aladdin*, which Ashman was unable to complete before he died from AIDS in 1991.

After Ashman's passing, Menken worked with different lyricists on a range of projects. Menken has won eight of his 19 Academy Award nominations, seven of his 16 Golden Globe nominations, 11 Grammy Awards, one of his five Tony Award nominations, and one of his six Drama Desk Award nominations.

Resources

Menken's website alanmenken.com offers a great deal of information. Menken's music is available in a variety of vocal selection, vocal score and anthology books.

Richard Maltby Jr. (b. 1937) and David Shire (b. 1937): *Starting here, starting now*

Stylistic approach

Although lyricist/librettist/director Maltby and composer Shire both had their greatest professional successes with other collaborators, their work together represents material of an extraordinarily high quality. Both of these writers are intensely musically literate, both being sons of big band leaders; they are also both highly intelligent, having met and begun their collaboration while undergraduates at Yale University. Highly infused with the popular and jazz styles of the 1970s and 1980s, David Shire's songs asks for vocal interpretations using those styles. Richard Maltby's lyrics are intensely smart; he has said that he has a tendency to write for characters who are almost too articulate, whose downfall is their intellect getting in the way of their emotional needs. Maltby's use of irony, wordplay involving homonyms and so on is not accidental. The characters who sing them are aware of their verbal dexterity and their wit, as evidenced in the songs "Crossword Puzzle," "Another Wedding" and "Back on Base."

While the other composers' works in this chapter are defined by their musicality, Maltby and Shire's songs are defined by their wit and humanity – both lyrical and musical. The characters that Maltby and Shire write are usually very self-aware, witty and literate; they use their humor and wit as a defense against the hardships of the world. They struggle with ethical dilemmas. While Shire is most comfortable in the worlds of symphonic music (as in his film scores) or songs with a contemporary or popular feel, the musical component in their songs almost always takes a back seat to the lyric content and the acting choices. Listen to Loni Ackerman singing "Crossword Puzzle," Margery Cohen singing "Autumn," or George Lee Andrews singing "I Don't Remember Christmas" from *Starting Here, Starting Now* for a sense of this style that weighs acting choices before musical choices.

Body of work

Many of Maltby and Shire's musicals never saw successful commercial productions. Aside from *Baby* and *Big* (*the musical*), their best-known shows are two revues compiled mostly of songs taken from their unsuccessful book musicals. Their musicals include:

Cyrano (written while undergraduates at Yale, received production by the Yale Dramatic Society, 1958 and later the Williamstown Theatre Festival)

The Grand Tour (written while undergraduates at Yale, received production by the Yale Dramatic Society and later the Williamstown Theatre Festival)

The Sap of Life
(off-Broadway, 1961)
How Do You Do, I Love You
(summer stock, 1967)
Love Match (Ahmanson
Theatre, 1968)
Starting Here, Starting Now
(off-Broadway, 1977)
Baby (1983)

Urban Blight (Manhattan
Theatre Club, 1988)
Closer Than Ever (1989)
Big (*the musical*) (1996)
Take Flight (London, 2007,
regional US premiere at
McCarter Theatre, 2011)
Waterfall (in development for
Broadway 2016)

Having been covered by various recording artists and transitioned from book musicals to revues, many Maltby and Shire's songs adapt well to being performed in different vocal registers. Some of their better-known songs include:

And What If We Had Love Like
That? ††/*
Another Wedding Song **/††
At Night She Comes Home
to Me ††
Autumn
Baby, Baby, Baby
Back on Base **
Barbara ††
Crossword Puzzle **
Dancing All the Time **
Easier to Love ††
Fatherhood Blues ††
Fathers of Fathers †/††
I Don't Remember Christmas ††
I Chose Right †

I Hear Bells ††
I Want It All **
If I Sing ††
A Little Bit Off **
Miss Byrd **
One of the Good Guys †/††
Patterns *
Starting Here, Starting Now
Stop Time *
The Story Goes On **
Throw It to the Wind *
Two People in Love **/†
What About Today **
What Am I Doin'? ††
What Could Be Better? **/†
With You ††/**

Biography

Both sons of bandleaders, Maltby and Shire were both born and raised far from New York City, Maltby in Ripon, Wisconsin and Shire in Buffalo, New York. They met and began working together while undergraduates at Yale University. After having two college works, *Cyrano* and *Grand Tour* produced by the Yale Dramatic Society, they moved to New York to pursue their careers in the theatre. *The Sap of Life* ran off-Broadway in 1961 for just over six weeks.

By the early 1970s, Shire had moved to California and become very successful composing scores for film and television in Hollywood. In 1976, while they had seen little popular success, their work was known in the industry. Manhattan Theatre Club proposed a revue of songs from their unproduced and unsuccessful shows; that revue ultimately became *Starting Here, Starting Now*. Maltby's directorial career took off too in 1978 when he conceived and directed *Ain't Misbehavin'*, which also began its life at Manhattan Theatre Club and won Tony Awards for Best Musical and Best Director. In addition to his work with Shire, Maltby wrote lyrics for *Miss Saigon*, *Nick and Nora* and *The Pirate Queen*, and he directed *Song and Dance*, *Fosse* and *The Story of My Life*. Maltby and Shire continue to work together, having *Waterfall*, a new project in development for a Broadway 2016 opening.

Resources

Direct resources on Maltby and Shire are scant; there are no biographies dealing exclusively with them, nor do they have websites. But there are many reviews of their work, and many interviews with both of them on youtube.com.

William Finn (b. 1952)

Stylistic approach

Composer and lyricist Finn's songs are challenging vocal material. Finn's songs almost give the appearance of being asymmetrical, written in a stream-of-consciousness manner; emphasis sometimes lands on the wrong syllable, phrases contain extra or missing clauses. There is great dramatic truth to his writing, but it can be elusive and coming to terms with it can take some work. Finn's work is different and his authorial voice is unique. He is drawn to writing for unique voices, and quirky performers like Alison Fraser, Mary Testa and Chip Zien are regular Finn performers. These performers and others are so successful at singing Finn's songs that they make it seem easy. In fact, there are many interesting twists and turns to Finn's music and lyrics, and they all need to be grappled with and come to terms with. But often, the things that take the most work to digest are the most interesting and multi-faceted.

Body of work

Many of Finn's shows are not terribly familiar. One of his earliest pieces, *In Trousers*, became part of a trilogy of one-act musicals, which included *March of the Falsettos* and *Falsettoland*. The latter two of these were later produced together as two acts under the title *Falsettos* on Broadway in 1992. Finn's works include:

Sizzle (produced at Williams College during Finn's undergraduate years)
In Trousers (off-Broadway, 1979)
March of the Falsettos (Playwright's Horizons, 1981)
America Kicks up Its Heels (off-Broadway, 1983)
Dangerous Games (1989)
Romance in Hard Times (off-Broadway, 1989)
Falsettoland (off-Broadway, 1990)
Falsettos (1992)

A New Brain (Lincoln Center, 1998)
Love's Desire (Public Theatre, 1998)
Muscle (Truman College, 2001)
Painting You for Love's Fire (The Acting Company)
Elegies: A Song Cycle (2003)
The 25th Annual Putnam County Spelling Bee (off-Broadway, 2004, Broadway, 2005)
Make Me a Song (off-Broadway, 2007)
Little Miss Sunshine (2011)
The Royal Family of Broadway (project abandoned, 2006)

Finn's songs are quirky, highly individual, funny and intensely personal. Between book musicals, revues and cover recordings, many of his songs have been sung in different settings by men and women in various registers. All of his songs, including the most obscure, are well worth getting to know. Some of Finn's most well-known songs include:

All Fall Down **
And They're Off ††
Anytime (I am There)
Change *
Everyone Hates His Parents †
Father to Son †
Four Jews in a Room Bitching
The Games I Play ††
Goodbye

Heart and Music ††
Holding to the Ground **
How Marvin Eats His Breakfast
I Have Found
The I Love You Song
I Never Wanted to Love You ††/†
I Speak Six Languages **

I'd Rather Be Sailing †/††
I'm Breaking Down **
I'm Not That Smart †
Infinite Joy
Love Is Blond ††
Love Me for What I Am *
Just Go
A Marriage Proposal ††
My Father's a Homo †

Set Those Sails *
This Had Better Come to
 a Stop †
Unlikely Lovers
What More Can I Say †
What Would I Do †/††
When the Earth Stopped
 Turning *
You Gotta Die Sometime ††

Biography

Born in Boston and raised in Natick, Massachusetts, Finn is one of the most autobiographical composer/lyricists in the American musical theatre; he writes overwhelmingly about the experience of being gay and Jewish in contemporary America. Finn graduated from Williams College where he majored in Literature and American Civilization. When Finn was 29, in 1981, the AIDS crisis began. It is not surprising that so much of Finn's material deals with loss; *The Washington Post* referred to him as "the musical theater's composer-laureate of loss."[12]

Resources

Very little has been written about Finn in book form, but there are plenty of magazine and newspaper articles, reviews, recordings, blogs and more.[13]

In summary

Historically, until this point the songs of the musical theatre were recorded and released by pop singers and became the popular material of the day; but for each of these writers, popular music was something outside the musical theatre, mostly rock and roll. The vocabulary of that popular music became the basis of the vocabulary that they brought to the musical theatre stage. Rather than writing songs that would become popular, they tended to write songs that reflected the sensibility of popular music.

All of the writers looked at in this chapter bring their own particular brand of the popular music sensibility to the Broadway musical stage. Galt MacDermot came to the musical theatre from the worlds of African music and jazz. Stephen Schwartz, on his own website, lists his wide and disparate range of musical influences. Marvin Hamlisch came to writing for the musical theatre through writing popular hits and Hollywood movie scores. In a 2015 interview on Broadway.com, William Finn talked about how his first produced musical, *In Trousers*, is a reaction to the Beatles.

As the first generation of musical theatre writers to grow up with rock and roll as the prevalent form of popular music during their adolescence, it was these writers who were able to create characters whose native idiom was rock based, or at least heavily influenced by that popular music. An understanding of the influences on these writers can inform the singer and help shape a performance that is, perhaps, truer to the writer's intent.

Notes

1 www.galtmacdermot.com/works.htm, maintained by MacDermot's recording label, Kilmarnock Records/MacDermot Music.

2 Scott Miller, *Let the Sun Shine In: The Genius of Hair*, Portsmouth, NH: Heinemann Drama, 2003.

3 Eric Grode, *Hair: The Story of the Show that Defined a Generation*, Philadelphia, PA: Running Press, 2010.

4 Jonathon Johnson, *Good Hair Days: A Personal Journey with the American Tribal Love-Rock Musical, Hair*, Bloomington, IN: iUniverse, Inc. 2004.

5 Stephen Schwartz at a Q & A session at an ASCAP event, cited by Carol de Giere, "Stephen Schwartz – Musical Influences and Styles," MusicalSchwartz.com, www.musicalschwartz.com/schwartz-musical-influences.htm, accessed January 3, 2015.

6 www.stephenschwartz.com/ accessed January 3, 2015.

7 www.musicalschwartz.com/ accessed January 3, 2015.

8 Carole de Giere, *Defying Gravity: The Creative Career of Stephen Schwartz, from Godspell to Wicked*, New York, NY: Applause Theatre & Cinema Books, 2008.

9 Marvin Hamlisch, *The Way I Was*, New York, NY: Scribner, 1992.

10 Maury Yeston, *Playbill*, May 31, 1997, pp. 18–20.

11 "Just a Bit About Alan Menken," *AlanMenken.com*, www.alanmenken.com/m/biography/, accessed January 17, 2015.

12 Peter Marks, "At Signature, 'Elegies' Puts the Good in Goodbye," *The Washington Post*, March 31, 2004, www.washingtonpost.com/archive/lifestyle/2004/03/31/at-signature-elegies-puts-the-good-in-goodbye/ca89b291-f6c2-4295-a129-37b69cfb009b/, accessed May 9, 2016.

13 See, for example, Ellen Pall, "The Long-Running Musical of William Finn's Life," *The New York Times*, June 14, 1998, www.nytimes.com/1998/06/14/magazine/the-long-running-musical-of-william-finns-life.html, accessed May 9, 2016.

Chapter 10

The mega-musical

Andrew Lloyd Webber, and Claude-Michel Schönberg and Alain Boublil

By 1980, a new kind of musical theatre was taking the world by storm, the mega-musical. Concept-driven musicals, which had brought the musical theatre forward through the 1970s, had become too financially risky with the exploding cost of production. The business model of marketing huge hits targeted towards the widest possible audience in identical productions replicated and installed around the world, demanded new kinds of musicals.

The mega-musicals represent some of the most successful musicals ever written in terms of length of run, the number of productions, the number of people who have seen them, and the revenue they have generated. Their popularity makes them a tremendous potential source of income for the musical theatre performer. Just as pop and rock stars in live venues must perform their greatest hits to please their audiences, and opera companies and symphony orchestras are obligated to present the most popular pieces from the repertoire, the most successful mega-musicals are continually presented on stages around the world. The mega-musical is a vitally important part of the canon for the musical theatre performer or concert artist to understand and sing well.

The drawing of the poor little waif from *Les Miserables* was recognizable on billboards on highways and airport terminals around the world, as was the pair of silhouetted dancers each outlined in the gleaming yellow cat's eye. Immediately identifiable worldwide product branding was an essential element of these shows' success.

Mega-musicals tended to be driven by scenic spectacle. They were through-sung, with most, if not all, of the dialogue sung in the operatic tradition of recitative. Deeply emotional, these shows call for a heightened style of acting not too far removed from melodrama. Much of the music from these shows was written to lie towards the top of the singers' vocal range, creating an intensely felt emotional quality.

While some of these musicals had little or no story, many returned to a deeply sentimental and self-serious style. Music took precedence over lyrics; great sweeping melodies seemed to express a particular sentiment in a deeply felt way without much development of plot or character. But the success of these musicals and their songs is unquestionable. People around the planet thrill to (and often sing along with) "I Dreamed a Dream," "Bring Him Home" and "The Music of the Night."

Often, singers known for their pop styling created many of the major roles in the mega-musicals. However the great majority of their replacements approach the material from a more classical legitimate tradition, allowing them to sustain so much technically difficult and emotional singing eight times a week.

This chapter explores the vocal demands and possibilities for the songs from the mega-musicals of the 1980s and 1990s. The greatest songwriters of mega-musicals, the ones examined in this chapter, are Andrew Lloyd Webber (b. 1948), and Claude-Michel Schönberg (b. 1944) and Alain Boublil (b. 1941). Both Lloyd Webber and the team of Schönberg and Boublil frequently call for vocalists who partake of a decidedly classical vocal sound informed by contemporary styling. Some of their shows, like *Jesus Christ Superstar*, are more rock based, while others, like *Aspects of Love*, call for a more classical vocal sound. Lloyd Webber's and Boublil and Schönberg's works are examined in this chapter, as is producer Cameron Mackintosh (b. 1946).

Andrew Lloyd Webber (b. 1948)

Stylistic approach

Andrew Lloyd Webber is arguably the most successful musical theatre composer ever. *Jesus Christ Superstar* both rocked and shocked the world. *Phantom of the Opera* holds records for grossing more money (more than $6 billion) and being seen by more people worldwide (more than 140 million) than any other, as well as for being the longest-running show on Broadway and the second-longest in London; it is still going strong in both cities and around the world.

Essential to Lloyd Webber's work is his solid grounding in classical music and the musical theatre classics, and how comfortable he is incorporating contemporary, pop and rock styles in his music. He writes gorgeous melodies, which sometimes mask how difficult they can be to sing well; people like the tunes and so they assume they can sing them well. Singing Lloyd Webber well takes great technique, control, mastery of a range of popular and rock styles and the taste to apply those styles enough without letting the stylization comment on the material.

Lloyd Webber has been writing musicals since 1965, and his body of work encompasses more than what we consider the megamusicals of the 1980s and 1990s. But as his greatest successes as a composer occurred during this period, his work is examined in this chapter. Like the other composers in this period, Lloyd Webber's scores feature "an eclectic blend of musical genres ranging from classical to rock, pop, and jazz, and with inclusion of electro-acoustic music and choral-like numbers in his musicals."[1] Lloyd Webber has written in so many different styles that many of his shows may appear to be completely different from each other. The operatic style Lloyd Webber uses in *Phantom of the Opera* is far from the pop pastiches of *Joseph and the Amazing Technicolor Dreamcoat* or the straight rock sounds of *Jesus Christ Superstar* or the musical theatre jazz styling of *Sunset Boulevard*. But underlying all of Lloyd Webber's work is a strong classical tradition fused with a leaning towards pop or techno-pop. Many roles in his shows have been created by singers with rock or pop inflections and have later been taken over with singers with a strong classical technique.

Andrew Lloyd Webber's first musical, the massive hit *Jesus Christ Superstar,* gave him a reputation as a writer of screaming rock songs. This score is as extreme in its need for rock styling as any other material in the musical theatre canon. While *Evita* continued this trend with Eva Peron and Che, ultimately Lloyd Webber's classical background made itself known. Lloyd Webber's music calls for a big bright sound from women; listen to Elaine Paige or Betty Buckley in *Cats,* and Paige or Patti Lupone in *Evita*. Laurie Beechman's narrator in *Joseph* is another example of the Lloyd Webber "ping." Male characters or female, Lloyd Webber writes for voices singing at the tops of their ranges. While some composers write well for character singers, where the song is driven more by the acting than the singing, Lloyd Webber does not fall into this category. The singer approaching Lloyd Webber's work needs to pay great attention to the shape of the musical line, the phrasing and the dynamics. There is usually at least some pop styling required of the voice, even in the most legitimate of Lloyd Webber's songs. Listen to the throb of the pop vibrato in Michael Ball's voice on the original cast recording of *Aspects of Love* for an example of this aspect of Lloyd Webber's writing.

Body of work

Andrew Lloyd Webber's career as a composer spans 40 years and continues to go strong. Although his earliest musicals predate the mega-musical by 15 years, his work is examined in this chapter; but as some of his earlier shows partake of other styles, each show will be examined stylistically individually.

The Likes of Us (1965; lyrics by Tim Rice)

When originally written, in 1965, *The Likes of Us* failed to attract financial backing and was not produced. In 1975, Andrew Lloyd Webber initiated a summer arts festival in a chapel on his estate in Sydmonton, dedicated to the presentation of new works to a small private audience. In 2005, Lloyd Webber resurrected *The Likes of Us* and presented it at his festival for the first time.

Musical numbers include:

Twice in Love Every Day	A Man on His Own
I'm a Very Busy Man	You Can Never Make It Alone
Love Is Here	Hold a March
Strange and Lovely Song	Will This Last Forever?
The Likes of Us	You Won't Care About Him
How Am I to Know	Anymore
We'll Get Him	Going, Going, Gone!
This is My Time	Man of the World
Lion-Hearted Land	Have Another Cup of Tea

Joseph and the Amazing Technicolor Dreamcoat (1968; lyrics by Tim Rice)

Joseph was created as a short pop oratorio for a school for boys aged seven to thirteen. The innocent infectious energy of the piece saw it developed into a concept album in 1969 and various evolving stage versions in 1970, 1971, 1972 and 1973, after the success of *Jesus Christ Superstar*. With almost no dialogue, *Joseph* is a sung-through musical. For this score, Lloyd Webber used a wide range of pop styles including Caribbean calypso, French chanson, pop ballad, American country and western, 1920s-style vaudeville, 1960s pop rock, an Elvis Presley imitation and others. Much of the fun of this score comes from applying all of these contrasting styles. Unlike much of Lloyd Webber's later work, this score is purely a pop score, originally intended for the fun of innocent young boys imitating more mature pop-singing styles. The subsequent stage productions have retained their pop/rock roots and call for all manner of pop and rock vocal styles. The narrator has a high pop belt-mix voice; Joseph is a tenor.

Songs include (see p. 10 for key to symbols):

Any Dream Will Do †	Poor, Poor Pharaoh/Song of the
Jacob and Sons **	King ††
Joseph's Coat (The Coat of	Pharaoh's Dream Explained †
Many Colors)	Stone the Crows
Poor, Poor Joseph	King of My Heart
One More Angel ††	Those Canaan Days ††
Potiphar ††	Who's the Thief?
Close Every Door †	Benjamin Calypso
Go, Go, Go Joseph	Any Dream Will Do †
Pharaoh Story	

Jesus Christ Superstar (1970; lyrics by Tim Rice)

The concept album of Lloyd Webber's *Jesus Christ Superstar* swept the world. The idea of comparing Jesus Christ with a pop or rock star was revelatory to some and sacrilegious to others, but very few people in 1970 had no opinion. The album and response to it became the cover story of publications like *Time* magazine and *The New York Times*. Vocally, *Superstar* is pure rock and roll. While *Joseph* had been a loving homage to the various styles that it imitated, *Superstar* was the real thing. While there are symphonic components to the orchestration, the singing is straight out rock and roll, except for "Herod's Song," which is straight-ahead vaudeville. Singing *Superstar* requires strong rock vocal instruments and a strong sense of rock styling. Growling, groaning, controlled shouting, frontally placed tones, pitch bending, portamento, riffing and other ornamentation – the Superstar score calls for all of these. Jesus, Judas, King Herod and Simon Zealotes are all screaming rock tenors; Mary Magdalene has a strong rock belt.

Songs from this show include:

Heaven on Their Minds †
What's the Buzz?
Strange Thing Mystifying †
Everything's Alright *
This Jesus Must Die †/††
Hosanna
Simon Zealotes †
Poor Jerusalem †
Pilate's Dream ††
The Temple †
I Don't Know How to Love
    Him **
Damned for All Time/Blood
    Money †/††

The Last Supper †
Gethsemane (I Only Want
    to Say) †
The Arrest ††
Peter's Denial
Pilate and Christ †/††
Herod's Song ††
Could We Start Again,
    Please? **/††
Judas's Death ††
Trial Before Pilate (Including
    the 39 Lashes)†
Superstar †
The Crucifixion †

Jeeves (1975; lyrics by Alan Ayckbourn)

Based on the characters of Bertie Wooster and his valet Jeeves, created by P.G. Wodehouse. Although the project was originally the idea of lyricist Tim Rice, Rice withdrew from the project early on, and Lloyd Webber collaborated with playwright Alan Ayckbourn, who wrote book and lyrics. Lloyd Webber's score was unlike anything else he had ever written; this very traditional score sounded like a musical from the Golden Age. This score calls for well-produced character singing. It does not partake of any of the rock and roll elements Lloyd Webber had used so successfully, nor does it have the more legitimate classical sweep of his shows that were to come. The show closed very quickly in the West End and did not have an American premiere until a failed production in 1996.

Songs from this musical include:

Code of the Woosters
Travel Hopefully
Female of the Species
Today
When Love Arrives
Jeeves is Past His Peak
Half a Moment
S.P.O.D.E.

Eulalie
Summer Day
Banjo Boy
Deadlier Than the Male
The Hallo Song
By Jeeves
What Have You Got to Say,
    Jeeves?

It's a Pig
Love Maze
Wooster Will Entertain You
Food of Love
Song of Spode
Literary Men

A False Start (1996 production)
Never Fear (1996 production)
That Nearly Was Us (1996 production)
The Wizard Rainbow Finale (1996 production)

Evita (1976; lyrics by Tim Rice)

Evita is Lloyd Webber's and lyricist Rice's biographical musical of the life of Argentina's Eva Peron. As with *Superstar*, it is a through-written rock opera. The score demands strong, legitimate singing technique with elements of rock singing applied judiciously. Eva Peron has an exceptionally high belt-mix, Ché is a tenor and Juan Peron is a baritone. Songs from *Evita* include:

A Cinema in Buenos Aires, 26 July 1952
Requiem for Evita
Oh, What a Circus †
On This Night of a Thousand Stars †
Eva and Magaldi/Eva Beware of the City **/†
Buenos Aires **
Good Night and Thank You
The Lady's Got Potential †
The Art of the Possible ††
Charity Concert
I'd Be Surprisingly Good For You **/††
Hello and Goodbye **
Another Suitcase, Another Hall *
Peron's Latest Flame †

A New Argentina
On the Balcony of the Casa Rosada
Don't Cry for Me Argentina **
High Flying Adored †
Rainbow High **
Rainbow Tour
The Actress Hasn't Heard the Lines **
And the Money Kept Rolling In (And Out) †
Santa Evita
A Waltz for Eva and Ché **/††
You Must Love Me **
She is a Diamond ††
Dice Are Rolling ††
Eva's Final Broadcast **
Montage
Lament

Tell Me on a Sunday (1979; lyrics by Don Black)

Tell Me on a Sunday was created by Lloyd Webber and lyricist Don Black as a one-woman show for Marti Webb, who had been playing Eva Peron for the matinees of the West End production of *Evita*. It was first heard at the Sydmonton Festival in 1979, was performed as a television special on the BBC in 1980, and was combined with a ballet piece of Lloyd Webber's, *Variations*, to create the musical *Song and Dance*, which opened in London in 1982. In 1985, Richard Maltby Jr. was brought in to Americanize *Song and Dance* for its Broadway version with Bernadette Peters. The show underwent revisions in 2003 for a London production, and again for a 2010 UK tour. All of these different versions resulted in a long list of songs that have appeared in the show at one time or another. They were all written for a woman's voice with a strong belt, great agility in the mix with very few vocally legitimate passages. The music is pop, and Lloyd Webber calls for pop styling throughout the score.

Songs from *Tell Me On a Sunday* and *Song and Dance* include:

Take That Look Off Your Face
Let Me Finish
It's Not the End of the World
  (If I Lose Him)
Letter Home to England
Sheldon Bloom
Capped Teeth and Caesar Salad
You Made Me Think You Were
  in Love
It's Not the End of the World
  (If He's Younger)
Second Letter Home
Come Back with the Same
  Look in Your Eyes
Let's Talk About You
Tell Me on a Sunday
I'm Very You, You're Very Me
Nothing Like You've
  Ever Known

The Last Man in My Life
Take That Look Off Your
  Face
I Love New York
Married Man
Goodbye Mum, Goodbye
  Girls
Haven in the Sky
Speed Dating
Tyler King
Third Letter Home
Unexpected Song
Who Needs Men
Fourth Letter Home
Ready Made Life
Fifth Letter Home
Somewhere, Someplace,
  Sometime
Dreams Never Run on Time

Cats (1981; lyrics by T. S. Eliot with additional lyrics by Richard Stilgoe and Trevor Nunn)

Lloyd Webber took the poetry of T.S. Eliot's *Old Possum's Practical Book of Cats* as his source material for this musical and set the poems almost intact as songs. The one exception was the hit "Memory," with lyrics by Trevor Nunn. The characters of

Grizabella, Bombalurina, Demeter and Jennyanydots are altos or mezzo-sopranos with high belt-mixes; Gus, Bustopher Jones, Mungojerrie, Rum Tum Tugger, Mr. Mistoffelees and Munkustrap are baritones, and Old Deuteronomy is a tenor. While the songs span a wide range of musical styles, they call for the newly emerging style of "pop/legitimate" that came to define Lloyd Webber's shows and the other mega-musicals. Songs from *Cats* include:

Jellicle Songs for Jellicle Cats
The Naming of Cats
Invitation to Jellicle Ball
The Old Gumbie Cat **
The Rum Tum Tugger ††
Grizabella: The Glamour Cat *
Bustopher Jones††/**
Mungojerrie and Rumplteazer **/††
The Awful Battle of the Pekes and the Pollicles
Old Deuteronomy
The Jellicle Ball
Memory *
The Moment of Happiness †
Gus: The Theatre Cat †
Growltiger's Last Stand
The Ballad of Billy McCaw
Skimbleshanks, The Railway Cat †
Macavity, The Mystery Cat**
Mr. Mistoffelees ††
Journey to the Heaviside Layer
The Ad-dressing of Cats

Starlight Express (1984; lyrics by Richard Stilgoe)

Starlight Express, a musical about a group of trains who all sing their stories and race to see who is the fastest. The score is based in pop and disco music, but also includes a country and western song, a rock ballad and an up-tempo gospel rouser. In terms of marketing and promotion *Starlight Express* is a mega-musical, but musically it is much more grounded in rock and roll than most of the other mega-musicals. All the principal women are mezzo-sopranos with strong rock belts except for Pearl, who is a soprano. Rusty and Electra are the tenor roles, and Greaseball and Poppa are the baritones. Mostly

it is written for big belt voices and requires rock, pop and gospel stylistic devices, namely portamento, sliding up to notes, embellishments and riffs. Vibrato should be used only sparingly on these songs.
   Songs from *Starlight Express* include:

Rolling Stock ††
Call Me Rusty †
A Lotta Locomotion **
Pumping Iron ††
AC/DC **
He Whistled at Me *
That Was Unfair **/††
There's Me
Poppa's Blues ††
Belle the Sleeping Car *
Boy, Boy, Boy ††
Starlight Express †
The Rap
Pearl Twirl ††/

U.N.C.O.U.P.L.E.D. **
C.B. **
Right Place, Right Time ††
I Am the Starlight †
No Comeback **
One Rock & Roll Too
   Many ††
Only He (Has the Power to
   Move Me) *
Only You †
Light at the End of the
   Tunnel ††
Make Up My Heart *
Next Time You Fall in Love */†

Cricket (Hearts and Wickets) (1986; lyrics by Tim Rice)

Cricket (Hearts and Wickets) was commissioned to celebrate Queen Elizabeth's 60th birthday. It was the last full musical Lloyd Webber wrote with lyricist Tim Rice. Sheet music from this musical is extremely difficult to find. *Cricket's* only production featured glam rock star Alvin Stardust as Vincent St. Leger, suggesting the same contemporary rock and roll/disco style as *Starlight Express*.
   Songs included:

The Summer Game ††
As the Seasons Slip
   Fruitlessly By *
The Sport of Kings */†
The Art of Bowling ††
All I Ask of Life ††

Fools Like Me *
A Ban for Life ††
The Making of St. Leger †
The Final Stand ††
One Hot Afternoon *

The Phantom of the Opera (1986; lyrics by Charles Hart)

Possibly the most famous musical ever written, certainly the most successful, *Phantom of the Opera* opened in the West End in 1986 and on Broadway in 1988; both productions are still going strong. The score is classically based, as its Paris Opera House setting would suggest. The Phantom is a tenor, Raoul is a baritone; and Christine and Carlotta are both sopranos. The title role, originated by pop star Michael Crawford, has since been played by actors with a much more legitimate sound. As with so many of the mega-musicals, the score of *Phantom* is intensely emotional, calling for a great dynamic range and singing at higher ends of the registers for longer periods of time. As with so many of these shows, the vocal feats called for require strong technique and impeccable phrasing. Songs from *The Phantom of the Opera* include:

Think of Me */†
Angel of Music *
The Phantom of the Opera */†
The Music of the Night †
I Remember/Stranger Than You
  Dreamed It */†
Prima Donna ††/*

Poor Fool, He Makes Me
  Laugh *
All I Ask of You */††
Masquerade
Wishing You Were Somehow
  Here Again *
The Point of No Return */†

Aspects of Love (1989; lyrics by Don Black and Charles Hart)

Aspects of Love is another Andrew Lloyd Webber musical with a classical-sounding score but cast with singers who excel in adding pop inflections. Even when not at his best, Lloyd Webber's music is always highly melodic. It is the pop inflection that makes these songs shine. The character of Alex Dillingham is a tenor, George Dillingham is a baritone, Jenny is a soprano role, and Rose is the mezzo-soprano. Songs from *Aspects of Love* include:

Love Changes Everything †/*
Parlez-vous Francais? **
Seeing Is Believing †
A Memory of a Happy
  Moment ††
Chanson d'enfance **
She'd Be Far Better Off
  with You †
Stop. Wait. Please. **/††

Leading Lady ††
Other Pleasures ††
There Is More to Love **
Mermaid Song *
The First Man You Remember ††
Falling
Hand Me the Wine and
  the Dice
Anything But Lonely *

Sunset Boulevard (1993; lyrics by Christopher Hampton and Don Black)

Solidly a mega-musical, *Sunset Boulevard* also has a legitimate score, this time with inflections of jazz to suggest the Hollywood of 1949. Again the singer is urged to approach this material from a contemporary pop perspective. The pop stylistic devices inform the classical sound and structure to give these musicals their distinctive sound. Norma Desmond is an alto, Joe Gillis and Max von Mayerling are the baritone roles, Betty Schaeffer is a mezzo with a strong belt-mix.

Songs from *Sunset Boulevard* include:

Let's Have Lunch	The Lady's Paying ††/**
Every Movie's a Circus	The Perfect Year **/††
Surrender **	This Time Next Year
With One Look **	Sunset Boulevard ††
Salome **/††	As If We Never Said
The Greatest Star of All ††	Goodbye **
Girl Meets Boy */††	Too Much in Love to Care */††
New Ways to Dream **	

Whistle Down the Wind (1996; lyrics by Jim Steinman)

In *Whistle Down the Wind*, with lyrics by pop songwriter Jim Steinman, Lloyd Webber went back to the rock and roll he had used so effectively in *Jesus Christ Superstar*. But this time he infused his score with gospel and country sounds. In the US, the show closed before it reached Broadway, but it received a very successful concept album featuring an array of pop and rock stars, and a relatively successful West End production in 1998. Songs from this show include:

The Vaults of Heaven	Unsettled Scores
I Never Get What I Pray For	If Only
Home by Now	Tire Tracks and Broken Hearts
It Just Doesn't Get Any Better Than This	Safe Haven
Whistle Down the Wind	Long Overdue for a Miracle
The Vow	When Children Rule the World
Cold	Annie Christmas
	No Matter What

Try Not to be Afraid
A Kiss is a Terrible Thing to
Waste
Charlie Christmas

Off Ramp Exit to Paradise
Wrestle with the Devil
Nature of the Beast

The Beautiful Game (2000; lyrics by Ben Elton)

The Beautiful Game is a coming of age story set among teenagers on a soccer team in Belfast, Ireland in 1969, during the rise of the IRA. In 2009 Lloyd Webber and lyricist Ben Elton revised *The Beautiful Game* and retitled it *The Boys in the Photograph*. Although set in 1969, the score frequently references more contemporary popular sounds like rap, football chants, lovely generic ballads and so forth. The lyrics and orchestration tend to suggest an Irish lilt, but little in the music itself does – it is on the singer to add this element. In fact the ballad melodies, pretty as they are, are so non-specific that one of them became the title song of *Love Never Dies*, the sequel to *Phantom of the Opera*. An understanding of Celtic folk music and folk styling would serve these songs well; if not Celtic, other folk styles could certainly be used. As with Bernstein's *West Side Story*, to which the critics compared this show, the score calls more for a youthful, enthusiastic, yearning sound, than a mature and completely controlled instrument. For this score, a rawer sound is an asset.

Songs from this show include:

The Beautiful Game
The Boys in the Photograph
Clean the Kit
Don't Like You
God's Own Country
Born in Belfast
Let Us Love in Peace
The Final (A Game of Two
Halves)
Off to the Party
The Craic
Our Kind of Love

The Happiest Day
To Have and To Hold
The First Time
I'd Rather Die on my Feet Than
Live on my Knees
The Selection
Dead Zone
If This is What We're
Fighting For
It Will Never End
All the Love I Have

The Woman in White (2004; lyrics by David Zippel)

By 2004, Lloyd Webber had honed the style of pop-infused legitimately based music, and the result is *The Woman in White*. With a stable of top performers like Michael Crawford and Michael Ball, who inhabit this style so naturally, Lloyd Webber wrote to their strengths. As with the other mega-musicals, this score calls for deeply emotional interpretations, with much of the emotion expressed in the singer's musical choices. The score does not contain much use of rock or pop, but the throb of the pop singer's vibrato is very much an asset to these songs. Marian Halcombe is a role for a soprano with a strong belt-mix, Laurie Fairlie is a soprano role, Anne Cathrick is a mezzo-soprano role, Walter Hartright is the tenor role and Count Fosco is the baritone role. This show opened in London and ten months later was completely revised and reopened as a new production. It ran a year and a half in London and only three months on Broadway. Songs from this show include.

I Hope You Like It Here */†	The Funeral/London – Fosco
Perspective */†	Tells of Laura's Death †
Trying Not to Notice †/*	Evermore Without You †
I Believe My Heart †/*	Lost Souls *
You See I Am No Ghost */†	If Not for Me for Her */†
A Gift for Living Well †/*	You Can Get Away with
All for Laura *	Anything †
The Document †/*	The Seduction †/*
If I Could Only Dream This	The Asylum */†
World Away *	Back to Limmeridge †/
The Nightmare †/*	

Love Never Dies (2010; lyrics by Glenn Slater)

Sequels are very rare in the musical theatre, and almost never successful. *Bye, Bye, Birdie* spawned *Bring Back Birdie*, *The Best Little Whorehouse in Texas* led to *The Best Little Whorehouse Goes Public* and *Annie* begat *Annie 2: Miss Hannigan's Revenge* and *Annie Warbucks*. All of these sequels failed fairly dismally. *Love Never Dies*, the sequel to *Phantom of the Opera*, has not found much success either, despite the fact that Lloyd Webber's score is highly melodic. As with *Phantom*, these songs call for highly trained legitimate voices. While pop inflections are terrific additions to an interpretation of this material, more important is the operatic nature of the score.

Songs include:

The Coney Island Waltz	Dear Old Friend
Heaven by the Sea	Beautiful
Only for Him/Only for You	The Beauty Underneath
The Ayrie	Why Does She Love Me?
Till I Hear You Sing	Devil Take the Hindmost
What a Dreadful Town	Bathing Beauty
Look with Your Heart	Love Never Dies
Beneath a Moonless Sky	
Once Upon Another Time	

Stephen Ward the Musical (2013; lyrics by Christopher Hampton and Don Black)

Stephen Ward is a chamber musical about the Profumo affair, a 1961 scandal involving Britain's Secretary of State for War, John Profumo, and a 19-year old would-be model, Christine Keeler, who had been introduced by osteopath and social climber Stephen Ward. Lloyd Webber calls on the sounds of the swinging sixties for this score, evoking some of his earlier rock material as well as some of the jazzier material from *Sunset Boulevard*.

Human Sacrifice ††	Mother Russia, While We Can ††
When You Get to Know Me ††/**	Love Nest /**
You're So Very Clever to Have Found This ††/**	Freedom Means the World to Me ††/**
This Side of the Sky ††/**	1963 **
Manipulation	Give Us Something Juicy **
He Sees Something in Me **	The Trial ††
Black Hearted Woman †	Too Close to the Flame ††

School of Rock (2015; lyrics by Glenn Slater)

Lloyd Webber's latest musical, *School of Rock*, based on the successful movie, opened in 2015 and has settled in for a long run in New York's Winter Garden Theatre, where *Cats* played for 18 years.

Biography

Born in London in 1948, Andrew Lloyd Webber's classical music roots run deep. His father was the director of the London College of Music; his mother was a piano teacher and his brother Julian is a world-renowned cellist. A piano prodigy, child violinist and french horn player, Lloyd Webber started a university degree in history at 17 but quickly changed universities to pursue a degree in music. In that same year, 1965, Lloyd Webber and lyricist Tim Rice began their collaboration, working on *The Likes of Us*, which would not premier until many years later at Sydmonton. A commission for a 20-minute pop cantata initiated what would become *Joseph and the Amazing Technicolor Dreamcoat*. By 1971, the pair had become an international sensation with *Jesus Christ Superstar*.

Lloyd Webber has managed to wed his classical background with all manner of popular and rock styles. He has become the most successful musical theatre composer ever as well as one of the wealthiest. His songs are known and sung around the world. Lloyd Webber has been knighted, won Tony Awards, Grammy Awards, an Oscar and the Kennedy Center Honors Award.

Resources

As one of the most successful composers ever, there is a great wealth of information on Andrew Lloyd Webber. The first biography on Lloyd Webber was published in 1985, but more recent biographies include Michael Coveney's *The Andrew Lloyd Webber Story*[2] and Stephen Citron's dual biography, *Stephen Sondheim and Andrew Lloyd Webber: The New Musical*.[3] Audio and video recordings of most of Lloyd Webber's writing are readily available.

Claude-Michel Schönberg (b. 1944) and Alain Boublil (b. 1941)

Stylistic approach

The French team of composer Schönberg and librettist/lyricist Boublil come to the theatre from the world of popular music. Their shows, particularly *Les Misérables* and *Miss Saigon* have come to epitomize the sound of the mega musicals.

Schönberg's music calls for pop vocal styles but requires legitimately trained voices to support the vocal and emotional size. Frequently the roles in their shows have been created by singers with strong popular music styling skills and later replaced with more "legitimate" singers. Much of their music sits at the high end of the singer's vocal range. Dramatically in most of their songs the singer shares the intensity of their emotion with the audience. A deeply felt, emotional performance is highly appropriate, even to the point of melodrama, as long as it does not shut down the vocal instrument.

Much of Schönberg and Boublil's work is vocally challenging. They aspire to operatic sound and symphonic scope, but within a pop idiom. Trying to achieve that size from within a pop idiom and sustain so much highly emotional material so high in the voice for so long is a challenge to any singer. Javert, Valjean, Eponine, Fantine and Cosette, in *Les Misérables*, all require pop inflections but need to push out a lot of sound and sustain long and difficult roles. The same is true of Chris and Kim in *Miss Saigon*. Listen to Kevin Gray's performance of "The American Dream" in *Miss Saigon* to get a sense of how difficult it is for The Engineer to tread the line between the need to stylize and the score's challenge to rise to the operatic scope.

Body of work

La Révolution Française (1973)

La Révolution Française is a through-sung rock opera, created first as a concept album and staged later that year at the *Palais des Sports de Paris*. Two additional collaborators worked on *La Révolution Française*. Claude-Michel Schönberg and Raymond Jeannot wrote the music, and Alain Boublil and Jean-Max Rivière wrote the book and lyrics. All of the songs are pop or rock songs, to which a symphonic element has been added in the studio, and later the theatre, paving the way for their works to come. All of the solo voices on the recordings of this show are driven by rock styles. While both the adult and children's ensembles occasionally sing in a more legitimate style, this musical is pure rock and pop singing. Knowledge of the French pop and rock singers of the 1970s and their vocal styles is very useful for the singer approaching this material. Throbbing vibrato, back-phrasing, phrasing ahead, speech-quality singing are required for the lower passages until the singer can soar on the higher passages. All of these elements of their later work are found in this recording. As with all of their later pieces, the show is completely sung through, with recitative-style pieces taking the place of any spoken dialogue. These songs are highly emotional and must be deeply felt by the singer; these are not the "intellectual" songs of Sondheim or Maltby and Shire, and shouldn't be approached in the same way.

Solo songs from this piece include:

Charles Gauthier †
Retour de la Bastille ††
Il s'appelle Charles Gauthier *
À bas tout les privilèges ††
Déclaration des droit de
  l'homme et du citoyen †
Ça ira, ça ira! ††
Quartre saisons pour un amour *
Serment de Talleyrand/Fête de
  la Fédération ††
Crieurs de journaux/La patrie
  est en danger ††
L'Exil †/*

Valmy/Proclamation de la
  République †
C'est du beau linge, mon
  général **/†
Le Procès de Louis XVI ††
Louis XVI/Exécution †
Chouans, en avant! ††
Fouquie-Tinville †
Au petit matin *
Que j'aie tort ou que j'aie
  raison ††
Le Fête de l'Être supreme ††
Révolution ††/*

Les Misérables (1980)

Like their first piece, *Les Misérables* first saw life as a concept album and was again mounted onstage in the *Palais des Sports* in 1980. The album came to the attention of producer Cameron Macintosh in 1983. After developing the piece for an English-language stage production over two years, Macintosh opened *Les Misérables* in London's West End. Productions on Broadway and around the world followed making *Les Misérables* one of the longest running and most successful musical entertainments ever created. Stylistically all of the musical elements discussed for their earlier work hold true for this one as well. The tenor roles are Jean Valjean and Marius; the baritone roles are Javert, Thenardier and Enjolras; Cosette is a soprano, Fantine, Eponine and Madame Thenardier are mezzo-sopranos.

Some of the solo songs of greatest interest from *Les Miserables* include:

I Dreamed a Dream **   Little People †
Who Am I †   A Little Fall of Rain **/†
Castle On a Cloud *   Drink With Me †/††
Master of the House ††/**   Bring Him Home †
Stars ††   Soliloquy (Javert's Suicide) ††
A Heart Full of Love †/**/*   Empty Chairs and Empty
On My Own **   Tables†

Miss Saigon

Schönberg and Boublil's *Miss Saigon* was written in the same style musically and dramaturgically. Some elements of the score suggest a vaguely Asian sound, particularly in the orchestration; but the score calls for legitimate singing with some minor pop styles laid overtop in the same way as *Les Misérables*. The roles of Kim and Ellen are mezzo-sopranos with a high belt-mix. Chris is a tenor while The Engineer and John are both baritones.

Songs from this score include:

The Movie In My Mind **   If You Want to Die in Bed ††
Why, God, Why? †   I'd Give My Life for You **
Sun and Moon **/†   Bui Doi ††
Last Night of the World **/†   Now That I've Seen Her **
I Still Believe **   The American Dream ††

Martin Guerre

Schönberg and Boublil's next musical, *Martin Guerre*, underwent a constant series of revisions. The writers rewrote their original version of the story of real-life historical figure Martin Guerre to bring out the theme of religious intolerance. Opening on the West End to poor reviews, the production closed after three months. It was completely revised, including a substantial amount of new material, and reopened in a new production on the West End several weeks later. Changes continued throughout the show's 675-performances run. An almost completely new version opened in Leeds in 1998 and toured the UK in 1999. *Martin Guerre* opened at the Guthrie Theatre in Minneapolis in yet another version, Macintosh claimed that "forty percent of the material was not in the original."[4] After being constantly changed while playing in five different US cities, the production closed down before opening on Broadway. The writers continued to change the show in various productions until 2006.

One of the difficulties of the score is that with so much plot to cover, it lacks the set-piece songs that made *Les Miserables* and *Miss Saigon* so successful, having an extraordinary amount of recitative. The same style as their other works, legitimate singing with pop stylistics overlaid, supported by a symphonic accompaniment, describes this score.

Some of the songs of interest from various productions of *Martin Guerre* include:

Live with Somebody You Love ††	Who? ††
I'm Martin Guerre †	All That I Love †/**
Without You as a Friend †	Justice Will Be Done †
How Many Tears **	Why? †/**
Don't †/**	Here Comes the Morning ††
The Day Has Come †/**	When Will Someone Hear? **
	Someone **

The Pirate Queen

The Pirate Queen premiered in 2005, starring Stephanie J. Block as Grace O'Malley and Linda Balgord as Queen Elizabeth I. Both performances garnered critical praise, but critics agreed that in 2005 the pop operetta had outstayed its welcome and just felt like a throwback to operettas from earlier eras. The show received poor reviews and never found its audience.

Some of the songs from this show include:

Woman **	The Waking of the Queen **
My Grace ††/**	Rah-Rah, Tip-Top **/††
Here on This Night **/†	Boys'll Be Boys

I'll Be There †
A Day Beyond Belclare **/†
Enemy at Portside /**
I Dismiss You **/††
If I Said I Love You †/**

The Role of the Queen **/††
Surrender ††
She Who Has All **
The Sea of Life **/††
Woman to Woman **

Marguerite

Marguerite took Dumas, fils' *La Dame aux Camélias* and updated it to Paris in the 1940s under Nazi occupation. Schönberg and Boublil co-wrote the libretto for *Marguerite* with Jonathan Kent; Boublil and Herbert Kretzmer wrote lyrics and Michel Legrand wrote the music. The show had a four-month run in London's West End and continues to be edited, reshaped and developed. While much of their style remains in this show, Legrand's world of popular music and jazz infuses a different sound, making this score more readily amenable to jazz styling than that of rock/pop.

Songs from *Marguerite* include:

Let the World Turn
Jazz Time
China Doll **/††
The Face I See **
Waiting **/††
I Am Here **/††
Take Good Care of Yourself */†

Dreams Shining Dreams ††
I Hate the Very Thought of
    Women ††
The Letter ††
What's Left of Love? ††
How Did I Get Where
    I Am? **

Biography

Composer and sometimes lyricist, record producer and actor Claude-Michel Schönberg was born in Vannes, France in 1944. Lyricist and librettist Alain Boublil was born in 1941 in Tunisia. According to Boublil, one day he heard a song of Schönberg's on the radio and contacted him to ask about the possibility of working together. They have become the most successful writing team in the history of the musical theatre.

Resources

There is a wealth of material on Schönberg and Boublil, including the website www.musicalworld-boublil-schonberg.com and Margaret Vermette's book *The Musical World of Schönberg and Boublil*.[5]

In summary

The scores of the mega-musicals tend to be operatic in scope; many of them are through-sung, with passages of recitative instead of dialogue. Their lyrics tend towards the poetic, making them very pretty to listen to, but often lacking in intellectual rigor or dramatic thrust. For these reasons, like their operatic ancestors, the singer's sound takes precedence. Because these shows tend to sit very high in the singers' ranges, they can be treacherously difficult to sing. Vocal styles range from strictly legitimate to pop, but always beneath the styling, these scores require strong vocal technique. To do these songs justice, they need to be big and well supported.

As important as vocal size is the extreme emotional intensity called for in these songs. These shows base their success on audiences who want to watch people feel very deeply. On *Britain's Got Talent* in 2009, Susan Boyle skyrocketed to fame singing "I Dreamed a Dream" from *Les Misérables*. Like so many before her, Boyle's performance captivated by the size of her voice and the emotional intensity of her delivery.

Notes

1 Uncredited, "Andrew Lloyd Webber, Biography," *IMDb*, www.imdb.com/name/nm0515908/bio, accessed January 3, 2015.
2 Michael Coveney, *The Andrew Lloyd Webber Story*, London, UK: Arrow Books, 2000.
3 Stephen Citron, *Stephen Sondheim and Andrew Lloyd Webber: The New Musical*, New York, NY: Oxford University Press, 2001.
4 Quoted in Bruce Weber, "When the Commercial Theater Moves In on Nonprofits," *The New York Times*, October 10, 1999, www.nytimes.com/1999/10/10/theater/theater-when-the-commercial-theater-moves-in-on-nonprofits.html, accessed May 11, 2016.
5 Margaret Vermette, *The Musical World of Boublil and Schönberg: The Creators of Les Misérables, Miss Saigon, Martin Guerre and The Pirate Queen*, New York, NY: Applause Theatre and Cinema Books, 2005.

Chapter 11

Musicals of the 1990s and 2000s – the new eclecticism

Elton John, Lynn Ahrens and Stephen Flaherty, Ricky Ian Gordon, Frank Wildhorn, Jonathan Larson, Jason Robert Brown, Jeanine Tesori, Michael John LaChiusa, Andrew Lippa, Adam Guettel and Tom Kitt

By the mid-1990s, the trend of the mega-musicals had just about played itself out. *Miss Saigon* would linger on Broadway until 2001 and *Les Misérables* until 2003, and *Phantom of the Opera* continues playing to packed houses all over the world, but fewer new mega-musicals were finding success. Across popular culture, the 1990s and 2000s were a time of "repurposed" or "recycled" culture, when artists reference, pull from and cite earlier works. This is true across a wide spectrum of popular and high art forms, and the musical theatre was no exception. In a time when popular culture in all areas took to recycling older genres and styles, a new generation of theatre composers and lyricists appeared on the scene doing exactly that in the musical theatre.

Of course the composers and lyricists examined earlier in this book had built on what had come before them, but the musical theatre of this period is defined like never before by repurposed styles "mashed up" and co-joined. The cutting edge was montage – placing already existing kinds of musical and lyric sounds together and allowing their new contexts to make them seem "new." All except one of the composers and lyricists examined in this chapter were born between 1956 and 1974 and grew up influenced by the pop and rock sounds of 1970–1990 in their formative teen years. Elton John, the one who was born earlier, came from the world of rock and roll.

The composers and lyricists in this chapter have all cited a wide range of influences, which are explored in this chapter. Facility with a wide range of styles is important for the vocalist in approaching the material of these writers. For the greatest stylistic facility with these songs, the singer of their songs should be as well versed in the artists of the 1970s-1990s as possible. Where previous chapters have attempted to identify the composer or lyricist's style, this chapter will attempt to identify their primary influences.

For example, almost every composer in this chapter singles out Stevie Wonder, in particular his album "Songs in the Key of Life," as a pivotal influence. The singer who is familiar with this album can see Wonder's sensibility reflected in their performance of these songs – the degree of vocal ornamentation, phrasing, tone, stylistic devices like portamento – all of these ultimately make or break a performance. The more familiar the singer is with all of the influences identified in this chapter, the bigger the singer's idiomatic vocabulary, the better.

Elton John (b. 1947)

Influences

Before ever working in the musical theatre, Elton John was one of the most successful rock artists ever as a singer, songwriter, pianist and producer in a pop music career that began in 1968. In 1994, John's first musical film, *The Lion King*, was released and almost instantly became a classic. John has written for the musical theatre on stage and screen frequently since then, but his influences and background are distinctly rock and roll. In an interview with Leah Harper of *The Guardian*, John discussed the recordings that have had the greatest influence on him. He mentions his mother playing Elvis Presley's "Heartbreak Hotel" for him in 1956, seeing and hearing Jerry Lee Lewis' "Great Balls of Fire" and watching Little Richard in performance. He also talks about the Simon and Garfunkel album "Bridge Over Troubled Water" as well as hearing Aretha Franklin's recording of the title song. Other influences he mentions are Leon Russell's "A Song For You," Bonnie Raitt's "I Can't Make You Love Me" and Stevie Wonder's "Songs In The Key of Life."[1]

Not surprisingly, many singers of Elton John's music have a wide range of rock styling at their disposal. John has a nice understanding of the rock voice, and writes scores that can be successfully sung eight times a week without stressing the voice. Listen to the original cast recording of any Elton John musical theatre score for this and you will hear even the character-driven parts applying rock styles to their sung material.

Body of work

Elton John has written some of the most popular rock songs ever. A short list of these include:

Bennie and the Jets	I Guess That's Why They Call It
Candle in the Wind	the Blues
Crocodile Rock	Philadelphia Freedom
Daniel	Rocket Man
Don't Go Breaking My Heart	Saturday Night's Alright
Don't Let the Sun Go	(For Fighting)
Down on Me	Someone Saved My Life Tonight
Goodbye Yellow Brick Road	Tiny Dancer
Honky Cat	Your Song

In 1994 John's first musical film, Disney's *The Lion King*, opened, and he began to enjoy writing musicals for both screen and stage. These projects have included (see p. 10 for key to symbols):

The Lion King (1994)

Circle of Life	Be Prepared
The Morning Report	Hakuna Matata
I Just Can't Wait to Be King	Can You Feel the Love Tonight

Aida (1998) [also known as Elton John and Tim Rice's Aida (1999)]

Every Story Is a Love Story **	Elaborate Lives †/**
Fortune Favors the Brave †	The Gods Love Nubia **
The Past is Another Land **	A Step Too Far **/†
How I Know You †/**	Easy as Life **
My Strongest Suit **	Radames' Letter †
Enchantment Passing	Written in the Stars **/†
Through †/**	I Know the Truth **

Billy Elliot (2005)

Shine **	Merry Christmas Maggie
Solidarity	Thatcher
Expressing Yourself	Deep Into the Ground ††
Born to Boogie	He Could Be a Star ††
	Once We Were Kings

Lestat (2005)

From the Dead ††	Embrace It
Beautiful Boy *	I Want More
The Thirst ††	I'll Never Have That Chance
Right Before My Eyes †	Sail Me Away
Make Me as You Are †	To Kill Your Kind
To Live Like This †	After All This Time
The Crimson Kiss **	From the Dead

Lynn Ahrens (b. 1948) and Stephen Flaherty (b. 1960)

Influences

Composer Stephen Flaherty and lyricist/librettist Lynn Ahrens met in Lehman Engel's BMI Musical Theatre Workshop, a program for developing musical theatre writers, in 1982. Of this generation of writers, Ahrens and Flaherty are one of the more prolific teams and are more firmly rooted in the traditional sounds of the musical theatre than any others. Their scores tend to suggest the locales where the stories take place while still being very much in the traditional musical theatre style. The Afro-Caribbean rhythms of *Once on This Island*, the Irish lilt of *A Man of No Importance* and the ragtime rhythms in the musical *Ragtime* are all used effectively, but they ornament the traditional musical theatre sound rather than replace it – they are references.

Flaherty has said in an interview,

> As a composer, my personal music interests are quite wide and varied. My background is in classical composition, although I grew up in the 1960s and 1970s with the sounds of R&B and was influenced by the whole singer/songwriter period, which I think has affected the kind of music I write. Each piece that Lynn and I have written together has its own unique musical vocabulary. *Once on This Island* is set on a fictitious Caribbean island, and in writing that piece, I was able to use a lot of contemporary world music sounds – Afro-Caribbean music, the sounds of Brazil – and combine them in a way that I think was fresh and theatrical at the same time. It's important to stay current, to keep your ears open to what musical influences there are today that are available.[2]

Ahrens and Flaherty write more to evoke a time and place than any other writer examined in this chapter. They have written for some extraordinary voices like LaChanze, Kecia Lewis-Evans, Brian Stokes Mitchell, Audra McDonald and Marin Mazzie. But the songs in their scores are more driven by acting choices than singing choices. Yes, the smart singer of songs from *My Favorite Year* will research popular music of the 1950s, but it is the character choices that will ultimately drive the performances. The same is true of most of their material: an understanding of the musical styles of the time and place are very important, but that information needs to be used to inform the acting choices.

Body of work

Their musicals tend to be favorites of musical theatre fans; and while their work is consistently produced, they have yet to have a major commercial hit. Their shows include:

Lucky Stiff (1988)

Lucky Stiff is a musical farce, based on Michael Butterworth's 1983 novel, *The Man Who Broke the Bank at Monte Carlo*. Ahrens and Flaherty's score offers broadly drawn characters in extreme situations within a traditional musical theatre sound.

Rita's Confession **	Speaking French **
Lucky †	Times Like This **
The Dogs vs. You **/†	Fancy Meeting You Here **
The Phone Call ††	Nice **/†
Monte Carlo! ††	A Woman in My Bathroom †

Once on This Island (1990)

In *Once on This Island* Ahrens and Flaherty combined contemporary pop sounds with Afro-Caribbean and Brazilian music, creating a unique sound that served to situate the setting on the fictitious island.

Waiting for Life	Forever Yours
Rain ††	Ti Moune
Pray	Mama Will Provide **

The Human Heart **   When We Are Wed **/††
Some Girls ††   A Part of Us

My Favorite Year (1993)

Ahrens and Flaherty's score for *My Favorite Year* evokes the musicals of the Golden Age of live television comedy in the 1950s. It tells the story of the backstage goings-on at a fictionalized version of the greatest live weekly television comedy show of the time. This score not only evokes the period, but also the manic, intense comic energy of its setting.

Twenty Million People †   If the World Were Like the
Larger Than Life †   Movies ††
Rookie in the Ring **   Shut Up and Dance †/**
Manhattan †   Professional Show Business
The Gospel According to   Comedy **
    King ††   My Favorite Year †
Funny/The Duck Joke **

Anastasia (animated musical film, 1997)

Journey To the Past **   Paris Holds the Key to
Once Upon a December **   Your Heart
In the Dark of the Night   At the Beginning
Learn To Do It

Ragtime (1998)

While in college, Flaherty played piano in a ragtime band. He put this training to good use in the musical *Ragtime*, which makes great use of the ragtime music as well other turn-of-the-century styles. In addition to ragtime, Ahrens and Flaherty make effective use of the sounds of Tin Pan Alley, "the klezmer [music] of the Lower East Side, bold brass band marches, delicate waltzes, up-tempo banjo tunes, period parlor songs and expansive anthems."[3]

Goodbye My Love **   His Name Was Coalhouse
Journey On †/††/**   Walker ††
The Crime of the Century **   Getting' Ready Rag ††
    Henry Ford ††

Your Daddy's Son *
New Music
Wheels of a Dream ††/*
The Night That Goldman
    Spoke at Union
    Square †/**
Gliding †
Justice ††

Coalhouse's Soliloquy ††
What a Game ††
Buffalo Nickel Photoplay, Inc. †
Our Children **/†
Sarah Brown Eyes ††/*
He Wanted To Say †/**
Back to Before **
Make Them Hear You ††

Seussical (2000)

With *Seussical* Ahrens and Flaherty reverted to a generic pop-musical theatre sound, which may to some degree account for the show's failure in its original Broadway incarnation. The show failed to find its voice on several fronts, although it has become quite successful and popular with schools and community groups.

Oh, The Things You Can Think
Horton Hears a Who †
Alone in the Universe †
The One Feather Tail of Miss
    Gertrude McFuzz *

Amazing Mayzie **
Amazing Gertrude *
Notice Me Horton **/†

A Man of No Importance (2002)

The score of *A Man of No Importance* effectively evokes its Dublin setting musically, lyrically and in the wonderful orchestration. Having a unique voice to hang their score on seems to bring out the best in Ahrens and Flaherty as it has allowed them to explore new vocabulary musically and lyrically.

The Burden of My Life **
Princess *
The Streets of Dublin †
Books ††/**
Love Who You Love ††

The Cuddles Mary Gave ††
Art ††
Confusing Times ††
Tell Me Why **
Welcome To the World ††

Dessa Rose (2005)

Dessa Rose tells the intertwining stories of two women, one white and one black in the antebellum South. The score is based on

"American roots music – blues, folk, different hymns, early kinds of gospel, the idea of call-and-response, which was a coded way that the slaves communicated so that the white people thought they were just singing."[4]

Comin' Down the
   Quarters ††
Ol' Banjar †
Something of My Own **
Ink †
Little Star †
Ladies **
At the Glen **
Capture the Girl ††
Fly Away **

Their Eyes Are Clear, Blue
   Like Sky **
Twelve Children **
Noah's Dove ††
The Scheme ††
In the Bend of My Arm **/††
Better If I Died **
Ten Petticoats **
A Pleasure **
White Milk and Red Blood **

The Glorious Ones (2007)

The Glorious Ones tells the story of a commedia dell'arte troupe. In an interview in *Playbill*, Flaherty said, "It's very Italian. It is probably my most 'European' score." Ahrens added, "Stephen has an uncanny knack for taking a particular period or place's 'sound' and making it theatrical and accessible and 'his.' "[5]

The Glorious Ones ††
Making Love **/††
Pantalone Alone †
Madness to Act ††
Absolom
Invitation to France
Armanda's Tarantella
Improvisation ††

The Only World She Writes
Opposite You
My Body Wasn't Why
Flaminio Scala's Ominous
   Dream ††
Rise and Fall
I Was Here

Rocky the Musical (2012)

For *Rocky* Flaherty took his musical vocabulary from the rock and roll of the mid-1970s, the time the story takes place. Flaherty has said in an interview, "I grew up in Pittsburgh in that same time period, so I really relate to these people. Out of everything that I have written musically, I think that this is actually the closest to who I am. In my heart I was sort of writing it for my neighborhood."[6]

Songs from *Rocky* include:

My Nose Ain't Broken	Fight From the Heart ††
Raining **	In The Ring ††
Patriotic ††	Happiness **/††
The Flip Side **/††	I'm Done **
Adrian ††	Keep On Standing ††

Ricky Ian Gordon (b. 1956)

Influence

Of the composers and lyricists in this chapter, Ricky Ian Gordon's music is closest to the world of classical music. He writes musicals, operas, art songs, ballets, choral music and piano pieces. *Billboard* cites two of his influences as Gershwin and Sondheim. Gordon's classical influences include Berg, Bartok, Britten, Weill, Bernstein, Copland, Hindemith, Shostakovich, Rorem, Prokofiev, Gershwin, Blitzstein, Messiaen, Tippet and Sondheim. His popular music influences include Joni Mitchell, The Beatles and Neil Young. While based in a strong classical composition background, Gordon's writing references bits of jazz and popular music from different eras.

While informed by a great wealth of influences, Gordon's music requires a degree of control and subtlety, which makes him a composer for highly classically trained voices. On his website, Gordon cites that his

> songs have been performed and or recorded by such internationally renowned singers as Renee Fleming, Dawn Upshaw, Nathan Gunn, Judy Collins, Kelli O'Hara, Audra McDonald, Kristin Chenoweth, Nicole Cabell, the late Lorraine Hunt Lieberson, Frederica Von Stade, Andrea Marcovicci, Harolyn Blackwell and Betty Buckley, among many others.[7]

Gordon's music requires dramatic choices to be expressed through musical ones – phrasing, shaping of sounds, dynamic choices. Approaching Gordon's music calls for a much more classical mindset than the other composers looked at in this chapter.

Body of work

For the legitimate singer with less comfort with popular styles, Gordon offers some exciting new American music that references popular styles without requiring mastery of those styles from the singer. His songs, however, require a singer with strong technique and a high degree of musicianship. His vocal music includes:

And flowers pick themselves ... (2005), a cycle of five songs for soprano and orchestra
Autumn Valentine Suite (1994), a suite for soprano and baritone
Blessing the Boats (2001), for soprano
Can You Look Me in the Eyes? (2004), for soprano
Five Americans (1985), a cycle of five songs for soprano
Genius Child (1993), ten songs for soprano
Green Sneakers (2007), for baritone
Home of the Brave (1998), for baritone
I Never Knew (1992), for baritone
I Was Thinking of You (1986), a cycle of six songs for soprano
Is It Morning? (1987), a cycle of six songs for soprano
Late Afternoon (2001), a cycle of six songs for mezzo-soprano
Night Flight to San Francisco (2000), text by Tony Kushner, for soprano
Orpheus and Euridice (2005) for soprano
Sweet Song (1991) a cycle of 27 songs for soprano
Through Mortal Waters (1986), a cycle of 6 songs for soprano
Too Few the Mornings Be (2000), text by Emily Dickinson, for soprano

Ricky Ian Gordon's operas include:

27 (2014)
Autumn Valentine (1992), an opera for soprano and baritone
A Coffin in Egypt (2014)
The Garden of the Finzi Continis (not premiered as of the writing of this book)
The Grapes of Wrath (2007)
Morning Star (2013)
Only Heaven (1995)
Rappohannock County (2011)
The Tibetan Book of the Dead (1996)

Ricky Ian Gordon's musicals have not found popular appeal. They are rich in subject and treatment and are best enjoyed by a highly literate audience, being layered with references to classical and contemporary styles. His musicals include:

Dream True: My Life With Vernon Dixon (1999; lyrics by Gordon and Tina Landau)

Dream True premiered off-Broadway at the Vineyard Theatre. *The New York Times* review said, "*Dream True*, which opened last night at the Vineyard Theater, is a truly perplexing experience. The story it tells is on the self-important side, yet the way it spins it is wholly original: the first musical, perhaps, to make a conscious appeal to the subconscious. Like the dream world itself, *Dream True* orbits in an alternate universe where rationality takes a back seat to sensation. 'Imagine a place, but it's really more of a feeling,' "[8] As this description might suggest, this score is expansive; it offers a feeling that extends into the dream state. There are few resolutions in the traditional sense, and mostly a sense of endless expansion. Stylistically, this is a classical score, with occasional bows to a country and western style. Songs include:

Wyoming	Space
We Can Fly	Peter's Dream
Finding Home	Dream True
The Way West	Have a Nice Day
The Best Years of Our Lives	Best for You
A Beautiful Life	Pride
He's Gone	Hold On
God Is There	We Will Always Walk Together

My Life with Albertine (2003; lyrics by Gordon and Richard Nelson)

My Life with Albertine premiered off-Broadway at Playwright's Horizons. As *Dream True*, evokes its setting, *My Life With Albertine* also evokes its setting, a private theatre in a private home in Paris in 1919. As with his first show, the voice production is legitimate, with occasional bows to Parisian cabaret styles. Songs include:

Is It Too Late? *	The Different Albertines †/††
My Soul Weeps */††	Sad Bolbee †/††

Song of Solitude †	The Street ††
I Want You **	Albertine's Lost Letter †
I Need Me a Girl †	If It Is True *

Gordon's most recent three musicals have all premiered, but none have been recorded or published, and even reviews of these shows are difficult to find. As Gordon is a composer of major interest, these musicals are important to be aware of. *States of Independence* (1993), lyrics by Gordon and Tina Landau, premiered at the American Musical Theatre Festival in Philadelphia. *Stonewall/Night Variations* (1994), lyrics by Tina Landau, premiered at Pier 25 in Tribeca, New York. *Sycamore Trees* (2010), lyrics by Gordon, premiered at the Signature Theatre in Arlington, Virginia.

Frank Wildhorn (b. 1958)

Influence

Composer Frank Wildhorn's strong suit is writing great songs in the light popular vein that too frequently do nothing to reveal character or advance the story. Wildhorn excels at pop anthems. Despite the many musicals that he has had produced, none have become major commercial hits. He has said that he has too many influences to list them all. He does say that in the forefront is Rachmaninoff, for his melodies. Other influences include Stevie Wonder, particularly "Talking Book," "Songs in the Key of Life" and "Inner Visions," the music of Marvin Gaye, the Doobie Brothers, Rodgers and Hammerstein and the great jazz masters.

Wildhorn's muses are Linda Eder and Whitney Houston. Both women are known for singing at the top of their range for long periods of time with tremendous control and precision; both are masters of pop styling. Eder first came to Wildhorn's attention as a 13-week winner of the television show *Star Search*. The two not only have worked together ever since, but were married from 1998 to 2004. Eder's 15 solo albums take advantage of her ability to adapt her four-octave voice to practically any style. The defining aspect of Wildhorn's songs is the bravura performances they demand. Listen to any original cast recording of a Wildhorn score and you will hear a degree of styling that many composers would never tolerate; Wildhorn's songs require it. On the *Bonnie and Clyde* original cast recording, Jeremy Jordan and Laura Osnes do not sing in the style of the 1930s, the setting of the show, they sing with all the pop inflections of 2011. Singers of Wildhorn's songs are recommended to think of them almost as contemporary pop songs. Give them the vocal technique and life that they might be given in a contemporary recording studio.

Body of work

Frank Wildhorn is incredibly prolific; he has written a lot of shows and had most of them produced.

Jekyll & Hyde (1990; lyrics by Leslie Bricusse)

Produced on Broadway. Songs include:

Lost in the Darkness ††	Someone Like You **
Take Me as I Am ††/*	Once Upon a Dream *
No One Knows Who I Am **	In His Eyes */**
This is the Moment ††	The Way Back ††
Alive ††	A New Life **

Svengali (1991; lyrics by Gregory Boyd)

Produced at the Alley Theatre in Houston. Songs include:

So Slowly ††/**	Vole Mon Ange **
If he Never Said Hello **	

The Scarlet Pimpernel (1997; lyrics by Nan Knighton)

Produced on Broadway. Songs include:

Storybook **	Where's the Girl? †
Prayer ††	Only Love **
Into the Fire ††	She Was There †
Falcon in the Dive †	I'll Forget You **
When I Look at You **	

The Civil War (1998; lyrics by Jack Murphy)

Produced on Broadway. Songs include:

Freedom's Child ††	I'll Never Pass This Way Again ††
Tell My Father †	Candle in the Window **
If Prayin' Were Horses ††/**	River Jordan ††
Father How Long? †	Sarah †

Camille Claude! (2003; lyrics by Nan Knighton)

Produced at the Goodspeed Theatre in East Haddam, Connecticut. This score is not published, and the only song recorded from this show was "Gold," which has been recorded twice by Linda Eder.

Dracula, the Musical (2004; lyrics by Don Black and Christopher Hampton)

Produced on Broadway. Songs include:

A Quiet Life ††	If I Could Fly **
The Mist *	There's Always
A Perfect Life **	Tomorrow ††/**
Nosferatu ††	Before the Summer Ends †
Life After Life ††/*	The Longer I Live †
The Heart is Slow to Learn **	

Waiting for the Moon: An American Love Story (2005; lyrics by Jack Murphy)

Produced at the Lenape Performing Arts Center, Marlton, New Jersey. This musical, previously titled *Zelda* and *Scott & Zelda: The Other Side of Paradise*, was inspired by the characters in F. Scott Fitzgerald's *The Great Gatsby*. The only song recorded from this score is Zelda's song "Easy" (**).

Cyrano de Bergerac The Musical (2006; lyrics by Leslie Bricusse)

Produced at the Nissay Theatre, Tokyo, Japan. The role of Cyrano is a high baritone, Roxanne is a high belter and Christian a tenor. Although the show opened in Japan, no songs from this score have been released.

Rudolph – The Last Kiss (2006; lyrics by Jack Murphy and Nan Knighton)

Produced at the Budapest Operetta Theatre. Although this musical about the Crown Prince of Austria has been performed in Hungary and Austria, no songs have been recorded or published.

Never Say Goodbye (2006; lyrics by Shûchirö Koiki)

Produced at the Takarazuka Grand Theatre, Takarazuka, Japan. This score is not available in an English language version.

Carmen (2008; lyrics by Jack Murphy)

Produced in Prague, Czech Republic. None of the music from this production has been published or recorded.

The Count of Monte Cristo (2009; lyrics by Jack Murphy)

Produced at the Theatre St. Gallen, Switzerland. Songs include:

When Love Is True †/**	Hell to Your Doorstep †
I Will Be There †/**	All This Time **
When the World Was Mine **	

Bonnie & Clyde (2009; lyrics by Don Black)

Produced on Broadway. Songs include:

The World Will Remember Me †/**	Too Late to Turn Back Now †/**
How 'Bout a Dance? **	That's What You Call a Dream **
You Can Do Better Than Him †/††	Was That Good Enough for You †/**
You Love Who You Love **	
Raise a Little Hell †	Bonnie †
The World Will Remember Us †/**	Dyin' Ain't So Bad **

Wonderland (2011; lyrics by Jack Murphy)

Produced on Broadway. Songs include:

The Worst Day of My Life **	The Mad Hatter **
Down the Rabbit Hole **	Hail the Queen **
Go with the Flow †	Off with Their Heads **
One Knight †	Finding Wonderland **

No music is available in either recorded or published form from Frank Wildhorn's three most recent musicals. They are *Tears of Heaven* (2011) written with Robin Lerner and Phoebe Hwang, Seoul, South Korea; *Mitsuko*, lyrics by Jack Murphy and Shuchiro Koike, (2011) Tokyo and Osaka, Japan; and *Excalibur*, lyrics by Robin Lerner (2014), Theatre St. Gallen, Switzerland.

Jonathan Larson (1960–1996)

Influence

As with so many of his generation Jonathan Larson's influences include Leonard Bernstein and Stephen Sondheim, and the rock influences from his adolescence, particularly Elton John, The Beatles, The Doors, The Who, Billy Joel, The Police, Prince. Later influences include Kurt Cobain and Liz Phair.

Composer and lyricist Larson struggled in his career, and ultimately turned to writing about his personal struggle in a rock monologue, in which he vented at the failure of earlier works. Ultimately this led to *Rent*. Tragically, Larson passed away the night of the first off-Broadway preview of *Rent*. One can only imagine how the tremendous success of *Rent* might have impacted future Larson shows.

Larson's songs require rock styling. They are as "singer-ly" as Ricky Ian Gordon, but the style is rock rather than classical. Anthony Rapp, Adam Pascal, Daphne Rubin-Vega, Idina Menzel and the others produce healthy rock sounds on the *Rent* original cast recording. Groaning, hitting the note under pitch and scooping up (in imitation of a guitar), bending notes, whining, screaming, vocal fry – all of these rock style devices and more are useful in Larson's music.

Body of work

Printed or recorded music from Larson's first two musicals is quite difficult to find, although copies of them do exist in the Library of Congress. *Sacrimmoralinority* (later retitled *Saved! – An Immoral Musical on the Moral Majority*) received a production at Adelphi University, where Larson was a student in 1981. It received a production the following year at Rusty's Storefront Blitz in New York. His next musical, *Superbia*, was a futuristic musical adaptation of George Orwell's *Nineteen Eighty-Four*, written in 1990; but the Orwell estate denied Larson the rights to the material.

In response to his lack of success, he wrote a "rock monologue" in 1991, which he performed seated at the piano with a small rock band. This piece was originally titled, *30/90*, was later retitled *Boho Days* and finally retitled again *tick, tick … BOOM!*, when it saw production in 2001, off-Broadway. Songs from *tick, tick … BOOM!* were all originally written for Larson to sing and can be readily adapted to any vocal register. They call for the same kind of rock stylization found in *Rent*. These songs include:

30/90	Sugar
Green Green Dress †/**	See Her Smile
Johnny Can't Decide	Come to Your Senses **
Sunday	Why †
No More ††/**	Louder Than Words
Therapy †/**	Boho Days
Real Life	

Jonathan Larson's *Rent* took Giacomo Puccini's opera *La bohème* and resituated it contemporarily in New York's Lower East Side, using the bohemian lifestyle of that neighborhood in place of Puccini's lower classes. *Rent* began off-Broadway and, after winning a Pulitzer Prize, moved to Broadway, where it played for 12 years, making it one of the longest-running Broadway musicals ever. Larson's score for *Rent* is contemporary alternative rock of the 1990s. Songs from *Rent* include:

Rent	You'll See †/††
One Song Glory †	Tango Maureen **/†
Light My Candle **/††	Out Tonight **
Today 4 U †/††	Another Day **/†

Sante Fe †/††
I'll Cover You †/††
Christmas Bells
Over the Moon **
La Vie Boheme
Seasons of Love
Happy New Year

Take Me or Leave Me **
Without You††/**
Halloween ††
Goodbye Love
What You Own †
Your Eyes †

Jason Robert Brown (b. 1960)

Influence

Composer, lyricist, playwright and arranger Jason Robert Brown said in an interview,

> I grew up mainly listening to disco; I was a Donna Summer freak. Then I wanted to be like Elton John or Billy Joel, so I tried to write those songs, but my pop songs never had any life to them without some sort of context. I then listened to Randy Newman and Joni Mitchell and Leonard Bernstein. At the end of the day, I listen to everything and I never know what's gonna get me going. It turns out that I've stolen more from Paul Simon than I've stolen from anyone else; there's something in his writing that always seems to push me forward.[9]

The New York Times cited Billy Joel and Randy Newman as influences of Brown's.

Jessica Molaskey, Andrea Burns, Brooks Ashmanskas, Norbert Leo Butz, Sherie Rene Scott and the others who sing Jason Robert Brown's material exceptionally well come at it with a great comfort and facility with the pop and rock styles from the 1980s to today. Listen to any of these singers to hear how simply referencing earlier rock styles informs these songs. For example, listen to Lauren Kenney's album *Songs of Jason Robert Brown* and you can hear echoes of Judy Collins, Billy Joel, Donna Summer.

Body of work

Songs for a New World (1995) is a musical theatre piece that exists at the junction of musical, revue and song cycle. In this first work one hears all of the myriad influences including a wide array of pop, gospel, jazz and rock styles, sometimes all in the same song. Songs include:

On the Deck of a Spanish
  Sailing Ship, 1492 †
Just One Step **
I'm Not Afraid of Anything **
The River Won't Flow †/††
Stars and the Moon **
She Cries ††

The Steam Train †
Surabya Santa **
Christmas Lullaby **
King of the World †
I'd Give It All for You ††/**
The Flagmaker, 1775 **
Flying Home †

Parade (1998) musicalizes the historical story of Leo Frank, a Jewish factory manager convicted of raping and killing a 13-year old employee. Frank was lynched by an angry mob inflamed by anti-Semitism. Brown's score pulls from both historical and contemporary influences including "pop, rock, folk, rhythm and blues and gospel."[10] Songs include:

The Old Red Hills of
  Home †/††
How Can I Call This Home? †
The Picture Show †/**
What Am I Waiting For? †/**
You Don't Know This Man **
Come Up to My Office **/†

My Child Will Forgive Me **
It's Hard to Speak My Heart †
It Goes On and On †
Do It Alone **
Pretty Music ††
This is Not Over Yet †/**
All the Wasted Time †/**

The Last Five Years (2002) is an autobiographical two-person musical about Brown's failed first marriage. Again, Brown mingles styles within songs, including folk, pop, rock, jazz, classical, klezmer and Latin. Songs from this score include:

Still Hurting **
Shiksa Goddess †
See I'm Smiling **
Moving Too Fast †
I'm a Part of That **
The Schmuel Song †
A Summer in Ohio **

The Next Ten Minutes †/**
When You Come Home
  to Me **
Climbing Uphill**
If I Didn't Believe in You †
I Can Do Better Than That **
Nobody Needs to Know †

Brown contributed five songs to the failed Broadway musical *Urban Cowboy* (2003), which featured the songs of more than twenty songwriters. Brown's songs are:

It Don't Get Better Than This †   That's How Texas Was Born
That's How She Rides †   Mr. Hopalong Heartache * *
I Wish I Didn't Love You †

In 2005, Brown released a solo album of previously written songs titled *Wearing Someone Else's Clothes*. Songs on this CD are:

Someone Else's Clothes   Nothing in Common
Long Long Road   I Could Be in Love with
Someone to Fall Back On   Someone Like You
Getting Out   I'm in Bizness
Over   Coming Together
Music of Heaven   Grow Old with Me

Brown's next Broadway musical, *13* (2008) about the trials of being 13 years old, featured a cast of actors and musicians all under 18 years old. Again using an eclectic blend of musical styles, the songs include:

13/Becoming a Man †   All Hail the Brain †
The Lamest Place in the   Terminal Illness †
    World * *   Good Enough * *
Get Me What I Need †   Tell Her †/* *
What It Means to Be a   If That's What It Is †/* *
    Friend * *   Brand New You * *

For his musical adaptation of *The Bridges of Madison County* (2013), Brown fused folk, country, pop and operatic styles. Songs include:

To Build a Home *   Something from a Dream †
Temporarily Lost   Falling into You †/*
What Do You Call a Man? *   Who We Are and Who We
Wondering */†   Want To Be †/*
Look at Me */†   Almost Real *
The World Inside a Frame †   It All Fades Away †

Brown's latest Broadway musical, *Honeymoon in Vegas* (2015) combines traditional musical theatre sounds with jazz, pop, rock, Hawaiian music, and the swing sounds of the Rat Pack's Las Vegas. Songs include:

I Love Betsy †
Never Get Married **
Anywhere but Here **
When You Say Vegas †
Out in the Sun †
Forever Starts Tonight †/††
Betsy's Getting Married **
Come to an Agreement ††

Friki-Friki **
You Made the Wait
    Worthwhile ††/**
Isn't That Enough? †
Airport Song †/**
Higher Love ††
I've Been Thinking **

Jeanine Tesori (b. 1961)

Influence

Jeanine Tesori's influences are as wide-ranging as her colleagues', but calling only on the sources appropriate for each show, her body of work seems to be lacking in any identifiable style. She has said, "'my style is linked to the dramatic event. There's always an aspect of the period that interests me." From the roaring '20s of *Thoroughly Modern Millie*; to the blues and Motown of *Caroline, or Change*; to the pop and R&B world of *Shrek* – no two of Tesori's musicals are alike."[11]

Most of the composers examined in this chapter have distinct musical personalities. Tesori, on the other hand, is a composer of tremendous craft who becomes submerged in each show. One is never aware of Tesori's personality in the score, just the high level of craftsmanship in the writing. Just as her identity is subjugated to the show in each of Tesori's scores, so the singer must be true to each score on an individual basis. *Thoroughly Modern Millie* could not be any more different from *Caroline, or Change* or *Shrek;* and yet every piece must be sung honestly for what it is.

Body of work

Violet (1997), lyrics by Brian Crawley, tells the story of a disfigured woman in Spruce Pine, North Carolina taking a bus trip seeking a cure from a televangelist in Tulsa, Oklahoma in 1964. Tesori's score fused folk, country, R&B, gospel, bluegrass and blues. In an interview lyricist/librettist Crawley talked about their conscious choice to shift musical style to mirror the journey of the bus geographically. Songs from *Violet* include:

Water in the Well **	Lay Down Your Head **
Surprised **	Hard to Say Goodbye **/†
On My Way **	Promise Me, Violet **/††/†
Questions 'n Answers ††/**	Look at Me **
Let It Sing †	That's What I Could Do ††
Anyone Would Do **	
Last Time I Came to	
Memphis ††/**	

Tesori began working on *Thoroughly Modern Millie* (2002), lyrics by Dick Scanlon, as an arranger with the expectation that the show would use pre-existing music from the 1920s. As the musical developed, the existing pieces that the collaborators found didn't suit the needs of the story, so Tesori and her collaborators began writing original pieces, which ultimately comprised the bulk of the score. Their influence was always the popular songs and dance band music of the 1920s. Tesori's songs from *Thoroughly Modern Millie* include:

Not for the Life of Me **	Forget About the Boy **
How the Other Half Lives **	I Turned the Corner †/**
They Didn't Know **	Long as I'm Here with You **
What Do I Need with Love †	Gimme Gimme **
Only in New York **	

Tesori's musical vocabulary for *Caroline, or Change* (2004), lyrics by Tony Kushner, included spirituals, blues, Motown, classical, klezmer and folk music. This musical, based on Kushner's memory of his childhood, tells the story of a black maid working for a Jewish family in New Orleans in 1963, during the Civil Rights Movement. Songs include:

Feet Beneath the Sea **	I Got Four Kids
Noah Down the Stairs	There Is No God Noah
The Dryer	Long Distance **

Dotty and Caroline * *
Moon Change * *
The Bus ††
No One Waitin' * *
'Night Mamma * *
Noah Has a Problem * *
Santa Comin' Caroline * *
Mr. Gellman's Shirt * *

I Saw Three Ships ††/* *
Dotty and Emmie * *
I Don't Want My Child to
    Hear That ††/* *
I Hate the Bus * *
Sunday Morning * *
Underwater * */†

For *Shrek, the Musical* (2008), lyrics by David Lindsay-Abaire, Tesori wrote,

> a score that blends a number of styles, including pop and R&B. "It's a quest story, a hero's journey." Where the songs sung by Shrek rely on folk rock to create a more private, heartfelt sound, the big numbers sung by the smorgasbord of fairy-tale characters who inhabit the land of Far, Far Away are a bit more over-the-top musical theater.[12]

Songs from *Shrek* include:

Big Bright Beautiful World
Story of My Life
Don't Let Me Go †
I Know It's Today * *
Travel Song †/††
Donkey Pot Pie * */†

Who I'd Be †/††/* *
Morning Person * *
I Think I Got You Beat ††/* *
When Words Fail ††
Build a Wall ††
Freak Flag

In her score for *Fun Home* (2015), Tesori uses the vocabulary of 1960s and 1970s pop but distorts it, turning it on its head in an effort to represent internal, psychological states in concrete musical terms. *The New York Times* said,

> Her work is both melodically sentimental and prickly with dissonance and tension. She layers contrapuntal voices to evoke every family's aspirations to complete harmony and the impossibility of achieving it. Ms. Tesori also makes witty use of the sounds of the 1960s and '70s, the decades in which Alison grows up ... [Her] most complex musical portraiture, though, is reserved for the divided self of Bruce, with melodies that change moods – from crisp, fatherly propriety to growling, guttural lust.[13]

Michael John LaChiusa (b. 1962)

Influence

Composer, lyricist and librettist Michael John LaChiusa creates complex and challenging music theatre pieces outside the mainstream. His wide-ranging influences include John Adams, Phillip Glass, John Corigliano, George Gershwin, Richard Rodgers and Stephen Sondheim. In an interview with Paul Leslie, LaChiusa said, "I loved most everything. I grew up in the 70s, so I love the pop music of that period. I also love classical music as well as the Broadway show tunes. I have pretty eclectic taste. I loved them all, everything from the Beatles to Fleetwood Mac to Bette Midler."[14]

LaChiusa's songs provide great technical challenge, and to sing them well the singer must own them completely and transcend the technical demands they require. LaChiusa has had great singers and actors perform his work, but the most successful have been those who can take this difficult material and develop performances that are "over the top." Listen to Mandy Patinkin and Toni Collete on the original cast recording of LaChiusa'a *The Wild Party* or Audra McDonald in *Marie Christine* and you will hear singers who have tremendous technical vocal control, but are able to transcend that and commit to larger than life performances.

Body of work

LaChiusa's operas and other non-musical theatre work include:

Four Short Operas: Break, Agnes, Eulogy for Mr. Hamm, Lucky Nurse (1991)
Desert of Roses (1992)
From the Towers of the Moon (1992)
Tania (1992)

Lovers and Friends (Chautauqua Variations), (2001)
The Seven Deadly Sins: A Song Cycle (2004)
The Cello Project (2005)
pre.view (2006)
Send (who are you? i love you) (2006)

He has written a number of musicals.

First Lady Suite (1993) is a chamber musical about four First Ladies of the United States, Eleanor Roosevelt, Mamie Eisenhower, Bess Truman and Jacqueline Bouvier Kennedy. This complex and difficult score presents musical and dramatic challenges to the actress. This score is purely classical in style. Songs include:

Over Texas **	Where's Mamie **
Four More Years **	My Husband Was an
Caroline **	Army Man **
The Smallest Thing **	Eleanor's Room **
This Is What We Are *	Great Ladies **

Hello Again (1994) tells the stories of ten sets of lovers spread over ten decades. LaChiusa takes this opportunity to reference the sounds from each decade in combination with his personal eclectic contemporary classical style. Songs include:

Hello Again **	At the Prom/Ah Maien Ziet! *
Zei Gezent (a bow to the	Listen to the Music ††
Andrews Sisters)	Safe †
In Some Other Life **	Silent Movie †
The Story of My Life */†	Rock with Rock †/**

The Petrified Prince (1994) opened and closed very quickly at Joseph Papp's Public Theatre, leaving a wake of devastating reviews and little evidence in terms of recordings or published music.

Marie Christine (1999) also closed very quickly, this time at Lincoln Center's Broadway venue, the Vivian Beaumont Theatre. It then moved to New Orleans. Loosely based on *Media*, and starring Audra McDonald, *Marie Christine* became one of the artistically important pieces of the year, even if it failed to find its audience. LaChiusa embraced Afro-Caribbean sounds to evoke the voodoo setting. Songs include:

Your Grandfather Is the Sun *	We're Gonna Go to
Beautiful *	Chicago †/*
Way Back to Paradise *	Cincinnati **
The Storm †/*	The Scorpion †/*
C'est L'Amour/To Find a Lover *	Tell Me †/*
Danced with a Girl †	Prison in a Prison *
Miracles and Mysteries *	I Will Love You*
I Don't Hear the Ocean †/*	Your Name †

In 2000 two musicals based on the Joseph Moncure March poem *The Wild Party* opened in New York. LaChiusa's opened on Broadway to mixed reviews. The score offers suggestions of 1920s popular music sounds interjected into LaChiusa's own particular eclectic blend of popular sounds from all periods, classical sounds and suggestions of vaudeville songs. Songs from LaChiusa's *The Wild Party* include:

Queenie Was a Blonde **	Lowdown-Down **
Marie is Tricky †	Gin/Wild †
Wild Party **/†	Black Is a Moocher **
Welcome to My Party **	People Like Us **/††
Like Sally **	The Movin' Uptown Blues ††
Breezin' Through	More ††
Another Day ††	How Many Women in the
Eddie and Mae **/††	World? †
Gold and Goldberg ††	When It Ends **
Moving Uptown **	This Is What It Is **
Wouldn't It Be Nice †	

Ben Brantley's *New York Times* review of LaChiusa's *Little Fish* (2003) complains that about halfway into this 90-minute musical it loses its shape and becomes a well-intentioned blob. LaChiusa's adamant refusal to consider traditional forms does not help this feeling. There is a wide range of musical styles in this musical comparing the crisis of giving up cigarettes to New Yorkers going through the crisis of the 9/11 attacks. There are some truly sparkling musical moments and some of the songs include:

Robert **	The Ninety-Year-Old Man **
It's a Sign **	By the Way ††
The Pool **	Remember Me **
Winter Is Here **	Anne **
Perfect **	Little Fish †
He ††	Poor Charlotte **
Cigarette Dream **	Simple Creature **
Flotsam **	In Two's and Three's **
I Ran †	

See What I Wanna See (2005) despite good reviews only managed a run of just over a month at Joseph Papp's Public Theatre.

LaChiusa's stylistic range expands further with this show as the range of characters expands over the centuries. The singing styles of these various characters reflect one style in one bar and another in the next. While the score is not commercially accessible, the music has extraordinary depth. Some songs include:

The Thief's Statement ††	Simple as This ††/**
See What I Wanna See **	Morito ††
Big Money ††	The Greatest Practical Joke **
You'll Go Away with Me ††	Central Park ††
Best not to Get Involved †	Coffee **
Louie **	There Will Be a Miracle **
No More **	

Bernada Alba (2006), based on Federico Garcia Lorca's play *The House of Bernarda Alba*, features an all-female company. Employing flamenco and other Western European folk styles, *Bernarda Alba* is a challenge to the singer, particularly the singer used to more traditional song structures and more unified, defined styles within songs. Songs include:

The Funeral	Adela
On the Day That I Marry	I Will Dream of What I Saw
Love, Let Me Sing You	One Moorish Girl
Let Me Go to the Sea	The Mare and the Stallion
Angustias	Lullaby
Maelia	Open the Door

Queen of the Mist (2011) and *Giant* (2012) both received positive reviews but have yet to receive any recording or published songs/scores.

Andrew Lippa (b. 1964)

Influence

Andrew Lippa was born in Leeds, England; his family moved to a suburb of Detroit when he was three years old. He is a classically trained pianist, but influences extend from every form of pop and rock music to the musicals *Dreamgirls*, *Sweeney Todd* and *Evita*. Like his other contemporaries, Lippa's music shifts effortlessly from one style to another.

Although Lippa has the same pop influences as the rest of his generation, his writing tends to be more grounded in the bright, frontal placement of traditional musical theatre vocal sound than most of his peers. Listen to the original cast recording of *The Addams Family*, for instance, and you could be listening to a Broadway musical from the 1970s or any period since. Lippa's songs are as driven by character as those of Ahrens and Flaherty, and singers need to be strong actors and storytellers.

Body of work

Jon & Jen, lyrics by Tom Greenwald, book by Lippa and Greenwald (off-Broadway, 1994) is a two actor/three character musical about a woman and her relationship to her brother in the first act, and her son in the second. The music evokes the time, which spans 1952 to 1990, through the use of eclectic styles. Songs include:

Welcome to the World **	Little League **/
Think Big **/††	Just Like You **
Dear God **/††	Bye Room ††
Hold Down the Fort **	Talk Show **/††
Timeline **/††	Smile of Your Dreams **
It Took Me a While ††	Graduation **/††
Out of My Sight **/††	The Road Ends Here **
Run and Hide **/††	That Was My Way **
Old Clothes **	Every Goodbye is Hello **/††

For the 1999 revival of *You're a Good Man Charlie Brown*, Lippa contributed two additional songs, "Beethoven Day" and "My New Philosophy."

In 2000, at almost the same time the Michael John LaChiusa's version of *The Wild Party* was preparing to open on Broadway, Lippa's was in rehearsal for an off-Broadway version of his own, running at the Manhattan Theatre Club. Songs include:

Queenie Was a Blonde **/†	Two of a Kind **/††
Out of the Blue **/†	Maybe I Like It This Way **
Raise the Roof **	What About Her? **/†
Look at Me Now **	The Life of the Party **
An Old-Fashioned Love Story **	

Originally produced in Mountain View, California in 2004, *A Little Princess*, with a book and lyrics by Brian Crawley, was an adaptation of the 1905 children's novel by Frances Hodgson Burnett. Although scheduled for Broadway, *A Little Princess* has not yet made it there. Songs from this show include:

Soon My love	Tables Were Turned
Live out Loud	Once and for All
Let Your Heart Be Your	Captain Crewe
Compass	Almost Christmas

Probably Lippa's biggest commercial hit was 2009's *The Addams Family*. For this show Lippa consciously tried to find a musical style for each of the characters. "This included giving Gomez a Flamenco-style Spanish score, Wednesday a more contemporary score, and Fester a vaudevillian score,"[15] as well as "the cabaret torch song 'Second Banana' for narcissistic Morticia; [... and] the lovely, Sondheim-ish ballad of contradictory emotions, 'Happy/Sad'."[16] Songs from *The Addams Family* include:

When You're An Addams	Happy/Sad ††
Pulled *	Crazier Than You ††/*
Where Did We Go Wrong **/††	Let's Not Talk About Anything
Morticia ††	Else But Love †/††
Waiting *	In the Arms †/*
Just Around the Corner **	Live Before We Die **/††
The Moon and Me †	Tango de Amor **/††

For his most recent Broadway musical *Big Fish*, with a book by John August (2013), Lippa goes back to earlier musical styles. August said, "I think what Andrew has been able to shape is a timeless American musical. It feels contemporary without being pop in any way and classical without feeling old."[17] Lippa added that the original film, the source material for the musical,

> just nodded in the direction [of country music] every once in a while. We believed that was the right way to go for the musical as well – to just give a flavor of country music. And what has emerged is, I think, a score within a score. There is what I call the emotional score, which is the family story, and there

is the fantasy score. When Bloom goes to the circus, obviously there is a circus music component and, in Act Two, there is a sequence in the Wild West, so that has a honky-tonk piano quality to it.[18]

Songs from *Big Fish* include:

Be the Hero ††   Daffodils ††/**
Stranger †   Fight the Dragons ††/†
Two Men in My life **   I Don't Need a Roof **
Out There on the Road ††   How It Ends ††
Time Stops ††/**

Adam Guettel (b. 1964)

Influence

Adam Guettel was born to the musical theatre, as the grandson of Richard Rodgers. In discussing his influences he has said,

> I listened to a lot of pop music – Stevie Wonder, Steely Dan, CSNY, The Who, Aerosmith – and also opera because I sang opera as a kid. I have come to identify a certain factor in my work, a tension between a kind of inevitable groove in the accompaniment, and a kind of smearing of measure lines, an eliding of different … melismatic elements on top. So we have this tension between a kind of wire-frame sub-structure that gives the audience a roadmap and something that is much more malleable on top.[19]

Guettel's work has ben noted for its complexity and chromaticism.

Like Ricky Ian Gordon's, Guettel's songs require a great deal of technique, and a level of vocal expressivity that call for a classically trained voice. Brian Stokes Mitchell, Kelli O'Hara, Audra McDonald, Christopher Innvar, Victoria Clark – these are the singers who have had the most success with Guettel's songs. The ability to implement choices about phrasing, tone and dynamics, acting – all while creating a beautiful sound – make for the most successful performance of Guettel's work.

Body of work

Floyd Collins (1996)

Although *Floyd Collins* ran for only 25 performances in its original off-Broadway production at Playwrights Horizons, it focused great attention on composer and lyricist Adam Guettel. *Floyd Collins* tells the story of a man who, while using the echos of his voice to explore Sand Cave in central Kentucky, becomes trapped, his foot wedged in position. While efforts to free Collins are underway, he is visited by his brother and fellow spelunker, William Burke "Skeets" Miller. The unusual story and tone of the treatment played into Guettel's strengths. His score, with additional lyrics by playwright Tina Landau, has been praised for its co-integration of multiple classical influences along with the sounds of bluegrass music.

Myths and Hymns (1998)

Myths and Hymns (originally titled *Saturn Returns*) is a revue of songs all dealing with the relationship between man and God. "The lyrics were inspired by Greek mythology and a nineteenth Century Presbyterian hymnal; the musical vocabulary sweeps from romantic art song and rock to Latin, gospel and R&B"[20] Guettel incorporates electronic jazz, piano ballads, gospel and traditional musical theatre. Songs include:

Children of the Heavenly King	Link
At the Sounding	Hero and Leander
Saturn Returns	Sisyphus †
Icarus	Come to Jesus *
Migratory V *	How Can I Lose You? **
Pegasus †/**/*	There's a Shout

In 2005, Guettel's greatest success, *The Light in the Piazza*, opened to rave reviews. "The score breaks from the 21st century tradition of pop music on Broadway by moving into the territory of Neo-romantic classical music and opera, with unexpected harmonic shifts and extended melodic structures, and is more heavily orchestrated than most Broadway scores."[21] Songs include:

Statues and Stories * Say It Somehow */†
The Beauty Is * The Light in the Piazza *
Passeggiata */† Let's Walk */††
The Joy You Feel * Love to Me †
Dividing Day * Fable *
Hysteria */†

Tom Kitt (b. 1974)

Influence

Tom Kitt has talked about growing up in a highly musical house, and being introduced to classical music at an early age. " 'My father has the most impressive record collection I've ever seen, spanning the worlds of classical music, jazz and vocal music.' But it was his brother and sister who introduced him to pop and rock music. 'My brother's love of classic rock-Billy Joel, the Beatles, Bruce Springsteen, Simon & Garfunkel-really influenced me as well.' "[22]

Like his contemporaries, Kitt's musicals are informed by a vast range of rock and popular music influences; those styles need to be accessible to the singer.

Body of work

Kitt's first Broadway show, *High Fidelity* (2006), lyrics by Amanda Green, came up against harsh critical response.

> Their score runs the gamut from pop music to rhythm and blues to romantic ballads, with each song in the style and musical vocabulary of a different pop or rock artist, including Bruce Springsteen, Beastie Boys, Indigo Girls, Talking Heads, Aretha Franklin, The Who, Guns N' Roses, Billy Joel, George Harrison, Percy Sledge, and others. However, all of the songs in the play were original composition, and none of the music by the classic artists spoken about by the characters is actually heard in the play – although (in a fantasy sequence) "Bruce Springsteen" shows up to advise the lead character of Rob on how to be like The Boss.[23]

Songs include:

The Last Real Record Store †/††	Number Five with a Bullet **
Desert Island Top 5	Nine Percent ††
Break Ups †	I Slept with Someone †
It's No Problem ††	Cryin' in the Rain †
She Goes **/†	Goodbye and Good Luck †/††
Ian's Here †/**	Ian's Prayer ††
	Laura, Laura †

Kitt's next musical was the Pulitzer Prize-winning rock musical *Next to Normal* (2009). This score includes:

Everything Else **	There's a World †
I Miss the Mountains **	Didn't I See This Movie? **
He's Not Here ††	Wish I Were Here **
You Don't Know **	Aftershocks †
I'm Alive ††	The Break **

For the 2012 musical, *Bring it On*, Kitt and Amanda Green co-wrote the score with composer/lyricist Lyn-Manuel Miranda. Taking place at a high school cheerleading competition, the score is an exploration of rock and contemporary popular music styles. Songs include:

What I Was Born to Do	Better
Tryouts	It Ain't No Thing
One Perfect Moment	Enjoy the Trip
Welcome to Jackson	Killer Instinct
Do Your Own Thing	We're Not Done
We Ain't No Cheerleaders	Legendary
Friday Night, Jackson	Eva's Rant
Something Isn't Right Here	Cross the Line
Bring It On	I Got You
It's All Happening	

In summary

The title of this chapter identifies this period as pulling from a range of sounds and lacking an identifiable style or sound. Since the majority of composers examined in this chapter began developing their adult musical sensibilities in the 1970s, it follows that the popular music of the 1970s is freely referenced in their works. Throughout the arts, particularly in popular art forms, the 1990s and 2000s were a time of "repurposed" art, when pieces of older popular culture found new life. Perhaps one of the clearest and most explicit example of this phenomenon is musical artist Jay-Z's rap remix of *Annie*'s "It's a Hard Knock Life." But the composers of this period pull from a vast range of popular, classical, folk, ethnic and other musical sources.

By 2016 composer and lyricist Lin-Manuel Miranda found tremendous success using the sounds of rap, hip-hop and house music as the musical vocabulary of George Washington, Thomas Jefferson and Alexander Hamilton. Miranda's use of these contemporary styles in a piece set more than 200 years ago, creates an electric and theatrically thrilling conflation of time periods, making the struggles of *Hamilton* and company so much more immediate to contemporary audiences. The actors who play these roles most successfully are at home in a broad range of styles, particularly the popular music styles. Actors like Idina Menzel, Heidi Blickenstaff, Norbert Leo Butz, Julia Murney, Aaron Tveit, Megan Hilty and Audra McDonald move easily from a legitimate sound in one phrase to an R&B riff in the next to an evocation of the great pop singers of the 1970s without skipping a beat. The twenty-first century musical theatre is defined by the "mash-up," the cross-contextualization of a vast range of sounds, styles and traditions. The twenty-first century musical theatre performer needs as many of these styles as possible available to them.

Notes

1 Leah Harper, "Elton John: Soundtrack of My Life," *The Guardian*, August 31, 2013, www.theguardian.com/music/2013/sep/01/elton-john-soundtrack-my-life, accessed April 22, 2015.

2 Stephen Flaherty, quoted in Jackson R. Bryer and Richard A. David, *The Art of the American Musical: Conversations with the Creators*, New Brunswick, NJ: Rutgers University Press, 2005, p. 3.

3 "Ragtime: The Musical," *Music Theatre International*, www.mtishows.com/show_detail.asp?showid=000228, accessed April 22, 2015.

4 Monty Arnold, "*Dessa*creation," *Playbill*, March 21, 2005, www.playbill.com/features/article/dessacreation-124812, accessed April 21, 2015.

5 Kenneth Jones, quoting Lynn Ahrens and Stephen Flaherty in "*Glorious Ones*, New Musical from Ahrens, Flaherty and Daniele, Opens in PA," *Playbill*, April 27, 2007, www.playbill.com/news/article/glorious-ones-new-musical-from-ahrens-flaherty-and-daniele-opens-in-pa-140374, accessed April 22, 2015.

6 Gerard Raymond, "Rocky: Ahrens & Flaherty Write a Musical Love Story," *Broadway Direct*, September 10, 2013, http://broadwaydirect.com/feature/rocky-ahrens-flaherty-write-a-musical-love-story, accessed April 24, 2015.

7 Ricky Ian Gordon Webstie, http://rickyiangordon.com/bio.php accessed July 21, 2015.

8 Peter Marks, "Oh, to Be Back Home in Wyoming," *The New York Times*, April 19, 1999, www.nytimes.com/1999/04/19/arts/theater-review-oh-to-be-back-home-in-wyoming.html, accessed April 28, 2015.

9 Michael Portantiere, "Brown, Guettel and LaChiusa Discuss Musical Theater at Drama Book Shop," *Theatremania*, March 16, 2004, www.theatermania.com/new-york-city-theater/news/03-2004/brown-guettel-and-lachiusa-discuss-musical-theater_4504.html, accessed April 25, 2015.

10 Christopher Isherwood, "Review: Parade," *Variety*, December 21, 1998, http://variety.com/1998/legit/reviews/parade-1200456199/, accessed May 23, 2016.

11 Julia Lowry Henderson, "Inside Jeanine Tesori's *Fun Home*," *Studio 360* (radio interview), April 16, 2015, www.studio360.org/story/jeanine-tesoris-fun-home/, accessed April 24, 2015.

12 Marshall Heyman, "Shrek's Theatre Queen: Composer Jeanine Tesori Returns to Broadway with a Big Green Ogre," *W Magazine*, December 2008, www.wmagazine.com/people/celebrities/2008/12/jeanine_tesori/, accessed April 27, 2105.

13 Ben Brantley, "'Fun Home,' a New Musical at the Public Theater," *The New York Times*, October 22, 2013, www.nytimes.com/2013/10/23/theater/reviews/fun-home-a-new-musical-at-the-public-theater.html, accessed July 27, 2015.

14 Paul Leslie, "Michael John LaChiusa: Musical Theatre and Opera Composer, Lyricist & Librettist," *The Paul Leslie*, www.thepaulleslie.com/michael-john-lachiusa/, accessed April 26, 2015.

15 Robert Simonson, "Playbill.com's Brief Encounter With Andrew Lippa," *Playbill*, December 9, 2009, www.playbill.com/article/playbill-coms-brief-encounter-with-andrew-lippa-com-176251, accessed May 12, 2016.

16 Steven Oxman, "Review: 'The Addams Family'," *Variety*, December 10, 2009, http://variety.com/2009/legit/reviews/the-addams-family-4-1200477895/, accessed April, 27, 2015.

17 Gerard Raymond, "Making Big Fish Sing: A New Broadway Musical," *Broadway Direct*, June 17, 2013, http://broadwaydirect.com/feature/making-big-fish-sing-a-new-broadway-musical-is-born, accessed April 28, 2015.

18 Raymond, "Making Big Fish Sing."

19 Michael Portantiere, "Brown, Guettel and LaChiusa Discuss Musical Theater at Drama Book Shop," *Theatremania.com*, March 16, 2004, www.theatermania.com/new-york-city-theater/news/03-2004/brown-guettel-and-lachiusa-discuss-musical-theater_4504.html, accessed April 25, 2015.

20 "Myths and Hymns," *Rodgers and Hammerstein*, www.rnh.com/show/69/Myths-%26-Hymns, accessed April 28, 2015.

21 "The Light in the Piazza" *TheBroadwayMusicals.com*, www.thebroad waymusicals.com/l/lightinthepiazza.htm, accessed April 28, 2015.

22 Suzanne Bixby, "Tom Kitt: 'Next to Normal's' Eclectic Tunesmith," March 9, 2012, *EdgeMediaNetwork*, www.edgeboston.com/?130790, accessed April 28, 2015.

23 Scott Kaufman, "(Video Scrapbook) "Cryin' In the Rain": 'Next to Normal' composer give B'way some 'High Fidelity', starring Will Chase in 2006," unsungbroadway.com, http://unsungbroadway.com/video-scrapbookcryin-in-the-rain-next-to-normal-composer-gives-bway-some-high-fidelity-starring-will-chase-in-2006/, posted December 7, 2013, accessed on July 5, 2016.

Chapter 12

Other popular styles

The jukebox musicals

In recent history, many Broadway seasons have seen the "one-of-a-kinds" – successful shows that have struck the public imagination without being part of a major trend. 2005's *The Drowsy Chaperone* started out as an extended skit at a bachelor party and made it successfully to Broadway. A cross between a paean to and loving satire of the American musical comedies of the 1920s, this Toronto-based musical developed a following. Trey Parker, Matt Stone and Robert Lopez's *The Book of Mormon* struck gold in 2011, bringing the comic sensibility of *South Park* to the stage. Just as *Spamalot* did in the 2005 season, *The Book of Mormon* captured the much sought-after male 18–35 demographic, insuring its success. The film *Once* was adapted for the stage in the 2012 season using the cast as musicians, a short-lived trend that had its last hurrah in that production. The 2013 season saw another pop songwriter, Cindy Lauper, enter the musical theatre with *Kinky Boots*, a fairly traditional, old-fashioned book musical. The 2014 season saw *A Gentleman's Guide to Love and Murder*. There will likely always be a yearly anomaly that by not fitting the pattern catches the public attention

Despite these one-of-a-kind shows, the most overwhelming trend of this period has been the jukebox musical. These shows, which create a plot, story or concept around existing songs, have overtaken traditional musicals that use scores written specifically for the characters and situations. Many of the jukebox musicals have plots (some fairly thin) written to weave the songs together. Because in the twenty-first century, it is the "jukebox" shows like *Jersey Boys* and *Mamma Mia* that have thrived, the genre has proliferated and given us other musicals like *Ring of Fire* and *A Night With Janis Joplin*.

Jukebox musicals use the catalog of a particular performer or songwriter, or a particular genre or theme. Frequently the songs are placed in a plot telling the story of the singer or songwriter's life story. Jukebox musicals have used country music (*Ring of Fire*), pop music of various traditions (*What's It All About? The Music of Burt Bacharach and Hal David*), jazz (*After Midnight*), rock music including classic rock (*Beautiful, Rock of Ages*), alternative (*American Idiot*), R&B (*Motown the Musical*), rap (*Holler If Ya Hear Me*), blues (*Blues in the Night*), gospel (*Crowns: The Gospel Musical*), American folk music (*The Times They Are A-Changin'*) and folk music of various other nations (*Fela, Mentiras el Musical*).

These shows have made the understanding of a vast range of musical styles absolutely essential; being able to listen, discern, study and learn styles is vitally important to the musical theatre performer of the twenty-first century. This chapter looks at what has appeared on the musical theatre stage. Since what has yet to appear could include any body of pre-existing music, the ability to listen, distill styles and fully embrace them is required in the musical theatre of today.

We need to differentiate between jukebox book musicals on one hand and revues that use previously existing songs on the other. While jukebox book musicals place pre-existing songs in the mouths of characters in the employ of a story, the jukebox revues simply celebrate the music without the context of character or story. Examples of revues would include: *Bubbling Brown Sugar* (using the songs of the Harlem Renaissance), *Eubie* (using the music of composer Eubie Blake), *Sophisticated Ladies* (featuring the music of Duke Ellington), *Jerome Kern Goes to Hollywood* (using the music of Jerome Kern) and *Side By Side By Sondheim* (using the music of Stephen Sondheim).

Early jukebox musicals include:

The Night That Made America Famous using the music of folk songwriter Harry Chapin, Broadway, 1975.

Elvis, using the songs recorded by Elvis Presley, West End, 1977.

Leader of the Pack, using the music of Ellie Greenwich, Broadway, 1984

Buddy – The Buddy Holly Story, using the songs recorded by Buddy Holly, West End, 1989

Return to the Forbidden Planet, using popular rock songs of the 1950s and 1960s, 1989.

Forever Plaid, using popular songs of the 1950s and 1960s, 1990.

Smokey Joe's Café, using music by Jerry Leiber and Mike Stoller, Broadway, 1995.

Play On!, using the songs of Duke Ellington, Broadway, 1997.
Boogie Nights, using the popular music of the 1970s, West End, 1998.
My Way: A Musical Tribute to Frank Sinatra, featuring the songs recorded by Frank Sinatra.1999.

Using popular songs is nothing new; composers of the 1910s and 1920s would reuse their most popular songs from time to time. Many shows have been created using the popular songs of great musical theatre composers (such as *My One and Only*, *Crazy for You* and *Nice Work if You Can Get It*, all from the catalog of Gershwin songs), and composer and theme revues have graced stages as long as there have been popular songs. But the genre took off in 1999, when Phyllida Lloyd's *Mamma Mia!* opened in the West End, using the music of 1970s Swedish pop group ABBA. The success of *Mamma Mia!* has been so overwhelming that it convinced producers that the best way to ensure success is to give audiences music that they already know. *Mamma Mia!* has played to over 54 million people, and it has appeared on six continents, in seventeen languages. It was this production that began the predominance of the jukebox musicals. Since *Mamma Mia!*, jukebox musicals have been produced featuring the music of (or recorded by) Janis Joplin (*Love, Janis*, 2001 and *A Night With Janis Joplin*, 2014), Queen (*We Will Rock You*, 2002), Billy Joel (*Movin' Out*, 2002), Peter Allen (*The Boy From Oz*, 2003), Rod Stewart (*Tonight's The Night: The Rod Stewart Musical*, 2003), the Disney catalog (*On the Record*, 2004), various pop artists of the 1970s or the 1980s, disco music, John Lennon (*Lennon: Through a Glass Onion*, 2014 and *Lennon*, 2005), The Beach Boys (*Good Vibrations*, 2005), Elvis Presley (*All Shook Up*, 2004), Frankie Vallie and the Four Seasons (*Jersey Boys*, 2005), Earth, Wind and Fire (*Hot Feet*, 2005), disco hits, Johnny Cash (*Ring of Fire*, 2006), glam metal groups of the 1990s (*Rock of Ages*, 2009), Michael Jackson (*Thriller, Live*, 2009), Bob Dylan (*The Times, They Are a-Changin'*, 2006), Blondie (*Desperately Seeking Susan*, 2007), Burt Bacharach (*What's It All About?: Bacharach Reimagined*, 2013), Frank Sinatra (*My Way: A Musical Tribute to Frank Sinatra*, 1999 and *My Sinatra*, 2015), Green Day (*American Idiot*, 2009), The Shirelles (*Baby It's You*, 2011), the Spice Girls (*Viva Forever*, 2012), Carole King (*Beautiful*, 2013), Duke Ellington (*Sophisticated Ladies*, 1981 and *Play On!*, 1997), the Motown catalog (*Motown, the Musical*, 2013), music of the 1930s, Tupac Shakur (*Holler If Ya Need Me*, 2014),

Billie Holiday (*Lady Day at Emerson's Bar and Grill*, 1986 revived 2014), Kurt Weill (*Lovemusick*, 2007), George and Ira Gershwin (*My One and Only*, 1983; *Crazy for You*, 1992; *The Gershwins' Fascinating Rhythm*, 1999; *George Gershwin Alone*, 2001 and *Nice Work If You Can Get It*, 2012).

As mentioned earlier, producers had long known the appeal of presenting audiences with familiar songs. More recently however, in the current wave of jukebox musicals, they have also learned that having one or two fewer creative participants at the table during production (the composer and lyricist) often spells success in the twenty-first century. Without a composer or lyricist participating in the shaping of a musical, the producers and other creative personnel have more freedom to shape the material as they see best. As a singer, this means that you are out on your own – you need to be able to take any artist or composer and distill their essence. As well as conveying the character that you are playing, you are also representing the song as it was originally recorded and are obliged to communicate the character of the original artist and their music. As a broad familiarity beforehand is the most valuable tool that any singer has, to this end listen to as much and as broad a range of music as you can listen to, not just your favorites. The ability to listen carefully, take what makes the essence of that music and implement it in an audition situation will make the difference between nailing the style (and booking the job), or not. "Cramming" the style can never replace having at least some familiarity with the music beforehand.

In 2010, *Million Dollar Quartet*, which had been making its way around the country (Florida, Washington state, Virginia, Chicago) brought to the stage a famed recorded jam session with Elvis Presley, Jerry Lee Lewis, Carl Perkins and Johnny Cash. Although the show only had relatively short runs on Broadway and the West End, it became very popular in regional theatre, owing to the popularity of the characters and the low cost of a show with just a unit set, six actors and two musicians. Many actors who were able to inhabit these singers' styles and get reasonably close to their looks found a great deal of work. And that is ultimately the point; the ability to pick up and put down styles and sounds, to listen carefully and not only imitate, but to wear a singer's style as one might wear a costume, is absolutely invaluable in the musical theatre of the twenty-first century.

Many first-class productions today have an in-house vocal supervisor, like Liz Caplan. Caplan is vocal supervisor of *Once*, *American Idiot*, *Motown: the Musical*, *The Book of Mormon* and

Aladdin. These members of the creative team help the singers to create and sustain the exact vocal quality and performance required by these shows, often requiring a carbon copy of the recordings by the original artists. The singer who aspires to be cast in these shows has to show a strong ability to not only mimic vocally, but to embody others' performances dramatically and emotionally.

One of the most successful jukebox musicals, worldwide, is Des Macanuf's *Jersey Boys*, which tells the story of Frankie Valli and the Four Seasons, using the songs that they made popular beginning in the 1962 with their first big hit, "Sherry." The cast needs to be able to transcend faithful vocal imitation and make the audience believe that they *are* Frankie Valli, Bob Gaudio and other Four Seasons.

An article in the *Baltimore Sun* talks about the difficulty of this kind of musical:

> 'The score is so difficult', says Katie Agresta ... 'Typically, a lead in a Broadway musical has maybe five songs. In "Jersey Boys," it's 27. And you have to act. That's why we developed what we call "Frankie Camp."' The 'camp' is held periodically in New York for actors who have shown potential. In addition to intensive sessions on acting and choreography, the camp focuses on the sound that made a short, Newark-born Italian-American one of the most instantly recognizable singers in pop music. 'Frankie had an amazing instrument with an amazing falsetto,' says 'Jersey Boys' music director Ron Melrose. 'Usually, a falsetto is soft and choirboy-ish, but there was a gritty, street sound to his.'[1]

To maintain their casting files for such a vocally grueling show, the *Jersey Boys* production supervisor, music and choreographic assistants and vocal coach Katie Agresta regularly hold "Frankie camp." The creative team invites a group of 50 actors who are 5'9", look Mediterranean and have a good falsetto voice to participate in the workshops. After the first several days, 40 of the participants are released and the remaining 10 go through a grueling week of voice work, choreography and acting sessions.

Very few shows other than *Jersey Boys* work so hard to prepare appropriate actors and singers. Most are left to their own devices, or to their own work with private vocal coaches, to nail the vocal styles required by these various shows. The ability to study, learn and imitate musical styles has become absolutely essential in today's musical theatre.

In summary

Today's composers demand stylistic diversity, practically from measure to measure. Shows calling for singers to recreate popular or famous recordings abound, and the most stylistically diverse singer is likely the one who will work the most. But this requires more than mere imitation.

How does the young singer begin to distill musical essences? Begin with listening to as much as humanly possible.

* Listen to tone – what is the tonal quality of the singer, or of the popular recordings or a composer's work? Performing the role of Billie Holiday in recent Broadway revival of *Lady Day at Emersons Bar and Grill*, Audra McDonald studied the singer's tone, diction, inflections and performance so thoroughly that she was able to inhabit the singer from within.
* Second is stylization – how much ornamentation is used by singers on the recordings? Performing the songs of Leiber and Stoller in a production of *Smokey Joe's Café* demands a singer provide a much greater range of ornamentation than a jukebox musical based on the songs of Doris Day, for instance.
* Do the original recordings lock into the groove, or does the singer back/front-phrase and seem to be floating above the groove, rather than locked into it? To affect the singing style of French chanteur Charles Aznavour, the singer must phrase behind the accompaniment. In fact, Aznavour's conductor is reported to have said that he had to wear headphones that blocked the singer's voice so as not to be pulled back. In contrast, most contemporary rock singers tend to lock in with the groove.
* Consider the inflection, phrasing, breathing, dynamics, approach to notes, use of vibrato, diction, and anything else that seems pertinent for the music you are listening to. Don't be afraid to copy vocal turns, flips, use of vibrato, and anything else that might be considered stylistically appropriate. To successfully perform in *Our Sinatra*, a singer has to listen to as many Frank Sinatra recordings as they can get their hands on, distill the style, borrow all aspects of Frank Sinatra's musicality, imitate them and ultimately make it live.

Oscar Wilde said, "Talent borrows, genius steals." Taking from your source material as many different ways of approaching the material, whatever is most germane to that musician, and applying it to the text at hand will lead to a more rounded representation of the style. Most important of all, however, try to locate the singer's soul. Do they sing to express their pain, joy, irony, incredulity, revelation or some other emotion? For example, one could listen to the French chanteuse Edith Piaf, and reasonably decide that she sings to proudly proclaim her survival, the fact that she is still here; that is a great place to start getting inside Piaf's skin and making the transition from simply imitating to finding your own "inner Piaf." Singing the Elvis Presley songs in the book musical *All Shook Up* requires the singer to know Presley's recordings intimately and suggest or reference them at times, without becoming *merely* an imitation of "the King." This level of ownership of the style can be done with any other singer or genre. It takes a lot of work, hours of listening, trying the vocal devices and affectations in your own voice, and then finding the truth of them. That is the greatest challenge facing a musical-theatre singer today, the ability to inhabit such a broad range of styles so completely.

The human voice has the capacity of creating a vast range of sounds, much larger than most singers take advantage of. Growls, snarls, hoots, slides, trills, percussive effects, vibrato, straight tone – the range of qualities is almost as limitless as the singer's imagination. In discussing vocal placement, voice teacher Paul Gavert expanded the singer's visualization by suggesting that there are as many possible placements as there are atoms in the singer's body. The range of human expression in song has such vast tonal and stylistic range, and yet so many singers get so caught up in making pretty sounds. The most successful singers are those who can access the widest stylistic and tonal vocabularies and the way to develop such a vocabulary is to listen to absolutely everything. Every kind of music is interesting and has something to teach the singer: vocal music, instrumental music, classical, contemporary, folk, jazz, fusion, opera, international. It will all be of use to the singer of the songs of the musical theatre, even if just as a point of reference.

Note

1 Tim Smith, "Actors in 'Jersey Boys' Learn Methods at Frankie Camp," *The Baltimore Sun*, November 8, 2013, http://articles.baltimoresun. com/2013-11-08/entertainment/bs-ae-arts-story-1108-20131107_1_ frankie-camp-frankie-valli-jersey-boys, accessed August 17, 2015.

Bibliography

Ainger, Michael, *Gilbert and Sullivan: A Dual Biography*, New York, NY: Oxford University Press, 2002.

Alonso, Harriet Hyman, *Yip Harburg: Legendary Lyricist and Human Rights Advocate*, Middletown, CT: Wesleyan Press, 2012.

Arnold, Monty, "*Dessa*creation," *Playbill*, March 21, 2005, www.playbill.com/features/article/dessacreation-124812, accessed April 21, 2015.

Ball, Michael, "Is Stephen Sondheim the Shakespeare of Musical Theatre?," *The Guardian*, www.theguardian.com/stage/theatreblog/2010/mar/29/stephen-sondheim-musical-theatre, accessed February 8, 2015.

Banfield, Stephen, *Jerome Kern*, New Haven, CT: Yale University Press, 2006.

——, *Sondheim's Broadway Musicals*, Ann Arbor, MI: University of Michigan Press, 1995.

Bell, J.X., "Cole Porter Biography," *The Cole Porter Resource Site*, www.coleporter.org/bio.html, accessed December 1, 2014.

Benjamin, Tom, *How to Sound Like Sinatra*, www.tom.com.au/kara-oke/sinatra.pdf, accessed December 27, 2014.

Bergreen, Laurence, *As Thousands Cheer: The Life of Irving Berlin*, New York, NY: Da Capo Press, 1996.

Bernstein, Leonard, *The Joy of Music*, New York, NY: Amadeus Press, 2014.

Bixby, Suzanne, "Tom Kitt: 'Next to Normal's' Eclectic Tunesmith," March 9, 2012, *EdgeMediaNetwork*, www.edgeboston.com/?130790, accessed April 28, 2015.

Blau, Eleanor, "Jule Styne, Bountiful Creator of Song Favorites, Dies at 88," *The New York Times*, September 21, 1994, www.nytimes.com/1994/09/21/obituaries/jule-styne-bountiful-creator-of-song-favorites-dies-at-88.html, accessed November 17, 2014.

Bordman, Gerald, *Jerome Kern: His Life and Music*, New York, NY: Oxford University Press, 1980.

Brantley, Ben. "'Fun Home,' a New Musical at the Public Theater," *The New York Times*, October 22, 2013, www.nytimes.com/2013/10/23/theater/reviews/fun-home-a-new-musical-at-the-public-theater.html, accessed July 27, 2015.

Brody, Seymour, "Jewish Heroes and Heroines of America," *Jewish Heroes and Heroines of America: 150 True Stories of American Jewish Heritage*, New York, NY: Lifetime Books, 1996, www.jewishvirtuallibrary.org/jsource/biography/berlin.html, accessed March 17, 2015.

Bryer, Jackson R. and Richard A. David, *The Art of the American Musical: Conversations with the Creators*, New Brunswick, NJ: Rutgers University Press, 2005.

Carmichael, Hoagy, Stephen Longstreet and John Edward Hasse, *The Stardust Road & Sometimes I Wonder: The Autobiography of Hoagy Carmichael*, New York, NY: Da Capo Press, 1999.

Cellier, François, *Gilbert and Sullivan and Their Operas; With Recollections and Anecdotes of D'Oyly Carte & Other Famous Savoyards*, Boston, MA: Little, Brown and Company, 1914.

Charles Strouse website, www.charlesstrouse.com/shows.php, accessed May 9, 2016.

Citron, Stephen, *Jerry Herman, Poet of the Showtune*, New Haven, CT: Yale University Press, 2004.

———, *Noel and Cole: The Sophisticates*, New York, NY: Oxford University Press, 1993.

———, *Stephen Sondheim and Andrew Lloyd Webber: The New Musical*, New York, NY: Oxford University Press, 2001.

Cohan, George M., *Twenty Years on Broadway and the Years It Took to Get There. The True Story of the Trouper's Life from the Cradle to the Closed Shop*, New York, NY: Harper and Brothers Publishers, 1925.

Comden, Betty, *Off Stage*, Milwaukee, WI: Limelight Editions, 2004.

———, *On the Sunny Side of the Street: The Life and Lyrics of Dorothy Fields*, Foreword, New York, NY: Schirmer Books, 1997.

Coveney, Michael, *The Andrew Lloyd Webber Story*, London, UK: Arrow Books, 2000.

De Giere, Carol, *Defying Gravity: The Creative Career of Stephen Schwartz, from Godspell to Wicked*, New York, NY: Applause Theatre and Cinema Books, 2008.

———, "Stephen Schwartz – Musical Influences and Styles," *MusicalSchwartz.com*, www.musicalschwartz.com/schwartz-musical-influences.htm, accessed January 3, 2015.

DeVenney, David P., *The New Broadway Song Companion: An Annotated Guide to Musical Theatre Literature by Voice Type and Song Style*, New York, NY: Scarecrow Press, 2009.

Dietz, Howard, *Dancing in the Dark: Words by Howard Dietz*, New York, NY: Quadrangle, 1974.

Eliot, T.S., "The Sacred Wood." *Goodreads*, www.goodreads.com/work/best_book/442581-the-sacred-wood, accessed October 28, 2015.

Ellington, Duke, *Music Is My Mistress*, New York, NY: Da Capo Press, 1976.

Everett, William A., *Sigmund Romberg*, New Haven, CT: Yale University Press, 2007.

Ewen, David, *Wine, Women and Waltz: A Romantic Biography of Johann Strauss, Son and Father*, Whitefish, MT: Kessinger Publishing, LLC, 2007.

Feinstein, Michael, *The Gershwins and Me: A Personal History in Twelve Songs*, New York, NY: Simon and Schuster, 2012.

——, "Harold Arlen," *Michael Feinstein's American Songbook*, www.michaelfeinsteinsamericansongbook.org/songwriter.html?p=45, accessed May 20, 2014.

Fordin, Hugh, *Getting to Know Him – A Biography of Oscar Hammerstein, II*, New York, NY: Da Capo Press, 1995.

Forman, Roanna, "Smith, Bessie," *jazz.com*, www.jazz.com/encyclopedia/smith-bessie, accessed December 25, 2014.

Friedwald, Will, *Jazz Singing: America's Greatest Voices: From Bessie Smith to Bebop and Beyond*. New York, NY: Da Capo Press, 1996.

Gordon, Joanne, *Art Isn't Easy: The Theatre of Stephen Sondheim*, New York, NY: Da Capo Press, 1992.

Gould, Neil, *Victor Herbert: A Theatrical Life*, New York, NY: Fordham University Press, 2008.

Gourse, Leslie, *The Billie Holiday Companion: Seven Decades of Commentary*, New York: Schirmer, 1997.

Greenspan, Charlotte, *Pick Yourself Up: Dorothy Fields and the American Musical*, New York, NY: Oxford University Press, 2010.

Grode, Eric, *Hair: The Story of the Show that Defined a Generation*, Philadelphia, PA: Running Press, 2010.

Grun, Bernard, *Gold and Silver: The Life and Times of Franz Lehár*, London, UK: W.H. Auden/Virgin Books, 1970.

Hamlin, Jesse, "Ben Sidran Revisits Jewish Influence on American Music," *SFGate*, March 26, 2014, www.sfgate.com/movies/article/Ben-Sidran-revisits-Jewish-influence-on-American-5351966.php, accessed May 20, 2104.

Hamlisch, Marvin, *The Way I Was*, New York, NY: Scribner, 1992.

Harper, Leah, "Elton John: Soundtrack of my life," *The Guardian*, August 31, 2013, www.theguardian.com/music/2013/sep/01/elton-john-soundtrack-my-life, accessed April 22, 2015.

Haun, Harry, "Charles Strouse Shares the Music of His Life," *Playbill*, August 29, 2008, www.playbill.com/article/charles-strouse-shares-the-music-of-his-life-com-152893, accessed May 9, 2016.

Hawtree, Christopher "Cy Coleman: Composer of Broadway Shows and Song Standards," *The Guardian*, November 22, 2004, www.theguardian.com/news/2004/nov/22/guardianobituaries.artsobituaries, accessed June 10, 2014.

Henahan , Donald , "Leonard Bernstein, 72, Music's Monarch, Dies," *The New York Times*, October 15, 1990, www.nytimes.com/learning/general/onthisday/bday/0825.html, accessed August 30, 2014.

Henderson, Julia Lowry, "Inside Jeanine Tesori's *Fun Home*," *Studio 360* (radio interview), April 16, 2015, www.studio360.org/story/jeanine-tesoris-fun-home/, accessed April 24, 2015.

Herman, Jerry, *Showtune: A Memoir by Jerry Herman*, New York, NY: Dutton, 1996.

————, "Tony Awards Acceptance Speech: *La Cage Aux Folles*," Gershwin Theatre, New York, NY, June 3, 1984, www.youtube.com/watch?v=v4SGTEv1164, accessed June 12, 2014.

Heyman, Marshall, "Shrek's Theatre Queen: Composer Jeanine Tesori Returns to Broadway with a Big Green Ogre," *W Magazine*, December 2008, www.wmagazine.com/people/celebrities/2008/12/jeanine_tesori/, accessed April 27, 2105.

Hirsch, Foster, *Kurt Weill Onstage: From Berlin to Broadway*, New York, NY: Knopf, 2002.

Hischak, Thomas, *The Jerome Kern Encyclopedia*, Plymouth, UK: Scarecrow Press, 2013.

Holden, Stephen, "Ella Fitzgerald, the Voice of Jazz, Dies at 79," *The New York Times*, June 16, 1996, www.nytimes.com/1996/06/16/nyregion/ella-fitzgerald-the-voice-of-jazz-dies-at-79.html, accessed December 27, 2014.

————, "Sarah Vaughan, 'Divine One' of Jazz Singing, Is Dead at 66," *The New York Times*, April 5, 1990, www.nytimes.com/1990/04/05/obituaries/sarah-vaughan-divine-one-of-jazz-singing-is-dead-at-66.html, accessed December 27, 2014.

————. "Their Songs Were America's Happy Talk," *The New York Times*, January 4, 1993, www.nytimes.com/1993/01/24/theater/theater-their-songs-were-america-s-happy-talk.html, accessed October 28, 2015.

Horowitz, Mark Eden, *Sondheim on Music: Minor Details and Major Decisions*, New York, NY: Scarecrow Press, 2010.

Horowitz, Murray, "Fats Waller Now, Fats Waller Forever," *Institute of Jazz Studies: Dana Library: Rutgers University Library*, http://newark-www.rutgers.edu/ijs/fw/contemp.htm, accessed December 30, 2014.

Howard, Elisabeth, *Sing!: The Vocal Power Method Male and Female Voice All Styles*, Van Nuys, CA: Alfred Publishing, 2006.

Isherwood, Christopher, "Review: Parade," *Variety*, December 21, 1998, http://variety.com/1998/legit/reviews/parade-1200456199/,accessed May 23, 2016.

Jablonski, Edward, *Alan Jay Lerner: A Biography*, New York, NY: Henry Holt & Co, 1996.

————, *Gershwin*, Lebanon, NH: Northeastern University Press, 1990.

————, *Harold Arlen: Happy With the Blues*, New York, NY: Da Capo Press, 1986.

————, *Harold Arlen: Rhythm, Rainbows and Blues*, Lebanon, NH: Northeastern University Press, 1996.

Jacobs, H.E., *Johann Strauss – Father and Son – A Century of Light Music*, New York, NY: Greystone, 1940.

Johnson, Jonathon, *Good Hair Days: A Personal Journey with the American Tribal Love-Rock Musical, Hair*, Bloomington, IN: iUniverse, Inc. 2004.

Jones, Kenneth, "*Glorious Ones*, New Musical from Ahrens, Flaherty and Daniele, Opens in PA," *Playbill*, April 27, 2007, www.playbill. com/news/article/glorious-ones-new-musical-from-ahrens-flaherty-and-daniele-opens-in-pa-140374, accessed April 22, 2015.

Jones, Quincy, *Q: The Autobiography of Quincy Jones*, New York, NY: Three Rivers Press, 2002.

Kaufman, Scott, "(Video Scrapbook) "Cryin' In the Rain"': 'Next to Normal' composer give B'way some 'High Fidelity', starring Will Chase in 2006," unsungbroadway.com, http://unsungbroadway.com/video-scrapbookcryin-in-the-rain-next-to-normal-composer-gives-bway-some-high-fidelity-starring-will-chase-in-2006/, posted December 7, 2013, accessed on July 5, 2016.

Kaye, Joseph, *Victor Herbert: The Biography of America's Greatest Composer of Romantic Music*, Whitefish, MT: Kessinger Publishing, LLC, 2007.

Kenrick, John, "Musical Closets: Gay Songwriters," *Musicals101.com: The Cyber Encyclopedia of Musical Theatre, Film & Television*, www.musicals101.com/gay5.htm, accessed March 21, 2015.

Kepecs, Susan, "Bobby McFerrin and the Simplest Form of Expression," *Isthmus*, www.isthmus.com/isthmus/article.php?article=24851, accessed September 1, 2014.

Kimball, Robert and William Bolcolm, *Reminiscing with Noble Sissle and Eubie Blake*, New York, NY: Cooper Square Press, 2000.

Kirby, Ed, *Ain't Misbehavin': The Story of Fats Waller*, New York, NY: Da Capo Press, 1975.

Lambert, Phillip, *To Broadway! To Life! The Musical Theatre of Bock and Harnick*, New York, NY: Oxford University Press, 2010.

Langley, K.E. Querns, "K.E. Querns Langley: Bel Canto Vocal Studio," *A World of Art – A World of Entertainment*, www.belcantovocalstudio. co.uk/bel-canto-history, accessed May 5, 2016.

Lawrence, Greg, *Colored Lights: Forty Years of Words and Music Show Biz, Collaboration and All That Jazz*, London, UK: Faber & Faber, 2004.

Lerner, Alan Jay, *The Street Where I Live*, New York, NY: W.W. Norton, 1978.

Leslie, Paul, "Michael John LaChiusa: Musical Theatre and Opera Composer, Lyricist & Librettist," *The Paul Leslie*, www.thepaulleslie. com/michael-john-lachiusa/, accessed April 26, 2015.

Leve, James, *Kander and Ebb*, Yale Broadway Masters Series, New Haven, CT: Yale University Press, 2009.

Loesser, Susan, *A Most Remarkable Fella: Frank Loesser and the Guys and Dolls in His Life: A Portrait by His Daughter*, Milwaukee, WI: Hal Leonard, 2000.

Lomax, Alan, *Mister Jelly Roll: The Fortunes of Jelly Roll Morton, New Orleans Creole and Inventor of Jazz*, Oakland, CA: University of California Press, 2001.

Luce, Jim and Dick Golden, producers, "Louis Armstrong: the Singer," *Jazz Profiles from NPR*, www.npr.org/programs/jazzprofiles/archive/armstrong_singer.html, accessed December 27, 2014.

Machlin, Paul, "The Music of Fats Waller," *Institute of Jazz Studies: Dana Library: Rutgers University Library*, http://newarkwww.rutgers.edu/ijs/fw/music.htm, accessed December 30, 2014.

Magee, Jeffrey, *Irving Berlin's American Musical Theatre*, New York, NY: Oxford University Press, 2012.

Marks, Peter, "At Signature, 'Elegies' Puts the Good in Goodbye," *The Washington Post*, March 31, 2004, www.washingtonpost.com/archive/lifestyle/2004/03/31/at-signature-elegies-puts-the-good-in-goodbye/ca89b291-f6c2-4295-a129-37b69cfb009b/, accessed May 9, 2016.

——, "Oh, to Be Back Home in Wyoming," *The New York Times*, April 19, 1999, www.nytimes.com/1999/04/19/arts/theater-review-oh-to-be-back-home-in-wyoming.html, accessed April 28, 2015.

Marotta, Sharon Zak, "Harold Arlen – Biography – Last Night When We Were Young," *The Official Harold Arlen Website*, www.haroldarlen.com/bio-9.html, accessed May 19, 2014.

Marx, Samuel and Jan Clayton, *Rodgers and Hart: Bewitched, Bothered and Bedeviled, an Anecdotal Account*, New York, NY: G.P. Putnam's Sons, 1976.

McBrien, William, *Cole Porter*, New York, NY: Vintage Press, 2000.

McHugh, Dominic, *Alan Jay Lerner: A Lyricist's Letters*, Oxford, UK: Oxford University Press, 2014.

Menken, Alan, "Just a Bit About Alan Menken," *AlanMenken.com*, www.alanmenken.com/m/biography/, accessed January 17, 2015.

Meyerson, Harold and Ernie Harburg, *Who Put the Rainbow in the Wizard of Oz?: Lyricist, Yip Harburg*, Ann Arbor, MI: University of Michigan Press, 1995.

Miller, Cynthia J., " 'Don't Be Scared About Going Lowbrow': Vernon Duke and the American Musical on Screen," Paper read at the conference *Popular Music in the Mercer Era, 1910–1970*, November 13–14, 2009, http://scholarworks.gsu.edu/cgi/viewcontent.cgi?article=1017&context=popular_music, accessed December 11, 2014.

Miller, Scott, *Let The Sun Shine In: The Genius of Hair*, Portsmouth, NH: Heinemann Drama, 2003.

——, "Inside High Fidelity," *New Line Theatre*, www.newlinetheatre.com/hifichapter.html, accessed April 29, 2015.

Mordden, Ethan, *Love Song: The Lives of Kurt Weill and Lotte Lenya*, New York, NY: St. Martin's Press, 2012.

———, *Opera Anecdotes*, New York, NY: Oxford University Press, 1985.

Morrison, Nick, "Get To Know: The Cole Porter Songbook," *NPR*, www.npr.org/2011/02/09/105032124/get-to-know-the-cole-porter-songbook, accessed July 26, 2015.

Morton, Jelly Roll and Alan Lomax, *Jelly Roll Morton: Library of Congress Recordings*, Washington, DC: Rounder, 2005.

Nolan, Fredrick, *The Sound of Their Music: The Story of Rodgers & Hammerstein*, New York, NY: Applause Theatre & Cinema Books, 2002.

Orel, Harold, *Gilbert and Sullivan: Interviews and Recollections*, Iowa City, IA: University of Iowa Press, 1994.

Oxman, Steven, "Review: 'The Addams Family'," *Variety*, December 10, 2009, http://variety.com/2009/legit/reviews/the-addams-family-4-1200 477895/, accessed April 27, 2015.

Pall, Ellen, "The Long-Running Musical of William Finn's Life," *The New York Times Magazine*, June 14, 1998, www.nytimes.com/1998/06/14/magazine/the-long-running-musical-of-william-finn-s-life.html, accessed 9 May 2016.

Pareles, John, "Arthur Schwartz, Composer of Broadway Shows, is Dead," *The New York Times*, September 5, 1984, www.nytimes.com/1984/09/05/obituaries/arthur-schwartz-composer-of-broadway-shows-is-dead.html, accessed May 19, 2014.

Portantiere, Michael, "Brown, Guettel and LaChiusa Discuss Musical Theater at Drama Book Shop," *Theatremania*, March 16, 2004, www.theatermania.com/new-york-city-theater/news/03-2004/brown-guettel-and-lachiusa-discuss-musical-theater_4504.html, accessed April 25, 2015.

Raymond, Gerard, "Making Big Fish Sing: A New Broadway Musical," *Broadway Direct*, June 17, 2013, http://broadwaydirect.com/feature/making-big-fish-sing-a-new-broadway-musical-is-born, accessed April 28, 2015.

———, "Rocky: Ahrens & Flaherty Write a Musical Love Story," *Broadway Direct*, September 10, 2013, http://broadwaydirect.com/feature/rocky-ahrens-flaherty-write-a-musical-love-story, accessed April 24, 2015.

Reich, Howard, "Joan Curto Celebrates the Genius of Cole Porter," *Chicago Tribune*, February 7, 2013, http://articles.chicagotribune.com/2013-02-07/entertainment/ct-ott-0208-jazz-scene-20130207_1_cole-porter-jewish-music-words-and-music, accessed December 1, 2014.

Reich, Howard and William M. Gaines, *Jelly's Blues: The Life, Music and Redemption of Jelly Roll Morton*, New York, NY: Da Capo Press, 2004.

Rick, Benjamin, *You're a Grand Old Rag: The Music of George M. Cohan*, www.newworldrecords.org/uploads/fileJGsEj.pdf, accessed March 17, 2015.

Rodgers, Richard, *Musical Stages: An Autobiography*, New York, NY: Random House, 1975.

Romberg, Sigmund, "A Peep into the Workshop of a Composer," *Theatre Magazine*, xlvii/6 (1928).

Rosati, Nancy "Spotlight on Tom Jones and Harvey Schmidt," www.talkinbroadway.com/spot/jonesschmidt1.html, accessed May 9, 2016.

Rose, Al, *Eubie Blake*, New York, NY: Macmillan, 1979.

Rosenberg, Deena Ruth, *Fascinating Rhythm: The Collaboration of George and Ira Gershwin*, Ann Arbor, MI: University of Michigan Press, 1998.

Rosenberg, Marion, "Lorenz Hart, Inside Out," *Capital New York*, July 3, 2012, www.capitalnewyork.com/article/culture/2012/07/6132084/lorenz-hart-inside-out, accessed December 6, 2014.

Secrest, Meryl, *Somewhere For Me – A Biography of Richard Rodgers*, New York, NY: Applause Theatre & Cinema Books, 2002.

Shipton, Alyn, *Fats Waller: The Cheerful Little Earful*, London, UK: Bloomsbury Academic, 2005.

——, *I Feel a Song Coming On: The Life of Jimmy McHugh (Music in American Life)*, Champaign, IL: University of Illinois Press, 2009.

Shout, John D., "Frank Loesser," *Broadway: The American Musical*, www.pbs.org/wnet/broadway/stars/frank-loesser/, accessed August 25, 2014.

Simonson, Robert, "Playbill.com's Brief Encounter With Andrew Lippa," *Playbill*, December 9, 2009, www.playbill.com/article/playbillcoms-brief-encounter-with-andrew-lippa-com-176251, accessed May 12, 2016.

Smith, Tim, "Actors in 'Jersey Boys' Learn Methods at Frankie Camp," *The Baltimore Sun*, November 8, 2013, http://articles.baltimoresun.com/2013-11-08/entertainment/bs-ae-arts-story-1108-20131107_1_frankie-camp-frankie-valli-jersey-boys, accessed August 17, 2015.

Sokol, Robert, "Rubbing Shoulders with Bernadette Peters," *Stephen Sondheim Stage*, www.sondheim.com/interview/sbswbp.html, accessed October 30, 2015.

Strouse, Charles, *Put on a Happy Face: A Broadway Memoir*, New York, NY: Union Square Press, 2008.

Sudhalter, Richard, *Stardust Melody: The Life and Music of Hoagy Carmichael*, New York, NY: Oxford University Press, 2003.

Swayne, Steve, *How Sondheim Found His Sound*, Ann Arbor, MI: University of Michigan Press, 2007.

Tamarkin, Jeff, "Extended Bio," *Bobby McFerrin Home*, http://bobbymcferrin.com/whos-bobby/press-kit/extended-bio/, accessed December 28, 2014.

Taylor, Theodore, *Jule: The Story of Composer Jule Styne*, New York, NY: Random House, 1979.

Teachout, Terry, *Duke: A Life of Duke Ellington*, New York, NY: Gotham, 2014.

Toft, Robert, *Bel Canto: A Performer's Guide*, Oxford, UK: Oxford University Press, 2013.

Tondreau, Chris, "Welcome to The Bel Canto Technique," *The Bel Canto Technique*, http://thebelcantotechnique.com, accessed March 10, 2015.

Traubner, Richard, *Operetta: A Theatrical History*, London, UK: Routledge, 2003.

Uncredited, "Anyone Can Whistle," *Sondheim.com*, www.sondheim.com/works/anyone_can_whistle/, accessed February 9, 2015.

Uncredited, *Instruments in Depth - The Saxophone*, "Bloomingdale School of Music," www.bsmny.org/exploring-music/features/iid/saxophone/2.php, accessed February 12, 2015.

Uncredited, "Strauss, II, J. Orchestral edition," *Naxos Classical*, www.naxos.com/catalogue/item.asp?item_code=8.505226, accessed March 7, 2015.

Vermette, Margaret, *The Musical World of Boublil and Schönberg: The Creators of Les Misérables, Miss Saigon, Martin Guerre and The Pirate Queen*, New York, NY: Applause Theatre and Cinema Books, 2005.

Wager, Gregg, "Kurt Weill," *The Orel Foundation\Kurt Weill\Biography*, http://orelfoundation.org/index.php/composers/article/kurt_weill/, accessed August 30, 2014.

Walder-Biesanz, Ilana, "Opera, Operetta, or Musical Theatre? – Blog," *Opera Vivrà*, www.operavivra.com/blog/opera-operetta-or-musical-theatre/, accessed October 20, 2015.

Waller, Maurice and Anthony Calabrese, *Fats Waller*, New York, NY: Macmillan Publishing Company, 1979.

Webb, Jimmy, *Tunesmith: Inside the Art of Songwriting*, New York, NY: Hachette Books, 1999.

Weber, Bruce, "When the Commercial Theater Moves In on Nonprofits," *The New York Times*, October 10, 1999, www.nytimes.com/1999/10/10/theater/theater-when-the-commercial-theater-moves-in-on-nonprofits.html, accessed May 11, 2016.

Winer, Deborah Grace, *On the Sunny Side of the Street: The Life and Lyrics of Dorothy Fields*, New York, NY: Schirmer Books, 1997.

Zinsser, William, *Easy To Remember: The Great American Songwriters and Their Songs*, Jaffrey, NH: David R. Godine, 2006.

Index of names

Index of show titles